IN GREAT
COMPANY

Unlocking the Secrets
of Cultural Transformation

Human Synergistics Australia Pty Ltd
Sydney NSW • Phone: +61 2 9271 5900
Melbourne VIC • Phone: +61 3 9675 0100
www.human-synergistics.com.au

Human Synergistics New Zealand Ltd
Wellington • Phone: +64 4 470 7700
Auckland • Phone: +64 9 309 9010
www.hsnz.co.nz

ISBN 0-9775753-0-6

Preface

It was over two decades ago that Human Synergistics International introduced the Organizational Culture Inventory® (OCI) as a tool for quantifying something that seemed important though difficult, if not impossible, to measure. At the time, we had no idea that the survey would later be translated into numerous languages and used by thousands of organisations around the world to guide their change and development initiatives. We are delighted that the OCI has been helpful to so many organisations and, in turn, appreciate the data and insights they have shared with us about how culture really works.

One of the most important learnings is that the consequences of culture extend beyond the organisation's own performance and the satisfaction, health, and well-being of its members. Organisations have a profound impact on the societies within which they operate. This impact is positive when the culture of the organisation enables it to serve a meaningful purpose for the larger society. It is also positive when the organisation demonstrates and disseminates values that support human rights, sustainability, and the world competitiveness of its host country or countries. Thus, through constructively redirecting their cultures, organisations can also change and improve the capabilities of, and the standard of living and quality of life in, the countries in which they operate.

These observations have led us to view our global mission as 'Changing the World—One Organisation at a Time™'. Our intention is to assist countries throughout the world in their efforts to improve and develop by providing their organisations with the expertise and tools they need to assess and constructively change cultural norms as well as the thinking styles of members, the impact of leaders, and the synergies achieved by their work groups and teams.

One of the most difficult challenges in 'changing the world', however, is finding the leaders who have the courage to do something about their own personal styles and the cultures of their organisations—and who are willing to share their stories with other organisations. Human Synergistics in Australia is fortunate to be in the great company of five organisations that have not only achieved transformational change but have also opened their doors to allow their journeys from Defensive to Constructive to be analysed, dissected, and documented. We extend our gratitude to these organisations as well as to the consultants who guided their cultural change initiatives and contributed to this research.

While no one has intentionally been keeping the process of successful cultural change a secret, it took the efforts of these companies and consultants, along with over a year of dedicated research by the authors, to crystallize the otherwise unavailable insights into the realities of effective organisational change and development that are presented in this book. It is difficult to change organisational culture; the failure rate is higher than we'd like and a better understanding of successful transformations has been needed. We hope that this book and the knowledge it shares enable and inspire you to constructively change the world, one organisation at a time.

Robert A. Cooke, Ph.D.
CEO and Director, Human Synergistics International
Associate Professor Emeritus of Management, University of Illinois at Chicago

Executive Summary

This book details the results of in-depth qualitative research, undertaken to identify the major drivers of successful culture change in Australian organisations.

The research was lead by Professor Dexter Dunphy, Distinguished Professor, University of Technology Sydney, in order to answer a series of questions regularly posed by clients of Human Synergistics International:

- How do organisations transform their cultures?
- What creates cultural transformation?
- What is the evidence about what works?

Each year Human Synergistics compiles research referencing organisational culture and leadership behaviour in Australia and New Zealand. Each year the results show little improvement in culture change. Employees and leaders consistently report their organisation's cultures are more Defensive than Constructive. This finding parallels Turner and Crawford's (1998) groundbreaking Australian research that showed 67% of change initiatives faltered. While many organisations know how to affect culture change, precious few actually do so. This frustrating dynamic is described by Pfeffer and Sutton (2000) as the 'knowing-doing gap'.

To determine how and why some organisations succeed in transforming their cultures, Human Synergistics examined a data set of 40 organisations that had not only measured their organisation's culture using the Organisational Culture Inventory® but had also remeasured it.

A small number of these organisations had achieved a quantum change so significant that the term 'transformation' could be used to describe it. They shifted their profiles from a predominance of Passive/Aggressive Defensive styles to being dominated by the Constructive styles. Five of these organisations agreed to take part in the study, to determine the drivers of cultural transformation. While sharing the ability to transform their cultures, these organisations – AdShel, MasterCard Worldwide (Australia), Balmain Leagues Club, Yarra Valley Water and Lion Nathan – are otherwise very different from each other in terms of their size, industry and corporate strategies.

The research methodology was designed to fully explore what it was about these organisations that allowed them to successfully transform themselves, with a particular focus on interviewing CEOs, change agents and selected staff through focus groups. The research team also reviewed:

- The rationale for undertaking cultural transformation
- Each organisation's mission, philosophy, structures, systems and technology
- Details of the cultural interventions undertaken and their impact
- The challenges faced and lessons learnt
- The impact of the cultural transformation on performance

The research finds that the challenge of changing human behaviour within organisations cannot be underestimated. While the research validates existing knowledge about organisational change and confirms that it is hard to achieve, it also challenges accepted paradigms.

The vital role of leaders in sponsoring change is reinforced. Through the case studies, decisive leadership from the CEO is seen as a prerequisite for transformational change, not an option. In particular, the CEO needs to demonstrate a personal commitment to changing his/her own behaviour and modeling the behavioural styles needed in the new culture. But the CEO can't work in isolation, the support of the leadership team and internal and external change agents all working together creates a core team that provides the support and high levels of energy needed to maintain the change process.

This core team must clarify the mission, purpose and values of the organisation, and ensure everyone understands their role within it. In practice this means creating coherence on a personal level and consistently reinforcing behaviours that support the new culture, not the old one.

The research also reinforces the importance of effective internal communication. Listening to and respecting all employees are identified as key change management skills. The language of change is also important: creating a common, shared change language within the organisation helps to ensure that everyone attributes the same meaning to change initiatives. Effective change programs use evocative language, rich in emotional symbolism, to capture the hearts as well as the minds of organisational members and help them make sense of the change taking place.

Change is unlikely to happen all at once. The research finds that transformational change does not follow a distinct or uniform set of phases. The leadership team needs to set the priorities for the change program, develop a transformation strategy specific to its organisation and be prepared to alter and adapt that strategy to match changing circumstances.

This uncertainty about the nature of change leads the research team to conclude that those organisations that successfully transform themselves also possess another important attribute – they are willing to take a step into the unknown. They are open to learning new things and have the ability to learn how to learn and to proactively seek out and manage change. This means they learn to be comfortable with uncertainty, emotional confrontation and turbulence.

The case studies also illustrate that moving to a Constructive culture creates more open communication, improved staff motivation and effectiveness, increased initiative taking, greater creativity and innovation, better teamwork and collaboration, and happier, more pleasant workplaces. The research strongly suggests that these improvements carry across into improved performance.

The research concludes that the key to long-term organisational sustainability lies in developing a capability that allows the organisation to continue to learn and grow, and proposes a new model towards a process change. This meta-capability of learning to learn also needs to be present at a personal level within the leadership team so that the leaders of the organisation can continue to reflect on and improve their personal behaviour in a way that mirrors that of their desired organisational culture.

Contributors

Quentin Jones – Australian Director, Human Synergistics International

Quentin Jones is Human Synergistics' Australian Director. Under his leadership, Human Synergistics Australia has grown to be a significant contributor to the field of culture and leadership development in Australia. It was his vision to undertake this research project, realising that what he had built over the past ten years would need to undergo its own transformation. The challenge was to build on Human Synergistics' reputation for excellence in measurement and move the company towards one that is also known for leadership in cultural transformation. This research makes a significant contribution to meeting the challenge.

His other inspiration in instigating this research project was to contribute towards Human Synergistics' new mission: Changing the World—One Organisation at a Time™.

Quentin can be contacted by email at quentin@human-synergistics.com.au

Dexter Dunphy - Distinguished Professor, University of Technology Sydney

Dexter Dunphy joined the University of Technology Sydney in January 2000 as Distinguished Professor. His main research and consulting interests are in the management of organisational change, human resource management, and corporate sustainability. He also has a special interest in comparative management, particularly in East Asia, where he has travelled widely. His research has been published in more than 70 articles and 20 books, including the Australian best-sellers (both co-authored with Doug Stace) *Under New Management: Australian Organisation in Transition,* and *Beyond the Boundaries: Leading and Re-creating the Successful Enterprise.* Dexter's most recent book is *The Sustainable Corporation: Organisational Renewal in Australia* (co-authored with Andrew Griffiths). His consulting includes advising on major organisational transformation and transitions, design of human resource strategies and systems, trouble shooting, and conflict resolution. He also has thirty years experience in working with senior executives, managers and other professionals in enhancing their managerial skills through executive workshops, consulting and counselling.

Dexter can be contacted by email at dexter.dunphy@uts.edu.au

Rosalie Fishman - Principal & Director, Future Pace Learning, GRF Management Services

Rosalie is a founding director of GRF Management Services and principle of Future Pace Learning. She is also an adjunct lecturer with the Australian Graduate School of Management, the University of Technology Sydney and a coaching affiliate of ENSO, the Executive coaching arm of Audrey Page and Associates.

Rosalie is a highly-skilled educator and consultant with over twenty-five years experience in the university sector and in private and public sector organisations. Her consulting and teaching focus ranges from organisational and leadership development, process facilitation, diversity management, and learning and change management, to in-depth work with individuals in an executive coaching/counselling capacity, and with groups to facilitate deep-level learning and change. Her current academic interest and research focus lies in transformational learning and change, with specific emphasis on the change process, lifelong learning methodologies and the interface between individual and organisational-level learning and cultural change.

Rosalie can be contacted at rfishman@medemail.com.au

Margherita Larné – Senior Consultant, Human Synergistics International

Margherita is a practice leader in organisational development with 17 years consulting experience with some of Australia's most respected retail, finance and insurance corporations and has extensive expertise in organisational development both as an in-house consultant and a Director of her own successful consulting business. She joined the Human Synergistics' Melbourne operations in early 2003 as Senior Consultant/State Manager and is now part of the consulting team in Human Synergistics' Sydney Office.

Margherita is passionate about systems and how they impact on individual behaviour. Being involved in this researched has informed her work as a practitioner and will assist in creating transformation in her clients.

Margherita can be contacted by email at margherita@human-synergistics.com.au

Corinne Canter - Senior Consultant, Human Synergistics International

Corinne is a Senior Consultant with Human Synergistics. Her expertise has been honed over 20 years of challenging senior leadership roles in Human Resources working across a number of industries and sectors including telecommunications, finance, the construction service industry and the public sector. She has specialised in the development and delivery of people management processes within organisations in the process of transformation. Corinne works closely with senior executive teams to enhance their leadership effectiveness, through the development and implementation of values, core team processes and business strategy.

Following on from this research project, Corinne's focus will be on building on and extending the insights gained from this work by developing frameworks, strategies and tools to support individuals, teams and organisations move towards greatness.

Corinne can be contacted by email at corinne@human-synergistics.com.au

Acknowledgements

This book is the result of a legacy, an idea created and left to us by J. Clayton Lafferty (1928-1997). The ultimate test of an idea is whether it outlives us. Almost forty years after Human Synergistics' founding in a Plymouth, Michigan farmhouse, the circumplex and its underpinning ideas continue to be discovered afresh, profoundly impacting people's lives across the world.

Of course, an idea needs others to make it a reality. Here we are indebted to Rob Cooke. Without Rob's stewardship of the circumplex, its impact may have been lost. Under the new ownership of Rob Cooke, there is a growing community of like-minded people enrolling into Human Synergistics' new mission of 'Changing the World–One Organisation at a Time™'.

In this part of the world, the idea was picked up in the late 1970s by three New Zealanders; Roy Lynch (1928 – 2003), Shaun McCarthy and Mike Gourley. Their leadership, hard work and commitment provides the foundation from which this book emerges. Without Shaun's vision, and Alastair Carey's outstanding implementation of our data 'warehousing' software, Production Manager, we would not have been able to collect and manipulate such large quantities of culture and leadership data. We acknowledge the amazing multi-tasking abilities of the many Client Service Managers who over the years have tirelessly worked with our client's profiles. In particular, special thanks to Mary Tzambazis and Clare Walsh, who directly managed this project's data.

Changing the world is a collaborative effort. In Australia and New Zealand, we have almost 1000 'collaborators' in this pursuit – our Accredited Practitioners.

Their commitment created the many organisational interventions from which we drew our research data set. Thanks to these extraordinary people for their passion, courage and friendship over many years. A special thanks to those who provided direct support in this research: Bob Barbour, Peter Fuda, Stephen Klemich, Ian Pimblett, Roma Gaster, Wayne Forrest and Chris Bowers.

Writing this book has been a delightful collaborative experience. I am indebted to Dexter Dunphy's willingness to hear my original idea, his wise council, leadership and timely proddings. For Corinne Canter's willingness to pick up this project and manage it. For Rosalie Fishman's expertise, and Joan Rasmussen's making small, important things happen. For René van Dijk's amazing designs and perseverance with our constant changes. For Ben Findlay's, Liz McLaughlin's and Cathy Ewart's editing and PR brilliance. For Debby DeFranco's wise advice. For Shaun McCarthy's sponsorship and on-going support for this research. And finally for the love and support of my co-author, business colleague and wife, Margherita Larné.

Quentin Jones
Australian Director, Human Synergistics International

Contents
In Great Company

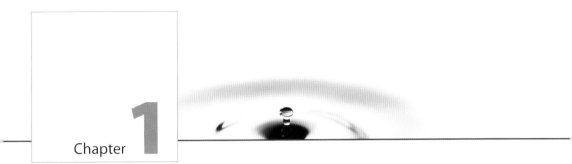

Chapter **1**

Introduction

Introduction — Written by Quentin Jones

This book is a response to our clients' challenge; 'How do organisations transform their cultures?', 'What creates transformation?' and 'What is the evidence about what works?' In the following chapters we seek to answer these questions and illustrate the process of cultural transformation in five Australian organisations – five organisations that we consider to be 'In Great Company'.

The challenge our clients are putting to us is not a small one. Human Synergistics has been measuring organisational behaviour internationally for over 30 years. Our consulting experience in Australia and New Zealand shows that organisations rarely achieve cultural 'transformation'.

Our annual compilation of organisational culture and leadership behaviour data shows no significant improvement (McCarthy, 2003; 2004; 2005). The average organisation's culture remains more Security than Satisfaction oriented. While there is a clear and consistent preference across most organisations for a corporate culture characterised by Constructive styles, in practice most cultures diverge from this. Staff and leaders consistently report that their organisation's culture is more Security than Satisfaction oriented. This Security orientation means people are investing more energy in protecting themselves by engaging in Passive/Defensive and Aggressive/Defensive strategies than in behaviours directed towards Satisfaction oriented needs, such as growth and Achievement.

Another data set, the one on which this book is based, found that some organisations achieved cultural transformation when they re-measured their cultures. However, most experienced only slight to moderate improvement, and a significant number went backwards. We will return to a more detailed discussion of these data later.

Both of these studies reflect the ongoing challenge of creating cultural transformation, and parallel Turner and Crawford's (1998) ground breaking Australian research that showed that 67% of change initiatives faltered at some point, reminding us that we have much to learn about culture change, and that the path of change is fraught with many challenges.

Of course, one of the biggest challenges is the human condition itself. The challenge of changing human behaviour cannot be underestimated. We will share very practical strategies and tactics in this book, but unfortunately, knowing how to effect culture change guarantees nothing. This frustrating dynamic is well described by Pfeffer and Sutton (2000) as the 'knowing-doing gap'. This is the phenomenon of organisational knowledge that is not being implemented, costing billions of dollars and creating failure of all kinds. At a very personal level, for example, we know what we should be doing to maintain our personal health, but we often do little in the way of exercise or diet modification. Organisations, as human systems, are no different.

People change organisations, and we have attempted to weave many of these human dramas into the five case studies that follow, because it is only through appreciating these wonderful human stories that we can glimpse the true key to organisational transformation; the transformation of the individual.

To illustrate; I recently had coffee with a now 'retired' executive. He told me he had left his job partly as a result of the transformational impact of the personal feedback process using the Life Styles Inventory™ (LSI). It had forced him to look at himself, his beliefs, values and worldview. Once exposed to looking at himself and the world through this new frame, he could no longer tolerate the disconnect between his own worldview and that of his organisation, and therefore felt compelled to leave.

Of course, the other path that leaders can take is to remain, and use their new worldview to transform their organisation. Whatever the path chosen, these five case studies illustrate the tremendous courage, vision and wisdom of the change agents, be they the CEO, senior executives, or external change agents. As you read these cases, we encourage you to read between the lines for the human story of these extraordinary people. To ignore this subtext is to ignore the key to transformation and the very human desire to make a difference in the world, and to leave a legacy.

CHANGING THE WORLD

Human Synergistics' mission is 'Changing the World—One Organisation at a Time™'. We believe individual effort can make a tremendous difference, particularly when individuals collaborate. The challenge our clients have put to us is the challenge facing us all, no matter what role we find ourselves in, the challenge of transforming organisations into truly sustainable entities that serve all constituents. This challenge is a shared one.

WHO SHOULD READ THIS BOOK

Whatever your role, our hope is that this book will be a significant aid in creating cultural transformation in your organisation. If you are a senior executive looking to address the significant cultural and leadership issues facing your organisation, we hope this book provides a vision that cultural transformation is possible. For internal and external change agents who are charged with the task of creating a path to this vision, we hope this book provides many practical tactics and most importantly, a path to follow. While every organisation will have its own journey, this book contains the stories of those who have already trail-blazed this challenging terrain. We can learn a great deal from these pioneers. We honour their courage by learning from them and applying and building on their wisdom, to create more transformation, faster.

At a personal level, I hope that it will inform, challenge and encourage you to go beyond your current practices and worldviews, to join with us as a community in 'Changing the World—One Organisation at a Time'.

HOW TO READ THIS BOOK

We have attempted to make the content as accessible as possible, recognising people's different reading styles. For example, if you want an executive summary of the five case studies, then turn to the summary tables at the end of this chapter. Also, each case study begins with a summary. Feel free to browse each case study and pick out the bits that interest you.

If you want more in-depth information about the research project's background, and its goal, then continue reading this chapter.

Chapter 2 is a synthesis by Distinguished Professor Dexter Dunphy and his research partner, Rosalie Fishman. In this chapter, Dexter and Rosalie sift the five case studies, identifying the keys, and proposing a new model for unlocking the secrets of cultural transformation.

The next five chapters, Chapters 3 to 7, provide a detailed description of each of the case studies, and outline the culture transformation journeys of five very diverse Australian organisations. We delve into the specific tactics they used, and present practical tools and concepts to apply to your own organisation's journey. While each story is unique, we have moulded these stories into two basic frameworks to gain clarity about what happened, and to make comparisons. The two frameworks used are the Test ➜ Action ➜ Re-Test adapted from the field of psychological research, and Dr Robert A. Cooke's 'How Culture Works' model (Cooke, 1997). We describe these models later in this chapter.

The book concludes with an epilogue critiquing how well we have addressed our clients' challenge, and pointing to the implications of this research for taking the findings from 'knowing' about, to the 'doing' of, transformation.

The appendices contain a glossary of terms, a summary of the Human Synergistics' International diagnostics used by the research organisations, a detailed description of the research methodology, and focus group interview summary data.

Our Cultural Challenge

The cultural challenge facing most organisations is to align what they espouse with what their employees experience. For the most part, employees tolerate considerable dissonance between an organisation's espoused values and what they experience in reality. In practical terms, the challenge for management is to ensure that the rhetoric of the recruitment interview matches the new employees' experience in the workplace.

In this section, we introduce the study's culture diagnostic, and explore the 'cultural disconnect' (Cooke & Szumal, 2000) using data collected from forty Australian and New Zealand organisations. We will also introduce a central model that explains the cause of this disconnect, and points to its remedy.

CULTURE AND HOW IT WAS MEASURED

For the purposes of this research, organisational culture is defined as: *"The behavioural norms and expectations, shaped in part by shared values and beliefs, that guide organizational members in how they should approach their work and interact with one another"* (Cooke & Szumal, 1993).

The Organizational Culture Inventory® (OCI; Cooke & Lafferty, 1987) was used to quantify these 'behavioural norms and expectations'. Organisations find that the OCI is a useful tool in making tangible the more abstract aspects of culture, such as shared values, assumptions and beliefs.

The OCI measures 12 different cultural norms, organised graphically onto a circumplex. See Table 1.

CULTURE AND PERFORMANCE

Importantly, organisational culture impacts performance. However, this is not a simple direct relationship. We believe the development of high performance, Constructive cultures lead to the attainment of an organisation's mission and that profit is a by-product not a key focus. Research and experience show the OCI's Constructive styles positively correlate with desirable organisational outcomes, such as, high staff and customer satisfaction, sales growth, profitability and shareholder value (Cooke and Szumal, 2000). Figure 1 depicts

Figure 1. Leadership-Culture-Performance Connection

LEADERSHIP   CULTURE   PERFORMANCE

the relationship between the leader's behaviour, its impact on the organisation's culture and ultimately on performance. It is also important to note how culture loops back and influences the leader's behaviour. We will explore in depth the Leadership-Culture-Performance connection in each of the case studies that follow.

PREFERRED CULTURE – THE CULTURES ORGANISATIONS WANT

Extensive data collected from over 1200 Australian and New Zealand organisations paints a very clear picture of our collective cultural aspiration. Consistently, managers and employees report their preference for Constructive behavioural norms: Achievement, Self-Actualizing, Humanistic-Encouraging and Affiliative. Experience shows that these Constructive norms map closely onto generally espoused corporate values and principles. Figure 2 shows the combined results from all OCI 'Preferred' inventories collected from Australian/New Zealand organisations in the period 1994 to 2005.

ACTUAL CULTURE – THE CULTURES PEOPLE EXPERIENCE

The Actual culture people experience is, in most cases, very different (see Figure 3). 'Actual' culture data show that behavioural expectations have completely reversed from meeting Satisfaction needs to being dominated by Security needs. Specifically, the expectation to be Humanistic-Encouraging is replaced with a drive for Opposition, Avoidance replaces Self-Actualizing, and the need for Achievement is replaced by Conventional and Competitive behavioural norms.

EXPLAINING THE CULTURAL DISCONNECT – HOW CULTURE REALLY WORKS

This 'disconnect' between an organisation's Preferred culture and the employees' experience is at the heart of Rob Cooke's 'How Culture Works' model (Cooke, 1997). This model is a simplified systems diagram that illustrates the impact that various factors have on culture (the antecedents or causal factors of culture) and the outcomes that result at the individual, group and organisational levels.

Table 1. Human Synergistics Circumplex	

SHORT DESCRIPTIONS OF THE OCI STYLES

Styles toward the top of the circumplex reflect behavioural expectations directed toward higher-order needs for growth and Satisfaction; those toward the bottom reflect behavioural expectations that focus on meeting lower-order needs for Security.

Cultural styles located on the right side of the circumplex reflect expected behaviours directed to interactions with People; cultural styles located on the left reflect expectations regarding Task-related behaviours.

See Appendix 2 for a complete description of the Organizational Culture Inventory® (OCI), Life Styles Inventory™ (LSI), Leadership/Impact® (L/I) and Organizational Effectiveness Inventory™ (OEI) used in this research.

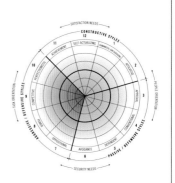

Humanistic-Encouraging (1 o'clock)	People are expected to be supportive, constructive, and open to influence in their dealings with one another.
Affiliative (2 o'clock)	People are expected to be friendly, cooperative, and sensitive to the satisfaction of their work group.
Approval (3 o'clock)	People are expected to agree with, gain the approval of, and be liked by others.
Conventional (4 o'clock)	People are expected to conform, follow the rules, and make a good impression.
Dependent (5 o'clock)	People are expected to do what they're told and clear all decisions with superiors.
Avoidance (6 o'clock)	People are expected to shift responsibilities to others and avoid any possibility of being blamed for mistakes.
Oppositional (7 o'clock)	People are expected to be critical, oppose the ideas of others, and make safe (but ineffectual) decisions.
Power (8 o'clock)	People are expected to take charge, control subordinates, and yield to the demands of superiors.
Competitive (9 o'clock)	People are expected to operate in a 'win-lose' framework and work against (rather than with) their peers.
Perfectionistic (10 o'clock)	People are expected to avoid mistakes, keep track of everything, and work long hours to attain narrowly-defined objectives.
Achievement (11 o'clock)	People are expected to set challenging but realistic goals, establish plans to reach those goals, and pursue them with enthusiasm.
Self-Actualizing (12 o'clock)	People are expected to enjoy their work, develop themselves, and take on new and interesting activities.

These 12 cultural norms cluster statistically into three categories:

Constructive cultures	Cultures in which members are encouraged to interact with others and approach tasks in ways that will help them to meet their higher-order Satisfaction needs (includes Achievement, Self-Actualizing, Humanistic-Encouraging and Affiliative cultures).
Passive/Defensive cultures	Cultures in which members believe they must interact with people in defensive ways that will not threaten their own Security (includes Approval, Conventional, Dependent and Avoidance cultures).
Aggressive/Defensive cultures	Cultures in which members are expected to approach tasks in forceful ways to protect their status and Security (includes Oppositional, Power, Competitive and Perfectionistic cultures).

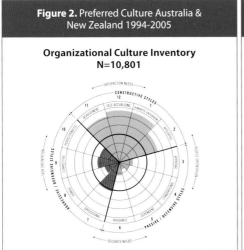

Figure 2. Preferred Culture Australia & New Zealand 1994-2005

Organizational Culture Inventory
N=10,801

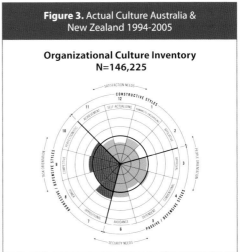

Figure 3. Actual Culture Australia & New Zealand 1994-2005

Organizational Culture Inventory
N=146,225

The Australian/New Zealand data have been overlaid onto the 'How Culture Works' model (Figure 4). This illustrates our organisations' aspiration for Constructive (Blue) cultures, and how organisational structures, systems, and other causal factors sabotage this aspiration, creating Aggressive/Defensive and Passive/Defensive (Red/Green) organisations and the consequent sub-optimal individual, group and organisational outcomes. Dr Robert A. Cooke summarises this dynamic: *"The behavioural norms that emerge in organisations are products of members' collective learnings regarding what it takes to get things done and succeed - or to stay out of trouble and survive - in the system. In discerning what behaviours are appropriate, members may react cautiously or even scep-tically to mission statements, change programs, and what managers 'say' they want. Instead, they infer what is expected on the basis of cues and signals from the forces they face on a daily basis. These forces - which include structures, systems, technologies, and skill/qualities - may or may not be consistent with the more fundamental aspects of the organization's culture"* (Cooke & Szumal, 2000, p. 153).

Cooke's research has identified a total of 31 'causal factors' organised into five categories:

- **Mission and Philosophy,** which includes measures of articulation of mission and customer service focus
- **Structures,** which includes measures of influence, empowerment, and employee involvement
- **Systems,** which includes measures of human resource management, appraisal and reinforcement, and goal setting
- **Technology,** which includes measures of job design and interdependence
- **Skills/Qualities,** which includes measures of the skills and qualities exhibited by members, including those in leadership positions

These causal factors are measured using the Organizational Effectiveness Inventory™ (OEI; Cooke, 1997). The OEI diagnostic allows organisations to measure both the causal factors that

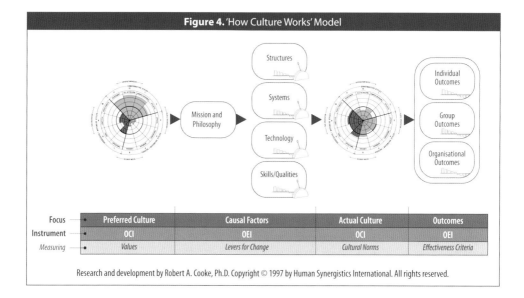

Figure 4. 'How Culture Works' Model

Focus	Preferred Culture	Causal Factors	Actual Culture	Outcomes
Instrument	OCI	OEI	OCI	OEI
Measuring	*Values*	*Levers for Change*	*Cultural Norms*	*Effectiveness Criteria*

shape their cultures, and the impact of their culture on members, groups, and their organisations as a whole.

Significantly, OEI data collected from Australian/New Zealand organisations show most causal factors falling below a research historical average (McCarthy, 2004). This accounts for the predominance of Passive/Aggressive Defensive norms in our national cultures. For example, the three strongest causal factors driving our organisations' Passive/Defensive and Aggressive/Defensive norms are:

1. **Systems (Appraisal and Reinforcement)** – (Non) Use of rewards: The likelihood that good performance will be noticed and reinforced in positive ways (that is, positive reinforcement)
2. **Skills/Qualities (Supervisory/Managerial Leadership)** – (Poor) Goal emphasis (task-oriented): The extent to which managers establish and communicate norms and expectations for excellence
3. **Technology (Job Design)** – (Low) Significance: The degree to which jobs are viewed by members as having an important impact on other people (either inside or outside of the organisation)

To summarise these data, the culture of the Australian and New Zealand organisations we have studied often fails to communicate goals for excellence or reward good performance, and in addition, organisational members don't perceive the impact that their work has on others.

For an organisation wanting to change its culture, the OEI complements the OCI by assessing causal factors, prioritising the cultural levers for transformation. We take this issue up next.

Bridging the Disconnect – Creating Transformation

The key to overcoming this disconnect lies in aligning an organisation's causal factors with its espoused values and culture. Seen as a system, organisations must ensure that all subsystems send the same behavioural messages. Leaders must orchestrate these divergent parts to produce a harmonious symphony. Unfortunately, most organisations have different parts playing off different musical scores, and what staff often hear sounds more like a cacophony. A few examples of mixed messages from our consulting experience include:

- Missions that espouse employee empowerment sabotaged by highly centralised *Structures* reinforcing Passive/Defensive norms
- Investments in team building wasted by reward *Systems* that foster individualistic competitive norms
- Aspirations to exceed customer expectations sabotaged by fragmented and simplified jobs producing meaningless, low-achievement, repetitive work (*Technology*)
- Leadership aspirations being reduced to micro-management by lack of development, and promotion of individuals with aggressive personal styles (*Skills/Qualities*)

What makes this alignment process so difficult is the range of competing agendas that need to be managed. Short-term versus long-term focus, effectiveness versus efficiency, productivity versus safety – these are but some of the competing demands managers have to juggle in designing and managing their organisations. The challenge is magnified by the need for managers to constantly update their modus operandi and their underpinning assumptions. In particular, in a rapidly changing world, what worked yesterday in one organisation is unlikely to work tomorrow, especially in another organisation. There is a constant need for managers to re-examine their practices in the light of new information, practices and research.

OUR CLIENTS' CHALLENGE IS OUR CHALLENGE

The challenge our clients have put to us is to answer the question: what creates cultural change? Constantly, in meetings with new and existing clients the request is for clear direction in how to go about changing their organisation's culture, including how to address the cultural disconnect they experience day to day.

Human Synergistics has developed a significant reputation for measuring and changing organisational culture. However, like most of our clients, our environment is also rapidly changing. For us to be sustainable and prosper we need to adapt, and indeed, transform ourselves and what we are known for. Our new purpose of 'Changing the World—One Organisation at a Time' cements our focus on the process of cultural transformation with researched-based measurement and practices.

DEFINING TRANSFORMATION

Transformation is a much overused phrase. However, it is a powerful concept, if used with understanding and respect. Human Synergistics was born in the 1970s, and was strongly influenced by the Organisational Development (OD) school of organisational improvement. Quade & Brown (2001) define OD in the following manner: *"Organizational development is a system-wide and values-based collaborative process of applying behavioural science knowledge to the adaptive development, improvement, and reinforcement of such organizational features as the strategies, structures, processes, people, and cultures that lead to organizational effectiveness."*

The main criticism of the OD movement is that it is essentially incremental in its approach to change, and that it failed to address the increased demands on organisations that emerged in the 80s, and have intensified since. Demands such as the explosion of information technology, globalisation, and consumer expectations have made it essential for organisations to 'change fast to survive' (Dunphy & Stace, 1998; Stace & Dunphy, 2001).

From these demands, a new school of organisational improvement emerged – Organisational Transformation (OT). OT's focus embraces the idea that sometimes organisations have to be more than 'tweaked' (French & Bell, 1994): *"Transformation can occur in response to or in anticipation of major changes in the organization's environment or technology. In addition, these changes are often associated with significant alterations in the firm's business strategy, which, in turn, may require modifying corporate culture as well as internal structures and processes to support the new direction. Such fundamental change entails a new paradigm for organizing and managing organizations. It involves qualitatively different ways of perceiving, thinking, and behaving in organizations"* (Cummings & Worley, 1993 p. 520).

Twenty-first century Australian/New Zealand organisations now face all of the old challenges and some new ones. With strong economic growth, and an aging workforce coupled with low unemployment, Australian workers are becoming more demanding of their employers. Whether one subscribes to the generational shifts popularised in terms such as Gen X and Y, expectations of workers are changing. People are more mobile, demanding more meaningful work in more physically-comfortable and emotionally-safe work places. To this end, senior executives, recognising the need to attract an 'unfair share' of talented people, have eagerly embraced such concepts as 'employment branding' and 'employer of choice'. While these strategies have merit, the more essential challenge faced by organisations is to find 'a fundamentally new paradigm for organising and managing organisations', that is, transformation.

DEFINING CULTURAL TRANSFORMATION

For this study, we have defined cultural transformation as the re-orientation of an organisation's culture from one dominated by Defensive norms meeting Security needs, to one oriented towards Constructive norms meeting Satisfaction needs. On the circumplex, such shifts are easily recognised by a shift in colour from Red and Green (Aggressive/Defensive and Passive/Defensive) to a predominance of Blue (Constructive norms). We wish to emphasise that this is not just a preference for these behaviours on our own part – this is what the majority of respondents in the organisations studied by Human Synergistics identify as the cultural change that they would like for their own organisations.

The Human Synergistics' Circumplex model measures a number of fundamentally different sets of behavioural norms; Task versus People, Constructive versus Defensive, and Security versus Satisfaction. Returning to our earlier definition by Cummings and Worley, each of these orientations are 'qualitatively different ways of perceiving, thinking, and behaving in organisations'.

McCarthy (2005) found significant differences in orientation when comparing Actual versus Preferred behavioural norms in Australian/New Zealand organisations as measured by the OCI (see Table 2).

When organisations address their cultural disconnects successfully, they are fundamentally re-orientating their organisation's culture, indeed, potentially transforming it.

Table 2. Actual vs. Preferred Behavioural Norms	
In terms of how people approach their work, senior management wants the culture to be one that encourages people to...	**In reality, however, people are encouraged to...**
■ Think ahead and plan	■ Treat rules as more important than ideas
■ Pursue a standard of excellence	■ Switch priorities to please others
■ Work for a sense of accomplishment	■ Never be the one blamed for problems
■ Enjoy their work	■ Follow orders, even when they're wrong
■ Take moderate risks	■ Push decisions upwards
■ Take on challenging tasks	■ Don't rock the boat
In terms of how people interact with each other, senior management wants the culture to be one that encourages people to...	**In reality, however, people are encouraged to...**
■ Maintain personal integrity	■ Play 'politics' to gain influence
■ Encourage others	■ Please those in positions of authority
■ Use good human relations skills	■ Maintain unquestioned authority
■ Be open about self	■ Maintain an image of superiority
■ Help others to grow and develop	■ Never appear to lose
■ Show concerns for the needs of others	■ Compete rather than cooperate

OCI survey items from Robert A. Cooke and J. Clayton Lafferty, Organizational Culture Inventory®, Human Synergistics International. Copyright © 1987-2006. All rights reserved.

Looking for Evidence of Cultural Transformation

Flowing from Human Synergistics' Mission of 'Changing the World—One Organisation at a Time', we set our Vision as 'Transforming Australian/New Zealand Organisations'. Using the Vision as an organising principle, we asked the question: 'Do we have any evidence of cultural transformation in our data base?' We were aware of a select group of client organisations that had not only measured (Test) their organisation's cultures using the OCI but had also re-measured them (Re-Test). On closer examination, we found a smaller subset that had not only re-measured, but in fact had made significant cultural change. In some cases, the quantum of change was so significant that, indeed, the term 'transformation' is a reasonable description of the change that took place.

The original data set of 40 Re-Test organisations is presented in Figure 5. Re-Tests occurred over a two-year period from 2003 to 2005. The sample's demographics are included.

This data set is encouraging. It points to the overall positive impact of cultural change

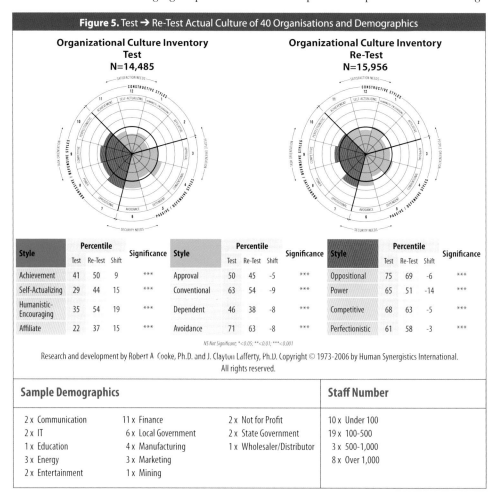

Figure 5. Test → Re-Test Actual Culture of 40 Organisations and Demographics

Organizational Culture Inventory
Test
N=14,485

Organizational Culture Inventory
Re-Test
N=15,956

Style	Percentile			Significance	Style	Percentile			Significance	Style	Percentile			Significance
	Test	Re-Test	Shift			Test	Re-Test	Shift			Test	Re-Test	Shift	
Achievement	41	50	9	***	Approval	50	45	-5	***	Oppositional	75	69	-6	***
Self-Actualizing	29	44	15	***	Conventional	63	54	-9	***	Power	65	51	-14	***
Humanistic-Encouraging	35	54	19	***	Dependent	46	38	-8	***	Competitive	68	63	-5	***
Affiliate	22	37	15	***	Avoidance	71	63	-8	***	Perfectionistic	61	58	-3	***

NS Not Significant; *<0.05; **<0.01; ***<0.001

Research and development by Robert A Cooke, Ph.D. and J. Clayton Lafferty, Ph.D. Copyright © 1973-2006 by Human Synergistics International. All rights reserved.

Sample Demographics

			Staff Number
2 x Communication	11 x Finance	2 x Not for Profit	10 x Under 100
2 x IT	6 x Local Government	2 x State Government	19 x 100-500
1 x Education	4 x Manufacturing	1 x Wholesaler/Distributor	3 x 500-1,000
3 x Energy	3 x Marketing		8 x Over 1,000
2 x Entertainment	1 x Mining		

efforts in Australia/New Zealand. All 12 circumplex styles show statistically significant shifts to a < 0.001 confidence level, using a statistical technique called a Student t-test. Interestingly, the biggest increases are in the People-orientated Constructive styles, with Humanistic-Encouraging and Affiliative replacing Power and Conventional norms. Disappointingly, the

Passive/Defensive and Aggressive/Defensive styles still outweigh the Constructive styles in the re-measured organisations, highlighting our ongoing culture change challenge.

IDENTIFYING THE RESEARCH ORGANISATIONS

The next step in our analysis led us to rank these 40 organisations by the degree of cultural shift. Changes in the percentile scores in the twelve cultural styles were used to calculate the percentage change from Passive/Defensive and Aggressive/Defensive to the Constructive styles. The results of this analysis are presented in Figure 6.

In summary, 75% of organisations showed some improvement in their cultures. On average,

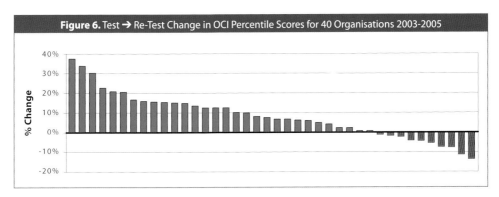

Figure 6. Test ➔ Re-Test Change in OCI Percentile Scores for 40 Organisations 2003-2005

these organisations improved by 13%. The remaining 25% of organisations regressed by an average of 6%. A 'topping and tailing' of the data set identified the five organisations that improved their cultures the most (Figure 7) and the five that regressed the most (Figure 8).

While five organisations were identified as having transformed the most toward their ideal culture, only three ended up in the research sample. The other two organisations did not allow the research team access, due to internal politics and external sensitivities. The sixth-placed organisation in the data set was then substituted and, serendipitously the second replacement was found when a Re-Test occurred during the project setup. This latter organisation appeared in third position in the ranking of cultural shift when included in the original sample of forty organisations. To summarise, the five transformational organisations chosen for this study represent five of the top six most-transformed organisations in the current data set of the now forty-one organisations.

Below is the final list of participating organisations, presented in order of how long they have been on their culture change journeys:

- Adshel
- MasterCard Worldwide (Australia)
- Yarra Valley Water
- Balmain Leagues Club
- Lion Nathan

Figure 7. Top 5 Test ➜ Re-Test Organisations

Organizational Culture Inventory
Test; N=1,691

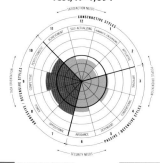

Organizational Culture Inventory
Re-Test; N=2,394

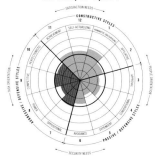

Style	Percentile			Significance	Style	Percentile			Significance	Style	Percentile			Significance
	Test	Re-Test	Shift			Test	Re-Test	Shift			Test	Re-Test	Shift	
Achievement	51	65	14	***	Approval	55	34	-21	***	Oppositional	76	53	-23	***
Self-Actualizing	39	63	24	***	Conventional	58	38	-20	***	Power	70	34	-36	***
Humanistic-Encouraging	38	70	32	***	Dependent	48	20	-28	***	Competitive	81	49	-32	***
Affiliate	22	47	25	***	Avoidance	65	41	-24	***	Perfectionistic	69	45	-24	***

NS Not Significant; *<0.05; **<0.01; ***<0.001

Figure 8. Bottom 5 Test ➜ Re-Test Organisations

Organizational Culture Inventory
Test; N=3,247

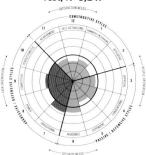

Organizational Culture Inventory
Re-Test; N=3,710

Style	Percentile			Significance	Style	Percentile			Significance	Style	Percentile			Significance
	Test	Re-Test	Shift			Test	Re-Test	Shift			Test	Re-Test	Shift	
Achievement	44	37	-7	***	Approval	43	49	6	***	Oppositional	70	74	4	***
Self-Actualizing	32	27	-5	***	Conventional	52	65	13	***	Power	52	65	13	***
Humanistic-Encouraging	41	35	-6	***	Dependent	37	46	9	***	Competitive	57	63	6	***
Affiliate	27	22	-5	***	Avoidance	65	78	13	***	Perfectionistic	50	59	9	***

NS Not Significant; *<0.05; **<0.01; ***<0.001

Using our earlier definition of 'transformation', these Top 5 organisations have transformed their cultures. On average, they have shifted their profiles from a predominance of Passive/Defensive and Aggressive/Defensive (Green/Red) styles to now being dominated by the Constructive (Blue) styles.

The burning question remains: 'What have these organisations done to create this magnitude of change?' The next section summarises the research approach taken to answer this question.

The Research Project Methodology

The following is a summary of the research methodology. A comprehensive explanation of the research methodology and samples of the instruments used can be found in Appendices 3-6.

RESEARCH TEAM

Dexter Dunphy and Rosalie Fishman were engaged to provide research expertise and an independent viewpoint for the design and conduct of the research. The central question, 'What created the transformation in the five target organisations?' was broadened to encompass the generation of a deeper understanding of the nature of corporate cultural change and results-based guidelines for how organisations can proactively direct their change efforts.

The research team also included five members from Human Synergistics: the Australian Director (Quentin Jones), two Senior Consultants (Corinne Canter and Margherita Larné), an Executive Assistant (Joan Rasmussen), and a Client Service Manager (Clare Walsh). Communications support was provided by Horizon Communication Group (Ben Findlay).

RESEARCH DESIGN

Given the intent of the project, a qualitative research framework was adopted. Qualitative research has high utility in this type of research, and its validity is measured not only by the findings it puts forward, but also by the success or otherwise of the decisions based on those findings. In effect, qualitative research allows for descriptions of what is salient, to enable the story to be told in context, and to generate ideas as to the 'what and how' of events and the possibilities of 'where to from here'.

What makes this approach to qualitative research unusual is the systematic basis on which the cases were selected. While traditional research on organisational change generally uses the case study approach, such cases are rarely chosen on any systematic basis, but rather on the story they can tell. In our sample, the case organisations were chosen from a population data set demonstrating superior performance using the normed Human Synergistics' OCI tool, thereby offering a validated database from which to proceed. See the previous section – Identifying the Research Organisations – for a full description of how the case organisations were chosen. Further, care was taken in the stringent research design, attention to detail in the research protocols, and triangulation of data in the handling of the research data, to maximise research reliability and validity. For a detailed discussion, see Appendices 3-6.

RESEARCH QUESTIONS

Effective field methodology aims to collect data to address the myriad research questions embedded in the larger question posed in a commissioned piece of work. In our case, the larger question 'What are the drivers of cultural transformation?' was intended to move past a theoretical or best practice prescriptive orientation, that is, the 'should do', to a potential explanation of what actually happens to enable, support and facilitate cultural change. To address these issues, taking Dr Cooke's model as a starting point, we needed to gather information on what was happening in each organisation with regard to its mission, philosophy, structures, systems, technology, skills and qualities. The research questions aimed to move beyond a validation of Cooke's model to more fully explore the question of how to make such cultural change happen. What was it about these organisations that allowed them to make the transformation? To find clues, we needed the transformational stories told by those involved in the change process. We needed to know what had changed, the processes involved, the energetic, motivational and emotional interplay, and the perceived costs and pay-offs for what could only be seen as a huge undertaking.

The following research questions guided the construction of the individual and focus group interview schedules and other data collection methods.

The Research Questions:

■ Background and rationale for measuring the organisation's culture; the 'Why start?' story
■ Impact of the culture survey results on the organisation
■ Detailed data on the organisation's mission, philosophy, structures, systems, technology, skills and qualities at period one (Test) and period two (Re-Test)
■ Detailed outline of cultural interventions undertaken and their impact
■ Description of the key change agents
■ Results and impacts of subsequent culture measures (Re-Tests)
■ Impact on performance
■ Challenges and lessons learnt

DATA GENERATION

To ensure a comprehensive story, the research team targeted the following data sources:

■ Review of relevant organisational data, including internal and external communications and performance data
■ Results of the initial OCI/OEI measures and subsequent Re-Tests
■ Results of other relevant inventories and diagnostics undertaken
■ Interviews with CEOs, CFOs and nominated key internal and external change agents
■ Focus group interviews with targeted team leaders and line managers

Case Study Structure

The Test → Action → Re-Test model has been used to describe the basic steps in the change process, and to provide a structure for the case studies. See Figure 9.

This model has been merged with Rob Cooke's 'How Culture Works' model to provide additional definition, and to explain how the circumplex diagnostics fit into these organisations' culture change journeys.

Phase 1	**Pre-Test:** This is an additional phase included to capture events and background leading up to the time the initial Test was conducted.
Phase 2	**Test:** This is the starting place, where organisations 'draw a line in the sand' using various diagnostics. The Preferred OCI measures cultural aspirations, the OEI measures the current state of Causal Factors, the Actual OCI assesses current behavioural norms, and the OCI/OEI combined quantify Individual, Group and Organisation Outcomes. At this time organisations may also include measures of other quantitative outcomes, such as staff turnover, customer satisfaction, and revenue. All five organisations in our sample completed the Preferred OCI and the Actual OCI inventories. Only two used the OEI to direct change. This is in part due to the OEI being a relatively new addition to Human Synergistics' integrated diagnostic system. In place of quantitative measures, these organisations used more qualitative (focus groups/workshops) and intuitive means to guide them in deciding which cultural levers to target.
Phase 3	**Action:** For ease of description and comparison, each organisation's actions are categorised under the Causal Factors groupings of Mission and Philosophy, Structures, Systems, Technology and Skills/Qualities.

Phase 4 	**Re-Test:** The 'How Culture Works' model is presented again to highlight the re-measurement of Causal Factors, Actual culture and Outcomes. This assesses the degree of change, and is the basis for the next Action phase. Three of the five organisations in this data set have undertaken more than one cycle of Test → Action → Re-Test, as depicted by the arrow looping back to the Action phase.
Phase 5	**Review:** The case studies finish with a review of the Change Agents, Lessons Learnt and Future Challenges faced by the organisations.

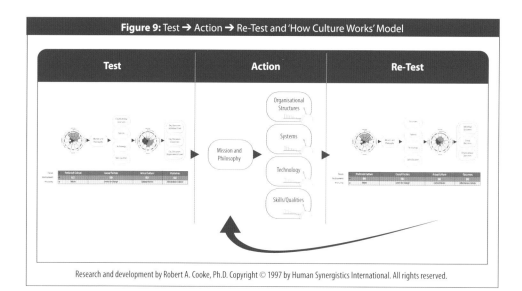

Figure 9: Test → Action → Re-Test and 'How Culture Works' Model

SYNTHESIS REPORT ON THE CASE STUDIES

In Dexter Dunphy and Rosalie Fishman's synthesis report, the five case studies are sifted and the learnings distilled, theory illuminates practical lessons, and decades of wisdom are crystallised into a new piece of theory.

Kurt Lewin once stated that there is nothing more practical than a good theory. We believe that this new theory will significantly improve the understanding and practice of cultural transformation, and contribute in practical ways to 'Changing the World—One Organisation at a Time'.

I hope you enjoy reading and absorbing the wisdom of the following pages as much as we did, and go on to explore each case study in detail.

Executive Summaries

Company	Summary	Organizational Culture Inventory Test → Re-Test Results
ADSHEL	Adshel is a very modern story of cultural transformation. It directly challenges the orthodoxy that Competitive and aggressive behaviours are the only behaviours that drive success. This case study also shows how a company, even though currently profitable, and with employee surveys reporting high levels of satisfaction, can nevertheless have real cultural issues – the 'Enron Syndrome'. The study documents how the CEO, Directors and staff at Adshel worked together to create one of the most significant shifts in culture yet documented by Human Synergistics.	 Test (2005) Re-Test (2006)
	This case study focuses on the Australia and New Zealand operations of MasterCard Worldwide and the stunning transformation it achieved over a two-year period of cultural change in Australia from 2002-2004, resulting in a significant increase in market share and local growth.	 Test (2003) Re-Test (2004)
 Yarra Valley Water	The public sector has provided fertile soil for jokes and jibes about the alleged lower levels of performance and sophistication. Yarra Valley Water, a retail utility company owned by the Victorian government, however, shatters many of these stereotypes. This case study documents the extraordinary journey of Yarra Valley Water as it transforms its organisation from a Defensive, old-style public service instrument into a dynamic, energized organisation.	 Test (2001) Re-Test (2005)
 TIGERS	This case study follows Balmain Leagues Club's journey from virtually a hand-to-mouth existence, where they were struggling to keep their doors open, to the emergence of a strategically-responsive, thriving organisation. We track Balmain's cultural metamorphosis as they harnessed their leadership's capacity to engage and energise their people in delivering a turnaround in performance that exceeded even the most optimistic hopes, and which ultimately has led to a viable future.	 Test (2000) Re-Test (2002)
 LION NATHAN	This case study locates Lion's cultural transformation in the broader context of the story behind the headlines – a story that charts an organisation's emerging strategic capability to do continuous change. There are many lessons to be learnt from what is the longest running case study on cultural transformation in our data set. Key among these lessons is what it takes to maintain the journey over a long period of time, and how a robust and Constructive culture precipitates resilient and courageous leadership.	 Test (1998) Re-Test (2004)

	ADSHEL	MasterCard	Yarra Valley Water	TIGERS	LION NATHAN
Industry	Advertising	Financial Services	Utilities	Hospitality - Clubs	Fast Moving Consumer Goods (FMCG)
Customers	National Network (Australia and New Zealand)	National Network (Australia and New Zealand)	1.6 million	35,000 per month	30,000
People	102	70	395	100	2,800 Australia, New Zealand, USA, UK
Assets	$100 Million	N/A	A$1.3 Billion	$25 Million	A$4.3 Billion
Revenue	N/A	N/A	A$381.5 Million	$18 Million per annum	A$1.8 Billion
CEO	Steve McCarthy	Leigh Clapham (Senior Vice-President and General Manager, Australasia)	Tony Kelly	Danny Munk (1995-2006), Tim Camiller (2006-Present)	Rob Murray (2004-Present); Gordon Cairns (1997-2004); Douglas Myers (1988-1997); Lion Nathan formed by the merger of Lion Breweries and LD Nathan in 1988
Internal Change Agent(s)	Culture Change Teams, Steve McCarthy	Leigh Clapham, Leadership Team	Anne Farquhar, Tony Kelly, Senior Executive Team	Danny Munk, Wayne Forrest, Executive Team, Duty Managers	Bob Barbour, People & Culture Director; Gordon Cairns, CEO (1997-2004); Lion Nathan Senior Leadership Team; Lion Nathan Human Resources Team; Rob Murray, CEO (2004-Present)
External Change Agent(s)	Stephen and Mara Klemich, Achievement Concepts	Peter Fuda, PCD	Ian Pimblett, Strategic Growth Pty Ltd	Roma Gaster, Karibu Education International Pty Ltd	Carolyn Taylor (1996-1998)
HSI Tools Used	Organizational Culture Inventory®(OCI) (Preferred and Actual), Life Styles Inventory™ 1&2 (LSI)	Organizational Culture Inventory® (OCI) (Preferred and Actual), Leadership/Impact® (L/I)	Organizational Culture Inventory® (OCI) (Preferred and Actual), Organizational Effectiveness Inventory™ (OEI), Life Styles Inventory™ 1&2 (LSI)	Organizational Culture Inventory® (OCI) (Preferred and Actual), Organizational Effectiveness Inventory™ (OEI), Life Styles Inventory™ 1&2 (LSI), Leadership/Impact® (L/I)	Organizational Culture Inventory® (OCI) (Actual), Life Styles Inventory™ 1&2 (LSI)
Outcomes	Increased staff satisfaction, role clarity, revenue and EBIT	Increased service quality, role clarity, successful pitches, market share, and global employee engagement survey results	Increased staff satisfaction, staff retention and engagement; increased efficiency and customer service	Business growth, decrease in operating costs, increased staff retention and satisfaction, increased brand currency	Increased profit, employee engagement and customer satisfaction

Chapter **2**

The Dynamics of Cultural Transformation

Introduction — Written by Dexter Dunphy and Rosalie Fishman

In this section we provide a synthesis of the research data from the five organisations chosen for study. Before doing this, however, we ask and answer some critical questions the reader needs to understand to follow our summary of the data and the conclusions we draw about how to conduct effective cultural transformation. The questions are: What is corporate culture? How is corporate culture formed? When should cultural change be attempted? How does planned change take place?

What is Corporate Culture?

This research deals with 'corporate culture' and its 'transformation', and so it is vital that we start with a clear understanding of what we mean by these terms.

A simple way to understand corporate culture is see it as 'the way we do business around here'. The members of every organisation have a set of shared implicit and explicit understandings of how to go about their work. If they didn't, the organisation would splinter, collapse and disintegrate. While this sometimes happens, mostly it doesn't. Why not? Some would answer: 'Because managers are telling employees what to do'. Of course managerial direction is important in setting the path and defining actions – it is one of the inputs into the evolution of corporate culture. But managers can't be everywhere at all times instructing people what to do and so most people go on working, often very effectively, without managerial supervision. So another way of thinking about corporate culture is that it is the set of attitudes and understandings that guide people's behaviour when those in authority are not taking charge; when their supervisor is not looking over their shoulder. More precisely, we define culture as: *"The behavioural norms and expectations, shaped in part by shared values and beliefs, that guide organizational members in how they should approach their work and interact with one another"* (Cooke & Szumal, 1993).

More specifically, culture has a number of key components. The first component, and the most difficult to access, is a set of beliefs or basic assumptions that govern much of what organisational members do. These assumptions are often held unconsciously, and are largely unexamined by those in the organisation. One way they surface is when a newcomer to the organisation acts naively, in a way that challenges an important assumption – and comes up against a sharp rebuke, or even some kind of punishment for apparent non-conformity, or is taken aside for an explanation: 'You have to understand that what you just did is not the way we do things around here'.

A clear example of the power of such a basic assumption comes from the Adshel case: In Adshel, before its transformation, it was assumed that the best way to maintain high performance was to encourage personnel in the organisation to compete within the organisation as well as with external competitors. In the relatively short history of the company, this had become a central assumption, even though it was never explicitly debated or verbalised. This assumption was central to the way people operated, and challenging it was a key to bringing about cultural change.

A second component of culture is values. Values act as rudders for behaviour, moving us toward things we 'ought' to do and away from things we 'ought not' do. In the case of MasterCard Australia for example, one of the key values, strongly held before the transformative change, could be expressed as: *"Everyone should comply with procedures and rules and seek approval from the hierarchy before making decisions."* This value on compliance limited personal initiative, innovation and risk-taking throughout the organisation. Transformation involved challenging this value.

Values flow forward into norms, which apply values to more specific organisational issues, and regulate day-to-day interaction between people. Norms specify what people expect from each other, and the kinds of behaviour needed to meet these expectations. An example would be: 'When I give you the list of orders generated by Sales each Tuesday, you will provide me with corresponding inventory levels by close of business Thursday.' One of the advantages of Human Synergistics' Organizational Culture Inventory® (OCI) is that it focuses specifically on measuring culture at the level of behavioural expectation – in the final analysis, organisations are defined by the ongoing flow of day-to-day behaviours of organisational members. This is where the rubber hits the road, and performance and satisfaction levels are defined. This is culture at its most concrete – beliefs and assumptions, values and norms are expressed in the way in which people behave, and in particular how they treat each other and customers.

Finally, there are some other components of culture that are more easily accessible, even to outsiders: symbols, artifacts, rituals and myths help to hold a culture together, and strengthen its hold on members of the organisation. In Balmain Leagues Club, the Board room was filled with symbols of the Club's football history. So in meetings, members were surrounded by evidence of the Club's past successes. Many of the photographs and trophies were associated with myths – stories of past glories 'purified' and 'meaning-enhanced' with re-telling over years, so that members now associated with the Club still make decisions in the context of the cultural trajectory of the past. It is not difficult to see how a behavioural norm of 'persist and endure' could arise in the context of a Club so deeply committed to football, and how this could flow into Perfectionistic expectations for staff members, even in the kitchen! But in the face of rapidly declining performance, with the probability of closure, even these deeply held traditions had to be challenged before a performance turnaround could be achieved. Transformation can mean breaking out of this kind of deeply internalised and compelling symbology.

Why is culture so important that sometimes conscious and deliberate efforts have to be made to transform it? We live in a world where most organisations at times encounter a rapid transformation of their environment, particularly their market environment. This is often experienced as an organisational crisis centering around performance. When an organisation is faced with a crisis, culture takes the driver's seat. For example, the September 11 crisis in 2001 confronted many multinationals with critical and immediate challenges – those that had built proactive, high-performance cultures with built-in capability for change found that these adaptive systems simply went into automatic drive. Their employees around the world were immediately feeding back information directly to head office about how local populations in different parts of the world were reacting, and taking local initiatives themselves where necessary, based on well-understood values. Within 24 hours, the most effective of these multinationals had assessed the situation, and were already putting into place coordinated actions on a world-wide basis to meet the emerging and unanticipated challenges. Many multinationals with traditional cultures unprepared for crisis failed to assess the situation accurately, reacted in uncoordinated ways if at all, and their performance suffered as a result. Their cultures did not have a built-in capacity to adapt and change, and to do so fast. The Lion Nathan case represents the development of this capacity for continuous change over a ten-year period.

All organisations today will face major shifts in crucial areas such as markets, products and technologies, and sometimes all these change simultaneously but unpredictably. The test of an organisation's culture is whether it is ready to respond to such changes, particularly when they are unforeseen, in a way that captures the new opportunities and resolves any critical problems that emerge. The core feature of those cultures that are sufficiently resilient and proactive to solve emerging problems and seize future business opportunities is the capability to manage change effectively, including transformational change when that is required.

How is Corporate Culture Formed?

To understand how to transform corporate culture, it is vital to know how corporate culture is formed in the first place, and how it evolves over time. Our own view is that corporate culture cannot be mandated from the top of organisations, but rather emerges from the shared experiences of those involved in the unfolding drama of organisational life. Culture is a collaborative attempt to make meaning from the business of doing business, and is most strongly influenced by collective experiences of success and failure that take place as people at all levels grapple with the exigencies of life at work.

National culture emerges in the same way. For example, for centuries the Chinese cultivated rice on a wide scale. Rice-growing is a collective endeavour, and depends on the large-scale coordination and disciplined hard work of a great number of people, not on individual entrepreneurs. No wonder then that Chinese culture has traditionally emphasised 'duty' - the value whereby the collective good takes precedence over the wants, interests and rights of the individual.

The culture at Yarra Valley Water before its transformation reflected its history as an engineering-based government water-utility – this was their equivalent to rice-growing. The emphasis at Yarra Valley Water was on mastering technical knowledge and on following procedures. This was a culture that maintained steady operational performance in a monopoly over several years. It was not, however, a culture suitable to operate a privatised organisation facing competition, and it was not a culture which would attract and retain skilled profes-sionals in an increasingly competitive labour market. The emerging environment was going to be radically different, and demanded that the existing culture be transformed to operate effectively in the new scene.

Their first response to this challenge was to move to a Competitive and aggressive culture, which had unintended negative consequences. This is an illustration of how well-intentioned attempts to modify culture may take a wrong turn and create cultural confusion. The Senior Executive Team realised that the new behaviours were not working, and this prompted them to explore other options and eventually to change their behaviour in ways that supported the development of a Constructive culture.

Corporate culture grows out of shared experiences, and can arise naturally, without any planned design process or intervention from senior management. However the behaviour of senior management is always a powerful influence on corporate culture, and often has unin-tended consequences. All these case studies show that many senior managers do not view their own behaviour accurately, and are surprised, even shocked at times, at how others in the organisation describe their managerial behaviour. They are also often unaware of how their behaviour influences other employees, and has a defining influence on the corporate culture. Part of the secret of successful planned culture change is to ensure that managers develop a more realistic view of how they behave, and how their behaviour affects the culture. They are then more likely to be committed to taking responsibility for modifying their behaviour, so it in fact helps form the kind of Constructive culture most aspire to create in the organisation.

We want to dispel a commonly-held illusion about the nature of organisations. We all treat organisations as if they were tangible things like desks, balance sheets or computers. Many years ago, the sociologist Emile Durkheim pointed out that organisations are 'social fictions'; organisations exist only because we agree to pretend that they exist, and to act as if they actually exist. An organisation is an idea in the heads of its members and stakeholders. Culture is embedded in the individual consciousness of organisational members and stake-holders. But culture is seldom uniform – there are often sub-cultures, for different individ-uals and groups who work for or relate to an organisation have somewhat different cultural consciousnesses. Our organisationally-relevant beliefs, values, and norms usually overlap to a large extent, but may also diverge in some areas; similarly, our understanding of the symbols, rituals and myths may vary. The challenge for managers in transforming low or medium-performance cultures into high-performance cultures is to engage organisational members in significant common experiences from which new shared meaning and perform-ance-enhancing norms emerge. The case studies we discuss show how this can be achieved.

At the individual level, culture can be thought of as the neuro-associative conditioning that emerges in each individual from their lived experiences and that, in turn, creates the habitual, mostly unconscious actions and reactions of our everyday functioning. Culture is embedded in the experiential knowing of our senses, and contains action sequences that are ready to be played out. It is rather like driving a car, where our conscious mind may be, for example, calculating the complexities of one of life's decisions while, at the same time, our deeper mind is reacting unconsciously to the demands of the road. Pursuing the analogy further, if another car suddenly cuts in on us, our blood pressure may shoot up and our heart rate increase; we 'rev-up' the engine, surge forward, and start raging at their driving, shaking our fist. This behaviour seems to come from nowhere. On reflection, we realise it may be counter-productive, even dangerous, but we can quickly justify it in the moment. Seldom do we evaluate it, and so we are likely to repeat it in similar circumstances. Even if we do consciously evaluate our behaviour, and decide that in future behaviour 'a' (accepting the event, slowing down and dropping back) is better than our enacted 'b' (raging), when a similar event happens, we may ignore this decision in the heat of the moment. Cognitive understanding is only one part, and often the least powerful part, of our consciousness. Consciously, we may well understand that we should do 'a' rather than 'b', but consistently find that we are reacting in our old, predetermined ways. Culture, too, operates like this.

Learning to behave differently involves creating new neurological pathways through experiences embedded in the five senses that carry an emotional intensity strong enough to form, maintain and indeed override old neural connections and associated behaviour patterns. Culture change involves unlearning and new learning of this kind. Such learning is clearly challenging, often confronting and painful in the moment, at other times exhilarating and joyous. It is in the repetitive experience of the new that change becomes embedded, and new habitual patterns of behaviour are formed.

We have emphasised the importance of the subjective or psychological basis of culture. However there is an objective side of culture that is equally important: organisational systems such as policies and procedures, human resource practices, technologies, etc. This objective side of the culture is co-created in the process of cultural change; its features are cultural artifacts which embody the beliefs, values and norms that constitute the core of the corporate culture. So culture resides in the hearts and minds of organisational members and stakeholders but it is also expressed and reinforced through codified organisational systems.

When Should Cultural Change Be Attempted?

Cultural change must be attempted all the time. Change is a continuous feature of modern society, and to survive and thrive, organisations also need to change continuously. The fate of those companies that don't at least match the pace of environmental change is to collapse or be taken over (Dunphy and Stace, 1990) Welcome to the world of unpredictable change and the chaordic organisation! In his book *Birth of the Chaordic Age*, Dee Hock (1997), the founder and CEO of Visa, coined the term 'chaordic' to describe how the pace of change means that managers have to manage organisations that combine both order and chaos.

There are two managerial imperatives that have to be carefully balanced in contemporary organisations: operating the ongoing organisation, and reshaping the organisation for the future (Turner and Crawford, 1999). Managerial theory in the past has mainly emphasised the first task – managing the ongoing operations - that is, building an ordered system that has the predicted outcome of getting the widgets out the door today. Traditional corporate cultures often reinforce this predictable order. But the challenge facing modern organisations is that if that's all that happens, the organisation will fail tomorrow when customers/clients tire of widgets and want bloggetts or, even more alarming, want services instead of products. Lion Nathan faced just this situation as Australians increasingly switched from standard beers to boutique beers and wines – even bottled water! And, in addition, customers showed they were prepared to pay a premium price for a lifestyle experience. Lion Nathan's existing capability in marketing and sales was below par so, in these circumstances, the challenge to build a strong capability in the area became critical.

We are dealing here with transformational change in particular. So when is transformational change necessary? Well, not all the time. Much of the time, incremental change will keep the organisation in alignment with its changing environment, and maintain high performance (Dunphy and Stace 1990; Stace and Dunphy 2001). But there are times when transformational change is necessary.

Many popular organisational writers, particularly from the USA, would argue that transformational change demands a 'burning platform', that is, it is called for only when the organisation faces a crisis which threatens to destroy its very basis – when organisational survival is at stake.

The fundamental challenges confronting organisations across all industries today require competency in accelerated transformation, and these challenges will only increase in the future

This is usually created by dramatic and often unpredicted environmental change – such as the loss of a key market, a major change in technology or the emergence of a new competitor. We agree that this is a signal of the need for transformational change and some of our cases illustrate this – for instance, Balmain Leagues Club and MasterCard Australia. But there is another basis for initiating transformational change – the pursuit of new opportunities. *"The demands of an ever competitive and changing environment are increasing the need for knowledge about how to lead and manage organisational change rapidly, efficiently, and effectively"* (Beer & Nohria, 2000).

Even organisations that are already performing well may seriously contemplate transformational change when their performance, even though already high, can be significantly improved, and/or when future opportunities are emerging that could be taken up proactively. When it comes to culture, we don't agree with the popular saying: 'If it ain't broke, don't fix it'. An example from this study is Adshel, which had a history of high performance, but signs were emerging that this performance might not be sustainable into the future. Current high performance is no guarantee of future success. Already, the existing culture was showing indications of future problems – the issue was to pick up these early signals, and to act to transform the culture before a burning platform became fully evident. It is hard to do this when all seems to be going well, but they managed to do it at Adshel.

So corporate transformation can be undertaken as a process of strategic opportunity-seeking rather than of crisis-management – as a way of ensuring that the culture becomes a major driver of change that will build a new platform for future success well before the current platform bursts into flames. We cannot always know what the future will bring – but we can ensure that the current culture embodies the constructive behaviours needed to resolve emerging problems and to pursue new strategic opportunities. We call this 'creating a culture of future readiness'. In this case, as the future unfolds, culture becomes an enabler of productive change, not a brake on it.

How Does Planned Culture Change Take Place?

Because culture is ultimately embedded in the consciousness of organisational members, the mindful reconstruction of culture involves the restructuring of consciousness. We have already indicated that culture emerges from the drama of organisational life – so the transformation of culture requires the creation of a new drama from which new meanings can emerge. The restructuring of consciousness involves reworking the neural connections formed as the old culture was acquired – a task which is not to be taken lightly. It is not just that people literally have to get their head around the change, but that the change has to literally get into the heads of people. This is not something that can simply be achieved by reformulating the mission of the organisation and printing it on plastic cards or by sending out a memo. We cannot over-emphasise that culture arises out of collective experiences of success and failure, therefore it can only be changed by a new set of such experiences. There is no short-cut. A critical mass of organisational members must be involved in this process, and most must undergo personal change, particularly those who are the visible leaders of the organisation – personal change

> **The demands of an ever competitive and changing environment are increasing the need for knowledge about how to lead and manage organisational change rapidly, efficiently, and effectively**
> (Beer & Nohria, 2000)

is not something that can simply be prescribed for other organisational members by the senior executive group and carried out by an external transformational consultant. Yet the most common message given by executives to external change consultants is: 'Go change the organisation for me!'

The psychological basis for cultural transformation is difficult enough to achieve, but not enough in itself. In the process, this subjective side of culture, the emerging new consciousness, needs to co-create the organisational systems that are the objective side of culture. If, for example, the reward systems (pay, incentives, recognition, promotion, etc.) remain unchanged, people will try the new behaviour but discover that it isn't rewarded, and therefore quickly revert to the old neural pathways and the old behaviours. At Adshel, for example, they found that they had to change the sales incentive systems to encourage cooperation rather than competition. The internal world of new beliefs, values and norms needs to find support in the external world of organisational systems if it is to survive and thrive. Transforming experiences must be translated into the cultural artifacts that make strategic coordinated behaviour possible.

In the cases we are about to summarise and discuss in more detail, the OCI and/or related instruments provide the basis for the creation of a new collective drama – it is the 'disconnect' between the desired and Actual culture that provides the collective awareness of the need to change, and the shock that begins the process of challenging the adequacy of the old ways. The new drama unfolds as the organisation seeks to move the culture in the desired direction. The personal engagement of the actors comes particularly from the Life Styles Inventory™(LSI), which illustrates for each individual how their behaviour contributes to locking the organisation into the old (Actual) culture and how they can play a role in the transformational drama of achieving the new (Preferred) culture. Individual and collective consciousness can then move synchronously. *"When culture is the focus of change, the need is to change the values, beliefs and behavioural norms of the way business is done. This requires a change in the way people think about the business, and does not occur unless a critical mass of the organisation becomes engaged – in their hearts, minds and action – in the change"* (Turner & Crawford, 1998, p. 90).

What Are The Critical Elements in Ensuring That the Planned Cultural Change Happens?

We now turn to a much more detailed analysis of what we have learned from our case studies about how to create successful cultural change. As we outlined in the methodology section, we have several sources of data:

- Human Synergistics' Test ➔ Re-Test data on the OCI, LSI, Leadership/Impact® (L/I) and Organizational Effectiveness Inventory™ (OEI) and, in some cases, instrumentation from other sources
- Data from research instruments devised specifically for this project by Dunphy and Fishman in collaboration with Human Synergistics' staff
- Interviews with CEOs, CFOs, and internal and external change agents
- Organisational records including performance data

We used all these sources to compile the individual case studies which follow this Synthesis Report and, from the case studies and summary data, we now report our general conclusions about the critical elements in corporate transformation. We will draw on the concepts we have developed above in our discussion of each section.

Making The Case For Transformation

The transformational journey is an awesome one, particularly viewed from upfront. For an organisation to commit to such a thoroughgoing change requires a convincing case to be made. People may not like where they are, but at least it is an environment they have learned to cope with. Who knows what a journey into an unknown future may bring?

As mentioned before, in some organisations there was a 'burning platform' that provided the major justification. Initially, Balmain Leagues Club, MasterCard Australia and Lion Nathan were facing business performance issues that threatened their viability. However, knowing this does not in itself provide an adequate diagnosis that defines a way forward; neither does it energise employees to commit to a change program, nor ensure the quality of relationships needed to allow new ideas to emerge and be dealt with constructively, so that an emergent strategy for handling the crisis unfolds. Clearly, what is required in these circumstances is a catalyst that not only clarifies and communicates the crisis, but also engages members throughout the organisation with its resolution. There needs to be enough fear to emphasise the seriousness of the situation, but also the hope that the crisis can be replaced with a positive plan to achieve a new level of success. The new plan, to be brought to fruition, requires a significant cultural shift – if the old culture persists, it will simply produce the old behaviour – the culture will act as a brake rather than as an enabler. Nevertheless, it is generally easier to demonstrate that change is necessary if there is a burning platform. This is not, however, a reason for allowing the organisation's performance to deteriorate to the point that its existence is threatened – managing an organisation back from this level of crisis is a risky business which often fails.

> **It is not the strongest species that survive, nor the most intelligent, but the one most responsive to change**
>
> (Charles Darwin)

A cultural audit such as that provided by Human Synergistics is an important step forward in providing a measure of the gap between where the culture of the organisation is, and where members would like it to be. It can therefore galvanise members into action to resolve the crisis.

For example, at MasterCard Australia, Leigh Clapham, the new Senior Vice-President and General Manager, clearly saw the need for a dramatic lift in business performance. He perceptively linked this to the need for cultural change and so he brought in Peter Fuda, an experienced change consultant, to help. Both agreed that the commercial imperative should be driven by cultural transformation and Fuda suggested using the OCI and L/I diagnostics. All 13 members of the Executive Team completed these instruments and were individually debriefed to obtain the leaders' views of the company and of their own management issues before the workshop took place. Then a two-day workshop retreat was organised for them where these results were put on the table. The results demonstrated a major gap between the way the organisation was currently operating and the way they wanted it to operate. It was also apparent from the L/I results how the behaviour of the 13 leaders was maintaining the current unproductive culture. This was the case for change – everyone including Senior Vice-President and General Manager was implicated. And all felt compelled to take responsibility to change the situation.

Similarly at Balmain, by 1995 Danny Munk, the CEO, was aware of the need for change and sensed that people were the fundamental problem, and that attitudes needed to alter. Wayne Forrest, Operations Manager at the time, had already been introduced to the LSI tool, which led him to a deep realisation that the behaviour for which he had been rewarded in the organisation ran counter to his core values. He convinced Munk to use the OCI to measure the culture. This led to a similar workshop being run which, as in MasterCard Australia, created a new awareness on the part of organisational members of how their behaviour impacted others and locked the inherited culture in place. While the buy-in proceeded a little more slowly at Balmain Leagues Club, eventually widespread commitment to change was generated, and a sense of personal responsibility developed. Most people participated in the change process by modifying their personal behaviour. Unless individuals own the change, it does not take place.

Business is also about maximising existing performance and pursuing new business opportunities. Not all organisations are in crisis. However, most organisations can do what they are doing more effectively, and benefit from scanning their environments for emerging opportunities. A cultural audit for these organisations can challenge what already seems an adequate work environment, and motivate people to strive for more. This was the case for two organisations in our research – Adshel and Yarra Valley Water.

Measuring the Culture – Generating Valid Data

In the 1980s, there was a surge of interest in culture change. However, these were mostly 'feel good' approaches to transformational change – the change agents were high on enthusiasm, but ignored two critical factors: the need to generate valid data on which to base a diagnosis of change requirements, and a clear line of sight to performance outcomes. As a result of these omissions, approaching transformational change through changing the culture was largely discredited.

There is renewed interest in culture change, but contemporary approaches are more tough-minded about filling in the previous gaps. Culture change is increasingly instrumented, that is, instrumentation is used to generate valid data about the current culture, particularly where it fails to support the creation and maintenance of high performance. This is where Human Synergistics' instruments make a powerful contribution – Human Synergistics have now generated a large data base, which allows comparison between organisations within and across industries. In addition, the connection between a Constructive culture and high-performance is more clearly understood, and strongly emphasized.

To reach a desired destination, first you have to know where you are – measurement of the Actual culture creates a benchmark against which progress towards a Preferred culture can be monitored. In addition, the availability of comparative norms allows a realistic assessment of how the culture of the target organisation compares with other organisations, particularly those that do generate high-performance outcomes.

Feeding Back the Results – The First Step in Engagement

While instrumentation can provide valid data, its generation is not in itself enough to create an impetus for change. Valid data is a necessary, but not sufficient, requirement to create engagement and commitment. The process by which the data is fed back to participants at all levels of the organisation is an important change intervention, which can achieve the desired outcomes, as participants in the process pointed out: *"The opportunity to carry out this cultural survey process including forming committees to continue focusing on this area has been a huge benefit - just by giving staff the chance to provide feedback… and making staff think about being aware of their own communication and behaviour"* (Focus Group Member, Adshel).

For valid data to have impact, the individual and collective data must be skillfully and sensitively fed back to those who generated it. This has to be done in a timely way. If it does not take place until months after the survey has been carried out, cynicism will set in, and the lapse of time may lead to the feedback being seen as irrelevant. The feedback also has to take place in a context where people feel safe and supported, as the impact of such personal feedback about the precious sense of self we have cultivated for so many years can be a powerful emotional experience.

The feedback process is best undertaken in stages, to ensure that the senior executive group is strongly engaged and committed first. At MasterCard Australia for instance the 13 top leaders completed the OCI and L/I surveys first and then received the feedback at an off-site residential workshop. Later the survey was extended to the next level leaders.

At Balmain Leagues Club, the LSI was used with the Executive Team, Duty Managers and other Administrative Managers first. The OCI, and later the combined OCI/OEI, was then administered to everyone in the organisation. Then the L/I was used with the Executive Team, intensifying their self-awareness and engagement. At Lion Nathan, the LSI was administered to the top 100 leaders in 1996. Later, the LSI process was extended to the next level of leadership, consisting of 500 people. At Yarra Valley Water, the OCI was first used to create an awareness of the issues across the organisation. In the process of identifying a cultural benchmark, it provided a measure against which leaders' behaviour could be measured. Yarra Valley Water followed implementation of the OCI with the implementation of the LSI throughout its leadership ranks.

At Adshel, the LSI was used first with the Senior Executive Team, and then later the OCI was rolled out nation-wide to all employees. This process was fully-resourced when commissioned, in order that it be done 'properly' (the Executive's words).

In all cases, skilled external change agents were commissioned to initiate the feedback process. However, it could also be driven mainly by one or more internal change agents. For example, at Lion Nathan, Bob Barbour used the Leadership Team to deliver leadership development training programs. Since that time, a number of Lion Nathan line managers have become accredited to use the LSI, enabling them to become internal coaches.

We cannot emphasise too strongly that the time and expense involved in commissioning the use of these instruments is wasted unless the feedback process itself becomes the first important intervention in changing the culture. Therefore the quality of the feedback process, and the care taken in creating a safe learning environment, is the first test of the integrity with which the organisation approaches the creation of a Constructive culture. Quinn writes: *"There is an important link between deep change at the personal level and deep change at the organisational level. To make deep personal change is to develop a new paradigm, a new self, one that is more effectively aligned with today's realities. This can occur only if we are willing to journey into unknown territory and confront the problems we encounter. This journey does not follow the assumptions of rational planning. The objective may not be clear, and the path is not paved with familiar procedures. This tortuous journey requires that we leave our comfort zone and step outside our normal roles. In doing so, we learn the paradoxical lesson that we can change the world only by changing ourselves. This is not just a cute abstraction; it is an elusive key to effective performance in all aspects of life"* (Quinn, 1996).

Implementing Change – Key Interventions

The Human Synergistics model for building high-performance cultures, derived from Cooke's research, has a comprehensive classification of implementation initiatives. The classification is not unique, and resembles others found in the literature. The terms in these classifications vary somewhat, but essentially cover the same range of implementation strategies or, as they are often called, 'levers for change', or 'process interventions'. Figure 1 outlines what these levers for change describe.

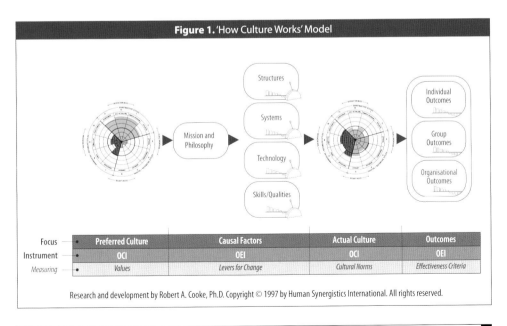

Figure 1. 'How Culture Works' Model

Focus	Preferred Culture	Causal Factors	Actual Culture	Outcomes
Instrument	OCI	OEI	OCI	OEI
Measuring	Values	Levers for Change	Cultural Norms	Effectiveness Criteria

Research and development by Robert A. Cooke, Ph.D. Copyright © 1997 by Human Synergistics International. All rights reserved.

The OEI assesses 31 specific factors found to be causally related to culture. These causal factors are organised into five general categories:

- **Mission and Philosophy** focus on the extent to which the organisation has successfully defined its identity and values to its members. The OEI examines Mission and Philosophy in terms of how clearly they are articulated to members, and their focus with respect to customers.
- **Structures** refer to the ways in which people, roles, and activities are ordered and coupled to create organisation. The OEI examines Structures in terms of the extent to which they permit (or restrict) influence, empowerment, and employee involvement.
- **Systems** refer to the interrelated sets of procedures that an organisation uses to support its core activities and to solve problems. The OEI examines aspects of human resource management, appraisal and reinforcement, and goal-setting systems.
- **Technology** refers to the methods used by the organisation to transform inputs into outputs. The OEI examines Technology in terms of various job design characteristics and the degree of interdependence among members.
- **Skills/Qualities** refer to the skills and qualities exhibited by organisational members— particularly those in leadership positions. The OEI examines Skills/Qualities in terms of communication, leadership, and sources of power within an organisation.

Participants in the focus groups were asked to choose the three most important process interventions from a list of twelve (see Appendix 5 – Focus Group Research Instruments). Summarised data from the focus group interviews shows that, in all five organisations, 'Leadership' was seen as one of the three most important process interventions in bringing about cultural change as outlined in Table 1 below.

Table 1. Cultural Change Process Interventions and the number of organisations nominating them in their top three choices.						
Process Interventions	**Top three across all organisations**	**Adshel**	**MasterCard Australia**	**Yarra Valley Water**	**Balmain Leagues Club**	**Lion Nathan**
Leadership/management style	5	2	1	1	2	3
Feedback using diagnostic tools	3			3	3	1
Communication	3	1	2	2		
Strategic redirection and focus	2				1	2
Change in reward structure	1					Significant
Level of employee involvement	1		3			

This indicates that there are some generally important interventions used in the transformational process. Leadership is of particular salience, followed closely by Feedback Tools and Communication, but there are also interventions specific to the needs of each individual organisation, that is, there is no universal recipe for effective cultural change.

This is also reflected in the variety of answers given to the first question discussed in the focus groups, which was: *"What are the major changes that occurred between the Test period (first administration of OCI) and the Re-Test period (second OCI administration)?"* Participants were then asked to rank the three most important changes. (See Focus Group Interview Summary Data; Appendix 6 – Table 1). There was a great diversity of changes listed. Nevertheless, there were some items highly ranked by participants in a number of the organisations. Adshel and Balmain ranked 'Feedback Using the Human Synergistics' Instrumentation' as number 1, and Yarra Valley Water ranked it as number 2. 'Leadership' also emerged as important here, chosen by Yarra Valley (#1), Lion (#2), MasterCard Australia (#3). 'Commercial/business redirection' was chosen by MasterCard Australia (#1) and Balmain Leagues Club (#2). The most important changes nominated by others were 'Role Clarity', 'Communication', 'Role Modeling', 'Accountability' and 'Key Personnel Leaving the Organisation'.

The number and variety of important changes listed in the focus groups, and in interviews with change agents and executives, suggests that the common elements in transformational change programs are balanced by a suite of other changes that are specifically related to the unique circumstances of each organisation. We conclude that executives planning to launch a culture change program would be well-advised to avoid the standardised 'off-the-shelf' packaged change programs often advocated by some consultancy firms. Effective transformational change programs need to be customised to the individual organisation. However, all programs must address the important critical variables of leadership, communication, behavioural feedback and setting strategic direction. As leadership was seen to be so important, we begin by discussing it first – in the Human Synergistics list of levers for change, it is classified under Skills/Qualities.

LEADERSHIP OF CHANGE

The role of the CEO and managers

Most texts on change refer to the critical role of the CEO in supporting change programs. Our research confirms this, and also fleshes out the distinctive contributions the CEO can make. We see these contributions as centering around: taking charge, authorising and resourcing the change, demonstrating personal commitment, modeling the behavioural changes needed for defining the new culture, and supporting others in making similar changes. We will deal with each of these in turn.

Taking charge: At Adshel, for example, it was CEO Steve McCarthy who quickly responded to fairly minimal signals of the need for change and took the lead in challenging the status quo, even though the organisation was highly successful. Steve described his role as follows: *"My key role in life is to be what I call the 'eggshell crusher', to jump all over the issues that people are tiptoeing around."*

He implemented the initial six-day Personal Effectiveness Program (PEP), where the 'high potential' staff involved, identified problems associated with the aggressive behaviour of the Directors, and the Competitive and Approval oriented culture. He quickly responded to a suggestion by Stephen Klemich, the external change agent who ran the PEP workshops, that it would be good to get a hard measure of culture. As a direct result, he involved himself and his Directors in completing Human Synergistics' LSI, and backed the continuing dialogue, and action that resulted, despite controversy and resistance on the part of some of his direct reports.

At MasterCard Australia, Leigh Clapham, responded to a cultural crisis that in large part was causing MasterCard Australia to lose significant market share. Clapham determined that outside help was needed and brought in an external change consultant Peter Fuda with a remit to address the behaviour of the 13 top leaders in the organisation, including Clapham himself, to build plans for changing the culture and to align the organisational structures and systems with the ideal culture. Leigh Clapham's personal passion, tenacity, belief in himself and others led the way in MasterCard Australia achieving an outstanding transformation.

At Balmain Leagues Club, there was a similar performance crisis – they were living hand-to-mouth, struggling to keep the Club's doors open, and facing potential closure. CEO Danny Munk inherited this situation, knew he had to take charge, and identified problems with the culture and the behaviour of his top team. He struggled with the situation for 18 months until he brought in Wayne Forrest and gave him the brief of implementing robust operational systems. This did not prove easy. The shift came when Wayne was introduced to, and undertook, the LSI. The changes he experienced were profound, and he now felt he had a platform from which to approach Danny Munk to undertake the OCI and the LSI at the Executive Team levels. It also helped him to clarify what needed to be done - people's behaviour needed to change, as well as structures and systems. Danny Munk's openness, his passion and commitment to make a difference, and his trust in his staff were reflected in his support of Wayne in those early days, when the way forward was not clear, and there were significant financial difficulties This capacity to step back, even when doubtful of the outcomes, and allow the staff to 'step up', was a critical factor in enabling him to lead the cultural transformation to a high-performing organisation.

At Yarra Valley, the incoming CEO was Tony Kelly, who had been a member of the senior team. On appointment as CEO, he catalysed a change that was already in train. Kelly's direct support and openness to the initiatives suggested by Anne Farquhar (General Manager, Human Resources) and his preparedness to 'walk the talk' and take his Executive Team with him were key factors in the success of the change program. He worked with staff to develop a new strategic intent for the organisation, worked with internal change agent Anne Farquhar to introduce Human Synergistics' diagnostic tools (OCI, OEI and LSI), and then on the basis of the diagnosis, worked to develop and initiate a systematic set of change interventions that transformed the organisation.

In Lion Nathan, we have an example of an organisation that managed transformational change over a 10 year period under the leadership of two successive CEOs. Gordon Cairns from 1995 to 2004, when he was succeeded by the current CEO, Rob Murray. Both outstanding leaders who initiated change, including the extended and extensive use of Human Synergistics' instruments, and who personally took charge of the strategic direction of a succession of change strategies that kept Lion Nathan responsive to change in a volatile and changing market.

We have described the relevant behaviour of the CEOs in all five organisations here to emphasise the importance of the CEO taking personal and direct charge of cultural change. The central role of the CEO is to take responsibility for the strategic redirection of the organisation and the corresponding cultural reorientation that is required. Decisive leadership from the CEO is a prerequisite for transformational change – not an option. This leadership is a signal to all others in the organisation that the change about to be undertaken is for real and, when the change is under way, that there is no turning back. There will be some who will be hoping, or fearing, that this is just another passing management fad and that tomorrow, or the next day, the business will go back to 'normal'; that it will be 'business as usual'.

When Cortes landed with a small band of armed conquistadors off the coast of what is now Veracruz in the New World of the Americas - a new and strange land where he hoped to find treasure - the first thing he did was to burn the boats that brought them there. He knew that many of his men feared the situation in which they found themselves, and would like to escape the uncertainties ahead. Burning the boats was a powerful signal that there was no turning back – only going forward. The resolution of the CEO gives just this signal.

Authorising the change: The power of the CEO stems partly from the authority invested in him or her by the Board or Minister. We often downplay authority in the modern world, but authority can unlock resources, and unleash action for change. No successful change program happens without the redistribution of human and other resources. In particular, effective change programs create networks of leaders and resources for change at all levels – more and more organisational members become change leaders as the momentum for change gathers.

What we see in all five cases we have studied is that the CEOs actively recruited and engaged other change leaders, beginning with their top team, and authorised them to act. This is not a formal process where they provide written certificates of authority, but rather an informal process where the personal and publicly-visible endorsement of the leadership of others confirms their right to act and to use resources. We can see this process very clearly in all organisations, for example with the endorsement of internal and external change agents.

In Yarra Valley Water, internal change agent Anne Farquhar exercised strong personal initiatives, including influencing the Senior Executive Team. However, her initiatives would have disappeared like water into sand if they had not been repeatedly endorsed by CEO Tony Kelly.

Power and authority are central features of organisational life. However, when we talk of CEOs 'taking charge of change', we do not mean that they need to control every aspect of the change process personally. In fact, this is a recipe for disaster. Management is the art of achieving things through others, and a successful change program operates through being given strong endorsement by the CEO, and then through the CEO's progressive and visible empowerment of other change agents, who are seen to be actively backed, resourced and rewarded. Thus taking charge of change progresses, as the CEO purposefully relinquishes direct control through delegating specific aspects of the change process to other players. Together with the CEO, these new players become actors in the organisational drama that is being scripted and enacted on the corporate stage. Eventually, the emerging culture takes the driver's seat, obviating the need for the CEO to be so visibly active in championing the cause.

Demonstrating personal commitment: All the CEOs in the study demonstrated their commitment through direct, up-front participation in the process of receiving feedback on their personal leadership style, and by making serious on-going efforts to change their behaviour toward a more Constructive style. Some of the feedback they received was surprising, even shocking to them, but they did not resile from the tough process of embarking on serious behavioural change. Adshel's Steve McCarthy was particularly articulate about his own shock when he realised the role his own behaviour was playing in supporting dysfunctional aspects of the former culture: *"We identified a lot of behaviour that had previously been condoned by many. That is the key to all this. This is behaviour that was condoned, supported. I was the cheerleader in all this stuff. I was saying how good are we because we do it like this? So there's no hiding behind anything."*

Gordon Cairns at Lion Nathan had a similar experience: *"As soon as you get the LSI you go: 'That's not me; that's how other people see me. It's not who I am'. So you go home and you show your wife and she says to you: 'That's who you are, and quite frankly, I and the kids have been telling you that for a long time...' So in a nice way your wife is saying: 'Look, we'd like you to change as well...' It seems to me, what more is there than a successful marriage and a successful career? That's a compelling reason to change."* Pain is part of the process of personal growth. It is painful sometimes to look into the mirror that others hold up to us. But there is joy beyond the pain when we abandon our PR self and generate more authentic relationships with those with whom we live and work.

A shift in the prevailing organisational paradigm does not take place without a corresponding shift in personal paradigms, and the CEO's paradigm is crucial. Roberts et al (2005, p. 715) argue that revisions of our view of ourselves are catalysed by trigger events which they refer to as 'jolts'. The feedback associated with the LSI in particular is often disconfirming of important aspects of the individual's view of themselves, and this constitutes just such a jolt, which can trigger a personal re-evaluation. Out of this re-evaluation can come the realisation, particularly critical for organisational change process, in the case of the CEO, that *"I must be the change I want to bring about in others"* (Ghandi). There can be no escape from doing the hard personal work on oneself that is needed to make this possible. Only those who have experienced a revolution within themselves can reach out effectively to help others change.

That brings us to the importance of modeling.

Modeling the behavioural changes needed for the new culture: All the CEOs in the cases we review here intuitively knew this to be true, and visibly struggled to make changes in their personal style. In the process, at times they appeared human and vulnerable; they would unthinkingly fall back into old behaviours – it is difficult to write over those old engraved neural pathways. Dunphy, in his first major book on change management (Dunphy & Dick, 1981), gave the initial chapter on change interventions the title: *Change Begins With Me.* Realising they had slipped back, they would inquire 'Am I doing it again?', laugh, and then try to produce the new, more Constructive, behaviour. Consequently, others could identify with them, learn from them, and learn to respect and love them.

Gordon Cairns again: *"Most people (leaders) recognise that you can't get good results without a great culture, but they think that culture is something that's out there and doesn't start with them, that's the difficulty. They say: 'We need a culture transformation program and oh, by the way, I'm not going to participate in it (as CEO) and neither is the senior team'. The whole point about that it that is it reinforces staff's belief that it is just another quick fix, another feel good, because the person/ people who need it most are not taking part. There is no such thing as 'the company'. The company is individuals. And it's individuals that have to change."*

Modeling the new behaviour has to start at the very top. The good news for CEOs is that none of us needs to be perfect. It is okay to stumble sometimes, to falter in the new perform-ance. That can help others to see us as more human, and to go on to identify with us, and internalise our model of the new behaviour. What is not acceptable is that the CEO persists in the old patterns and says: 'Don't do as I do, do as I say.' Australians, in particular, are very sensitive to what they sometimes refer to as 'the bullshit factor'. 'Are you fair dinkum?' is a profound question in this country. Australians need more inspirational examples of the power of personal transformation, not more excuses for cynical disillusionment.

Supporting others in making the changes: Finally, the CEO has to support others to make the changes they need to make if they are to contribute to the cultural transformation. This is more likely to happen where the CEO herself/himself has struggled with the difficult process of personal behavioural transformation; there is an immediate empathy with the struggles others are having, and a commitment to help.

To those around her/him, the CEO acts as a coach, a mentor and an encouraging influence. To do this where there is a significant power difference (as there always is with the CEO), there must be no threat. Jamie Tomlinson, CFO at Lion Nathan, describes how Rob Murray created this sense of trust: *"Rob's style is very open. He is very strategic and trusts, and wants people to do the right thing. In that kind of environment, people are happy to talk; there's no fear."*

The CEO's supportive role creates a climate of psychological safety, which is a critical element in allowing others to change.

The role of other senior executives

What we have written about the role of the CEO can be readily extrapolated to others in the top team. They also need to be personally involved and committed to the feedback process, and active in passing the change downward in their units. They also need to model the new, more Constructive behaviours, and to support others in making personal change. *"Change starts at the top, and so the leaders were coming out and sharing their circumplexes and like, they were saying, 'If I can, you can too'. The whole process became very personalised"* (Focus Group Member, Lion Nathan).

We have many examples of the active commitment, involvement and modeling of members of the Senior Executive Teams in all five organisations.

For example, Pat McCafferty, General Manager, Strategy & Communications at Yarra Valley Water, described the active role he played in keeping the cultural change moving along: *"I schedule about 30-40 interviews; people come in and talk to me about things like their understanding of strategy and direction, their role and I speak to them about leadership and commu-nication and the feedback feeds straight into an annual review. It takes a lot of time, but it is of enormous benefit."*

In describing what his managers and supervisors were doing as a result of the culture change, Tim Camiller, newly appointed CEO of Balmain Leagues Club, had this to say: *"We have an environment and a practice that whenever there is an issue, we apply our learned Human Synergistics skills to address these issues. We have a de-brief that says what's working, what's not working. Even in our performance appraisals, we talk about this, and what you can say about yourself that you couldn't say last year. We apply it in lots of circumstances. Instead of just working in the business, we are working on the business. It's about saying: 'I know that I have 20 tasks to perform this week, but I need to find time to reflect on how I can improve the business – sit back and design systems, sit back and grow people."*

What is evident from the comments of the two executives we have quoted is how the change of consciousness in managers and supervisors creates reflection on the way the strategy, structures and systems are working, and results in an active reworking of this objective side of the corporate culture. This illustrates the process of co-creation that occurs - as more managers experience a change of consciousness, it becomes apparent to them that some of the strategies, structures and systems are increasingly out of alignment, and so they work actively to redesign them to support the growing edge of the Constructive culture.

Many executives try to change consciousness by simply manipulating strategies, structures and processes as if there is a one-way causal path from these organisational elements to the human mind. Redrafting the corporate strategy, redrawing the organisational chart and putting in a new appraisal or incentive system may produce some tactical changes in employee behaviour, but seldom produces engaged people who have deeply internalised a new strategic vision for the future of the company. The blueprint for change must emerge from the collective experience of those who are undergoing the change – it can't be simply created on PowerPoint at head office and emailed throughout the organisation.

The role of other change agents
Our research shows that, while the leadership of line managers is essential, other change agents also played important roles in the cultural transformation process. We interviewed both internal and external change consultants for these organisations. All five organisations used at least one external change consultant all but two of the organisations (Adshel and MasterCard Australia) also had a key internal change consultant. This raises the question of what knowledge and skills these consultants provided, and whether internal and external consultants played differentiated roles.

The external change agents: There was a principal external consultant in four of the five organisations. We will look at each in turn and then compare the roles they played.

In Adshel, Stephen Klemich was a serendipitous introduction. One of his company's ex-staff members had gone to work for Adshel as CEO Steve McCarthy's Personal Assistant (PA), and had recommended Klemich's company in response to the CEO's initiative in looking for a change consultant. Klemich was first commissioned by McCarthy to design and run two six-day Personal Effectiveness Programs (PEP); then to design and run a six-day Executive Development Program (EDP). He later organised follow-up workshops for former PEP participants, and another follow-up workshop for former EDP participants. After the two initial PEP programs, Klemich presented to a strategy meeting of directors, and gained permission to roll out an OCI survey through the company. Klemich worked with his wife Mara, and also brought in another external consultant, Joanna Price, to address the issue of role clarity.

Klemich's role evolved from training provider initially, to strategic change agent and trusted adviser to the CEO. Klemich had the courage to challenge the client company's assumptions and norms, and to engage people at all levels in meaningful dialogue about the culture of the organisation. He was skilled at building trust so that difficult, previously 'undiscussable' issues could be openly confronted.

In MasterCard Australia, Leigh Clapham had known of the work of external consultant Peter Fuda prior to being appointed as Senior Vice-President and General Manager. Six months after taking on his new job, Clapham called Fuda in to discuss his diagnosis of the organisation's situation. Fuda worked closely with Clapham to measure the culture of MasterCard Australia and to identify the impact of the top 13 leaders on it. Out of this intervention individual, group and company plans were developed focusing on achievable behavioural changes needed to shift the culture toward their ideal. These plans were commercially as well as behaviourally focussed. Once again Fuda was asked to design and run off-site workshops with the Leadership Team, carry the OCI surveys through the company and work with managers to develop the new roadmap of how the changes were to be achieved. MasterCard Australia is unusual in that there was no internal change agent (apart from Clapham himself) so that Fuda's role involved some of the tasks that would usually be carried out by an internal change agent.

Balmain Leagues Club had a couple of strong internal change agents in Danny Munk and Wayne Forrest. It was Wayne however who was introduced to the LSI by KPMG – who were already working in the organisation. Wayne's personal journey enabled him to conceive of a different way to lead and manage people. In 2000, he commissioned Roma Gaster, who he had met while undertaking his LSI Accreditation at Human Synergistics, to join the team as an external consultant to support the developing culture. Her expertise allowed for a new voice in offering feedback and support, running workshops and coaching for behavioural change. This joint initiative resulted in the outstanding transformational change achieved in the organisation.

Lion Nathan drew from a range of expert suppliers in a variety of culture building approaches. They engaged Carolyn Taylor of Corporate Vision (Taylor's company at that time) to conduct workshops, and she introduced the LSI in connection with these. Clearly, these workshops were a 'paradigm-busting' experience. Through most of the ten years of change however, Bob Barbour, the internal change agent, played a powerful role in maintaining momentum, and his team played a hands-on role in de-briefing and developing staff.

In Yarra Valley Water, the external consultant, Ian Pimblett, worked with Anne Farquhar, General Manager Human Resources. These two change agents formed a close and dynamic partnership, with Farquhar playing the role of social architect, and Pimblett the role of builder sub-contractor. Pimblett was responsible for similar initiatives to those discussed above – introducing and managing administration of the OCI/OEI, and designing and running workshops. He also worked closely with individuals, coaching them in interpreting their scores and designing action programs.

What then can we conclude about the role of the external change consultant?

It seems from our case studies that external change agents can bring three critical assets which form the core of their contribution to the transformational journey. The first is an independent point of view, an 'innocence', in relation to the existing corporate culture. They have not been socialised into the culture, and do not share the prevailing assumptions, values and norms. Consequently, they are in a position to question and challenge the Actual culture, including if necessary any contribution the CEO's behaviour is making to sustaining it. For this asset to be realised, the consultant needs to work directly to the CEO, and have the courage to challenge the prevailing order and to confront the CEO and other senior executives if necessary. This is only likely to be successful where there is a rapport and relationship of mutual respect and trust between the CEO and the external change agent. Alternatively, the external consultant can work mainly to the primary internal change agent who, in these cases, is generally the Human Resources Manager who in turn has direct access to the CEO. The external change agent, again, is only likely to succeed where there is a relationship of mutual support and trust.

The second asset these consultants brought was knowledge and expertise of how to manage a transformational change process. This kind of knowledge and expertise is rare, and is only built through accumulating substantial experience in the conduct of significant change programs, and reflecting on and learning from that experience. Knowledge of relevant theory and research also helps in ordering accumulating wisdom about how to make significant change.

The third asset brought by these external change agents was a high degree of interpersonal skill, and personal maturity and wisdom (Dunphy and Pitsis, 2003). Corporate change is always a political process, achieved through interpersonal relationships. The skills needed to be an effective change agent are broad and complex. Further, mastery in this area only develops through experience, and over time.

The combination of relevant knowledge, expertise and skill needed to contribute actively to culture change at all levels of the organisation is often claimed, but seldom manifested. Truly effective transformational change consultants are hard to find. There is a need for a systematic development program to produce more master change agents.

The internal change agents: Yarra Valley Water, Balmain Leagues Club and Lion Nathan each had an internal change agent who also played a key role as catalyst for change.

In Yarra Valley Water, this was Anne Farquhar, General Manager, Human Resources. Farquhar joined the organisation with a specific brief to change the culture. She has a 'straight talking' style, and her position in the organisation provided a strong base from which to influence the Senior Executive Team. She impressed all by her initiative and competence, and quickly built trust throughout the organisation. She and Ian Pimblett, the external consultant, formed an effective working partnership, and together decided that the OCI could be useful in launching the cultural change. Because Anne was new to the organisation, she had some of the qualities that we identified in the external change agents. She was also a 'cultural clean skin', and therefore able to stand outside and evaluate it more objectively than those caught up in it. She also had relevant knowledge, expertise and skills. Her internal position gave her the added advantage of having a position of authority and, given that her responsibility was Human Resources, a particularly important power base from which to leverage cultural change, and to ensure that the 'objective' side of culture - structure and systems - was modified to support the emerging Constructive culture.

In Lion Nathan, Bob Barbour (People & Culture Director) was the key internal change agent over a period of several years, under the leadership of two successive CEOs. Bob took the initiative of introducing the idea of cultural change to then CEO Gordon Cairns, bringing in the outside change consultant, Carolyn Taylor, and introducing the Human Synergistics instruments. Subsequently, he consistently followed through, managing a constant evolution of the structures and systems to ensure that the new culture maintained its adaptiveness.

At Balmain Leagues Club, as partly outlined above, the prime initiative for cultural change was provided initially by Wayne Forrest, the newly appointed Operations Manager and eventually shared by Danny Munk, CEO from 1995 to 2006. The use of the OCI and LSI led to a revolution in how the managers went about attempting culture change. Forrest describes this as follows: *"In the past, we always tried to rectify things by changing structure, but now we had come to the recognition that the old catch phrase of 'strategy before structure' was what we had to deal with. It was a real simple question – if leadership was about helping people to grow, then the only people we didn't have involved in that process were the people who were in a direct leadership role – the duty managers. Nor did we measure it, nor was it part of their performance criteria. So we set about putting some things in place to address that gap."*

Forrest and Munk, in collaboration with their executive colleagues put in place a series of interventions which transformed the people, built new capabilities, and redesigned the systems to create a culture of initiative and high performance.

Neither MasterCard Australia nor Adshel had an internal change agent – in both cases the respective CEOs saw the change as so important that they took on elements of this role themselves, but also delegated a good deal of what might in other circumstances have been done by an internal change agent to their external change agent. Adshel had relatively small staff numbers, which made this feasible – it would hardly be possible in a large complex organisation such as Lion Nathan, or even a medium-sized organisation such as Yarra Valley Water.

Internal change agents orchestrate the diverse actors and projects in a comprehensive organisation-wide change program. They make connections between staff and management, and between internal and external change agents. They match and complement the skills and expertise of the external change agent, and ensure that all interventions are integrated into the day-to-day evolution of the cultural change. They are actor, producer and director, all at once.

What can we conclude therefore about the role of internal change agents?

First, that while they are not essential to the change process in smaller organisations, they can play vital roles in the cultural transformation process. Particularly if they have recently come to their role from outside the organisation, in the absence of a high-level external consultant, they can also provide the initial stimulus for change. If they hold a key staff role in the organisation, they can use that as an effective base for action; the position of Human Resources Director is a particularly suitable base, as that function can and should provide leadership for the process of transformation. Finally, they also need a high level of interpersonal and project management skills, and the ability to build a personal relationship with the CEO and other members of the Executive Team, and to win the trust of other members of the organisation. All three internal change agents we have described achieved this.

Overall, it is apparent that a critical catalyst for transformational change is the existence of a close working relationship between the CEO and at least one other change agent, who can be either a high-level external change agent or an effective internal change agent, preferably the Human Resources Director. We suggest that in a large, complex organisation, a combination of all three can be a powerful contributor to change. It is vital that the members of this team have a strong rapport with each other, trust and respect each other, and understand the different contributions they can each make to the transformation process.

Widening the circle of leaders

While this core team is important, its success must be judged by the effectiveness with which it widens the circle of change leaders throughout the organisation. Great leaders don't make followers – they make other leaders. The energisation of the Senior Executive Team is the critical factor here, for it is a prerequisite for enabling the change to be moved out across the organisation as a whole. The combination of a CEO, change consultants and a fired up senior team is what Kotter refers to as a 'guiding coalition'. Kotter writes: *"Because major change is so difficult to accomplish, a powerful force is required to sustain the process. No one individual, even a monarch-like CEO, is ever able to develop the right vision, communicate it to large numbers of people, eliminate all key obstacles, generate short term wins, lead and manage dozens of change projects, and anchor the new approaches deep in the organisation's culture… A strong guiding coalition is always needed – one with the right composition, level of trust, and shared objective. Building such a team is always an essential part of the early stages of any effort to restructure, re-engineer, or re-tool a set of strategies"* (Kotter, 1996).

In writing about leadership for cultural change, Bate argues that leaders need to become more *"process sensitive, that is, responsive to the shifting concerns and requirements of the internal change process… cultural change is a dynamic process that requires a dynamic conception of leadership… A uniform, homogenous view of leadership must give way to one of dynamism, diversity and heterogeneity, in which all the necessary roles are brought into play to effect cultural change. Different kinds of leadership will be needed at different stages of the change process. The challenge lies in putting together a leadership process that reflects the changing requirements of the cultural process, where individuals and groups resource and service these requirements in a variety of ways"* (Bate, 1994).

Change in key personnel

Seldom do all key personnel commit to organisational transformation. In these cases, there were some managers in key positions who did not support cultural transformation, and remained loyal subjects of the old order. In some cases, these are people who have devoted much of their career to the organisation, and played a key role in the formation of the existing culture. Often, they are also reluctant to engage in personal transformation. They are committed to the maintenance of the existing culture, and like themselves the way they are, or are afraid to embark on a journey of personal change. Clearly, the organisation has a debt of gratitude to these people, and a duty of care. However, if transformational change is necessary to avoid organisational disaster, or to pick up important new business opportunities, and they actively undermine or simply block this change, then they must go.

One of the advantages of creating a Constructive culture is that it allows this situation to be openly addressed, and to be treated as a problem-solving situation. The LSI feedback itself can lead to an individual taking the initiative to leave voluntarily, realising that there will be a lack of fit between his or her style and the emerging interpersonal style to which others are committed. Failing this, they can be counselled realistically about their future, and assisted to find a suitable position elsewhere. Feedback can even help provide the self-insight a CEO needs to decide that it is time to leave. This was how Gordon Cairns of Lion Nathan described his decision to go: *"I am not the right person to take the next step for Lion Nathan. I believe a CEO's best work is done in the first years. My primary role is to hold up the mirror and make bold decisions. After seven years, I have built a reputation I want to protect. This is likely to make me risk averse."*

There were several examples of people leaving the organisations during the change process, sometimes voluntarily, and at other times after being counselled to leave the organisation. Sometimes the feedback process left some people realising that they would prefer to work elsewhere. Others were unable or unwilling to change to meet the demands of the new culture, including restructured roles or increased performance standards.

INSTITUTING EFFECTIVE COMMUNICATION, BUILDING ENGAGEMENT

Transformative change takes place through communication. Before discussing how communication affects organisational transformation, we want to correct a misconception about the role of communication in culture change.

The misconception is that communication is primarily about managers telling others in the organisation to change. In the first place, communication is not simply telling. As fundamental to effective communication as telling, perhaps more important, is listening.

As Palmer et al point out: *"If communication about change entails a dialogue, then listening becomes a central communication skill"* (Palmer et al, 2006). The managers and change agents in all these organisations did a lot of listening – much of this was informal and some was formalised (survey feedback is actually 'organised listening'). One of the most significant communication strategies to change the culture in these organisations was in fact the OCI collection process itself, which informed everyone of what kind of culture people aspired to create.

God gave us each two ears and one mouth and it was a hint

This can be the first and most important step in creating widespread engagement in the change process. This is exemplified at Adshel, where all staff participated, and the process was fully-resourced. All staff also attended workshops where the results of the survey were presented. Steve McCarthy, the CEO, attended all of these workshops. At the workshops, staff were involved in small-group activity, which included listing 'five things management can do to develop the culture', and 'five things the staff can do to develop the culture'. Listening can lead to informed decision-making and responsible action.

The process of collective communication and action-planning was itself a culture change intervention at Adshel – the way the workshops were run, and staff involved, signalled a major departure from the way things were done there. Up until this point, influence and power had been centralised with the CEO and the Sales department. But at the workshops *"staff were given input right from the beginning – they were heard. Many of them said: 'We've been heard; they're listening to us'. This starts to shift the culture immediately. It's a better place because we've been heard. And then, something was actually done – quickly – as a result of those issues. People realised that discussing things in this forum would mean that it would be dealt with"* (Focus Group Member, Adshel). The norms of the old culture were already changing, and the change was visible, and noted. People at all levels of the organisation were given voice.

Other approaches to communication were also important.

At Yarra Valley Water, this process of ensuring managers listened to lower level employees was institutionalised in the form of 'skip level interviews'. Skip level interviews are where staff have the opportunity to speak to the manager of their manager. The introduction of these interviews didn't compromise the manager's authority, but enabled staff to be heard by the key decision-makers of the company.

These new leaders will have, not the loudest voice, but the most attentive ear

(Warren Bennis)

One of the advantages of creating a Constructive culture is that it encourages dialogue and increases the amount of listening within the organisation, particularly to messages from front-line staff and customers. This increases the amount of valid data available for decision-making, and opens up the previously hidden interpersonal underworld of gossip, private deals and rorts, cynicism and unexpressed hopes to realistic examination. Listening is a change-management skill.

Telling is, however, also part of transformational change and, as Palmer et al write: *"One under-recognised management communication skill is storytelling. People tell stories in conversations to keep the organisation from repeating historically bad choices and to invite the repetition of past successes"* (Palmer et al, 2006, p. 294). Cultures carry these story-lines – changing the culture involves creating new stories that become the new myths which carry the organisation onward.

We also discovered that the language of the change agents is often rich with symbolism, imagery and metaphor – the stuff good stories are made of. To create change, there must be a credible intellectual agenda, but it is not enough to speak to people's minds - change agents must also reach to the hearts of those in the organisation, and touch emotions. To do this they create a rich rhetoric, a persuasive language that is 'in sync' with the type of changes they wish to bring about. Marshak points to the importance of this kind of language, and argues that when the images and metaphors that managers use are misaligned with the type of change they desire, this contributes to the failure of the change program (Marshak, 1993).

But the most powerful communication is not necessarily words – actions often speak more powerfully than words. Effective change agents understand that they are creating a drama in which symbolic events can concentrate the attention of those in the organisation, creating new, shared experiences that regenerate meaning, shifting the culture. Symbolic events can signal that the times have changed, and that we too must change.

A simple example comes from Yarra Valley Water, where a group of employees had gone off to a workshop, and resolved to return and front up to the then Managing Director Peter Harford to question the way the organisational mission had been developed without consultation. He himself had realised that it had failed to create the commitment he had hoped for. When they raised this issue first, he listened, then took out a copy of the mission statement, tore it up, and threw the pieces into the bin. This was seen as a commitment on his part to listen, to be prepared to change, and to consult. He did not need to send out a memo to make these points – the story spread rapidly throughout the organisation, being told and retold.

At Yarra Valley Water, they also instituted what they called 'Blue Zone' days. Blue is the colour used in the Human Synergistics Circumplex to signify Constructive behaviour. They conducted these days twice a year, and they were attended by about 150 people. The intention was to demonstrate and clarify, through fun and engaging activities, what is meant by appropriate cultural behaviours. These activities explored the 12 styles associated with the OCI and LSI tools, and helped create a common understanding about what 'Blue Zone' behaviour really is.

Anne Farquhar spoke of the systematic use of such symbolic events as a way of keeping the pot of change on the boil, and demonstrating to staff that change was continuing: *"Regular visibility and events occurring… so that every three or four months there was something that was happening… You never stop using this type of stuff, it has to be continuous."*

This points to another important aspect of the change dialogue – creating a common change language. Language undergirds culture, for language conveys meaning, and culture centres on meaning. One reason that change programs fail is that the different interest groups don't succeed in creating a common language. One way to think about organisational change is to view it as different speech communities in negotiation with each other. Some change programs, particularly in large organisations, resemble the tower of Babel. Different change practitioners are brought in, each with their own professional and esoteric language. Strategic Change consultants, Business Process Re-engineering consultants, Organisation Development consultants, IT consultants – each has their own agenda for change expressed in technical terms the other groups don't understand, and they are often running competitive change agendas. Not surprisingly, most members of the organisation don't follow what they are talking about, and often couldn't care less. They just hope the whole lot of them will eventually go away, so life can revert to normal.

Heracleous and Barrett describe how this kind of cacophony affected one change program in the UK that finally failed: *"We saw stakeholder groups talking past each other, rather than to each other, because of their almost diametrically opposed discourses, at both the deeper structure levels and communicative action levels, and their lack of common ground on which to base a dialogue"* (Heracleous and Barrett, 2001).

One of the advantages of the Human Synergistics' tools and their use is that they provide an engaging set of shared experiences and a relatively simple vocabulary (Red, Green, Blue at the simplest level) that has powerful and concrete meaning, because it relates directly to the personal behaviour of each individual. The concepts are expressed in behavioural terms, and so are not abstract. In many of the organisations we studied employees and managers demonstrated this through the use of terms such as 'becoming Blue' or would refer to individuals as 'being a bit Red' or 'that was a bit Green'. This often provided a springboard for leadership teams in particular, to reach agreement on how they would interact with one another. In the Balmain Leagues Club for example, the Executive Team used a process they named 'calling the line'. As part of their team development workshops they identified behaviours that were seen to be Constructive and therefore 'above the line' and behaviours that were seen as Defensive (below the line). As part of their team commitment to working in the Constructive they agreed to 'call the line': when any one of them slipped into Defensive behaviours.

As mentioned above, the focus groups regarded the introduction of the Human Synergistics' tools as one of the most important process interventions. Providing accurate feedback to each person is key to developing high-level skills of self-awareness, relating to others, and problem-solving. This ability to see ourselves accurately, and confront external realities realistically, is what we refer to as 'reflexivity', and is the ground from which change can occur. It is central to building the ongoing capacity for constructive interpersonal communication.

MODIFYING OTHER ORGANISATIONAL SYSTEMS

We now move on to the other interventions specified in the Human Synergistics model, beginning with interventions to change the Mission and Philosophy of the organisation. Most of the organisations made some intervention under each of these headings at some point in the change program. The sequence varied from organisation to organisation and the emphasis given to interventions under each heading varied according to the needs diagnosis made by the guiding coalition of change agents.

Changing Mission and Philosophy

The Mission and Philosophy lever involves articulation of the mission and values of the organisation, and the degree to which it is customer service-focussed.

Perhaps the most significant change in Mission and Philosophy occurred at Lion Nathan, where the initial change workshops in 1996 identified the need for change to be firmly anchored in a sense of purpose and values. Input from employees about what values should be core to the company was followed by intense debate in the leadership team. Eventually, it was agreed that the core purpose should be 'making our world a more social place'. This may read rather like 'motherhood and apple pie', however the real test of whether a company's mission and strategy really mean something is whether they actually lead to closing off some desirable options because these options lie outside the definition. In Lion Nathan's case, the mission passes this test, as it led to a decision not to move into the lucrative poker machine market, because poker machines were not seen to make clubs and pubs more sociable places. Over time, a lot of work was devoted to clarifying Lion's core purpose and vision so that they could be summarised on a one-page blueprint that could be used in decision-making.

The Mission and Philosophy lever was also important in the change process at MasterCard Australia. When Leigh took over MasterCard Australia he was surprised that many of those in the organisation did not have a perspective on the business and how it was tracking. He therefore instituted face-to-face communication sessions with employees and during these sessions ensured that there was clarity around global and local business goals and priorities and a clear understanding of their aspiration to achieve a 40% market share. Values supportive of these goals were then reinforced through the employee recognition board and 'Team of the Quarter' award.

It is vital to clarify the Mission and Philosophy of the organisation, and to ensure that the organisation's purpose and values are understood by all in the organisation. If the transformative process is to succeed, each individual member of the organisation must know where the organisation is headed, what it is attempting to accomplish, and how their work can contribute to that. Achieving this basic requirement necessitates planning, time, resources and skill.

Changing Structures

Structures refer to the ways in which people, roles and activities are ordered, and their impact on the distribution of power and influence, empowerment and employee involvement. Structure represents the repetitive interactions of people around the process of getting the work done.

Significant structural changes have been made at Lion Nathan over the ten years of its change program. Under its current CEO Rob Murray, for example, the Victorian hotels were sold off, and the firm moved out of China.

But structural change is not always on this scale. At MasterCard Australia task forces were created to agree action areas and to implement the agreed actions. There were a variety of other action-oriented meetings set up also including cross-functional forums, regular reviews of progress on plans and bi-annual meetings to consolidate the change agenda, celebrate success and share learnings.

At Adshel, Structure was not a significant lever, as the prevailing structure was seen as appropriate. However, there was a substantial impact connected with the structure in that the pivotal role of Sales Director changed hands, and the leadership style of the new Director was much more closely aligned with the aspirational culture. The change process also brought about a significant change in the distribution of power within the structure. The dominance of the sales function was lessened through a number of changes that redistributed influence more widely across the company as a whole.

At Balmain Leagues Club, people's jobs were redesigned, and their roles upgraded to line management responsibilities so they became strongly involved in decision-making processes. They were upskilled and empowered. Duty Managers were involved in strategic planning alongside the CEO, General Managers and Board members. As a result, the strategic decision was made to broaden their revenue base by investing in and repositioning the food and beverage business, establishing a café, and a satellite club at Homebush. In a short time, the planning and decision-making processes became a cultural expectation – part of the unconscious operating style of 'the way we do things around here'.

Changing Systems including reward structures

Systems refer to the interrelated set of procedures that an organisation uses to support its core activities and to solve problems; human resource systems are particularly important in this regard.

At Adshel, substantial systems changes took place around goal-setting, where there was much greater clarity, and around human resource practices, specifically recruitment, and performance appraisal, remuneration, training and development. In particular, the overhaul of the sales commission system, to ensure that it supported more collaborative behaviour, made a major contribution to transformational change.

At Balmain Leagues Club, the central focus of the change was at two levels – the Executive and the Duty Managers. In particular, the changes that took place in the leadership styles of the Duty Managers impacted directly on line staff and customers. Interventions here were around the introduction of intensive training and development, ongoing performance reviews, honest discussions on how to increase the coordination between the two levels of management, and a new approach to problem-solving (the de-brief). In addition, an induction program for new employees was introduced that assigned every new employee to the care of a Duty Manager, who became their model and coach.

At Lion Nathan, there were step changes in human resource practices between 1998 and 2005. Each phase built on the 'step' laid down before it. The Systems introduced have covered capability analysis, competency assessment and development, talent management, performance management, recognition and review, and resourcing, leadership and achievement programs. Altogether, this represents a major ongoing investment in the development of a coherent and integrated set of human resource systems. It is this kind of coherent suite of human resource systems that can reinforce and consolidate the gains made by culture change.

Changing Technology including job design

Technology refers to methods used to transform inputs into outcomes and outputs, and includes job design.

At Adshel, a new IT-based 'panel booking system' was introduced. The panel booking system allows Adshel's entire collection of 11,000 advertising panels to be booked every fortnight on behalf of contracts for advertising sold to clients. The old system, although IT based, was operated by five data-entry clerks in a back office, and was open to manipulation on the basis of status and favours. It failed to maximise the profitability of sales contracts for the company, because it was distorted by a bonus system that encouraged intense competition within the company. The new system allows full transparency and access by all staff across the organisation, and operates to maximise profitability.

Adshel's results were also being affected by a lack of role clarity – people often didn't know what was expected of them. This is often the case in small organisations that have expanded rapidly. A reduction in the number of different positions and the collaborative development of new position descriptions achieved an average 9.8% improvement on the relevant items measuring role clarity in the OCI.

Summary: Change Interventions

Managers have at their disposal a number of ways of intervening in the ongoing life of the organisation in order to produce cultural change. We have argued that leadership and communication are central levers for shifting the cultural axis. The change literature generally supports the importance of these strategic interventions. Beyond these universals, there are several others that can be brought to bear. All five organisations provide some examples of interventions in these remaining areas, but the importance of each area varies from one change program to another.

Transformational change clearly depends on creating alignment across the full range of organisational activities; it is vital to create coherence and consistency across the full range from Mission and Philosophy, through Structures, Systems and Technology. But the logic and sequencing of transformative change programs will vary according to circumstances. Not everything can be changed at once – skilled leadership is usually in short supply, particularly at first, and resources are not limitless. Therefore, the guiding coalition in each change program must set priorities for change, intervening in areas that seem of most strategic importance, and moving on to another area when wins have been had. Step-by-step, the various facets of organisational being are brought into increasing alignment.

IMPACT OF CHANGE

Change programs have goals, and in the change programs we studied, one immediate goal was to transform the corporate culture. This was not a goal pursued purely for its own sake, but rather as a means to creating high-performance organisations.

We will deal with each of these goals separately, and then examine what we have learned about the links between corporate culture and business performance.

Impact on the culture

Culture change is the flavour-of-the-month in some business circles, and CEOs can command large audiences when they speak about how the corporate culture of their organisations has been transformed. Our own experience is that when members of some of these organisations are asked about the culture change program, their response is a puzzled: 'What culture change program?' It seems that the transformation is largely a fantasy in the mind of the CEO.

In the case of the organisations we have studied here however, we have hard data that clearly demonstrate statistically highly-significant shifts in culture on multiple dimensions (see Table 1).

This data are, however, from responses to questionnaires, and so we thought it wise to follow up this 'hard' evidence with questions to those involved in the changes about whether they perceived the culture changes, and how they evaluated the impact on organisational life.

It was evident from the focus group discussions that, in the five organisations, the cultural change that had occurred was clearly visible to all participants. They pointed in particular to: behavioural changes in themselves and other organisational members; changes in leadership and management style; increased awareness on the part of organisational members of the

Table 1. Top 5 Test → Re-Test Culture survey results

Style	Percentile			Significance	Style	Percentile			Significance	Style	Percentile			Significance
	Test	Re-Test	Shift			Test	Re-Test	Shift			Test	Re-Test	Shift	
Achievement	51	65	14	***	Approval	55	34	-21	***	Oppositional	76	53	-23	***
Self-Actualizing	39	63	24	***	Conventional	58	38	-20	***	Power	70	34	-36	***
Humanistic-Encouraging	38	70	32	***	Dependent	48	20	-28	***	Competitive	81	49	-32	***
Affiliate	22	47	25	***	Avoidance	65	41	-24	***	Perfectionistic	69	45	-24	***

NS Not Significant; *<0.05; **<0.01; ***<0.001

impact of their behavioural style on others; increased commitment to change and 'buy-in' to the change process; modified reward systems; and increased role clarity.

The behavioural change was seen as having positive outcomes in other areas, such as: increased accountability; respect for and empathy with others; higher trust levels; and communication effectiveness. These points are summaries of many written responses of individual Focus Group Members and their subsequent discussions of the changes they had listed (see Focus Group Interview Summary Data; Appendix 6 – Table 6).

For many, the feedback process had been a transforming experience, with positive benefits outside the workplace as well as within it. The following quote was typical: *"The Human Synergistics program has not only changed the way I think and act at work but also when I am at home. My way of thinking has changed, and it has helped me with personal relationships as well. For me, it was a 'life experience'"* (Focus Group Member, Balmain Leagues Club).

An important part of the impact on culture is the transformation of leadership style that occurred in all organisations. At MasterCard Australia for example the leadership style shifted from Passive/Defensive and Aggressive/Defensive to strongly Constructive with all four of the Constructive styles over the 50th percentile. Similar changes occurred in all five organisations.

> **The cultural journey has been great, and significant. We could not have achieved what we currently are without this. Well done, Exec – it's working!**
>
> (Focus Group Member, Yarra Valley Water)

There is no doubt that these change programs did transform the culture of these organisations. The change is measurable, significant, clearly perceived by organisational members at all levels, and had a profound effect on the working and personal lives of many of those involved.

Impact on results – business performance

One of the most difficult and debated issues in organisational change is how to measure the impact of a change program on corporate performance (Beer & Nohria, 2000). We speak of change programs as if they were discrete interventions in a static organisation. In fact, an organisation is never static, but always in process. Its environment is in constant change, and people at different levels are adjusting their behaviour to those changes. New members with new ideas are being recruited and some existing members leaving, taking knowledge and skills with them. New technologies are being adopted; old technologies being phased out. Even without any significant planned change intervention, performance can improve or decline. On top of all this endemic change, the CEO and other change agents design and implement a deliberate program of planned change aimed, usually, to improve the organisation's performance. How can we know whether the particular actions associated with the planned change program are responsible for a change in performance levels, and not the myriad other changes taking place in the organisation anyway?

And then there is the question: How are we to measure performance? Do we measure results in the short or longer term? Do we use financial measures alone, or some broader measure such as increase in corporate capability, or the Triple Bottom Line?

In our research study, we set out to gather what evidence we could to examine the links, if any, between the five planned change programs and corporate performance as they defined it. To this end, we interviewed the CEO and CFO in each organisation, and gathered what evidence they could provide about the impact of the culture change program on performance. We also asked the Focus Group Members if they could discern any impact on performance of the changes in culture they had identified.

We will start with the responses from the focus groups. In responding to the question: 'What impact did the cultural change have on business performance?', participants in focus groups largely emphasised the impact on individual performance. Examples were: improved staff motivation and effectiveness, increased initiative, innovation, creativity, achievement, and decisiveness. They also emphasised that they were now working in happier, more pleasant workplaces, and that teamwork and collaboration had improved, both internally and cross-functionally. At both Yarra Valley Water and Balmain, improved staff retention and customer service were also noted. Improved financial outcomes were specifically mentioned by Focus Group Members in Balmain Leagues Club and MasterCard Australia but in other organisations there did not seem to be a strong awareness of such an impact (see Focus Group Summary Data; Appendix 6 – Table 5). Overall, the change program was seen as having had substantial impact on personal effectiveness at work, and on the structures and systems of all five organisations.

What of the responses of the CFOs? CFOs are normally the tough-minded, 'no nonsense' members of the organisation whose job emphasises, of course, meeting the financial goals set for the organisation by the Board or Minister. We found that, rather than being skeptical of what some cynics might see as the 'soft and mushy' human relations emphasis of these change programs, these CFOs were highly impressed by the human impact of the program in their own lives, and by the impact on the interpersonal relationships and teamwork throughout the organisation. Somewhat to our amusement, in a couple of cases we found it difficult to steer the conversation away from these 'soft' issues, and get the CFOs to focus on the impact of these cultural changes on 'hard' performance data.

We now turn to the performance data we were able to glean from interviews with the CEOs, and CFOs, and from company documents and records. Different organisations measure performance in differing ways, so we have had to work with the measures that they themselves used. Consequently, the results are not directly comparable across organisations.

The organisation with the longest history of culture change interventions is Lion Nathan. Starting with the 'hard' measures, at the start of the change program, in the years 1996 and 1997, financial results were poor. As the change program began to affect the organisation, net profits moved from a low of A$110 million after tax to $220 million in 2004, and the share price increased from $3.34 to $7.38. However, after Rob Murray took over in 2004, he made some tough strategic decisions, such as selling its Victorian hotels, and leaving China. He also revised the double-digit growth projections to a more conservative 5%, so the company could reinvest and secure its long term sustainability. This again raises the question of how far out should performance measures be taken? Clearly there was a major increase in financial success over an extended period, but the company now faces a situation where its new strategy has reduced performance outcomes, for the short-run at least to ensure strong long-term sustainability.

Lion Nathan also measured 'customer satisfaction' over the course of the past five years. The organisation's overall performance on this measure has been maintained at an average of 8 out of 10. Hewitt Associates were employed to measure 'employee engagement', and scores for Lion Nathan peaked at 78% in 2003, but have since declined to 68% in 2004-2005. The peak put Lion Nathan within Hewitt's Best Employer category, but the current score is below Lion Nathan's target for engagement of 75%. However all of these figures are well above the average figure for all organisations surveyed.

At Balmain Leagues Club, $2 million worth of efficiencies were made over two years, through doing things differently, and improving cross-functional relationships. The function business grew 15% year on year due to better customer service and greater responsiveness. A satellite club was established in Homebush without the provision of any additional staff resources. Newly appointed CEO Tim Camiller stated: *"Five years ago we would not have been able to open another club without throwing in a number of external resources. We can now comfortably do it ourselves and be confident that we can put a couple of staff in to manage and establish a new club facility."*

Adshel was a very profitable company at the beginning of the change program. It was, and, remains one of the most profitable companies in the Clear Channel and APN group, and consistently outperforms the market. Its revenue and EBIT growth has been double-digit over the past two years of the change program – revenue grew 15% and 17%, and EBIT 31% and 45% for the two calendar years 2004 and 2005. Quality of service and employee satisfaction is also measured in the OCI, and improved over the course of the change program by 4.7% and 6.6% respectively.

At Yarra Valley there was a 75% reduction in recruitment costs over the period of the change program due to decreased staff turnover – down from 26% to 6%. Sick leave also reduced from 6.43 sick days per employee to 4.5 per employee. There were also substantial improvements in a variety of reputation measures on the Millwood Brown survey. Employee engagement rose from 57% to 76% over this period.

At MasterCard Australia, since 2002, MasterCard Australia increased its success rate with new business agreements from 33% to 67%. Its market share of total credit cards in Australia increased from 29% to 40% in 36 months. Employee engagement scores increased exponentially over the period of the change program. Employee satisfaction improved 12.6% and quality of service improved by 14.2%.

Summary of performance impact

We can conclude that most of these organisations showed sizeable improvement on most measurable performance outcomes over the period of the change program – in some cases the improvement was dramatic. Lion Nathan shows one exception where there was a minor decline in the measure of engagement after a period of growth. We cannot, however, demonstrate that these changed performance measures were directly attributable to the culture change programs. Certainly, many in the organisations thought the change programs did impact performance, and in one case (Balmain Leagues Club) it was seen as rescuing the organisation from imminent closure. *"The Tigers changed significantly from a semi-stagnant organisation into one with limitless potential"* (Focus Group Member, Balmain Leagues Club).

We do think that there is a good deal of evidence of increased motivation and personal effectiveness at work, more open communication, clearer definition of strategies and work roles, and more innovation and creativity. It would be unusual if these did not have a positive impact on performance. We have many examples of actions taken as result of the change programs – actions that would not have otherwise been taken – that did impact directly on performance for example by increasing sales (for example MasterCard Australia) and decreasing wasteful internal competition (Adshel). We think that such evidence points toward the impact of many cumulative acts taken by individuals at all levels as a result of the change program that together represent a significant new input into the commercial success of these organisations.

Balkundi and Harrison recently reported a meta-analysis of 37 studies of team effectiveness, and conclude that *"teams with densely configured interpersonal ties attain their goals better and are more committed to staying together; that is, team task performance and viability are both higher"* (Balkundi & Harrison, 2006). The process of survey feedback we have described here is conducted with intact teams and, because of the intensity of the workshop processes, leads to more densely configured personal ties. For example, at MasterCard Australia the top team had never met together in a social situation until they attended the off-site feedback workshop. Consequently, we can expect that the increased density of group ties is one factor leading to increased performance.

So these change programs did transform the cultures in these organisations and, as far as we can estimate, had a positive, often major, impact on performance as the organisations themselves defined it.

This raises the next question: How do Constructive cultures impact an organisation's capability to sustain itself over the longer term?

Creating the Learning Organisation –
A Culture of Future Readiness – Sustaining the Change

CONSTRUCTIVE BEHAVIOUR AS THE BASIS FOR THE LEARNING ORGANISATION

When we reflect on lessons learned through these case studies, it is apparent that the key to long-term organisational sustainability lies in developing a capability that allows the organisation to continue to learn and grow. An organisation needs the kind of capability development that fosters ongoing learning and change if it is to continue to face the challenges of the future. We refer to this as a 'meta-capability', because it develops from building a range of other capabilities, and then takes over as the central organising principle of the culture. This represents a step change in the evolution of cultural maturity.

Argyris (1992) calls this meta-capability 'learning how to learn'. It is a consciousness of what we have learned, combined with a consciousness of how we learned it, and an ability to extrapolate this knowledge to maximise learning in the future. In 1990, Senge wrote a seminal work on *The Learning Organisation*, which spells out in more detail what is involved. He argues that there are five key elements involved:

1. An interplay between the individual's development of personal mastery and the development of organisational mastery. Individual mastery depends on generating a desire to more fully understand our self, focus our energies, and clarify our vision. This contributes to organisational mastery, which is a similar development at the organisational level of a corporate sense of identity, vision and strategy.

2. An understanding of our mental models, that is, the deeply ingrained assumptions and beliefs that underscore how we view the world and act within it.

3. The centrality of building a shared vision of the future, and the commitment that brings when owned by all.

4. Team learning and extraordinary results that can only be achieved through team action, and the power of effective dialogue to make that happen.

5. A 'systems framework' that places individual and team endeavour within the organisation and its environment, and allows change efforts to target the critical variables that will make the most difference.

The learning organisation can be thought of as having developed 'fit-readiness' – a capability similar to that of a finely-tuned athlete that brings the capacity to meet environmental challenges to new levels of excellence.

Of the organisations we researched, Lion Nathan had the longest history of transformative change and seemed to have created this meta-capability. Rob Murray, Lion Nathan's current CEO, remarked: *"We have a very strong strategy. We have a group of people deployed around making it happen. We're honest enough to call whether the results are good or bad, and honest enough or brave enough to throw away some of the paradigms we have had about how you measure success."*

So how did Murray see Lion Nathan going forward? He saw the next strategy as bedding down this learning by incorporating it into all aspects of the business: *"The next stage of our journey is all linked to standardising the way we do things: 'The Lion Nathan Way for Sales', 'The Lion Nathan Way for Brand', 'The Lion Nathan Way for Fast Change and Managing Change'… Just standardising things."*

At Yarra Valley Water, at an earlier phase of cultural change, the meta-capability is still being developed. Tony Kelly, the MD, looking forward said: *"As the culture improves, staff expectations increase as well. Their expectations of us as managers are probably more critical. They are not worried about the basics; they become more worried about the icing on the cake. So the better you become, the harder it is. Our improvement strategies need to be more sophisticated from now on, that's for sure."*

And Anne Farquhar clearly conceptualised the next steps towards putting those 'more sophisticated' strategies in place: *"We will continue to integrate appropriately-timed opportunities for improvement through self-awareness, development of leadership competencies, measurement of progress, and recognition of achievement. There will be an emphasis on communication, particularly to develop understanding of the way we unconsciously process information and use our personal filters to alter reality."*

For Balmain Leagues Club, the most significant change on the OEI occurred on External Adaptability, which includes the rapid and efficient implementation of new programs, proactive identification of, and adaptation to, changes in the external environment, and effective response to external opportunities and threats. Given its prior inability to cope effectively with changes in its external environment, this shift in orientation was critical to its continuing to be able to survive and thrive – an important step in developing this meta-capability.

At Mastercard Australia at the time of our interviews (March 2006), there was an emerging awareness that, after the major effort of bringing about change, the momentum for change was dropping off – the learning was being lost and needed re-creating. Leigh Clapham said: *"It was quite extraordinary when I spoke to three or four of the people who had been on this journey about where we are now. They all said that we are not firing on all cylinders. If we had put as much effort in our working groups, focussed on certain outcomes between there and now, we would have continued to grow our effectiveness. Our effectiveness on a scale of one to ten – if it was eight in May 2004 – has probably slipped to a seven. Our team members who had been involved in the process noticed the difference and they acknowledge that we didn't have task forces working between May 2004 and February 2006 on maintaining those levels of effectiveness and recognising the impact of leadership on the culture and eventual outcomes of new people coming in as well."*

It can take years to create a learning organisation which has the meta-capability of 'learning how to learn' built in as a core feature of the culture, and it can never be taken for granted.

HOW CAN CULTURAL CHANGE BE MONITORED AND SUSTAINED?

To what extent can we generalise from the results of this study to the management of change generally? We need to answer this question to know where and how to apply what has been learned.

We note first that this is a study of five organisations that have undergone successful organisational transformation selected from a larger list of forty-one organisations that used Human Synergistics' instrumentation more than once. Can these cases said to be representative of all organisations that successfully undergo organisational change?

The answer to this question is 'no'. To explain why, we refer the reader to research reported in Dunphy and Stace (Under New Management, op cit) and Stace and Dunphy (Beyond the Boundaries, op cit) which examined cases of successful and unsuccessful organisational change in a range of industries. Figure 1 is the basic matrix model which displays the two dimensions that have been shown empirically to be fundamental to understanding organisational change – the 'Scale of Change and the Style of Change Management' (Horrigan, 2005). Dunphy and Stace measured these dimensions and arrayed the organisations they studied (mainly large corporations) on this matrix. Examples of successful and unsuccessful organisational change programs were found in all quadrants of this model.

Figure 2 shows how the organisations that were studied clustered on the matrix. Note that these organisational change programs fell into five clusters. Those programs that are labelled 'Taylorism' were not changing fast enough to keep up with changes in their environment and were unsuccessful, so we will not discuss these further here.

Of the other four types, there were examples of successful change programs in all areas, although most medium to high-performance organisations were found in the area of 'mid-range change' covered by the Developmental and Task-Focussed Transitions. The organisations in this area were undergoing incremental, not transformational change. The change programs in the five organisations studied in Human Synergistics' research achieved significant cultural transformation. Cultural transformation can be achieved in a single burst of rapid change over a limited period (for example twelve months at Adshel), or in bursts of rapid change interspersed with periods of incremental change (for example over ten years at Lion Nathan).

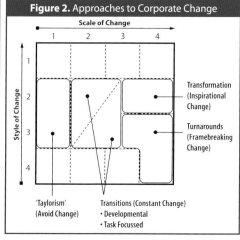

If we look at the area covered by Charismatic Transformations and Turnarounds in the Dunphy and Stace model in Figure 1, the executives of the Turnaround organisations were using a strongly directive or coercive leadership style, that is, they were forcing change on their organisations against opposition from groups with entrenched power. There was relatively little evidence of this in the organisations studied, although there were cases of individuals opposed to the changes, some of whom left or were counselled out of the organisations. The approaches to change in the five Human Synergistics cases are primarily examples of inspirational change.

This raises the question of whether the Human Synergistics' approach, so successful in these cases, can be applied with equal success in those organisations where there are significant interest groups that oppose transformational change. The method involves widespread voluntary commitment to change on the part of the majority of organisational members, so what happens when some significant opposition was encountered by groups or individuals that did not cooperate or oppose attempts to redefine the culture? The issue of power is central in organisations and, when the power structure is divided, collaborative approaches of this kind can founder and fail. Significant opposition was encountered in some of the organisations we studied - this varied, from opposition on the part of one or more senior executives or widespread resistance from staff, unions, some supervisors or segments of the workforce. Sometimes this was extreme. For example, Danny Munk commented on their early change attempts at Balmain: *"During mid 1996 to the end of 1996, I can't say that we did too much with cultural change; in the prevailing climate at that time we had our hands full dealing with intense opposition. We had people with talent but they didn't believe anything that came out of our mouths or anything that was written. We had an area that was so anti-change because they believed that any change would take away from anything they had worked so hard for."* The problem was not only with the commitment of the workforce to the old culture, which was deeply internalised, but also with the Club's clients, as Danny continues: *"We had a number of stakeholders – people who had used the club for many years – who wanted it to stay as it was."*

How were situations like this turned around?

The most significant factors appear to have been:

1. Unswerving commitment to the culture change process on the part of the CEO involved. For example a few years into its transformation, Gordon Cairns was faced with some tough decisions which were defining moments: How would he manage a few high profile members of the Leadership Team, who consistently and visibly behaved counter to the values, but who delivered great financial results? He agreed that Lion needed to manage them out of the organisation. Gordon Cairns had to be seen to do the right thing even though it meant losing some very high performers. In some instances, he had known these individuals for some time. He describes this as being a painful process: *"Parts of the experience have been very painful, parting with friends, looking in the mirror… The acceptance of responsibility."*

2. Use of the Human Synergistics' instruments, particularly the OCI and LSI, to provide feedback, which directly linked people's observable behaviour to behavioural outcomes. For example Danny Munk described Wayne's 'hallelujah moment' when he discovered

the LSI: *"Wayne became very passionate about LSI because it enabled him to provide a vehicle for people to see how they impacted on others and how others impacted them and sometimes the outcomes of this impact, without using the words right or wrong. Because in our industry sometimes when you use the words right or wrong you find yourself facing the union."*

3. Personal transformation on the part of some resisters. In Yarra Valley Water for example, one of the team leaders commented on the inspirational effect of a senior manager who had been on record previously as resisting the change: *"Our GM lead the change. He had said previously 'I am too old to change'. His change was an inspiration to everyone within the group. Everyone thought if he could change then we could as well."*

4. Departures from the organisation, often but not always voluntarily, on the part of key figures who either opposed the changes or who persisted in behaviour that was persistently Red or Green despite receiving feedback - in other words, who either did not wish to modify their behaviour or were not able to do so. Some of these people were high performers who produced solid financial outcomes but whose methods of doing this were aggressive and who created defensive behaviour on the part of others. It was a measure of the CEOs' commitment to building the constructive process that, as a last resort, they were prepared to take tough action to ensure that it was protected.

5. Progressive building of trust by 'walking the talk' – the Senior Executive Team and other managers actually changing their behaviour and modeling the new culture in their actions.

The organisations studied demonstrated that the Human Synergistics model is effective in bringing about change even in organisations where there is significant opposition from one or more interest groups. Opposition is most likely to be overcome if there is strong visible commitment first and foremost from the CEO. The intensity of their personal commitment to transformation is key in ensuring that opposition to the change is dealt with fairly, constructively and efficiently.

The Emergent Logic of Transformational Change

The question may reasonably be asked: Have we discovered anything new from our research that is not already in the existing literature on change?

Firstly, we point out that the aim of research is not only to create new knowledge, but also to confirm or disprove existing conclusions from previous research studies. Our research, for example, confirms the importance of CEO commitment in bringing about change and the existing evidence about the importance of communication in the change process.

However we have come up with some controversial findings. The first is the support provided by these case studies for the principle of starting the transformation process by concentrating on culture. Leading US change guru John Kotter argues strongly that change programs should not start by concentrating on culture, but should only focus on culture in their final phase. 'Cultural change comes last, not first', in his view. He goes on to write that:

"One of the theories of change that has circulated widely over the past fifteen years might be summarised as follows: The biggest impediment to change in a group is culture. Therefore, the first step in a major transformation is to alter the norms and values. After the culture has been shifted, the rest of the change effort becomes more feasible and easier to put into effect. I once believed in this model, but everything that I have seen over the last decade tells me it's wrong. Culture is not something you manipulate easily. Attempts to grab it and twist it into a new shape never work, because you can't grab it. Culture changes only after you have successfully altered people's actions, after the new behaviour produces some group benefit for a period of time, and after people see the connection between the new actions and the performance improvement. Thus most cultural change happens in stage 8, not stage 1" (Kotter, 1996, pp. 155-156). Note that Kotter advocates a sequence of 8 steps to bring about organisational change.

We disagree with Kotter, and think that these cases represent a refutation of Kotter's argument about attempting culture change last rather than first. (We do not however disagree with his perception that culture change is difficult to bring about). Note that Kotter assumes that change managers or change agents outside the culture are trying to 'grab it and twist it', that is, manipulate it. However, as we have argued, culture is not primarily an objective 'it', but has its foundations in the consciousness of organisational members. Culture change can be attempted first if those members are engaged in a personal change process, and willingly take responsibility for cultural transformation. We are not alone in taking this position – Cohen has also taken a similar view to ours in a thoughtful analysis of this hotly debated issue: *"Where complex new behaviour is needed and there is high dependency on the goodwill of organisational members, change will require both structural and process interventions, each stimulating and supporting the other. Structural interventions are unlikely to be a viable starting point for change"* (Cohen, 2000, p. 187).

Cohen's view also supports our notion of the reciprocal nature of what we have called the subjective and objective side of culture change. We believe that transformation proceeds through the co-creation of these two aspects of culture – one does not precede the other. Arguing that one precedes the other is like arguing that butterflies preceded flowers, or vice versa. The truth is that both evolved together, becoming increasingly diversified and interdependent as they did so. The same happens with cultural evolution.

This leads us to another distinctively different conclusion from one advanced strongly in the organisational change literature. We reject on both theoretical grounds and the evidence of these cases that transformational change proceeds through a distinct and uniform set of phases such as those outlined by Kotter (1996) and Kotter and Cohen (2002).

Kotter's view has an elegant and appealing simplicity about it. The world of organisational change is however inevitably messy, and generates a more fuzzy logic.

Change programs are more open ended than models like Kotter's imply – they have an emergent rather than a planned logic. There is a place for careful planning in change programs, but it isn't possible to predict what will happen when a range of interventions are launched. Project management skills are important, but these projects are more open-ended than, say, a standard building project. Change agents need to remain responsive to the emerging drama, which inevitably develops its own unfolding 'psychologic' as new waves of actors join in. We think the analogy of improvised drama captures more of the spirit of how the transformation proceeds – each actor who joins in brings something distinctive from their own experience and complicates and redirects the change process. In change programs in large organisations, there is usually a central plot emerging, but also sub-plots playing out within different organisational units. The general direction of the change may be apparent at any time, but the next steps are not necessarily predictable. It is necessary to track the trajectory of change, and design new interventions to readjust the direction if it strays off target. Good change programs are rather like heat-seeking missiles; their trajectory is off about 90% of the time, and needs constant monitoring and readjustment to come in on target.

We suspect that change programs in larger organisations may need more planning, while the smaller can rely more on being responsive to emergent issues. But, regardless of organisational size, the guiding coalition at least needs some kind of template of the change process that can be filled out with a range of specific interventions designed as the change evolves. However, even with the more carefully planned change programs in large organisations, the change agents have to remain flexible and responsive to the emerging drama, and modify their planned actions to capture the spirit of the moment.

Important in the corporate drama is the discourse of change. The discourse created in effective change programs is the language of poetry and legend; rich in emotional symbolism, powerful in appealing to the senses. It expands beyond rationality to engage the hearts as well as minds of organisational members, and involves them in a new and exciting debate about the organisational future and their contribution to it. As this discourse proceeds, a shared language comes into being which holds the symbols, stories and myths that express the values of the new culture. In transformational change programs, the discourse is directed to what Weick calls 'sensemaking' – the process of generating new meaning from novel situations where the old meanings no longer apply (Weick, 1995).

Leadership is central, as the change literature has always emphasised – but the cases show that personal transformation of the CEO and other senior people precedes cultural transformation and is a prerequisite for it. When this transformation has taken place or is under way, then the guiding coalition that provides much of the ongoing impetus for change can move into action. Usually the guiding coalition consists of the CEO, the Senior Executive Team and external and internal change agents. As the transformation becomes more inclusive, gathering in a wider group, the guiding coalition's role becomes one of maintaining the momentum. At some stage in the process of the diffusion of change a 'tipping point' is reached, where a critical mass of organisational members ensures that the transformational process becomes self-sustaining, with only minimal input from the guiding coalition (Gladwell, 2000). Like a spinning wheel on a bicycle, after momentum is gained, the smallest touch is sufficient to maintain the speed with which the wheel turns.

The distinctive characteristic of the Human Synergistics' approach is its emphasis on a process vision. The Human Synergistics' approach to culture change is 'content free', and focuses on the relationships people have with one another – the quality of these relationships determines whether the process of co-creation will result in a Constructive culture that supports high-performance. The vision is for a quality of interpersonal exchange, not for 'business' issues such as market share or financial returns. It is not that business objectives are seen as unimportant, but rather that their achievement has been shown to depend on creating a quality of interpersonal process that provides the optimum environment for the development and realisation of such a strategic vision. It does not in itself ensure that the organisation follows a viable business strategy, but it increases the probability that strategic errors will be identified early and rectified, and that the new strategic options will be identified. Success is guaranteed by a Constructive culture coupled with a viable business strategy.

Our five case study organisations demonstrate that such an emphasis on a process vision can drive the successes we have been describing here.

Our research shows the power of a Constructive culture in creating commitment and engagement in employees, and strongly suggests that this carries across into increasing performance levels. This finding builds on the base of previous research at Human Synergistics. We point out that the creation of a Constructive culture may require transformational change, particularly if there is a substantial disconnect between the Actual and the Preferred culture. Poor performance results also point to the need for transformational change, particularly in combination with a sizable disconnect. But maintenance of a Constructive culture does not always require continual transformation – it does require continual change, but in some circumstances this change may be incremental rather than transformational. Previous research suggests that maintaining unrelieved transformational change for long periods can lead to problems of decreasing engagement and commitment (Dunphy & Stace; Stace & Dunphy op cit).

We have argued that building competence for managing ongoing change is the most important meta-capability for modern organisations, and the basis for a learning organisation. The Human Synergistics' focus on process interventions that both create the capacity in individuals to seek feedback and change, plus build organisational systems that support change, can ultimately lead to the creation of this meta-capability, that is, the ability for the organisation to change continuously. The key to progressing beyond the resistance to change that can be observed in most organisations is to create a culture that, rather than maintaining itself by resisting change, keeps itself 'future fit' by proactively seeking change, and to back that attitude with the knowledge, skills and systems to make the change happen.

Toward a Process Model of Change

So, we have data that are relevant to understanding organisations that are undergoing consultative and charismatic transformations, and where widespread cooperation with the change process can be generated. The results of our research provide significant insights into how effective cultural change processes can be managed under these conditions.

It is relevant to return at this point to Cooke's 'How Culture Works' model. The Cooke model provides a useful guide to the management of change, because it outlines the range of factors that executives can use to influence culture change. Building on this model, these case studies demonstrate the dynamic processes that are associated with each of these levers for change. We can extend this model to more specifically highlight this dynamic interplay between key factors that managers can use as a guide to action in building a process which will support the creation of the meta-capability of 'learning how to learn', and building the capacity for conducting successful ongoing change.

It is here that we return to our summary of results above, and rephrase the outcomes of the study in process terms. We have essentially described three parallel processes that need to be run simultaneously to achieve transformational change.

The first is the process of 'Leading', which involves several sub-processes. The first, 'making the case for transformation', is a necessary preliminary to change. It is here that administering the OCI and related instruments is particularly useful. The second sub-process is 'exemplary modeling' by the CEO and the Executive Team. In each case, the CEO and members of the top team personally underwent a transformational process of personal change. This was not modeling in the sense of 'going through the motions', but genuinely committing to personal change before advocating it for others. The third sub-process was forming a guiding coalition of change agents made up of the Executive Team and selected skilled internal and external change agents. Finally, this Change Leadership Alliance cascaded the change process out through the organisation, with line managers leading the change in their own areas, supported and resourced by the other skilled change agents.

The second parallel process is 'Engaging'. This also has sub-processes. The most important of these is widespread 'listening', which lays the foundation for constructive dialogue and increased personal involvement on the part of a critical mass of those in the organisation. Various approaches were used in the cases, but they all involved increasing the volume of upward and lateral communication in particular, and reducing the restrictive impact of authority and power structures in blocking open communication flows. 'Telling', the second sub-process, involves developing a unified and shared vocabulary for talking about change that picked up and focussed the increasing emotional involvement of organisational members through the use of stories, metaphor and imagery. The third sub-process is ensuring the continued development of high-level 'skills for relating'. Constructive cultures demand a higher capability to relate to others, solve problems and engage in constructive dialogue. For the purposes of simplicity, we will refer to this second process simply as Engaging, for the main purpose of communicating is to create informed engagement.

The third parallel process, 'Redesigning', was developing a suite of interventions to work on the levers for change identified by Cooke. What we found however, was that in each organisation this suite of interventions differed – there was no universally applicable set of interventions – rather they had to be 'tailor made' for each organisation. The third parallel process we are describing here is a natural and logical result of the first two processes - Leading and Engaging - for they evolve into a collaborative diagnosis of what needs to change and into a set of intervention strategies to effect these changes. What needs to change is unique to the situation of each organisation.

These three processes are grounded in 'Reflexivity', which is the capacity to become aware of self in relation to others, and in relation to the organisation. Feedback instruments, used sensitively by skilled change agents, build the self-awareness and ability to face reality that is the basic prerequisite for change. In addition, such instrumentation enables the organisation to monitor whether progress is being made toward the Ideal culture, and this allows feedback loops to be developed to bring the culture change program back on course if the previous interventions have not had the intended effects. In the five cases studied here, the Human Synergistics' instrumentation was a powerful reflexivity tool catalysing the three parallel processes underlying cultural change. Figure 3 shows these relationships visually; this diagram encapsulates the major learnings we have derived from the study, and provides the key to successful transformational change toward Constructive cultures.

META-CAPABILITY MODEL FOR CULTURAL TRANSFORMATION

The cultural transformation model proposed here (the 'Meta-capability Model') gives us a framework to develop practical strategies to create cultural transformation. We have summarized the model and included the parallel processes that need to be run simultaneously to achieve transformational change.

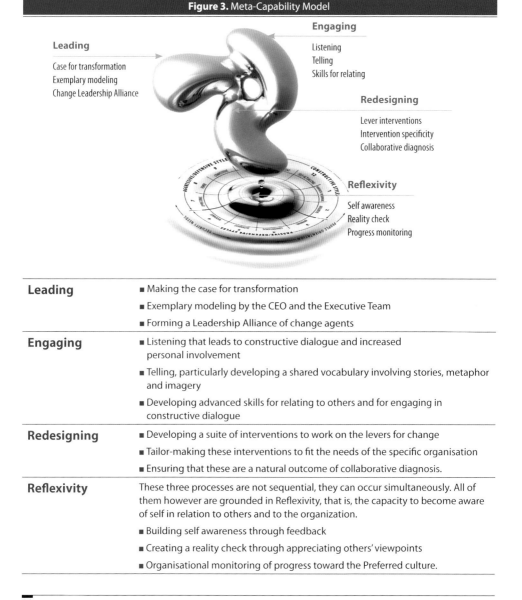

Figure 3. Meta-Capability Model

Engaging
Listening
Telling
Skills for relating

Leading
Case for transformation
Exemplary modeling
Change Leadership Alliance

Redesigning
Lever interventions
Intervention specificity
Collaborative diagnosis

Reflexivity
Self awareness
Reality check
Progress monitoring

Leading	■ Making the case for transformation ■ Exemplary modeling by the CEO and the Executive Team ■ Forming a Leadership Alliance of change agents
Engaging	■ Listening that leads to constructive dialogue and increased personal involvement ■ Telling, particularly developing a shared vocabulary involving stories, metaphor and imagery ■ Developing advanced skills for relating to others and for engaging in constructive dialogue
Redesigning	■ Developing a suite of interventions to work on the levers for change ■ Tailor-making these interventions to fit the needs of the specific organisation ■ Ensuring that these are a natural outcome of collaborative diagnosis.
Reflexivity	These three processes are not sequential, they can occur simultaneously. All of them however are grounded in Reflexivity, that is, the capacity to become aware of self in relation to others and to the organization. ■ Building self awareness through feedback ■ Creating a reality check through appreciating others' viewpoints ■ Organisational monitoring of progress toward the Preferred culture.

Chapter **3**

About Life

ADSHEL

Contents
Adshel

Written by Quentin Jones

Executive Summary

Adshel is a very modern story of cultural transformation. It directly challenges the orthodoxy that Competitive and aggressive behaviours are the only behaviours that drive success. This case study also shows how a company, even though currently profitable, and with employee surveys reporting high satisfaction, can nevertheless have real cultural issues – the 'Enron Syndrome'. The study documents how the CEO, the Directors, and the staff at Adshel worked together to create one of the most significant shifts in culture yet documented by Human Synergistics.

Industry	Advertising
Customers	National Network (Australia and New Zealand)
People	102
Assets	$100 Million
Revenue	N/A
CEO	Steve McCarthy
Internal Change Agent(s)	Culture Change Teams, Steve McCarthy
External Change Agents(s)	Stephen and Mara Klemich, Achievement Concepts
HSI Tools Used	Organizational Culture Inventory® (OCI), Life Styles Inventory™ 1&2 (LSI)

Culture Results

Organizational Culture Inventory
Test (2005)

Organizational Culture Inventory
Re-Test (2006)

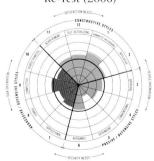

Outcomes	Increased staff satisfaction, role clarity, revenue and EBIT

Adshel

Pre-Test

Phase **1**

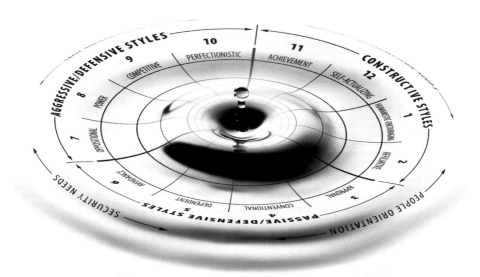

Introduction

Adshel operates Australia and New Zealand's most successful street furniture advertising business. Founded 30 years ago in the UK, the company's prime objective is 'to assist councils, municipalities, transit authorities and retail developers to maximise the potential of their assets through the sale of advertising on high quality street furniture and public amenity structures'.

Figure 1. Adshel business

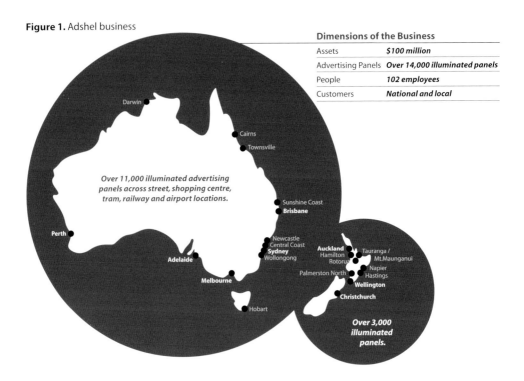

Dimensions of the Business

Assets	**$100 million**
Advertising Panels	**Over 14,000 illuminated panels**
People	**102 employees**
Customers	**National and local**

Over 11,000 illuminated advertising panels across street, shopping centre, tram, railway and airport locations.

Over 3,000 illuminated panels.

The company is a relatively young entity, now in its 9th year of business. Established as a joint venture between APN News & Media and Clear Channel, Adshel supplies an extensive range of world class street furniture at no cost to cities or the community, and is currently cleaning and maintaining over 7,000 bus and tram shelters across Australia and New Zealand.

Internal and External Operating Environment

By most measures, Adshel has been, and continues to be, a successful company in the very competitive advertising industry. Dominating its market segment, Adshel is one of the most profitable businesses in the Clear Channel and APN group, with long-term contracts (15 years) which would seem to assure a successful future. So, where was the problem? Why did the CEO consider it necessary to invest in his company's leadership and culture?

Questions about the business's sustainability came into focus with feedback from an external change agent, Stephen Klemich. Back in 2002, Steve McCarthy, the CEO, commissioned Klemich to run a six-day Personal Effectiveness Program (PEP). At that time, McCarthy wanted to address the perceived need to recognise and develop high potential staff.

... staff didn't like the culture

Stephen Klemich says that, *"There weren't particular performance issues, but Steve recognised that there were leaders who needed training and skills. What triggered this was when a member of staff went on a one-week RYLA (Rotary Youth Leadership Awards) program for up-and-coming youth in the community – they nominate people to attend. This member of staff came back transformed, and Steve recognised that he needed to be doing that for more, or all, of his staff members."*

In 2002, the first PEP took a dozen staff off-site to a venue in southern New South Wales, where they underwent an intensive indoor and outdoor training experience. Despite some initial suspicions by those selected that this was a 'remedial' program, the staff involved returned thrilled with the experience. From this program, signals started to emerge that there were some underlying cultural issues that needed to be addressed. Staff indicated they liked the company, but expressed concerns about its culture - concerns that would later be confirmed by the Human Synergistics' Organizational Culture Inventory® (OCI) measurement.

The senior team totally disagreed, they were perfect

"The Directors' aggressive behaviour, the Competitive-Approval 'bow-tie'. Staff didn't like it. It was interesting to hear them say they were paid very well, but they didn't like the Competitive culture. Some people thrived on it, people in their late 20s early 30s, but most people didn't like this culture" (Stephen Klemich, Achievement Concepts).

A second PEP in 2003 reinforced these messages, and it was during Klemich's debrief with McCarthy that he first suggested using the OCI as a quantitative measure of culture. In Klemich's view, undertaking the OCI would quantify and illuminate what staff were saying. In fact one of the messages that emerged from the PEP courses was that the senior team should do something like this. Predictably, this suggestion met with some resistance from the senior team: *"There was a strong push from those who had attended (PEP) saying that the senior team should do something like this. The senior team totally disagreed, because they thought they were perfect – in fact, perfect is an understatement. We were sitting here feeling pretty shit-hot, actually"* (Steve McCarthy, CEO).

Reasons for Measuring Culture

Apart from the PEP feedback, there was no significant case for measuring the culture. The business was successful, most staff claimed they were satisfied, and the market was strong. However, strategically, the business needed to mature to become sustainable. Adshel had evolved rapidly through an entrepreneurial phase, followed by a growth phase, and was now moving into maturity. McCarthy recognised the need to address the people and cultural issues if Adshel was to transition successfully and remain sustainable.

Over its short history, the company had grown from a couple of people into a 100 person organisation, and the approaches and systems that supported the company in the early days were under challenge from the new people coming into the business. There were real inconsistencies in expectations, depending on whether you were one of the original staff, or a new recruit.

An important turning point in thinking was the May 2004 Executive Development Program (EDP). Run in the West MacDonnell ranges of Central Australia, this six day 'agenda free' program created an opportunity for the Executive to look at the business, their people, and ultimately, themselves. Undertaking the Life Styles Inventory™ (LSI) confronted their thinking about what had made the business successful up to that point, that is, their aggressive and Competitive behaviour. This opened up a critical discussion.

If you don't drive people, you won't be successful

The proposition that the very behaviour that had underlaid their success to date might prove counter-productive in the next phase of corporate growth was fiercely debated - one director described it as a 'joke' that the debate was occurring at all, and walked out of the discussion.

According to Stephen Klemich the belief was: *"The thinking was 'If you're not Competitive, and you don't drive these people, then you won't be successful. Our success is because we are aggressive, and we have been rewarded for these behaviours.'"*

Steve McCarthy hung in there throughout this emotional debate, realising that something wasn't right about the current culture, and *"the more we spoke, the more he was catching it"* (Stephen Klemich, Achievement Concepts). Whilst some directors resisted the idea of change, others were open to the possibility that what had made the firm successful in the past may not be the key to future success. As the executives sat around a camp fire in Australia's outback, the seed of a new possibility was planted.

2005

Phase **2**

Adshel
Test

Collecting the Culture Results

Agreement to undertake the OCI was forthcoming after Stephen Klemich presented information on it at a strategy meeting in October 2004. Options were discussed, and it was agreed to do one audit so as to be able to have a culture benchmark to work from. Characteristically, the desire to 'benchmark' emerged from the existing Competitive way of thinking, that is, 'we can compare ourselves and see how great we are doing'.

The Directors also insisted that the OCI survey be done 'properly', that is, all the necessary resources should be committed to it. In February 2005, a nationwide focus group roll-out commenced. In a three-hour session, all staff completed both the Actual and Preferred OCI. In this way, Adshel achieved an unusually high 100% response rate, but more importantly, took a major step towards engaging all staff in the culture change process.

The importance of how the culture survey is undertaken, and its impact on the culture, is well illustrated here. The priority given to the focus groups as evidenced by the CEO's attendance was itself a culture change intervention. Steve McCarthy believes that if the survey had been taken in May, after the focus groups, the culture would have improved with no other action needing to be taken!

The Culture Survey Results

A total of 102 Adshel staff completed the Preferred and Actual versions of the OCI, and the results are presented in Figures 2 and 3.

Adshel's Preferred culture circumplex (Figure 2) reflects a strong Constructive, or Blue, orientation. This is consistent with national trend research, showing that aspirational organisational cultures are strongest in the following behavioural norms: Humanistic-Encouraging, Self-Actualizing, Achievement and Affiliative. Conversely, Aggressive/Defensive (Red) and Passive/Defensive (Green) styles are well within the 50-percentile ring as represented by the thicker third ring from the centre.

Adshel's Actual culture (Figure 3), however, showed up very differently. In contrast to their Preferred culture, the Aggressive/Defensive styles of Competitive and Power dominated, backed up by a strong Passive/Defensive cluster dominated by Approval and Avoidance. Security needs dominated, with a stronger Task than People Orientation. Interestingly, the profile has a distinctive Competitive (9 o'clock) and Approval (3 o'clock) 'bow-tie'. The dominance of these two styles in the profile is often found in advertising, sales, and marketing groups.

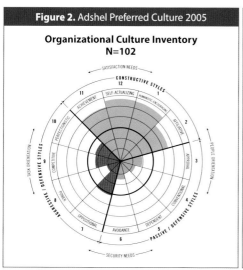

Figure 2. Adshel Preferred Culture 2005

Organizational Culture Inventory
N=102

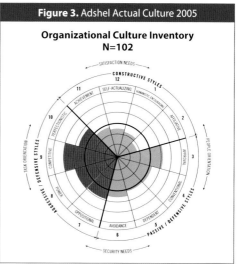

Figure 3. Adshel Actual Culture 2005

Organizational Culture Inventory
N=102

Impact of Culture Survey Results

For Steve McCarthy, receiving the OCI results was a defining moment: *"The 'come to God' day was the day we got these results - that was the big calling day. Prior to that there was an evolutionary process. There was no business crisis that was forcing us to turn around and go, 'Jesus! - the wheels have just fallen off when we thought it was going well'. This feedback happened in a period of great business success."*

Steve took a couple of days to come to terms with the results, and to absorb the impact of seeing the massive divergence between the Preferred and Actual cultures. Then it was the Directors' turn to examine the results. Their reaction involved the usual questions and challenges around such feedback; specifically, some questioned the tool's accuracy, and suggested that the staff had filled in the form incorrectly. Acceptance 'that it must be right' only occurred when the Directors' Actual OCI profile was placed over the total company's profile, confirming that the Directors themselves shared a similar view of the culture.

> **The big calling day was when we got these results**

Anna Lee, Adshel's CFO, summarises clearly the process of coming to terms with the results: *"Management said 'Oh my God!' But if you asked people, it wasn't really that surprising. But we were all in kind of denial. It was one of those things that was always in the back of your mind, but when it comes screaming at you how Competitive we really were, it was surprising."*

Next it was the staff's turn to receive the results. Again, staff debriefing was done 'properly'. All staff participated in an office-based, half-day debrief, facilitated by Klemich and attended by the CEO.

How Did the Culture Survey Results Play Out in Adshel?

The Competitive motivation dominated Adshel's culture. Like many sales-oriented groups, competition is seen as critical to success. There were high levels of internal competition which were driven by executive behaviour and supported by the company's systems, especially the bonus and reward systems. These had been supported by the CEO himself, saying: *"It had got to the point where more energy was being expended on internal competition than on external competitors."*

Examples of how these Competitive and Approval behaviours played out included:

Competitive

- Sales people being incentivised to compete with each other internally and individualistically
- 'Bizarre' behaviours, such as hiding stock, putting stock on hold, and using campaigns that didn't exist
- Manipulation and bullying of administration staff when sales personnel were asked to complete normal administrative requirements, e.g. *"Are you asking me to complete an AMEX bill rather than focusing on going after this multi-million dollar deal?"*
- Silos reinforced between sales and 'back of house' personnel

Approval

- Everyone's purpose (in support functions) was to please Sales
- An attitude of 'Don't do anything to upset sales, because that will go up to the Sales Director then to the CEO'
- 'Sucking up' to back office functions by some sales staff to ensure their work was attended to ahead of that of other sales people
- Pressure to socialise over drinks; if you didn't attend, you were ostracised
- 'In-group' and 'out-group' favouritism. The 'in-group' was significantly better rewarded

Culture Outcomes

Another intriguing aspect of Adshel's results was in relation to the cultural outcomes reported by staff. Adshel's 2005 cultural outcomes are presented in the gap bar chart (Figure 4). These cultural outcomes, as reported by staff, fell into three broad themes:

- Strong Quality of Service outcomes, for example high scores on: 'To what extent would you personally go out of your way to make sure that a customer/client feels good about the service you've provided?'

- Moderately strong Employee Satisfaction, for example high scores on: 'To what extent are you satisfied being a member of this organisation?'
- Weak Role Clarity, for example low scores on: 'To what extent do you clearly know what is expected of you as a member of this organisation?'

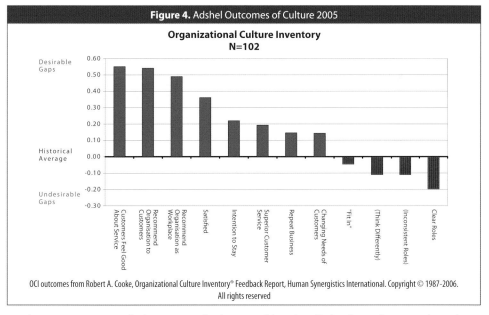

Figure 4. Adshel Outcomes of Culture 2005

An apparent contradiction emerged – how could such a Defensive culture produce above average outcomes? A Defensive culture normally produces poor climate outcomes, for example staff dissatisfaction, but in fact the staff had relatively high levels of satisfaction. This 'Enron Syndrome' can be explained by the strong extrinsic and short-term focus of the culture. Steve McCarthy again: "… *as it was pointed out, we were a happy bunch because we spent a lot of time, money and effort on little trinkets and things to make people happy. And it's, like, the view we had as a senior team that we will have to continue to offer more and more trinkets to keep people happy.*"

The sustainability of the strong customer focus was also in question. Staff began to question the cost of meeting unrealistic customer demands. Driven by the strong Approval style, the staff were being encouraged to please customers and meet their demands, no matter what the cost to the organisation and its people.

Lack of Role Clarity was a very clear negative cultural outcome from the Competitive and Approval 'bow-tie'. In attempting to meet competing senior managers' demands, staff received inconsistent messages about what was expected. This produced pressure to think and behave differently to how they would have preferred. These indicators pointed to the challenge of transforming Adshel from a culture focussed on extrinsic rewards and short-term results (a Competitive culture), to a more sustainable culture with a focus on intrinsic rewards and longer-term objectives (an Achievement culture).

2005-2006

Adshel

Phase **3** # Action

The Cultural Change Strategy

Adshel's cultural change strategy is an emergent one. No strategy was dictated by head office – rather, they initiated a learning process that was sustained over a number of years. This injection of new ideas was allowed to take root, nurtured by the CEO, and eventually led to many of the fundamental assumptions driving the business being challenged. It takes time for such transformational ideas to challenge the status quo, and it wasn't until 2005 that action was taken to address the issue of culture directly.

The Program of Initiatives

The Actions that have contributed to Adshel's cultural transformation are presented in Table 1 and are framed in Dr Robert A. Cooke's 'How Culture Works' model (Cooke, 1997) Figure 5. This illustrates how Adshel used a range of managerial levers to achieve cultural transformation. In summary, there was a strong focus on aligning Systems, especially HR Systems, and Training and Development initiatives, and on developing Skills/Qualities, in particular Leadership Style and Communication.

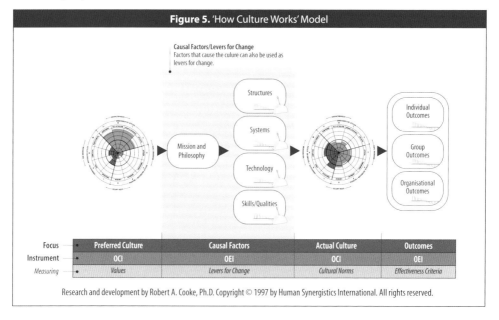

Figure 5. 'How Culture Works' Model

Research and development by Robert A. Cooke, Ph.D. Copyright © 1997 by Human Synergistics International. All rights reserved.

The following discussion of Adshel's actions focuses on tangible changes that can be clearly identified and written about. As with all real culture change, there is a less tangible aspect to transformation, one that is more difficult to measure and write about. We attempt to capture this intangible aspect of culture change in the 'learnings' section of this case study.

Adshel is a case study about how to create an environment that releases the energy, currently trapped in traditional organisational cultures. This release of human energy achieved one of the biggest cultural shifts documented by Human Synergistics over a 12-month period. So how did Adshel do it?

Table 1. Summary table of Initiatives 2002-2006

Levers (Causal Factors)	2002	2003	2004	2005	2006
Mission & Philosophy Initiatives that relate to clear articulation of the organisation's identity and values				■ Establishing cultural vision – Preferred OCI ■ Test - Actual OCI	■ Re-Test – Actual OCI
Structures Initiatives that relate to how people, roles and activities are ordered to create Organisation				■ Role Clarity – PDs ■ Culture Teams established ■ Some restructuring and reporting changes	
Systems ■ Human Resource Systems ■ Selection & Placement ■ Training & Development ■ Performance Management	**T&D** ■ PEP#1	**T&D** ■ PEP#2	**T&D** ■ PEP#3 ■ EDP#1 (LSI 1) ■ PEP#1&2 FU (LSI 1)	**T&D** ■ PEP#4 **HR Systems** ■ Remuneration ■ Performance Appraisals	**T&D** ■ PEP#5 ■ EDP#2 (LSI 1&2) ■ PEP#3&4 FU
Technologies Methods to transform effort/input into outcomes/output				**IT systems** ■ New panel booking system	
Skills/Qualities Including methods of communication (up, down and for learning)				■ Focus groups ■ OCI roadshows ■ New Sales Director ■ CEO behaviour change	■ Focus groups ■ OCI roadshows

Mission & Philosophy

Adshel did not implement significant shifts in strategic direction over this time, as it was already highly successful in achieving its business goals. The focus of the change process was on how success was being achieved – the Executive view was that current methods of achieving business success were not sustainable in the long term, and were having unintended consequences that limited internal collaboration and innovation.

A PROCESS VISION - THE CIRCUMPLEX FRAMEWORK
The OCI circumplex was adopted as a key framework to guide leadership and staff behaviour – to provide a 'process vision'.

Experience shows that most values endorsed by organisational members completing the Preferred OCI plot onto the Constructive (Blue) styles of the circumplex, that is they fall into the Achievement, Humanistic-Encouraging, Self-Actualizing and Affiliative styles. The comparison of scores between the Preferred OCI and the Actual OCI on the Constructive styles provides quantification of how much alignment there is between what is espoused and what is being experienced by staff. In particular, the comparison indicates the degree of energy being wasted on defensive actions being used by management and staff to protect themselves in a threatening internal organisational environment.

It is important to be aware of how Adshel approached the collection of the culture inventories. Inventories are often collected via reply-paid envelopes or remote internet collection. In addition, while all staff usually complete the Actual culture inventory, the Preferred culture inventory is generally completed by a sample of the population. Responses to the Preferred OCI have low standard deviations, and so a sampling approach is statistically acceptable.

Stephen Klemich's approach to inventory collection differed in that all staff completed both the Actual and Preferred OCI inventories in a half-day focus group attended by the CEO.

Knowing the circumplex, you sense when something is wrong

Adshel's approach went beyond simply aiming to collect a statistically valid sample; its goal was to embed the circumplex model into the organisational learning process. Having everyone complete both inventories, especially the Preferred, ensured that all staff reflected on what behaviours they really wanted in Adshel. The process of completing inventories such as the OCI can create significant insight and education for the person completing the inventory, and is a change intervention in its own right.

Steve McCarthy clearly articulates the power of having the circumplex framework embedded in the organisation, indeed in everyone's consciousness, including his own: *"If you know the circumplex styles, you can sense when something is not right."*

Structures

Many organisational change initiatives focus on the organisational structure. In Adshel's case, only minor structural changes were made – there was no 're-arranging of the deck chairs'. As far as structural changes were concerned, the main focus was on clarifying existing roles, and redistributing centralised power from the Sales department to all other key functions. This change to Adshel's 'social architecture' (Charan, 2006) was critical to Adshel's cultural transformation.

In summary, Adshel addressed the following structural levers to create its cultural transformation:

- Position Descriptions
- Culture Teams
- Restructuring
- Redistribution of Influence

We discuss each of these in turn.

EMPOWERMENT THROUGH KNOWING WHAT I AM SUPPOSED TO DO

Clearly establishing what were staff responsible for, contributed significantly to the culture change from Test to Re-Test. As noted earlier, lack of role clarity was identified as a key outcome from Adshel's Competitive and Approval culture. In the past, rather than systematically addressing the need for role clarity, staff development, and career progression, Adshel had addressed staff motivation by giving people different job titles. This strategy fed the Competitive and Approval culture, reinforcing the use of extrinsic rewards as short-term motivators.

An external consultant, Joanna Price, was brought in to review position descriptions. Prior to preparing to brief her, Steve McCarthy believed that Adshel had set up about 20 position descriptions. To his surprise, he found that he was way out in his estimate: *"I went through our internal phone list and found that we had 57 job titles. That's one job title for every two people in the organisation. We would give people a new title to make them feel more important, but nothing else would change - today you're a coordinator, tomorrow you're a senior coordinator. Is there any difference in your job? None at all. Does it make you feel better? It does for a week."*

The position description development process communicated the new cultural norms. Every manager was interviewed. The 'tough' questions were asked to find out what everyone actually did, and duplications across different roles were eliminated. This created a transparent and disciplined system that the CEO could readily monitor. Importantly, the final say was with those who had to perform in the newly defined roles.

According to CFO, Anna Lee: *"It was really driven by Steve. We went to our staff and consulted with them. We said, 'This is what we have done, do you agree with this?' And they would say, 'Yeah, that's what I do. It's really clear now, that's what I do'. We were also able to say to them, 'Having it written down is going to assist in your performance appraisal.'"*

Overhauling the position descriptions resulted in clarification of the following:

- Position Title
- Department
- Purpose of the Position
- Reporting Relationships
- Key Responsibilities
- Financial Accountabilities
- Knowledge, Skills, Experience and Qualifications

The clarification of everyone's roles was identified by all those interviewed as a critical lever in moving towards a more disciplined and transparent culture. As one member of the Focus Group commented: *"People feel better about their job when they know what they're supposed to do."*

Given the speed at which the organisation had grown, both in terms of numbers and the complexity of its business, it should come as no surprise that role clarification had such an important impact on the development of the new culture.

ESTABLISHING CULTURE TEAMS

Culture teams were established at a national level, and in all states, to engage staff so improvement ideas could be reviewed and implemented. These groups comprised line staff from each functional area. A critical reason for their success was the strong support and resourcing provided by the Executive Team.

One of the key insights from the survey was that senior management's practices were sometimes out of touch with how staff wished them to behave. Critically, the culture teams bridged this gap between staff and senior management, and made innovative suggestions for changes to systems.

An example of how the Culture Teams operated is provided by the Sydney Culture Team, comprising of six staff, which considered over 110 culture improvement ideas. Some initiatives that the Sydney team was proud of included:

- Publication of a Sydney Culture Review Newsletter
- Affirmations promoting core values published around the office (in advertising formatting!)
- Introduction of a monthly Friday afternoon social event for all staff in the 'Chill Out' room
- Re-focusing the regular Friday afternoon review away from a pressured comparison of each team's sales figures to a more social, fun event, still with a strong focus on achievement, but with less pressure on staff to compete
- Introduction of a Comments Box (that was a complete 'fizzer'!)

STRUCTURAL CHANGE

Some organisational restructuring occurred in New Zealand and Melbourne, but for the most part, this was not a significant lever. The most significant structural change was the resignation of a member of the Executive Team. The replacement's leadership style had significant impact on building a more Constructive culture, and will be explored later in the Skills/Qualities section.

REDISTRIBUTION OF INFLUENCE

Influence is an intangible concept. Most staff look to their organisation chart for guidance as to who has power; however this is usually only a partial indication of how real power and influence is exercised in the office. Informal and undocumented influence structures form what is often referred to as 'social architecture', that is, the collective ways in which people work together (or compete) across an organisation to get the work done. As in most organisations, the social architecture at Adshel had evolved from the activities of key figures in the early history of the company.

Since the company's foundation, the Sales Department and the CEO had held a disproportionate amount of influence and power. Adshel saw itself as a sales organisation ('Sales are King') and to prosper, staff ensured they had the approval of a powerful patron.

Anna Lee summed up: *"The culture was such that no one wanted to upset Sales, because as soon as that happened, the Sales Director would be notified, and the Sales Director would speak to the CEO, and whoever was 'pissing Sales off' would be in trouble with the CEO."*

After the survey results were analysed, both tangible and intangible actions were taken to redistribute the influence and power. Tangible actions included the:

- Establishment of National and State based Culture Teams
- Creation of role clarity via revised position descriptions that clearly documented accountabilities, delegations and responsibilities, resulting in staff feeling confident and 'safe' in their roles
- Revision of the remuneration scheme to reward staff on the basis of a broader set of indicators than sales figures alone
- Introduction of an appraisal system with a stronger development and career planning focus
- Communication with, and engagement of, staff in the OCI culture results and the implementation of improvement strategies

The intangible actions taken were, by their very nature, harder to identify and document, but had substantial impact on the amount of influence staff believe they have. Some that have been identified include:

- New and consistent messages from the CEO and the new Sales Director about wanting staff to have a voice and responsibility for Adshel's future. This shift was well articulated by a member of the focus group after attending a mini-sales conference: *"Staff realised that they were empowered to make decisions for the company. As a result, a lot of people walked away realising that things were going to be OK. The message was: 'If you think you're doing the right thing then go ahead and do it'. It slows the business down if that empowerment is not there. This change has continued and grown throughout the business."*
- Greater openness about decision making. For example, the CEO circulated key decisions from monthly board meetings to all staff.
- Directors were excluded from the OCI debriefs to create a feeling of psychological and emotional safety for staff.

Systems

An organisation's human resource management systems (selection and placement, training and development, appraisal and reinforcement) and goal setting systems are critical drivers of organisational culture. For Adshel, significant system changes that contributed to cultural transformation occurred in the areas of:

- Remuneration
- Training and Development
- Performance Appraisal
- Goal Setting
- Recruitment

Changes to other business systems can also play a significant role in reinforcing new cultural norms. In Adshel's case changes to the 'Panel Booking' system were significant in this regard. We now discuss these Systems changes.

OVERHAULING ADSHEL'S REMUNERATION SYSTEM

Leadership behaviour and reward systems are often the two keys to culture change (Dr Rob Cooke, personal communication); Adshel is no exception in this regard. Adshel's original remuneration system, especially for its sales people, strongly reinforced the Executive's expectations about competitive performance.

The old system was based on individual sales personnel selling a limited number of 'advertising panel' packages (for example, on bus shelters) worth up to $300,000 each. Commissions were paid on the number of packages sold each fortnight.

CEO, Steve McCarthy observed the following: *"We have a limited number of those packages available to be sold, so in a sales sense, if there's nothing left to sell, I can't generate more revenue. I can't make more money, and for the month of April let's say, if I sold none then I get no commission, and if the guy next to me has sold ten, he gets a shit-load of commission. Well I might be happy for a second and say 'well done buddy', and say 'that's great for the team', but personally I will go home to my wife and my bank manager and say 'I'm not happy'. So we have all of these internally developed systems and procedures to generate a highly competitive internal organisation; we're competing more with ourselves than with our external competitors!"*

With the assistance of an external consulting firm PriceWaterhouseCoopers, this commission system was overhauled. The system's focus shifted from rewarding individual performance to rewards based on team and organisational performance. The major focus was to adjust the fixed:variable ratio. Previously, it had been as high as 30:70 for key sales people. This created a strong survival mentality, with some months being 'feasts' and others 'famines'. The new ratios are almost the reverse of what they were under the previous system. Fixed components now range from 60 to 70 percent with the variable components (commissions and bonuses) being 30 to 40 percent of the total. In relation to bonuses, a much broader range of Key Performance Indicators (KPIs) has been introduced to complement sales revenue, such as leadership behaviour, team building, staff training and development, coaching, and collaboration with other departments. These bonus configurations can be in the order of 50:50 (sales revenue:other KPIs) depending on the nature of the person's role.

Staff realised that they were empowered to make decisions for the company

As a result, the staff now receive significantly different messages about what is important. The revised remuneration system, changes the emphasis from achieving short-term dollar results – the 'Sales are King' model that previously prevailed – to a more sustainable, longer-term focus on high collective achievement, whereby managers are encouraged to invest in developing their staff, inter-departmental relationships, and ongoing customer relationships.

At a very human level, people felt they could move from asking, 'How am I going to pay the mortgage this month?' to a more developmental and collaborative focus. In Human Synergistics' Circumplex terms, this is a shift from a Security (Red/Green) focus to a Satisfaction (Blue) focus.

Most significantly, the new rewards system moved from being heavily biased towards sales to a situation where all staff could enjoy the benefits of making a contribution to the success of the business. As one Focus Group Member said: *"Back office staff now have a sense that somewhere in the back of my mind, I am thinking, if I can help this sales person to be more successful, then I will share in the organisation's profits."* This is a far cry from the old system, where sales people were the only ones who enjoyed the benefits, and saw back office staff as there to be manipulated to ensure that they reached their monthly sales target.

TRAINING AND DEVELOPMENT

The key to understanding Adshel's journey of corporate transformation is to understand the role of individual leadership and personal transformation in bringing about the changes. The PEP (Personal Effectiveness Program), and EDP (Executive Development Program) were the primary vehicles used to create an environment where individual transformation could occur.

As discussed earlier, it was through feedback from the early PEP sessions that the initial rumblings of cultural discontent were first heard by the CEO.

PEP

The program's design shows a significant insight into the transformational process:

Objectives	To develop Adshel's up-and-coming staff in terms of skills and personal development. Note: Steve McCarthy initially went looking for a new leadership program from an outside provider, but decided instead to focus on individual effectiveness, and retained the title PEP, to properly reflect the intent of the program
Location	Southern New South Wales
Duration	Six days
Group size	12 maximum
Process	Outdoor and indoor components focussed on getting participants to work as a team in problem solving. In the early programs, the idea of Constructive (above the line) and Defensive (below the line) behaviour was introduced, but the LSI itself was not introduced until the follow-up program.
Leadership participation	CEO attended both the beginning and the end of the program

"Steve opened the program, explaining his objective of developing people and leaders, more on a personal level than an organisational level" (Stephen Klemich, Achievement Concepts).

On the last day, Steve returned for the action planning session. Here, participants presented their action plans and got feedback from their peers and from Steve. Stephen Klemich added that: *"Steve's presence added a lot of value to this, because it gave people the opportunity to see his sincerity, his Humanistic-Encouraging side."*

PEP is now an annual event.

PEP Follow-up

In 2004, a three day PEP follow-up program was introduced, bringing participants from the 2002 and 2003 programs together. At this program, participants were introduced directly to the LSI 1 for the first time. Another PEP follow-up program that will incorporate both the LSI 1&2 feedback to participants is planned during 2006.

EDP - THE EXECUTIVE'S TURN

As often happens in organisations, staff return from profound development experiences pushing for senior management to undertake the same program. At Adshel, this suggestion met resistance from the Executive, as we discussed earlier. However by 2004, after three PEPs had occurred, Steve succumbed to staff pressure.

Again, the EDP featured many transformational design elements.

Objectives	To create an 'isomorph' of the organisation's culture in a new and unfamiliar setting. This enables the organisation's members to see their cultural dynamic from a fresh perspective
Location	West MacDonnell Ranges, Central Australia
Length	Six days
Group	Full Executive Team
Process	The EDP is a 'no-agenda' program, where executives are taken out of their office and placed in a challenging physical environment. In Adshel's case, the Executive was flown to Alice Springs and given $1,000 to gear-up, hire vehicles, and buy food for a six-day expedition. Their immediate objective was to photograph the entire team at 20 strategic locations across the West MacDonnell Ranges

A key benefit of this process is the way in which the team's behaviours, and the impact members have on each other, become very clear. As Stephen Klemich puts it: *"The results in the outdoors are very clear and specific. If you're lost you're lost, if you miss a location you miss a location. It's pretty straight forward, and the feedback, of success or missing the target, is obvious."*

Many learnings were drawn from the collective experience in this environment. For Adshel's Executive, the EDP proved to be a profound turning point in two ways: Firstly, it was the first occasion on which the assumption that 'Competitive equals Success' was challenged. With six days and no detailed agenda, the Executive had plenty of time to reflect on the business, the organisation's culture, and ultimately themselves. Stephen Klemich waited for the right moment to pull out the LSI 1 for self-reflection, and open up this critical conversation. As discussed earlier, this created considerable debate and defensiveness. However, there was plenty of time to work through the issues. *"We went through the process, explaining why certain behaviours were effective, ineffective, etc. It was all conversational, people were asking more and more questions, and from there you start to relate it to other people, family and colleagues"* (Stephen Klemich, Achievement Concepts).

This conversation has continued well beyond that program; however it was a critical turning point in terms of understanding for a number of Directors, and in particular for Steve McCarthy.

Secondly, this was when the Sales Director decided to leave the organisation. One of Adshel's first employees, he had contributed hugely to the success of the business. He was also a strong advocate for competitiveness in the culture.

The EDP had a follow-up program early in 2006.

EDP Follow-up

Objectives	To give the Executive behavioural feedback (LSI) and to create a challenging team interaction, where the impacts of Constructive and Defensive behaviours could be explored
Location	The Castle, Budawang Ranges, NSW
Duration	Three days experiential plus two days strategic planning
Group	Full Executive Team
Process	Introduction to the concepts taught in the PEP program, LSI 1&2 debrief, then a team activity – scaling The Castle

Perhaps a little foolishly in hindsight, Steve McCarthy had suggested that the first EDP lacked physical challenge. Stephen Klemich took up this challenge by having the team hike with backpacks for the first half-day to a base camp at the foot of The Castle (a precipitous mountain in the area). Overnight, while camping in a cave, the Executive had their LSI debrief in preparation for their eight-hour ascent the following morning.

Steve McCarthy recalls: *"We were all given the feedback prior to actually heading off, and what we agreed to do was stick it somewhere in our backpacks and take it with us, to possibly look at when we had some time up the hill. So then we did our summit climb, and we all got to the summit, which was a pretty mind blowing experience, because it was physically very demanding. It required us to have harnesses, ropes, and helmets. Some of us we were well out of our comfort zone, absolutely terrified, but we got to the summit as a group, which was just wonderful."*

The following day was spent reviewing the experience with the LSI feedback at hand. A challenged but strengthened Executive then retired to the comforts of Bannister's Resort for two days of strategic planning.

HOW DO I GET ASSESSED AND DEVELOPED?

Adshel is a young company in two senses: It came into existence relatively recently (1997), and 48% of staff fall into the Generation Y age group. Consequently, the Executive Team faces the challenge of managing a workforce that is increasingly dominated by Generations X and Y. These generations are generally characterised as being less concerned about security, seeking more flexibility in work and travel, and very importantly, demanding development.

Steve McCarthy, who at 43 is on the cusp of being a Gen X, puts himself in the position of a typical member of the organisation: *"My expectations are that if I'm in this organisation you will train me, you will develop me and you will give me a career. But on my terms and my expectations, and at the end of my three month review I'll put some demands to you."*

A new procedure for the Performance Review Report was developed, with a strong focus on development and career progression – the old system having been seen as very limited in what it covered, 'open ended', and too subjective. Staff were involved in developing the new system and managers were given extensive training

People suddenly realised that somebody did care about our development

in the system, and in conducting an effective performance review conversation. Anna Lee describes the improvement on the old system: *"We developed a brand new form which actually took the whole performance appraisal time from about an hour to something like three hours, which was good, because it enabled people to really open up and talk about all the different issues."*

The first round of six-monthly appraisals using the new format was completed in December 2005. While the conversations took longer, there were no complaints from management, as they acknowledged that they needed to spend more time with staff on this important exercise. Again, this practical commitment sent important messages to staff: *"People were suddenly realising that finally somebody out there does give a shit about what I want to do. The managers have always cared, but they haven't had the means to look at it properly"* (Anna Lee, CFO).

GIVING STAFF THE RIGHT TOOLS

Adshel's Panel Booking system had been a key business system that reinforced the previous Competitive and Approval cultural norms. Described as a 'dinosaur' by the CFO, this system handled the booking of Adshel's entire 14,000 advertising panels every fortnight. The system was operated by five back office data-entry people. *"That's where a lot of the strings were being pulled, because there was no visibility in the booking system. In other words, only five people in the business could access that database, and because that team were kind of the data enterers, they were often influenced by the sales people and the size of their contract. They might be asked to push a contract of a lesser value aside to concentrate on what was conceivably a more important, valuable contract, etc. Obviously, if the person with the lesser value contract found out that their contract was pushed aside, they didn't like it"* (Anna Lee, CFO).

The new IT system allows access for all staff across the country, and full transparency.

Anna Lee continues: *"Everyone can go in and see what's booked, and what people are working on. That's a huge change, and obviously things like that prevent too much wheeling and dealing. There's no manipulation to 'get in there before that other team'. The only way you can get in before another team is to literally do so - by convincing the client to sign, or to put a hold on it. It's a significant shift in that respect."*

GOAL SETTING

An important outcome of the revamped Position Descriptions, Performance Appraisals and Remuneration System was to reset and clarify individual goals. This brought a stronger Achievement focus, with goals becoming clearer, more realistic, and more aligned with the company's common goals. Fear and confusion were replaced by greater confidence in dealing with others, especially managers.

RECRUITMENT

Adshel's recruitment focus has shifted to include a strong element of 'cultural fit'. The new system is a two-fold process that asks, firstly, 'Can the candidate do the job?', and secondly, 'Does the candidate fit Adshel's new culture?' Steve McCarthy estimates that 95% of those who don't get jobs fail because of poor culture-fit.

Three-month probation reviews are taken very seriously, and generally involve review by the Board. Again, a majority of problems arise from fit, not from whether the person can do the job.

Skills/Qualities

COMMUNICATION

Communication is the life blood of any social system – organisations in particular. In its culture change program, Adshel also addressed many aspects of its formal and informal communication.

As noted earlier, one of the most significant communication strategies employed in culture change at Adshel was the OCI data collection process itself. Culture can be defined as 'the way we do things around here'. Consequently, how an organisation does anything, including undertaking culture surveys, can usually be predicted by its culture.

The Directors' demand that the survey be done 'properly' was a significant departure from the previous culture, and provided a sign of the beginning of a cultural shift that many in the organisation would have picked up.

Adshel is a model in how to engage staff in the OCI collection and results debriefing. Two basic communication workshops were designed. Firstly, the Focus Group, which was more than a vehicle to collect the OCI data, it was an education and engagement activity; and secondly, the Roadshows, where the CEO presented the results of the survey to all staff.

2005 Focus Groups

Objective	To inform staff of the survey's purpose, demonstrate CEO support, complete and collect OCI Actual and Preferred inventories, and foreshadow how the results will be communicated
Attendees	All staff participated in State-based workshops and New Zealand
Duration	Half-day
Process	• Introduction by CEO (Note: Steve McCarthy attended all sessions) • Introduction to culture (what culture is and isn't; what the OCI measures) • All participants filled out the Actual and Preferred OCI (resulting in a 100% response rate for both diagnostic inventories) • Results feedback process explained • Presentation of stories and journeys of other transformational organisations

2005 Roadshows

Objective	To debrief staff on OCI results, and identify levers for change
Attendees	All staff participated in State-based workshops and New Zealand
Duration	Half-day
Process	• CEO introduction (Note: Steve McCarthy personally attended all sessions) • Reminder of what culture is by Stephen Klemich • Preferred culture activity (Preferred culture was drawn on a wall chart) • Presentation of 2005 OCI Test results ***Small group activity 1:*** • What do you think the results are? • Why do you think you got those results? • How do you think you are going to change? • Present regional results ***Small group activity 2 (Directors undertook this exercise first then presented to staff):*** • What are five behaviours we need to change to develop the culture? • Review the similarities and differences between management's and staff's lists of behaviours

2006 Roadshows

Objective	To provide feedback on the OCI Re-Test results, demonstrate CEO support, and decide what levers to focus on
Attendees	All staff participated in State-based workshops and New Zealand
Duration	Half-day
Process	• CEO introduction (Note: Steve McCarthy personally attended all sessions)
	• Reminder of what culture is
	• Preferred culture activity (Preferred culture was drawn on a wall chart)
	• Presentation of 2006 OCI Re-Test results
	Small group activity 1:
	• What do you think the results are?
	• Why do you think you got those results?
	• How do you think you are going to change?
	• Present regional results
	• Presentation of Directors' levers for change (by Steve McCarthy)
	Small group activity 2:
	• What are five things management can do to develop the culture?
	• What are five things that staff can do to develop the culture?

This rigorous process of engagement, communication and action planning with all staff in these workshops delivered a number of important outcomes. Fundamentally, these processes were counter-cultural, as they challenged the way things were done

We've been heard, and something was actually done!

in Adshel. Even from the commencement of the program, starting with the survey to collect data from the 2005 Focus Group, staff reported a shift in attitude: *"Staff were able to have input right from the beginning. They were heard. Many of them actually said, 'We've been heard, they're listening to us'. This starts to shift the culture immediately. It's a better place because they've been heard. And then, something was actually done! And quickly - as a result of those issues being raised"* (Stephen Klemich, Achievement Concepts).

Steve McCarthy believes that there would have been an immediate improvement in the OCI results if the Re-Test had been done in May 2005, even if no other action had been taken.

DIALOGUE: A KEY TO ORGANISATIONAL TRANSFORMATION

Adshel's focus on communication is one of the keys to its transformation. We will never know the motivation of the Executive who demanded that the OCI survey be done 'properly', but it gave Stephen Klemich permission to go to work at a deep level with the organisation. Part of the success of the change program resulted from giving staff, as Steve McCarthy says, a genuine *"voice"* in the organisation's future. Previously, influence and power had been centralised with the CEO and the Sales Department. Organisational communication initiatives are often dissatisfying because they are top-down; by contrast, the Adshel Focus Groups and Roadshows were empowering, because they initiated bottom-up communication that was listened to and acted on. The new norms embedded in the processes had a significant impact in creating a sense of empowerment: *"People realised that discussing things in this forum meant that they would be dealt with"* (Focus Group Member).

LEADERSHIP

There are myriad leadership definitions, but Rob Cooke's definition summarises the impact of Steve McCarthy's leadership on Adshel: *"Managers cannot be considered to 'lead' unless they in some way transform, shape, or influence the organisational context of members, and the ways in which they approach their work and interact with one another"* (Cooke, 2005).

We have already discussed many of the structural and system changes that Steve McCarthy instigated and supported as CEO to change the context for staff. But it is critical to also understand the person behind the leader, for without Steve's inspiration, support and courage, Adshel would not have transformed its culture. Stephen

The CEO's buy-in to the Blue behaviour made me feel empowered

Klemich speaks to Steve McCarthy's intangible leadership quality: *"There's just that innate quality in Steve as a leader in that he considers people, product and profit equally, which has been one of the major contributing factors to the success of the change."* So what can we learn about this 'innate leadership' thing that Steve McCarthy has?

To do this, we need to return to the genesis of this transformational story. As we have discussed, Adshel was financially successful. There was no 'burning platform' for change, but Steve McCarthy wanted to create a development program for 'our up-and-coming staff'.

This speaks to his:

- **Understanding of the people side of business**, and his **development values**, illustrated by a willingness to make an on-going investment in people development and staff careers.
- **Sensitivity and openness to environmental feedback**, illustrated by his sensitivity to staff feedback from PEP and other sources.
- **Willingness to have his assumptions challenged**, illustrated by his engagement with the LSI in Central Australia and then confronting Culture results.

- **Courage to act on his convictions** about the culture. As one of the Focus Group Members put it: *"It's a gutsy thing for an organisation to do, for any leader to do."*
- **Willingness to challenge the status quo** and deal with issues in a conflict-averse Approval culture. As Steve puts it: *"My key role in life is to be what I call the 'eggshell crusher', to jump all over the issues that people are tiptoeing around."*
- **Modeling of the new behaviours**, illustrated by being more engaged with staff: *"Steve takes the time to speak to everyone in the office, which means that people trust him when he makes decisions like bringing in the OCI – people feel that they have a relationship with him"* (Focus Group Member).
- **Seeing new possibilities** in unanticipated change, illustrated by Steve's initial fear that sales would be seriously impacted with the resignation of the Sales Director. However, he quickly saw this as an opportunity to bring in a different leadership style.
- **Taking responsibility for his behavioural impact:** *"We identified a lot of behaviour that had previously been condoned by many. That's the key to this process. This is behaviour that was condoned, supported. I was the cheerleader in all of this stuff, I was saying how good are we because we do it like this. So there's no hiding behind anything,"* said Steve McCarthy, CEO.
- **Openness to feedback**, illustrated by Steve undertaking the LSI 1&2 in early 2006.

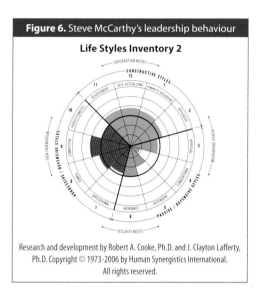

Figure 6. Steve McCarthy's leadership behaviour

Research and development by Robert A. Cooke, Ph.D. and J. Clayton Lafferty, Ph.D. Copyright © 1973-2006 by Human Synergistics International. All rights reserved.

THE LEADER'S LSI RESULTS
Steve McCarthy's LSI 2 profile (Figure 6) shows a predominantly Constructive (Blue) and Task orientation. These strengths confirm staff feedback, and would account for his effectiveness as a leader. Significantly, the Competitive extension remains at the 75th percentile. If not managed, these behaviours will overpower the Humanistic-Encouraging values that Steve wants to promote.

EXECUTIVE TEAM'S LSI 2
Significantly, the Executive Team's group LSI 2 (Figure 7) shows a stronger Aggressive/ Defensive (Red) orientation. As Stephen Klemich comments: *"The LSI 2 of the directors is no surprise. It is unfortunate that we do no have LSI 2 data from last year on them, as it would have been so much worse."*

However, there is clear feedback from staff about management's changed behaviour: *"To see the changes in management behaviour and have them embrace and encourage the feedback from the survey has been great"* (Focus Group Member).

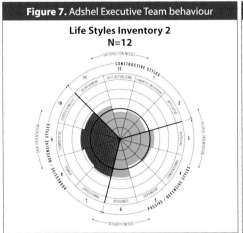

Figure 7. Adshel Executive Team behaviour

Figure 8. Adshel Executive Team culture results

This could reflect the lag effect between culture and actual behaviour as measured by the LSI 2. The behavioural expectations (OCI Actual) reported by the Executive Team are very Constructive (Blue) as shown in Figure 8. This is an important lesson about cultural transformation; expectations for behaviour must shift first. This 'hidden force' then leads managers and staff to behave in particular ways. The challenge for all players is to decide whether they are going to align themselves to the new expectations.

A NEW LEADER, A NEW APPROACH

Leadership style is the most important driver of organisational culture. Leaders shape expectations by what they reward and punish, what they pay attention to and what they ignore (Schein, 2004). This is especially the case in young, developing organisations that have undeveloped systems and processes - organisations like Adshel.

It is very clear that the new Sales Director's leadership style has positively impacted the Constructive styles. Staff report significant improvement in management and leadership style across the organisation:

- More relaxed and less abrasive
- Identifying and communicating strategies and future plans
- Paying attention to office behaviour
- Leading the change
- Openness of the Director
- More consultative
- More 'Blue' behaviour in senior roles in Sales
- Increase in awareness
- Shift from directive to consultative
- More consultative, relaxed, open management style
- Now team players

At a very personal level, the transformational process led by Steve McCarthy allowed individuals to heal the emotional hurt caused by the Red/Green culture and Aggressive management styles. *"Having Steve deliver the culture results, and his buy-in to the Blue behaviour, made me feel empowered to know that even though my boss was against these styles, I knew that his behaviour was wrong. All my fears and anger about how I was being managed were all of a sudden out on the table. Even though he was talking about the company, it was very personal for me; it made me realise that I'm okay – it empowered me. Eventually my manager left of his own accord"* (Focus Group Member).

MAKING CHOICES ABOUT THE CULTURE

One of the toughest dynamics in culture change is dealing with individual values and behavioural fit. As an organisation's culture evolves, acceptable values, and how they are expressed in behaviours, change dramatically. Culture is the pressure to conform, to fit in. When this changes, individuals are forced to make decisions about conforming to the new expectations, or choosing to find other cultures that better align with their personal values. Of course, an organisation is often an outward expression of the leader's values and, as noted by the Focus Group Member above, conflict will occur when these values are not shared by key decision-makers. Attitudes, values and behaviours evolve and shift, forcing people to make choices.

This was the case for a number of Adshel's senior team. Having been instrumental in setting up the company, their influence in shaping the organisation, its culture and its success had been significant. However, as the organisation and its culture evolved, they wrestled with questions about whether this was an environment where they could continue to be satisfied, given its new cultural direction. As a result some decided to leave the organisation.

2006

Adshel

Phase **4**

Re-Test

Culture Re-Test Results

Adshel's OCI Re-Test was conducted in February 2006, 12 months after the initial measure. Again, there was an exceptional response rate (99%), despite completion of the survey being made voluntary this time.

The Re-Test circumplex (Figure 9) shows a dramatic shift in culture from a profile dominated by Passive/ Aggressive (Green/Red) to one dominated by the Constructive (Blue) cluster. Specifically, there is a substantial decrease in Competitive norms and an increase in Humanistic-Encouraging norms. Table 2 describes these two styles.

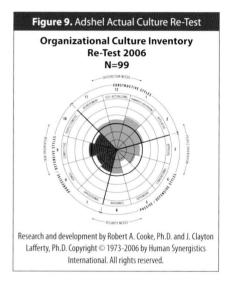

Figure 9. Adshel Actual Culture Re-Test

Organizational Culture Inventory
Re-Test 2006
N=99

Research and development by Robert A. Cooke, Ph.D. and J. Clayton Lafferty, Ph.D. Copyright © 1973-2006 by Human Synergistics International. All rights reserved.

Statistical Significance

Figure 10 shows Adshel's Test ➔ Re-Test OCI results. The results show a statistically significant shift in all styles in the desired direction. Points of note are:

- Strong improvement in people-orientated Constructive styles: Humanistic-Encouraging and Affiliative.
- Relatively low improvement in the Achievement style. This should be the focus moving forward, as this style most correlates with organisational effectiveness. The goal should be to ensure that Achievement motivation is significantly greater than Competitive.
- Significant decreases in the related styles of Dependent and Power, reflecting the redistribution of influence we explored earlier. That is, managers are less controlling (reduced Power), causing staff to feel less 'helpless' (reduced Dependent).

Reaction to The Re-Test

Not surprisingly, the reaction to the Re-Test feedback was very positive. The following quote speaks to the reality that culture change is often a three-to-ten-year project. However, it can be dramatically shorter if the organisation is courageous, focussed and prepared to put in the resources. *"It was made clear that change was not going to happen overnight – when the changes came through the way they did, it was a huge achievement. Seeing the results made sense, but it blew us all away. We all expected minor changes, but not change that was so big. Now that we think about it, you can understand why the result is as good as it is"* (Focus Group Member).

Table 2. Comparison of Primary Cultural Styles

From a culture dominated by Competitive in 2005 to Humanistic-Encouraging in 2006

A Competitive culture is one in which winning is valued, and members are rewarded for out-performing one another. People in such organisations operate in a 'win-lose' framework, and believe they must work against (rather than with) their peers to be noticed. An overly Competitive culture can inhibit effectiveness by reducing cooperation, and promoting unrealistic standards of performance (either too high or too low).

A Humanistic-Encouraging culture characterises organisations that are managed in a participative and person-centred way. Members are expected to be supportive, constructive and open to influence in their dealings with one another. A Humanistic-Encouraging culture leads to effective organisational performance by providing for the growth and active involvement of members who, in turn, report high satisfaction with, and commitment to, the organisation.

Strongest behavioural norms:

People are expected to:
- be a 'winner'
- be seen and noticed
- win against others

Strongest behavioural norms:

People are expected to:
- encourage others
- be supportive of others
- help others to grow and develop

Figure 10. Adshel Actual Culture Test ➔ Re-Test

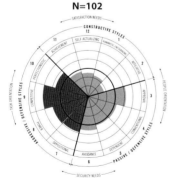

Organizational Culture Inventory
Test 2005
N=102

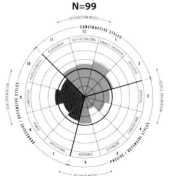

Organizational Culture Inventory
Re-Test 2006
N=99

Research and development by Robert A. Cooke, Ph.D. and J. Clayton Lafferty, Ph.D. Copyright © 1973-2006 by Human Synergistics International. All rights reserved.

Style	Percentile			Significance	Style	Percentile			Significance	Style	Percentile			Significance
	Test	Re-Test	Shift			Test	Re-Test	Shift			Test	Re-Test	Shift	
Achievement	45	59	14	*	Approval	77	44	-33	***	Oppositional	73	43	-30	***
Self-Actualizing	38	62	24	**	Conventional	57	30	-27	***	Power	75	34	-41	***
Humanistic-Encouraging	32	74	42	***	Dependent	54	14	-40	***	Competitive	90	56	-34	***
Affiliate	21	56	35	***	Avoidance	65	45	-20	*	Perfectionistic	66	45	-21	*

*NS Not Significant; *<0.05; **<0.01; ***<0.001*

Business Outcomes

We see a dramatic improvement in Adshel's culture, but why the investment? Ultimately, the investment was aimed not at changing the culture for its own sake, but to modify the outcomes being produced by the culture.

The most commonly requested culture-outcome relationship is to demonstrate that there is a link between culture and profitability. Whilst research has established links, the search for a simple, direct causal relationship reflects an assumption that needs to be tested in today's businesses (Cooke & Szumal, 2000). A commonly held belief, by both managers and staff, is that their organisation exists to make profits. Perhaps a more sustainable concept is that organisations are here to serve a number of constituents, and when they do this well, profit will be an outcome. Of course, in many cases the short-term

> **We all expected minor changes but not change that was so big**

pressure from shareholders for quick returns is structured into CEOs' bonus schemes and into sales managers' monthly budgets. This can drive an aggressive attitude of 'don't worry about tomorrow, mortgage it, so today's sales look good!'

While many managers would like to see a simple, clear link between culture and profitability, Steve McCarthy has a radically different view of the world: *"Good people, great environment, the business looks after itself. If your focus is only on numbers, then all this stuff gets thrown away, and you end up with a miserable organisation that is driven by numbers. And that works okay in a good market, but the minute the market turns, if that's what you drive your business on, you've got nothing left. You turn around and you say there's no soul in this joint. We don't actually have any passion for people to come to work other than to come to work to make a buck and pay the bills."*

Again, on his role: *"My job is to employ good people and create the environment where they can do great things. They're the only two reasons I'm here! If I do both of those things well, everything else, including the numbers, takes care of itself. All of those things flow from that."*

So, profit is seen as an outcome from building a great culture over the longer term.

As we have already noted, Adshel is a 'successful' company. But how is 'success' defined? A popular interpretation is that 'success' means profits, and increasing shareholder value. A more embracing definition would define these as outcomes from having a purposeful and sustainable organisation that respects all key stakeholders: staff, customers and shareholders.

Shareholder Outcomes

Historically, Adshel has taken good care of this group. Adshel is one of the most profitable companies in the Clear Channel and APN group, consistently outperforming the market. Revenue and EBIT growth is double-digit over the past two years (see Figure 11).

Anna Lee, Adshel's CFO, believes the dramatic improvement in profit growth is due to the

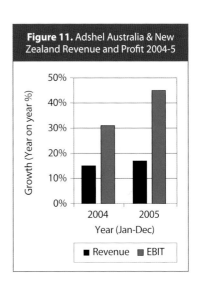

Figure 11. Adshel Australia & New Zealand Revenue and Profit 2004-5

shift in staff attitude towards the company: *"We now have a collective culture with real pride and passion for Adshel. People are now accountable and responsible 'cost managers' who are not going to throw us into ridiculous contracts. The attitude has shifted from 'Who cares, it's just the company?' to staff looking after the company."*

Staff and Customers

Staff's experience of Adshel's culture has changed dramatically. In the 'Action' section of this case study, we described improved outcomes from each of the improvement actions. These outcomes included:

- Rationalising Position Descriptions - giving staff role clarity
- Improved communication
- Re-distribution of influence - leading to staff feeling more empowered
- Providing enhanced training and development - creating a sense that the company is committed to their development

As one Focus Group Member notes: *"Competitiveness has decreased, pressure and fear has reduced; this has resulted in an ability to concentrate on moving forward, rather than having to focus on keeping your job – [providing] empowerment to all staff."*

The OCI provides valuable quantitative outcome data. As we have discussed in the 'Test' section, Adshel's initial survey showed a paradoxical relationship between moderate to high staff satisfaction within an Aggressive/Passive Culture – the 'Enron Syndrome'. The Re-Test of the OCI outcomes shows consistent improvement, in particular for those outcomes identified as problematic in the initial survey (see Figure 12).

These cultural outcomes, as reported by staff, fall into three broad themes: Role Clarity, Employee Satisfaction and Quality of Service.

- **Role Clarity** improved the most: 9.8% (average improvement across the three items that make up this construct). The item with the biggest change in this cluster and across all 12 outcome questions is, '… do you receive inconsistent messages regarding what is expected?' (improved by 10.5%). This is a predictable outcome as Adshel's culture shifts away from a Competitive and Approval culture, where staff were confused by conflicting management expectations, to one where expectations are clear, documented, and agreed to. The primary driver has been the focus on Systems improvement, especially appraisal, remuneration, and position descriptions. Obviously, revised Systems alone are not going to support Role Clarity unless there is the requisite redistribution of Structural Influence, which indeed occurred.

- **Employee Satisfaction** improved by 6.6% (average of the construct's three items). The biggest item shift is, '… are you satisfied being a member of this organisation?' (improved by 7.4%). So, despite the claim in 2005 that staff were 'satisfied', staff reported significant subsequent improvements in their satisfaction level.
- **Quality of Service** improved by 4.7% (average of the construct's four items). The biggest item shift is, '… does your organisation have a reputation for superior customer service?' (improved by 9.6%). Interestingly, this category has the greatest variation, and includes one item that went backwards, '… would you personally go out of your way to make sure that a customer/client feels good about the service you've provided?' (-0.2%). This paradox can be explained by understanding how Approval drives staff to please the customer at all costs, even at the expense of themselves and the back office, who have to deliver on unrealistic promises made by Sales. The 'giving away the shop' approach to customer service is not sustainable, and needs to be replaced by a more rational and planned approach. As one of the Sales Executives grappling with this issue stated: *"Just because you do it fast, doesn't mean it's necessarily right."*

This is a healthy improvement, reflecting a more mature approach to customer service. However, this transition to Achievement needs to be managed well, because most customers feel that they cannot get enough service, and renegotiating their expectations can be misinterpreted.

Stephen Klemich observes a maturing of Sales' attitudes towards customers: *"They have lost a lot of that 'smart Alec' style. And I think this is reflected in some of the new business they have won, for example, the government business, and the airports contract. They have lost that upstart brashness. Clients are more comfortable with a more mature approach."*

The CEO's Big Outcome

Steve McCarthy aspires to making Adshel an employer of choice. He wants his people to really want to come to work, not to be 'lemon suckers', who come to work with sour faces and do just enough work to avoid getting fired. Reiterating that: *"I want that our staff are ready to leave, but happy to stay."*

Steve now has both a measure of where the organisation is at and the tools to realise his vision. Or perhaps this has already been realised, as one of the Focus Group Members declared: *"We love this company. You don't get out of bed in the morning if you don't want to go to work."*

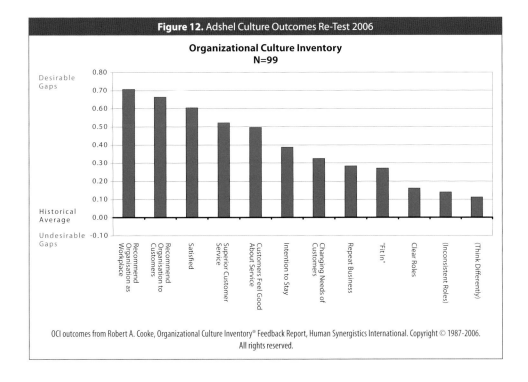

Figure 12. Adshel Culture Outcomes Re-Test 2006

Organizational Culture Inventory
N=99

Adshel

Phase **5**

Review

Change Agents | Lessons Learnt | Future Challenges |
Towards A Sustainable Organisation

Change Agents

Internal Change Agents	Steve McCarthy, CEO Adshel
	National & State Culture teams

External Change Agents	Stephen Klemich, Achievement Concepts

The constant challenge of change requires organisations to build the capacity to change as a core capability to ensure survival. It is worth reflecting on Adshel's evolution from a start-up nine years ago to a maturing, prosperous organisation today. Of course, this doesn't happen without leadership and change agency.

There are always many players in any change effort, and ideally all are acknowledged and celebrated. They range from the disgruntled employees who had the courage to speak up at the first PEPs about their disquiet, to the managers who were quick to take action once the feedback became clear, to the external agents who came in to provide technical expertise and support, and ultimately to the CEO who led decisively, allowing himself to be influenced, and allowing others to take initiative and act.

Here we touch on only three key change agents: the CEO, the main external change agent, and the Culture Teams.

Steve McCarthy - CEO Adshel
We have already discussed Steve McCarthy's role in this transformation at length - see the Skills/Qualities section.

Stephen Klemich - External Change Agent
Stephen Klemich's introduction to Adshel was one of those serendipitous events. A member of his company left to work for Adshel as the CEO's Personal Assistant (PA). So when Steve McCarthy went into the market looking for someone to replicate the experience of the staff member who came back 'transformed' from the RYLA experience, his PA recommended Stephen Klemich's company, Achievement Concepts.

The relationship with Achievement Concepts and Stephen began in 2002, with the running of the first PEP, and evolved from one where he was simply a training provider to one where he was a strategic change agent and trusted advisor. Stephen and his wife and business partner, Mara, brought a different set of values and assumptions into Adshel, and began to sow the seeds of transformation. What they also brought was a different 'how', as we have already discussed.

Following are a number of defining features of Stephen Klemich's approach:

- Courage to challenge the client's assumptions and norms, even if they are strongly and emotionally held.
- Ability to facilitate conversations at all levels: one of the keys to having effective conversations/dialogue is making the time to have them—such as a six-day, no-agenda wilderness trek, allowing people the time to unwind in a new environment, and provoking new ways of seeing the world.
- Facilitation of conversations designed to build independence: *"That's exactly our philosophy. We don't want to foster dependency, we actually want to foster achievement within that organisation. If we foster dependency, then we are being hypocritical in relation to the very thing that we are espousing as consultants. That's why we call ourselves facilitators, rather than consultants. If we can help facilitate them in coming up with meaning, that's going to help them change"* (Stephen Klemich, Achievement Concepts).
- Building self-responsibility in staff – *"No one else is going to change it but ourselves"* (a Focus Group comment relating to Stephen Klemich).
- Creating a safe environment for conversations to be had. During the Roadshows to debrief the OCI results, Stephen invites the Directors, including the CEO, to leave the workshop for an hour so staff can state their issues, which always include leadership behaviour. They then return to hear what staff have said. It is hoped that trust has developed between staff and management to the extent that next year's debrief will not require the Directors to leave the room. As one of the Focus Groups described their relationship with the facilitators: *"Delivery of results was easier because of our relationships with Stephen and Mara – having them there made the process easier; staff had trust and faith in them."*
- Working deeply - which means going beyond the mundane to the profound. Stephen and Mara worked with individuals to resolve ego defences, and find meaning and purpose. One executive's story speaks to the outcome of personal transformation: *"Upon retiring, he underwent a significant personal transformation, losing weight, stopping smoking, and finding new meaning for his life"* (Stephen Klemich, Achievement Concepts).

National and State Culture Teams

We have already discussed the important role these pieces of the 'social architecture' played in Adshel's transformation, but it is worth relating an anecdote about one of the members of the Focus Group. The story illustrates the culture shift from Dependent to Achievement, and the creative energy that is released when staff are given a voice. At the end of the focus group's session, one of the Sydney Culture Team came up and expressed a concern that what they had been doing was without input from a consultant, and enquired whether that was alright! Some level of dependency still lingers in the question, but it is overshadowed by the responsibility this group has assumed in initiating culture-improvement action.

Lessons Learnt

What are the key lessons to be learnt about cultural transformation from Adshel's case study?

MEASURING THE UNMEASURABLE

Managers frequently remark that 'if you can't measure it you can't manage it'. Certainly, this was the challenge for Adshel. Despite the organisation's success, staff reported that they felt there was something wrong. The circumplex provided a framework and language to articulate these concerns. One Focus Group Member observed: *"When staff saw the results, they didn't realise that their behaviour could fit into those behavioural styles – e.g. treat others the way you would like to be treated – it made people realise how their behaviour affects others."* And, *"It wasn't just words, there was meaning to the results. We had tangible examples to show what the behaviours are like."*

With this more sophisticated language, staff became more aware of their behaviour and its impact on others. Awareness is the first step in change.

MEASURING THE RIGHT THING

The limitation of staff satisfaction surveys is well illustrated here. If Adshel had just used a staff satisfaction survey, it is unlikely that significant change would have occurred. These limitations are described by the CEO: *"If we had just done the satisfaction survey and just asked those questions, we would have done no further work, because we would have thought; that's pretty good. We were a happy bunch."*

Culture and climate are very different but interrelated constructs. In Rob Cooke's 'How Culture Works' model, climate is seen as an outcome of culture, that is, an effect, not a cause. CEOs often report frustration with satisfaction surveys, as they provide little insight into how to change the culture. Adshel's culture and climate data are particularly interesting because of the culture's mixed impact on climate outcomes. The 'Enron' effect occurred where a Defensive culture produced a limited number of positive, short-term climate outcomes, for example, staff satisfaction.

HOW SYSTEMS SHAPE BEHAVIOUR

During the twelve months between the Test and Re-Test, Adshel made radical changes to the systems that encode behavioural norms into the very fabric of the organisation. The review of systems went beyond the HR systems (position descriptions, remuneration, and appraisal) to include business systems such as the Panel Booking IT system. The messages that organisational systems send cannot be underestimated. They are critical to achieving alignment between the organisation's cultural aspirations, as articulated in the Preferred culture circumplex, and members' personal motivations. As a member of the Focus Group put it: *"The more you set up systems that support Blue behaviour, the quicker it will weed out people who don't fit."*

REDISTRIBUTION OF INFLUENCE

Organisations spend significant resources on reviewing their systems and structures, often to little or no avail in cultural terms. This is because the systemic issues of influence and power are not addressed. Plenty of organisations have perfectly adequate systems to support Constructive behaviour, but formal and informal bases of power overwhelm these messages. For example, aggressive managers may see performance appraisal conversations as a 'tick and flick' exercise to comply with HR requirements.

What is unique in Adshel's case is the radical redistribution of influence from the Sales Department and the Senior Executive to all staff. Power relationships are usually socially conditioned and largely unconscious. Adshel was able to significantly re-engineer these power relationships to achieve an unusually high level of staff engagement and empowerment.

BUILDING SOCIAL ARCHITECTURE FOR ORGANISATIONAL DIALOGUE

The establishment and empowerment of the Culture Teams was a critical new piece of 'Social Architecture' (Charan, 2006) within Adshel that redistributed influence and power down the organisational chart. These 'white spaces between the boxes on the organisational chart' strategies are critical vehicles to balancing power within the formal structure. Along with the communication strategies of Focus Groups and Roadshows, these structures are integral to facilitating Peter Senge's (1990) process of Dialogue, an essential mechanism for transformation.

Senge speaks to the critical role of 'discussing things', or dialogue, in organisational learning and renewal. He describes a process whereby 'in dialogue, people become observers of their own thinking'. Importantly, to have transformational value, this dialogue must deal with what Chris Argyris (1990) calls 'undiscussables', that is, the organisation's underlying assumptions, norms and values. If this is done with 'valid knowledge' sourced from diagnostics such as the OCI, from independent outsiders, and most importantly from the organisation's members themselves, then breakthroughs occur. In the process, current assumptions, norms and values are re-examined and, where appropriate, over-turned, updated or replaced.

This happened in Adshel:

- 'Undiscussables' were discussed – arguably the best example of this was the belief that being aggressive and Competitive motivates staff and leads to success. When this assumption was exposed and challenged, it was replaced with a belief that staff were self-motivated, and could be trusted to act in the company's best interests.
- 'Valid knowledge' exposed contradictions - this process is best described by a member of the Focus Group saying: *"People thought the culture was fine, everyone was happy – but there was an undercurrent, which came out from the results. People had felt certain things about the organisation, but couldn't put them into words until they sat down and saw the results, and then it made sense."*
- Independent outsiders brought in new assumptions - Stephen Klemich and the other external change agents brought a set of empowering values into Adshel: *"That's why we call ourselves facilitators rather than consultants. If we can help facilitate them in coming up with meaning, that's going to help them change."*

- Worldviews were changed - members of the Focus Group eloquently articulated Adshel's shift in consciousness and perspective: *"It was a shift in the way things are looked at"*; and *"What's happened to ego? It's disappeared, but every so often it comes back."*

The outcome was a powerful process of engagement and empowerment, and most importantly, it gave staff a voice!

DEEP DEVELOPMENT LEADING TO PERSONAL TRANSFORMATION

Personal transformation occurs when an individual is confronted by the reality of the 'disconnect' between their self-concept and their behaviour as observed by others. Feedback processes like the LSI *"expose us to ourselves"* (Stephen Klemich), creating emotional disturbance that demands resolution. This is often described as a sense of waking up to the reality of our unhappiness with our current predicament. The predicament is often that we want to live by a particular set of values, but find ourselves in an environment that forces us to behave in contrary ways to meet our Security needs. The resolution of this emotional disturbance, this lack of alignment of personal aspirations with reality, is the fuel of personal change. The outcomes of this process can vary from adoption of a specific new behaviour to a change in our life's purpose.

> **The circumplex is a confronting philosophy, the more you hear it, the more it confronts you**

Stephen Klemich, one of Australia's longest users of Human Synergistics' tools, explains the power of the circumplex to create dissonance: *"It [the circumplex] is a confronting philosophy because of its profound truth. The more you hear it, the more it confronts you, as you explore where you are basing your security and ego status, and we teach this at quite a deep level."*

Critical for this process is time and space, sufficient to enable people to slow down enough to allow this natural process of self-reflection to occur. These transformational assumptions were incorporated into the PEP and EDP programs, and had a marked impact on those participating. This is confirmed by a Focus Group Member: *"Self-assessment – looking at the way they behaved. Behaviour is significantly different now to before the survey."*

LEADERSHIP

The final key is leadership. Without leadership, Adshel's transformation would not have happened. *"Senior management, led by Steve, realised that they had to change their management styles"* (Focus Group Member).

Our society and organisations call out for real leadership by men and women who will step up and be committed to improving how their organisations and society operate. Leadership involves living with integrity and challenging the status quo in order to create unique organisations and a society based on Constructive values. It involves leaders examining themselves to ensure they are truly walking their talk, embracing new possibilities, and having the emotional and psychological courage to stand out and truly lead.

Whatever can be said about creating transformation, if the leader is without the rare combination of qualities of personal insight and courage, little changes: *"It's a gutsy thing for an organisation to do, and for any leader to do"* (Focus Group Member).

Future Challenges

Adshel has achieved an extraordinary shift in culture. It still has many challenges to overcome if it is to continue its development.

The following initiatives have been identified by the Directors in the 2006 Roadshows as the next critical steps in their journey:

- Focus on Achievement
- Senior team has completed individual LSI - view of self compared to those of five others - we all have work to do
- Take feedback from the groups and continue to drive a "Blue Environment"
- Maintain use of committees/teams to tackle issues that need broad involvement and buy-in
- Maintain the fun and work hard to stay 'cool' - review HR systems and processes
- Identify "Iconic Moments" for the business and the team and treat appropriately

Staff were also asked during the last round of Roadshows to identify what management can do to continue the culture change, and secondly, what staff can do. These data were collected and prioritised by staff from Sydney, Melbourne and New Zealand, and it was only after this that the Directors' list was presented. The following is a summary of the key themes.

What Management Can Do...

MANAGEMENT STYLE

Continue to build openness in the culture by management's style, for example, by committing to open discussions and having open doors. Plus leading by example, and maintaining integrity with what management espouses, 'doing versus talking'.

Recommended Action: focus on supporting and coaching all managers with the implementation of their LSI action plans. Ensure systems, such as appraisal and remuneration, shape behaviour in-line with Adshel's Preferred culture.

ACHIEVEMENT MOTIVATION

Ensure that goal setting, planning and problem solving supports realistic expectations of staff, that expectations are realistic in relation to available resources. Demonstrate sensitivity to the impact on people of business decisions. Continue to work on business systems.

Recommended Action: build an awareness of what the Achievement motivation is, and how it is fundamentally different to the Competitive and Perfectionistic motivations. Build Achievement skills by training staff in goal setting and problem-solving skills, and continue to encode Achievement into all of Adshel's systems, policies and client relationships.

TRAINING AND DEVELOPMENT

Continue to focus on all aspects of development, making it more equitable for all departments.

Recommended Action: continue development processes, ensuring they are seen as fair. Promote all aspects of development beyond just attending workshops, for example, on-the-job training.

What Staff Can Do...

TAKE RESPONSIBILITY

Self-responsibility is a strong theme. For example, everyone is to take responsibility for being direct, open and honest in office communications, and have the courage to address behaviour and actions of others, address issues, and solve problems.

Recommended Action: continue to re-engineer the organisation to redistribute influence, responsibility and consequences down the organisation. Identify, promote and reward behaviours that reflect self-responsibility.

ADSHEL FOCUS

Undertake a commitment to focus on Adshel as a whole. To respect each other and our roles, taking time to gain knowledge of other departments, and increase collective pride and passion.

Recommended Action: promote the mission and purpose of Adshel, and celebrate its collective achievements. Challenge Competitive, silo thinking and behaviour.

Towards A Sustainable Organisation

Organisational sustainability has emerged as a popular concept in the light of recent corporate collapses. Adshel's CEO has clearly identified sustainability as a motivation in addressing his organisation's culture. So, what is sustainability?

Dexter Dunphy (1998) suggests the new model of sustainable organisations is a natural ecosystem: *"An organic, self-renewing biological system, such as a rainforest or a coral reef."*
This metaphor is in stark contrast to the popular conception of organisation as machine. Adshel's transformation reflects a dramatic balancing of the organisational ecosystem. What we see is the balancing of the various parts of the system, particularly reflected in the redistribution of influence across the organisation. If such imbalances are not addressed, parts of the system become stressed , and continual demands deplete the sub-system, leading to failure. This is most commonly seen in organisations that pressure staff to achieve unrealistically high goals while being unable to exert much influence, in an atmosphere of fear and blame. In the short-term, staff expend a lot of effort; however, symptoms of strain emerge, and burnout, disengagement and finally, separation result.

This was characteristic of Adshel in the early days – a stressed system, 'successful' because it was in a prosperous market niche with a fresh young workforce. What the CEO realised was that the system would not survive a downturn in the market or increased competition for employees; hence his interest in measuring the culture as a way of understanding more clearly what he intuitively felt.

We see a maturing organisation responding to the demands of its internal constituents for a 'voice' in how the organisation is run. We also see the beginnings of Adshel engaging differently with its external environment, in particular, its clients. The maturing of client relationships is seen in the shift from the unsustainable over-servicing Approval behaviour to a more Achievement-oriented behaviour that respects both internal and external stakeholders' needs.

At this stage in Adshel's evolution we see evidence of it 'balancing' internal and external factors. As the culture further embraces the underlying assumptions of the Constructive (Blue) cultural styles, it will continue to strengthen all of its sub-systems, its interface with the broader environment, and its natural evolution towards becoming a sustainable organisation.

Chapter **4**

Priceless

Contents
MasterCard Worldwide

Written by Margherita Larné

Executive Summary

This case study focuses on the Australian and New Zealand operations of MasterCard Worldwide and the stunning transformation it achieved over a two year period of cultural change from 2002 to 2004, resulting in significant market share and growth in Australia.

Industry	Financial Services
Customers	National Network (Australia and New Zealand)
People	70
Assets	N/A
Revenue	N/A
CEO	Leigh Clapham (Senior Vice-President & General Manager)
Internal Change Agent(s)	Leigh Clapham, Leadership Team
External Change Agents(s)	Peter Fuda, PCD
HSI Tools Used	Organizational Culture Inventory® (OCI), Leadership/Impact® (L/I)

Culture Results

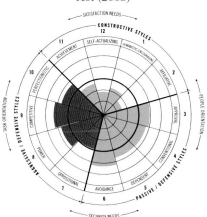

Organizational Culture Inventory
Test (2003)

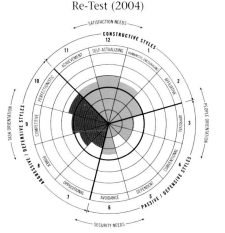

Organizational Culture Inventory
Re-Test (2004)

Outcomes	Increased service quality, role clarity, successful pitches, market share, and global employee engagement survey results

Phase **1**

MasterCard Worldwide
Pre-Test

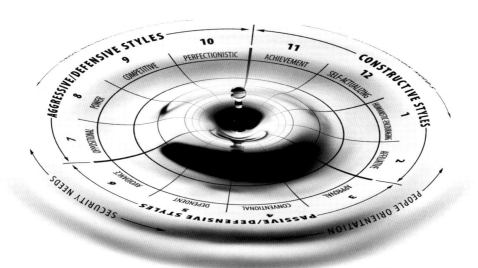

Introduction

"I sat down with Peter Fuda, of consulting change leadership firm Professional Change & Development (PCD), in September 2002 when I had been here six months, I started in March – and said we have a defeatist attitude; we have pitched about a dozen new business opportunities in the last couple years and won one or two. We're just not competitive. We have no confidence in dealing with the banks. And we just don't have any confidence together as a team and we have just got to do something about it" *(Leigh Clapham, Senior Vice-President and General Manager, Australasia).*

This case study focuses on the Australian and New Zealand operations of MasterCard Worldwide and the stunning transformation it achieved over a two year period of cultural change from 2002 to 2004, resulting in significant market share and growth locally.

Background

MasterCard Worldwide is a global payments company with one of the most recognised and respected brands in the world. It manages a full range of payment programs and services, including MasterCard® credit cards, MasterCard® debit cards, Maestro® online debit cards, Cirrus® ATM cash access, and related programs.[1]

MasterCard Worldwide is organised geographically into the following regions: Asia/ Pacific; Europe; Latin America and Caribbean; North America (U.S. and Canada); and South Asia, Middle East and Africa. The Corporate headquarters is in Purchase, New York, with technology operations located outside of St. Louis, Missouri. Regional headquarters include Waterloo, Singapore, Miami, and Dubai.[2]

Today MasterCard Worldwide has approximately 4,000 employees working in more than 37 MasterCard Worldwide offices around the world including a strong presence in Asia Pacific, with offices in Sydney, Singapore, Seoul, Tokyo, Taiwan, Shanghai, Guangzhou, Kuala Lumpur, Hong Kong, Bangkok, Jakarta, Manila and Beijing. It serves more than 23,000 customer financial institutions around the world in over 210 countries and processes as many as 32 million authorisations of financial transactions a day, enabling consumers to make purchases instantly, any time, almost anywhere, in both the virtual and real worlds.[3]

It's amazing to think that the first real credit card was 'born' in 1951 and amazing

---

1 MasterCard FAQs [Online], Available: http://www.mastercardintl.com/newsroom/faqs.html; 2 ibid; 3 ibid

still to realize that MasterCard Worldwide came into being in the late 1940s when several U.S. banks started giving their customers specially-issued paper that could be used like cash in local stores. But it wasn't until 1951, when the Franklin National Bank in New York formalised the practice by introducing the first real credit card. For the next decade several franchises evolved where a single bank in each major U.S. city would accept cards as payment with certain merchants they'd chosen to work with. On August 16, 1966 one of these franchises formed the Interbank Card Association (ICA). The unique thing about ICA was that unlike other similar organisations, it was not dominated by a single bank; rather member committees were established to run the association.[4]

ICA was renamed MasterCard International to reflect the commitment to international growth. The 80s saw further expansion into Asia and Latin America and in 1987 MasterCard International became the first payment card to be issued in the People's Republic of China. By 1993, China was the second largest country in sales volume for MasterCard International and in 1988, the first MasterCard card was issued in the Soviet Union.[5]

In June 2002, MasterCard International converted from a membership association to a private share corporation, in connection with its merger with Europay International and on 25th May 2006 listed on the New York stock exchange. On the 27th June 2006, MasterCard International was rebranded to MasterCard Worldwide.

External and Internal Operating Environment

The MasterCard Worldwide operations in Australia and New Zealand has approximately 65-70 people. The largest part is the customer facing side of the business which totals about 30-35 people. The reporting line for the Senior Vice-President and General Manager of Australasia, is to the Regional President who is based in Singapore.

Market share had been slipping precariously away from MasterCard Australia for the previous few years, with a very powerful competitor in Visa. They were operating in a hostile regulatory environment where the Reserve Bank of Australia was reforming the credit card industry and were facing regulatory intervention. They had won just 30% of new business agreements in the preceding three years or put another way, over a 12 month period they had lost 11 out of 12 new business agreements.

For ease of reading, the Australian and New Zealand operations, will be referred to as MasterCard Australia, but includes the New Zealand operations.

The Case for Transformation

The Australian operation had become quite bureaucratic and compliant. The prevailing culture and leadership style were not promoting effectiveness. The local team was feeling constantly under pressure and was becoming very reactive. Their Global Employee Engagement results

4 "About Us" MasterCard corporate document; 5 ibid

in April 2002 reflected this challenging state.

Urgent change was required to drive business performance. The Global Board of MasterCard Worldwide decided that Australia and New Zealand were priority markets for the company. They set new and ambitious goals for the organisation with limited resources and timeframes within which to achieve them. Expectations of success were high…

Enter a new Senior Vice-President and General Manager. In March 2002, Leigh Clapham was appointed Senior Vice-President and General Manager of Australasia, based in Sydney. With his 28 year career in advertising and recognised as being a leader in getting new business in the door, he was going to be a key driver in transforming the Australian and New Zealand business.

2003

MasterCard Worldwide

Phase **2**

Test

The Approach

Leigh Clapham decided that the way to turn around the company was to get outside help. He approached Peter Fuda, and his consulting change leadership firm Professional Change & Development (PCD), which was just the expertise he needed. Leigh felt that the focus needed to be on culture. Whilst MasterCard Australia's strategy and people were sound, he believed its leadership and execution could be improved and that culture was at the heart of the problem. So he decided the emphasis needed to be on measurement, behavioural change and systems alignment.

One of PCD's first tasks in working with CEOs is to make them 'literate' as soon as possible. Peter says this is about creating a frame of reference through which CEOs see their world: *"Through a process of exploration we understand their pain, so they agree that we understand what their issues are. Then the ability we have is to say: well if I were to show you on a model the pain that you're feeling, this is what it is: you actually have no clearly articulated vision of the future. When I look at the documents on your website and your annual report I actually don't know who it is you're trying to be, who your stakeholders are etc. You've just articulated that you have real issues around your leadership but you have no measures of the impact on your most important people etc... You talk about cultural issues but you have no diagnostic. So I use language which is relevant to a CEO – data, performance etc. So what we start to do now is frame up the problem in our language so when we present the solution they are now seeing it through our eyes."*

With MasterCard Australia the lead in time was quite short because Leigh was already 'literate': *"The difference with Leigh was that I had a long term relationship with him before we started. Leigh was a colleague - we were part of the same group of companies. I invited Leigh in a couple of times to see what it was we did here and he was fascinated by it. I invited him in to see what we were doing with Bayer and a couple of their big leaders' forums where we had the top 100 and he was fascinated by it. When he left the parent company of George Patterson where he was the managing director of their Integrated Communications Division and went to MasterCard Worldwide, one of the first calls he made was to us. He said 'there are some big gaps and big issues here and it is on the people side. I think the strategy is pretty sound but we're not winning business'. So he knew lots of the things to look for. He was reasonably literate."*

So the process was somewhat compressed with MasterCard Australia, in that Leigh was already very confident that they had the right strategy and they didn't need to focus on purpose and vision. Instead, the process was focussed primarily around leadership and culture. The other focus was around systems, structures and symbols.

The basic idea with MasterCard Australia then was to measure the current culture and the leadership impact of the 13 top leaders in the Australian and New Zealand operations. This would give them the most organisational leverage, and they would be able to track that over time.

Firstly, culture was measured using Human Synergistics' Organisational Culture Inventory® (OCI) which measures 'what is expected' of members of an organisation or more technically, behavioural norms and expectations. These reflect the more abstract aspects of culture such as shared values and beliefs, associated with three general types of cultures — Constructive, Passive/Defensive, and Aggressive/Defensive. Additionally, the inventory assesses outcomes associated with these different cultural norms, including members' role clarity, role conflict, perceptions of service quality, and satisfaction.

The leadership component was measured using the Human Synergistics' Leadership/ Impact® (L/I) diagnostic. L/I helps leaders to become aware of the impact they have on the people they lead and the leadership strategies they use to create this impact. It measures how others believe they themselves are encouraged to behave as a result of the individual's leadership (see Appendix for complete description of these diagnostics).

Secondly, these data were then used to build individual, team and Australian and New Zealand company plans focusing on achievable behavioural changes that needed to get the Actual culture to the Preferred culture.

Thirdly, the Australian offices' systems, structures and symbols were redesigned and then aligned to the Preferred culture so that positive behavioural changes were supported and reinforced.

PCD kick-started the process with Leigh and his team with a two day workshop in Bowral, Sydney in January 2003. Considerable pre-work had gone on prior to the off-site workshop, with PCD sending out individual packs to each of the 13 leaders and following these up with an individual meeting, to get each leader's view of the company and their own issues before the workshop. All this was by way of 'warm-up' to the process. So everything was in place for the 'download' of data to occur.

The Culture Survey Results

"And the sense of realisation when we went through this program for the first time at Milton Park in Bowral was phenomenal. When people learnt things about the organisation, about themselves about why they felt certain ways about things, how they reacted to our customers and relationships with customers and probably a daunting sense of our competitors. So all of a sudden it was all laid bare in front of them. And then they realised it was their behaviour that was causing all this" (Leigh Clapham, Senior Vice-President and General Manager, Australasia).

The Bowral workshop was a momentous occasion for the 13 leaders of the Australian and New Zealand operations. It was the first time that the senior team had come together away from the office and in a social setting.

There was no great surprise when the Preferred OCI completed by four members of the senior team (including Leigh) prior to the Workshop was shared with the group. What is shown in Figure 1 is typical of most organisations when they describe a Preferred organisational culture. The four people who completed the Preferred OCI believed that MasterCard Australia's culture should ideally be:

- **Humanistic-Encouraging (Constructive);** which involves expectations for being supportive of others, giving positive rewards to others and encouraging others.
- **Achievement (Constructive);** which involves expectations for taking on challenging tasks, establishing plans to achieve those tasks and pursuing them with a standard of excellence.

The Actual OCI however, was a different story. Once again prior to the Workshop, 21 people, including the 13 Workshop participants and some other key employees, assessed MasterCard Australia's Actual culture using the OCI.

Figure 1. MasterCard Australia Preferred Culture January 2003

Organizational Culture Inventory
N=4

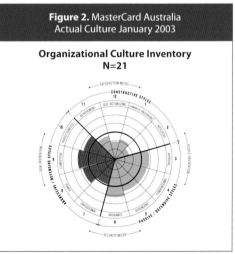

Figure 2. MasterCard Australia Actual Culture January 2003

Organizational Culture Inventory
N=21

The Actual culture of MasterCard in Australia and New Zealand (see Figure 2) was described as being:

- **Avoidance (Passive/Defensive);** which involved expectations for pushing decisions upwards, never being blamed for mistakes and laying low when things got tough.
- **Competitive (Aggressive/Defensive);** which involved expectations for being a 'winner', being seen and noticed, and maintaining an image of superiority.

If we think of the context within which MasterCard Australia found itself, these results seem to make sense. On the one hand it was operating in a market place that was highly regulated by the Reserve Bank of Australia, so being creative, taking risks and doing things differently perhaps were not options. Rather, doing what you're told (Dependent) and following procedures (Conventional) to ensure compliance of government regulations may have been the order of the day. Internally, it had its challenges of being part of a multinational requiring compliance and adherence to Head Office procedures.

Perhaps MasterCard Australia's external and internal environment may have been promoting not only a Passive/Defensive culture but also an Aggressive/Defensive one, where people were expected to get things approved by Head Office (Approval), to perform flawlessly (Perfectionistic) and follow procedures without question (Conventional). This could explain why the

So all of a sudden it was all laid bare in front of them… they realised it was their behaviour that was causing all this

business was stagnating as there may have been little risk taking, which may have created a situation where its competitor Visa was on the front foot. Andrew Cartwright's, Vice-President, Finance, comments here allude to the challenge that MasterCard in Australia and New Zealand had in acquiring new business because they were not prepared to push the envelope: *"The success of our business is a lot around winning business deals and I think Leigh has mentioned how we won 10 out of 13 in the first year. It was good in a way that there were a lot of new deals coming up but I think if we had done it in the previous 24 months it would have been three out of 13. It was almost a complete swap."*

So being in this competitive credit card industry in Australia and New Zealand meant that MasterCard Australia needed to compete for 'wallet-share' with Visa. Although an organisation's external environment may dictate aggressive and competitive strategies, internally aggressive and Competitive cultures do not produce the best results. We know that organisations with Aggressive/Defensive cultures tend to place relatively little value on people and operate on the philosophy that the road to success is through finding errors, weeding out 'mistakes', and promoting internal competition – a 'win-lose' frame of mind (Cooke, 1998).

Certainly this was the case with MasterCard Australia, having a highly Competitive culture with a focus on 'winning' and very little focus on achieving the outcome (Achievement). An example of how the highly Competitive style played out was when MasterCard Australia won a new business agreement with a major Australian customer, but it was disappointed and puzzled as to why the new deal was not having an impact on its market share. After they had won the deal they just walked away, expecting it to all fall into place. They were focussed on the wrong outcome, winning the deal, rather than building a long-term relationship based on on-going service. Meanwhile behind the scenes, MasterCard Australia's competitor was targeting the same customer and promoting its product. As Peter says, they realised that they needed to take an Achievement focus and meet with every one of their customer's managers and make sure they understood the benefits of promoting the MasterCard Worldwide products and the consequences if they didn't promote their products. They started to track this on a monthly basis and continued to interact with their new customer. And then the outcomes started to show as a result of working differently with this customer. It was then they began to understand that the difference between Achievement and Competitive, is that the former is being focussed on the outcome which is market share, and the latter is focussed on beating a competitor. Peter Fuda reflected: *"They won the deal and walked away and expected it to all fall into place. So the deal didn't get translated into market share, because they were not focussed on Achievement they were focussed on being Competitive... the penny dropped. 'Now we get it, the difference between Achievement and Competitive, is being focussed on the outcome we want which is market share, not beating Visa, which is a Competitive issue.'"*

We know that organisational culture typically has a strong impact on outcomes such as employee's role clarity and conflict, satisfaction, and evaluations of service quality. Outcomes associated with Passive/Defensive and Aggressive/Defensive cultural norms provide little benefit to organisations, their members and their customers. Figure 3 shows MasterCard Australia's outcomes as measured by the OCI. The biggest gap was in the area of service quality (Superior Customer Service), where the perception from employees was that MasterCard in Australia and New Zealand was not known for its superior customer service. Perhaps this

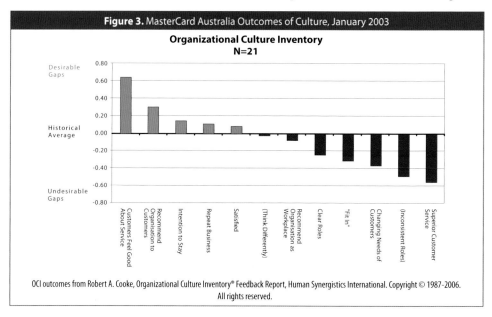

Figure 3. MasterCard Australia Outcomes of Culture, January 2003

may be attributable to a perceived need to conform, which may have made it difficult for MasterCard Australia to respond readily to the needs of their customers and effectively take advantage of market opportunities.

The second biggest gap was role conflict (Inconsistent Roles), where employees felt they received 'mixed messages' from different people about how they were expected to behave. Within MasterCard Australia this may have been driven by the confrontational 'win-lose' environment (Competitive and Power) where people contradicted one another and there was a feeling of having to choose who to listen to. If this was the case then it may have had a flow on effect to role clarity (Clear Roles) as employees then perhaps felt unsure about their responsibilities and authority (Avoidance).

There was very little disagreement with the culture results from the 13 members of the top team, as Andrew Cartwright reflects: *"[After] a lot of these cultural off-sites you come back to the office and you just revert back to habit. Whereas I think perhaps that there was the acknowledgment that we needed to change and we were going to change, and the actions items that followed were a key driver in changing the culture. In terms of a learning to come out of the case study I think that it was better done than anything that I had been associated with before."*

The Leadership Results

GROUP DATA

"I think from the 12 or 15 people that attended the first off-site there was a great amount of personal accountability – everybody except one showed their circumplex to the team. This was voluntary, Leigh went first. This was encouraged and from day one it was said, 'We will talk through your feedback. One of the first stages is you have to accept it first before you act on it. One of the ways you can accept it is to talk about it and validate it. Some of you at the end of the session may be prepared to show everyone.' We showed it to maybe two or three people in groups and discussed it in these small groups. In the last session Leigh got up. So he led it and then someone shared theirs and then another – everyone around the room shared — it was spontaneous. So timing was right – personal accountability was there right from the outset" (Andrew Cartwright, Vice-President, Finance).

Not surprisingly the MasterCard Australia group leadership data told the same story as the culture data and highlights spectacularly the proposition that leaders create and shape organisational culture. The Ideal Impact profiles of the 13 managers were very similar to their Preferred culture - strong extensions along the four Constructive behaviours and relatively weak extensions along the Passive/Defensive and Aggressive/Defensive behaviours, as seen in Figure 4. In particular the primary Ideal impact was Achievement followed by the secondary Ideal impact of Humanistic-Encouraging.

As can be seen from Figure 4 there is a 'gap' between the Ideal Impact profile and the profile showing the current impact on others. The primary behavioural impact as a leadership team was Avoidance, which typically means that people are led to take few chances, feel apprehensive, insecure about their position and authority and are led to stay away from

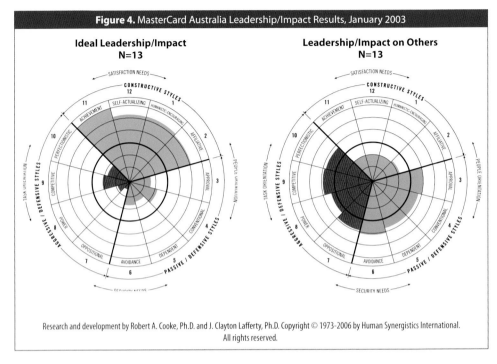

Figure 4. MasterCard Australia Leadership/Impact Results, January 2003

Ideal Leadership/Impact
N=13

Leadership/Impact on Others
N=13

difficult situations that could make them look bad. In addition, the secondary behavioural impact was Approval, which typically means that people are led to go along with others, refrain from taking controversial or unpopular actions, and put forth only those ideas and suggestions that are likely to 'please' others.

The results suggest that the leadership strategies used by the 13 MasterCard managers in the Australian and New Zealand operations were predominantly Restrictive, promoting Defensive behaviours, rather than Prescriptive strategies which promote Constructive behaviours. Restrictive strategies in the context of the L/I diagnostic are those that constrain or prohibit activities and behaviours with respect to goals, opportunities, and methods. Prescriptive strategies are those techniques that guide or direct the activities and behaviours of others toward goals, opportunities, and methods for task accomplishment.

Prescriptive strategies generally are more effective than Restrictive strategies. This is partly because the former serve to define a direction for the system, establish structures for organisational learning and adaptation, and support processes for problem solving and the integration of organisational components. Possibly most important, however, Prescriptive strategies on the part of leaders create and reinforce an organisational culture that communicates Constructive norms and expectations to members.

Previous findings with L/I indicate that leaders generally see themselves as being more Prescriptive than they are viewed by others. Prescriptive leadership behaviours generally are assumed to be functional and desirable; leaders, therefore, often overestimate the frequency with which they exhibit such behaviours. Similarly, there is a tendency for leaders to underestimate the frequency with which they behave in Restrictive ways—but this discrepancy between self-reports and descriptions by others is not as great as it is for the Prescriptive behaviours. It needs to be remembered that all leaders use a combination of Prescriptive and Restrictive strategies.

As can be seen from Figure 5, the double barchart summarises MasterCard Australia's overall results for the 13 managers with respect to the use of the 10 Prescriptive and Restrictive leadership strategies. Prescriptive results are presented on the top charts and Restrictive strategies on the bottom charts. The bars on the top chart show the frequency with which Prescriptive strategies are used. Longer bars extending upwards indicate the greater the frequency with which Prescriptive strategies are exhibited according to self-report and others who described the individual. The bars on the bottom chart depict the frequency with which Restrictive strategies are used. Longer bars extending downwards indicate the more frequently Restrictive leadership strategies are used. Within each chart, the left bar depicts self-report and the right bar summarizes the results of others, and the bar to the left tends to be 'taller' than the bar to the right.

As a Leadership Team, there were a number of strategies that could explain their leadership impact, as depicted in their circumplexes in Figure 4. For example, Stimulating Thinking, in particular Vertical Thinking, is about a lack of creativity and conforming to conventional ways of doing things, and could explain their Conventional and Perfectionistic impact. Also, Providing Feedback, in particular Negative Feedback, involves communicating negative evaluations of people's activities and performance when people are not meeting standards and could account for their

I was more empowered to share mine and then came the personal accountability

Dependent as well as Competitive and Oppositional impact. So the leadership strategies provided the team with a 'tangible' explanation of why their impact was what it was, as highlighted in Figure 4.

Despite the process being initially quite confronting, Andrew Cartwright resonated with his results as seen by the following comment: *"…because you looked at your own [circumplex] – and I think most of us would be – ashamed is maybe too strong a word – defensive about it. 'Is this really what my peers think of me?' I think with my strong Green I could understand that is exactly what I was doing. Once a couple of others shared it – some of them were really strong on Red – that was a little surprising but the fact that they were prepared to share that – then I was more empowered to share mine and then came the personal accountability, perhaps because I was prepared to show everyone my style."*

And this from a Focus Group Member: *"When we got the results initially, you don't see too much Blue, so it was a good starting point. I think we all embraced it, all of us got up and said a few words at Bowral from the heart. I think we were all committed, action plans were put in place and there was a deliberate commitment to change."*

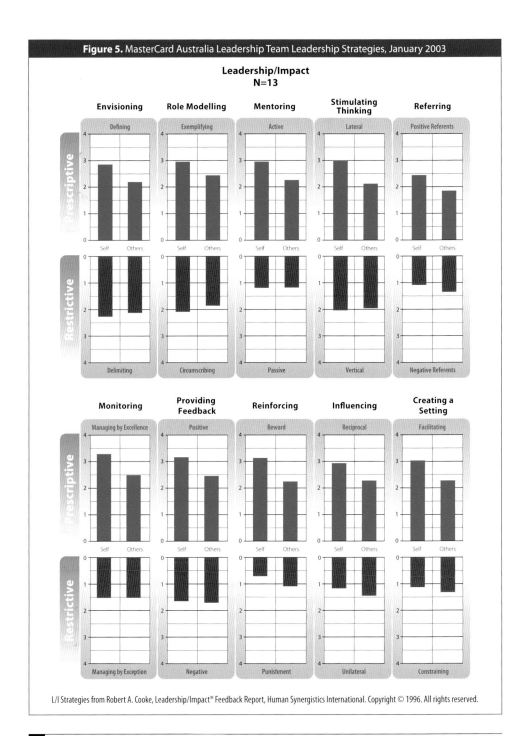

Figure 5. MasterCard Australia Leadership Team Leadership Strategies, January 2003

Leadership/Impact
N=13

LEIGH CLAPHAM'S DATA

"Leigh had a certain style and he was a bit surprised by the results that he got back and there was good reason to move from that style to a more team culture… he drove a lot of that" (Focus Group Member).

As we can see in Figure 6, Leigh's Ideal impact in 2003 was Constructive, so his aspiration was to have a leadership style that creates an environment that stimulates people's needs for growth and achievement and encourages them to think and behave in ways that will enable them to satisfy those needs.

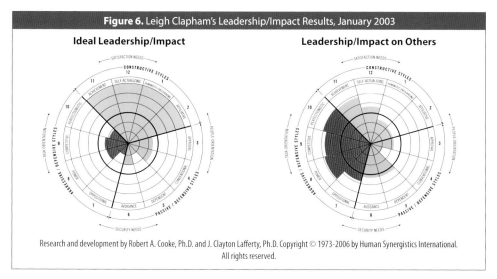

Figure 6. Leigh Clapham's Leadership/Impact Results, January 2003

Ideal Leadership/Impact

Leadership/Impact on Others

In Leigh's Actual impact there is a strong task focus and a large amount of Achievement and Self-Actualizing, with an orientation to achieving the results, as reflected in this comment about Leigh: *"Leigh's background was winning business overnight, whereas in financial service it takes months to get it and that's not his culture at all. He had an autocratic style to start with, he just came in and made decisions but he also brought a winning culture to the business"* (Focus Group Member).

At times, however, an over emphasis on tasks may lead to a focus on individual objectives and detract from collaboration and coordination.

Figure 7 profiles the leadership strategies Leigh was using. For example, his Achievement impact was being driven by his Envisioning, and in particular Defining strategies, which are about identifying and sharing a vision for the organization. Also, Stimulating Thinking, in particular Lateral Thinking, is about encouraging people to challenge assumptions, looking at things in new ways to stimulate creativity and inspiring others to creatively translate problems into opportunities, leading to Leigh's Achievement and Self-Actualizing impact on others. The strategy of Monitoring, and in particular Managing by Exception, involves highlighting mistakes, deviations, and things that are out of place and led to his Oppositional, Power, and Perfectionistic impact.

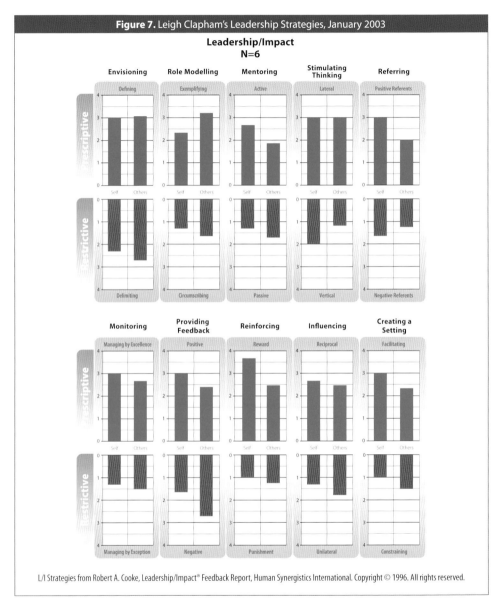

Figure 7. Leigh Clapham's Leadership Strategies, January 2003

It's fair to say that these results took Leigh by surprise but he acknowledged that his leadership tactics were an important influence on MasterCard Australia's culture and in turn the behaviour and performance of his team, and were in need of further development and refinement.

Phase **3**

MasterCard Worldwide
Action

Program of Initiatives

Over the next 12 months, from January 2003 to May 2004, the leadership team sprung into action to begin MasterCard Australia's transformation journey – in reality it had already begun at their Bowral Workshop.

One of the most striking things about MasterCard Australia was that they took a 'business as usual' approach to its actions following the debrief of the results. The Action items were identified on day two of the Bowral workshop and the 13 leaders committed to two to three actions each.

"*We just thought that it was business as usual, it was something we all agreed to do and we were all in it together, and it wasn't sort of anal, it really was business as usual. The expectation was that we weren't going to action them in the first month – then there would have been negativity – it was going to be done in three to six months in terms of the journey. And there was a great acceptance that we needed to do it*" (Andrew Cartwright, Vice-President, Finance).

The following sections highlight the key Actions implemented by MasterCard Australia and have been framed in terms of five causal factor categories that make up Dr Robert A Cooke's 'How Culture Works Model': Mission and Philosophy; Structures; Systems; Technology and Skills/Qualities, as shown in Figure 8, in the 'How Culture Works Model'. They have also been summarised in Table 1.

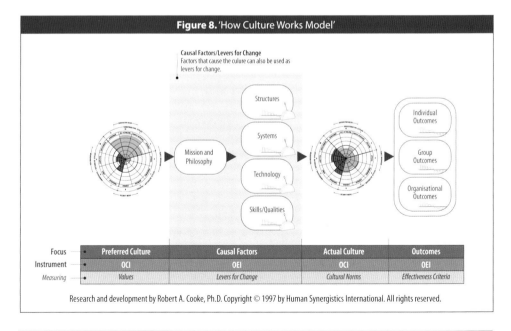

Figure 8. 'How Culture Works Model'

Research and development by Robert A. Cooke, Ph.D. Copyright © 1997 by Human Synergistics International. All rights reserved.

These five causal factor categories shape and reinforce an organisation's current operating culture and its effectiveness. When causal factors are in alignment with an organisation's values, the current operating culture looks very similar to the Preferred culture profile.

However, when these factors are not aligned with organisational values, the current operating culture becomes disconnected from the Preferred culture, creating the 'cultural disconnect'. This was the situation with MasterCard Australia – a disconnect between MasterCard Australia's

Table 1. Summary Table of Initiatives 2003-2004		
Levers (Causal Factors)	**2003**	**2004**
Mission & Philosophy Initiatives that relate to clear articulation of the organisation's identity and values	■ Establishing cultural vision – Preferred OCI ■ Test - Actual culture ■ Articulating business goals ■ Sharing stories of employees who exemplified the values	■ Re-Test Actual OCI
Structures Initiatives that relate to how people, roles and activities are ordered to create Organisation	■ Quarterly team workshops ■ Bi-annual workshops ■ WIP meetings ■ Cross-functional forums ■ Defined roles and responsibilities ■ Common area for employees ■ MasterCard social club	
Systems ■ Human Resource Systems ■ Selection & Placement ■ Training & Development ■ Performance Management	■ Team of Quarter award ■ Employee Recognition Board ■ Joint setting of KPI's ■ Revised Performance Management System – focus on KPI's, values and behaviours	
Technologies Methods to transform effort/input into outcomes/output	■ Job redesign	
Skills/Qualities Including methods of communication (up, down and for learning)	■ Two-way flow of communication ■ Cascading L/I to the next level of leaders ■ Leaders undertaking one-to-one coaching ■ Leaders sharing L/I data and action plans	
OEI causal factors from Robert A. Cooke and Janet L. Szumal, Organizational Effectiveness Inventory™ Feedback Report, Human Synergistics International. Copyright © 1995-2006. All rights reserved.		

espoused values for a Constructive culture as we saw in Figure 1 and its current operating culture as we saw in Figure 2. When this happens, it points to a misalignment between Preferred Constructive culture and Mission and Philosophy, the day-to-day Structures, Systems, Technology, and Skills/Qualities, leading to a current Defensive culture.

Outlined below are the actions MasterCard Australia implemented, so that the business could move to be more aligned with its Preferred values and build a Constructive culture.

Mission & Philosophy

The Mission and Philosophy lever focuses on an organisation defining its identity and its values to its employees. To this end, MasterCard Australia implemented the following initiatives that spoke to this lever.

DESCRIBING AN ASPIRATIONAL FUTURE AND A FOCUS ON ACHIEVEMENT

One of the areas that was a surprise to Leigh was that the MasterCard Australian and New Zealand operations didn't have a perspective on the business and how it was tracking. One of the simple actions that he implemented was having regular face-to-face employee communication sessions. During these sessions he ensured that there was clarity around global and local business goals and priorities and a clear statement of their

We wanted to achieve 40% market share... everybody embraced it

aspirational future of a 40% market share. This is reflected by Leigh: *"There was a low level of knowledge about the business across the various business units. Literally telling the folks what our corporate goal was – we wanted to achieve 40% market share across Australia and New Zealand sometime in 2004, everybody embraced it and at each staff meeting we would have a countdown and it was agreed that we would celebrate when we got there."*

EXEMPLIFYING THE VALUES

This involved celebrating achievements and sharing 'stories' of employees who exemplified the values and philosophies of their organisation thus reinforcing the Self-Actualizing and Affiliative norms. Initiatives such as the Employee Recognition Board and the Team of the Quarter award, was introduced: *"In terms of communication we have now implemented a quarterly, staff presentation, because we are on three floors and in terms of the business results, and recognising the team in the quarter so it was more a quarterly business update, to catch people in the act of doing something well as opposed to catch them doing something wrong"* (Andrew Cartwright, Vice-President, Finance).

Structures

The Structures lever refers to the ways in which people, roles, and activities are ordered and coupled to create organisation. Specifically key initiatives included:

'SOFT' STRUCTURES TO AID IMPLEMENTATION

"…They embraced it with enthusiasm. But it was a very enthusiastic response and a very enthusiastic application. Those task forces all agreed action areas and implemented all those action areas" (Leigh Clapham, Senior Vice-President and General Manager, Australasia).

"When you go away to any training course, you'll take notes, you'll stay awake for a while, you'll pay attention and then you go back to work and all of a sudden, the phone rings, the emails start and you forget. But with this one, I think Leigh was particularly determined, I think we all were, to try and make it work. And so we came back and forced ourselves to have regular meetings and feedback sessions. I think we were all pretty open and honest about it too. We had little sub groups to help achieve our list of actions" (Focus Group Member).

The term Structures is used here to describe the various forums in which people came together to achieve an outcome. It appears that the various task forces set up by the Leadership Team had a momentum of their own and were about implementing initiatives that were seen as part of people's everyday jobs. Other structures included the following:

- Quarterly team workshops to maintain focus and momentum.
- Bi-annual Workshops to consolidate the change agenda, celebrate success and share learnings.
- Operationalising team and culture action plans by reviewing progress each week in senior team meetings.
- Regular WIP (work in progress) meetings were 'restructured' to focus on 'outcomes' as opposed to 'tasks'.
- People conducted cross-functional forums to review 'bids' pre and post contracts, so that there was an emphasis on collaboration and collective learning from people's experiences. This represented a shift away from working in silos and a move to an internal partnership approach to business.
- They also defined roles and responsibilities and developed a greater understanding of what other people did in different parts of the business.

'HARD' STRUCTURES FOR DEVELOPING RELATIONSHIPS

'Hard' or physical structures such as the creation of a common area for employees to mingle during lunch times or to have drinks after work. This literal 'breaking down of walls' provided people with the opportunity to develop relationships with other parts of the business and to foster collaboration - simply getting to know people. Another example was the 'resurrecting' of MasterCard Australia's social club.

Systems

Systems refer to the inter-related sets of procedures that an organisation uses to support its core activities and to solve problems. In this area there was a focus on:

CELEBRATING SUCCESS

One of the most commented on initiatives was the implementation of processes to reward and recognise good performance. This was undertaken in a more public fashion through the setting up of recognition awards. For example, a Team of the Quarter reward was established to celebrate the achievement of stretch targets and an Employee Recognition Board was created to recognise those employees who were living the company's values.

The symbolic value of celebrating success was highlighted when MasterCard Australia achieved its target of 40% market share and they honoured this with a party at Sydney's Luna Park, a theme park on Sydney Harbour.

OWNERSHIP OF GOALS

Employees were involved in setting their individual KPI's (key performance indicators) to reflect performance objectives and agreed standards of behaviours. This was to ensure that employees were challenged by their work, yet were confident they could accomplish what was expected of them. This process involved managers and employees together setting clear, specific, and challenging goals and standards, and in doing so would have led to the establishment of Achievement and Humanistic norms.

ALIGNING PERFORMANCE MANAGEMENT SYSTEM

A related area to the previous initiative was that of aligning the MasterCard Australia's performance management system to critical measures, circumplex behaviours and values, thus ensuring the 'cultural connect' and alignment to the espoused values and behaviours. So there was a review of the Performance Management System, which focussed on KPI's and value and behaviours.

Technology

This lever is about the methods used by an organisation to transform inputs into outputs in terms of various job design characteristics and improving the degree of interdependence among members. To this end, there was a significant redesign of jobs, particularly in the IT area, which resulted in significant staff cuts off-shore. This allowed them to focus on their core business.

Skills/Qualities

Skills/Qualities refer to the skills and qualities in terms of communication and leadership.

TWO-WAY FLOW OF COMMUNICATION

The following represent the vertical and horizontal lines or the two-way flow of communication that account for the strengthening of MasterCard Australia's Achievement and Humanistic-Encouraging cultural norms:

- There was transparency with the sharing of financial, customer, leadership and culture data across the organisation.
- The stretch 'market share' target of 40% was agreed and communicated to the whole organisation. Quarterly face-to-face information sessions conducted by Leigh, updated the whole office on the business results and the progress towards their 'stretch' target. This was an important mechanism which ensured buy-in to corporate goals.
- The MasterCard Australia's email facility was expanded to all employees to allow free flow of communication to all employees.

MEASURING PERSONAL STYLE AND BEHAVIOURS

"Every 2 weeks the list came out, what's happening on that, are we doing that, who's doing that and I think we were highly energised after the two days off-site to act on our own personal initiatives in different ways. I didn't come in every morning and look at my plan and change the behaviour. I guess it was more subconscious" (Andrew Cartwright, Vice-President, Finance).

Measuring the intangible, that is, cultural norms and behaviours, was an important step in shifting people's mindset and worldviews. MasterCard Australia maintained a focus on this and ensured that the measurement and in turn, the follow-up action planning took place. In particular other key initiatives included:

- Measuring the behaviour of the next level leaders and debriefing them in a process similar to the process for the 13 senior leaders.
- Each leader undertook one-to-one regular meetings to explore their leadership results and actions, and connected them to business performance.
- Leaders openly sharing L/I data, challenges and action plans. For example people had their circumplexes pinned to their walls illustrating the physical embracing of the change.
- There was the introduction of Red/Blue/Green cards to describe to a person what behaviour they were using as a way of reinforcing the accepted behaviours and highlighting the 'unacceptable' behaviours. This facilitated the giving of feedback in the team in a constructive way.

2004

MasterCard Worldwide
Re-Test

Phase **4**

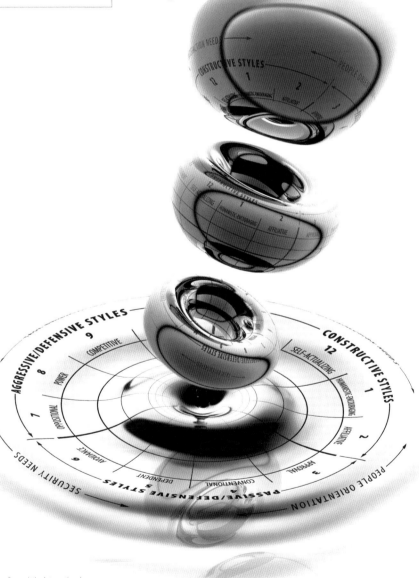

The Culture Survey Results

MasterCard Australia's culture Re-Test in May 2004, 16 months after the original survey, reflects the essence of transformation.

MasterCard Australia's Re-Test OCI in Figure 9 shows a dramatic shift in culture from a profile dominated by Passive/Defensive (Green) and Aggressive/Defensive (Red) to one dominated by the Constructive cluster (Blue). Specifically, there is a dramatic shift in focus from an Avoidance (Passive/Defensive) dominated culture to one dominated by Self-Actualizing norms; a shift from competing with others, Competitive (Aggressive/Defensive) to a collective focus on achieving organisational goals; Achievement (Constructive), supporting one another, Humanistic-Encouraging, and working collaboratively, Affiliative.

The Test → Re-Test results in Figure 9 show a statistically significant shift in all styles in the desired direction. What makes an immediate and breath-taking impact when looking at both circumplexes is the absolute reduction in all the Passive/Defensive behaviours and most of the

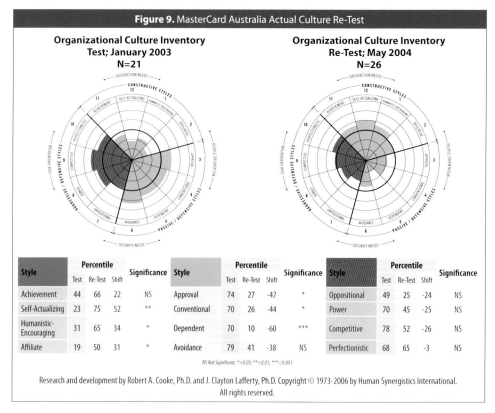

Figure 9. MasterCard Australia Actual Culture Re-Test

Organizational Culture Inventory
Test; January 2003
N=21

Organizational Culture Inventory
Re-Test; May 2004
N=26

Style	Percentile			Significance	Style	Percentile			Significance	Style	Percentile			Significance
	Test	Re-Test	Shift			Test	Re-Test	Shift			Test	Re-Test	Shift	
Achievement	44	66	22	NS	Approval	74	27	-47	*	Oppositional	49	25	-24	NS
Self-Actualizing	23	75	52	**	Conventional	70	26	-44	*	Power	70	45	-25	NS
Humanistic-Encouraging	31	65	34	*	Dependent	70	10	-60	***	Competitive	78	52	-26	NS
Affiliate	19	50	31	*	Avoidance	79	41	-38	NS	Perfectionistic	68	65	-3	NS

*NS Not Significant; *<0.05; **<0.01; ***<0.001*

Research and development by Robert A. Cooke, Ph.D. and J. Clayton Lafferty, Ph.D. Copyright © 1973-2006 by Human Synergistics International. All rights reserved.

Aggressive/Defensive behaviours and the dramatic increase in the Constructive behaviours.

The strongest improvement has been a decrease in Dependent, Approval and Conventional, resulting in a flow on improvement in Self-Actualizing and Achievement. This speaks to an employee sense of feeling less 'helpless' and not being constrained, to more confidence in their ability and their sense of self.

There have also been significant shifts in the people-oriented Constructive styles of Humanistic-Encouraging and Affiliative, reflecting the greater focus on being supportive and working collaboratively, resulting in a decrease in Avoidance, Power and Competitive.

The Leadership Results

GROUP DATA

We see the same transformation theme in the MasterCard Australia Leadership Team's leadership data Re-Test in 2004. Once again the leadership impact in Figure 10 has dramatically shifted from a Passive/Defensive and Aggressive/Defensive impact to a strongly Constructive impact and reflects the same shifts in the culture, as we saw in Figure 9. There is a flip from a Security orientation to a Satisfaction orientation, with all four Constructive styles over the 50th percentile.

This stunning shift can be attributed to two key ingredients: firstly, the individual action planning process that was facilitated by PCD after the Bowral workshop and secondly, the willingness of the individual leaders to make that shift.

The action planning process that PCD facilitated was results driven. Following the Bowral workshop each leader was tasked with seeking out their respondents and having candid conver-

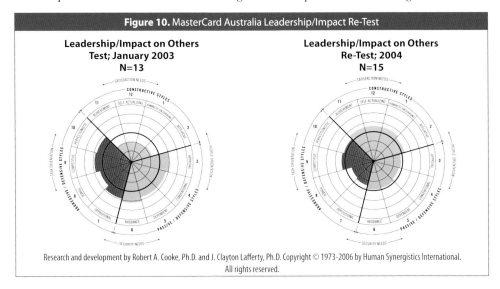

Figure 10. MasterCard Australia Leadership/Impact Re-Test

Leadership/Impact on Others
Test; January 2003
N=13

Leadership/Impact on Others
Re-Test; 2004
N=15

Research and development by Robert A. Cooke, Ph.D. and J. Clayton Lafferty, Ph.D. Copyright © 1973-2006 by Human Synergistics International. All rights reserved.

sations on leadership areas which their respondents believed needed improvement. Each leader then used this information to identify specific areas to change and then developed an action plan. Once the action plan was in place, each leader met with a PCD Account Director who coached them and helped them refine their actions in line with the leadership strategies, as Peter Fuda describes here: *"So maybe someone does not do regular team meetings or regular sales conferences so then they have to put new interventions in their diary – so they walk out saying I need to put this in my diary – 12 one-on-ones every quarter and a leadership conference for say December and they need to put this in their diary until it gets filled up. And then we talk to them about how they are going to use the Prescriptive strategies. So basically diary, tasks, using the strategies old and new – because most of the strategies are already there, leaders just use them unconsciously but they need help in using them more prescriptively and need help in articulating what their vision is. And after a while with this new agenda they realise that in their meetings they are getting better outcomes and achieving more. What happened? They are using these Prescriptive strategies and becoming consciously skilled."*

Leigh's style and new way of operating was a significant contributor to our turnaround

Once these action plans were in place the leadership team came together again approximately three months after the Bowral workshop. At this follow-up session each leader was asked to address their peers and reflect on what they learnt regarding key insights about themselves and the key actions that they had identified. The group was then asked to give positive feedback to each individual leader. As can be imagined, this was an extremely powerful process.

The commitment of each individual leader to their own transformation needs to be underscored here and is the other key factor that has contributed to the results in Figure 10, as is highlighted by this quote: *"Within a week of coming back from the Conference because I have been maybe Green, avoidant or approval defensive, I went on the front foot and said [to Leigh] that I need X Y and Z in quite a forceful manner because I wanted to lift my game. As quick as a flash Leigh shot me back an email and said 'Oh Andrew that is a bit red!' jokingly and I shot back straight away and I said 'better than Green' in a joking sort of a manner - we immediately wanted to get away from our type. So the colour thing was part of our language"* (Andrew Cartwright, Vice-President, Finance).

LEIGH CLAPHAM'S DATA

"Leigh's style and new way of operating was a significant contributor to our turnaround – the fact that he changed his style in 2003 and 2004 had a flow on effect to increased business… there was significant buy in to his direction and vision" (Focus Group Member).

Leigh's Re-Test leadership results indicate an increase in all Constructive styles and in fact three out of the four are above the 50th percentile as shown in Figure 11. He has had an increase in his Achievement and Humanistic-Encouraging impact. In addition there has been a decrease in his Passive/Defensive impact of Avoidance and Dependent.

Leigh's profile also highlights an orientation that is slowly moving in a Satisfaction

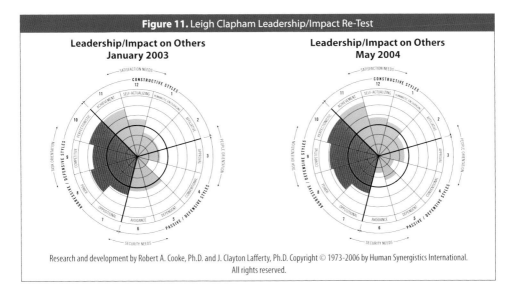

Figure 11. Leigh Clapham Leadership/Impact Re-Test

oriented direction but with a strong Task Orientation. Of significant note here is that his Achievement impact is above his Perfectionistic impact and is in fact over the 90th percentile – indicating an absolute focus on outcomes – an impact that you would hope a Senior Vice-President and General Manager would have!

Some of this shift can be attributable to Leigh's concerted actions around conducting regular one-to-one meetings with all of his direct reports and taking more of a coach and mentoring approach to these relationships, as Peter Fuda reflects: *"When we come to the success factors I think a very strong task focus has been a major asset. We had to temper it and channel it, and actually give him (Leigh) tasks around people in order for him to understand it, he had to diarise things and then it worked in their culture."*

It's important to remember that this is a snapshot in time and it can take a number of Re-Tests before this shifts. Something that someone with a strong emphasis on Task Orientation might consider is the notion of what J. Clayton Lafferty, the creator of the circumplex, called the 'humanising of the achievement style', that is the combining of Achievement with a Humanistic-Encouraging impact. Achievement on its own won't 'grow' people. In addition the Perfectionistic impact encourages a focus on the minutest of details, at the expense of the strategic challenges. Also there could be a cost in terms of additional pressure and stress, on the individual.

Leigh's challenge moving forward is to balance the task impact with a people impact. A way of doing this is to 'ramp up' the Humanistic-Encouraging impact and let go of the 'doing', with more emphasis on coaching and delegating. An overly Aggressive/Defensive task impact won't be sustainable and in fact, drive and momentum will be lost because it has not been devolved.

Business Outcomes

The ultimate test of any transformation effort is in how did it impact on the organisation's performance and business outcomes? How do we define performance?

Certainly profitability is one element of an organisation's performance but it's a narrow focus. Dr Robert A Cooke's research indicates that performance is not just about profitability but rather profitability is a given if there is what he calls 'systems effectiveness'. Systems effectiveness is the integration of 'subsystems', which include employees, units, departments and how the organisation adapts to the 'supersystem', that is its customers. These both in turn are a pre-condition for and impact on profit. Systems effectiveness then, is a direct result of an organisation's culture.

The effectiveness of MasterCard Australia's subsystems and supersystems can be gleaned from the OCI Re-Test outcomes. As can be seen in Figure 12 there is a spectacular improvement! In 2003, seven out of the twelve outcomes were gaps or 'below the line' and in 2004 all twelve outcomes were 'above the line'.

These cultural outcomes, as reported by employees, fall into three broad themes;

- **Quality of Service** was the most improved by 14.2%, (average improvement across the five items that make up this construct). The item with the biggest change in this cluster and across all 12 outcome questions is, '… does your organisation have

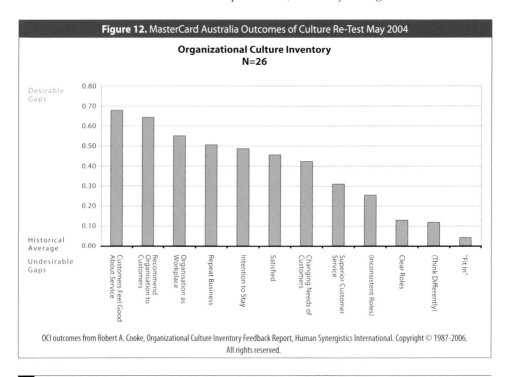

Figure 12. MasterCard Australia Outcomes of Culture Re-Test May 2004

Organizational Culture Inventory
N=26

OCI outcomes from Robert A. Cooke, Organizational Culture Inventory Feedback Report, Human Synergistics International. Copyright © 1987-2006. All rights reserved.

a reputation for superior customer service' (27.7%) and was also the biggest gap in the 2003 results. The second biggest item shift was '...does the organisation respond effectively to the changing needs of its customers' (25.2%), which was the third biggest gap in 2003. These shifts are a testament to the decrease in Conventional and Approval, and an increase in Achievement.

■ **Role Clarity** improved by 13.1% (average improvement across the three items that make up this construct). The biggest item shift is, '... do you receive inconsistent messages regarding what is expected' (25.9 %) and was the second biggest gap in 2003. This is a predictable outcome as MasterCard Australia's culture shifts away from a Competitive and Approval culture where employees were confused by competing management expectations, to one where expectations are clear, documented and agreed to.

■ **Employee Satisfaction** improved by 12.6%, three item average. The biggest item shift is, '...would you recommend this organisation as a good place to work' (17.9%), which was the fifth biggest gap in 2003.

Not surprisingly these outcomes have been reflected in MasterCard Worldwide's employee engagement scores, as measured by the company's Global Engagement survey. The results were already quite good in April 2002, however in October 2004 when the program had been in place for approximately 18 months, the results increased exponentially over that period as shown in Table 2.

Table 2. MasterCard Worldwide Employee Engagement Survey Results		
Australia/New Zealand	**April 2002**	**October 2004**
Understand what work Group Manager expects of me	88	96
Stay focussed on critical tasks that need to be accomplished	71	96
People work together as a team	71	87
MasterCard creates an environment where people want to give extra effort	53	86
In the past year we have improved processes and enhanced overall productivity	53	73

Another salient outcome for the MasterCard Australian and New Zealand operations was its improved working relationship with the Regional Office. The focus on collaboration and 'people work(ing) together as a team' as indicated in Table 2, allowed them to work more effectively with the Regional Office and in doing so, focus on achieving the business outcomes as a united and laser-focussed organisation. As Leigh comments: *"The Regional Office in Singapore had the capability to help us but we had to learn how to unlock this positive support. As we changed, Singapore became more valuable in supporting our strategy. The Regional President was incredibly supportive in this process."*

The pie charts in Figure 13 indicate that since 2002, MasterCard Australia has increased its success rate with new business agreements from 33% to an impressive 67%! So since embarking on this journey and implementing the various initiatives, MasterCard Australia has been successful in two out of every three new business agreements.

The Regional President was incredibly supportive in this process

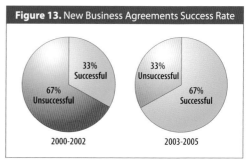

Figure 13. New Business Agreements Success Rate

And impressively its market share of total credit cards in Australia increased from 29% to 40% in 36 months as shown in Figure 14. This means there have been over two million additional MasterCard cards in people's wallets in Australia within three years.

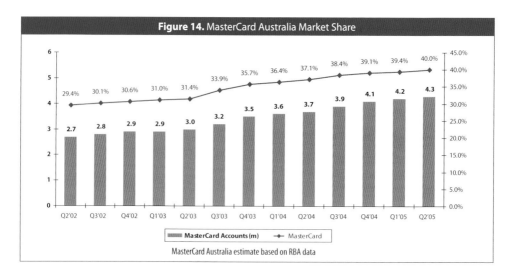

Figure 14. MasterCard Australia Market Share

MasterCard Australia estimate based on RBA data

MasterCard Worldwide

Review

Phase **5**

Change Agents | Lessons Learnt | Future Challenges

Change Agents

Internal Change Agents	The Australian and New Zealand Leadership Team, Leigh Clapham
External Change Agents	PCD

Most stories of transformation have a protagonist that envisions a future state and in doing so, sows the seed of dissatisfaction with the current state, and MasterCard Australia is no different.

The protagonist change agent is clearly Leigh Clapham the Senior Vice-President and General Manager. As the internal change agent he was the primary influencer and driver of the transformation agenda. The MasterCard Australia Leadership Team also played a very important 'support' role to Leigh and were also instrumental in guiding the journey.

Externally, the PCD team provided the enabling framework and mechanisms from a change leadership perspective.

The Internal Change Agents

THE LEADERSHIP TEAM

"And fortunately, it could have gone the other way, they could have said 'this is a good time to get out of here, this is all too hard, and we're never going to change'. But quite the contrary, they were a talented group of people who came together as a team and that it how they moved to this point and it was their enthusiasm in joining individual task forces on individual action areas that we identified would make the most difference" (Leigh Clapham, Senior Vice-President and General Manager, Australasia).

In the above quote, Leigh is acknowledging the significant contribution his leadership team made in being role models. This speaks to the notion of the 'guiding coalition' that Kotter (1996) talks about in his book *Leading Change*. The striking thing is the unwavering commitment from these leaders and a passion not only for their own personal transformation but also for MasterCard Australia's transformation.

There was a higher level of consciousness of how we reacted and interacted with others...

One picks up the willingness to explore 'untrodden' territory in terms of their personal leadership styles as well as an enthusiasm to role model these within their teams: *"There was a higher level of consciousness of how we reacted and interacted with others – rather than say 'no' upfront, there was a change in attitude and we were more positive"* (Focus Group Member).

LEIGH CLAPHAM

"It's almost a given that the champion has to be the leader, isn't it because if it starts from the top then there's no better place to lead by example and embrace the whole thing" (Focus Group Member).

There's no denying that Leigh Clapham is very much a 'results' man. There is a sense of energy, drive, enthusiasm and an 'I mean business' attitude about him. It's these attributes and style that he brought into MasterCard Australia and enabled its transformation. He was certainly seen as the driver of the change and was very much the 'internal change agent'.

"He came in when the business was sliding, his background being 30 years advertising going from deal to deal to deal with a lot of energy and he just brought that into this business. Luckily at that time significant business opportunities opened up. So we took all his learning into the banks which were much more passive organisations and we went in there with so much energy and commitment and enthusiasm and customer understanding that we turned them around and surprised them with what we were able to offer them" (Focus Group Member).

> **They were a talented group of people who came together as a team**

He was also someone who was able to put forward a different perspective and challenge MasterCard Australia's paradigms and worldviews. Leigh did this exceptionally well when he encouraged his people to challenge the status quo: *"We said right at the outset of the two day conference that we shouldn't be limited by the things that are necessarily outside our control as being excuses. It was more about changing the way we worked together and if we had crutches that we would always lean against as excuses, then we would never progress"* (Andrew Cartwright, Vice-President, Finance).

There's a certain tenacity about Leigh that is subtle and it's this tenacity and determination that allowed him to work behind the scenes and challenge the status quo. This same tenacity allowed Leigh to push forward the transformation agenda within and outside of MasterCard Australia, to slowly evolve the organisation into being a key contender in the market-place.

The sense that one gets is that his style was infectious. The often bandied term 'a can-do' attitude seems clichéd to use but here it aptly described the effortlessness with which Leigh went about doing what he did. It seems like it was exactly what people were in need of: someone who was able to paint a picture of 'possibilities' and opportunities that were theirs to have if they wanted – especially if we think about his challenge to his team of capturing 40% of the market. *"I keep mentioning Leigh, he had come out of advertising where I remember his first speech he ever gave to the staff when he was first introduced on his appointment he said 'I am really looking forward to coming as I really see we have only one competitor whereas in terms of when I have had to do new business pitches from an advertising point of view I am competing against 7,*

8, 9 other agencies'. So this gave us a little bit of confidence. The fact that he has come out of that environment where it is very much pitch driven really to increase our aptitude in this area" (Andrew Cartwright, Vice-President, Finance).

So the MasterCard Australia people were eager to be led, which in turn inspired them to lead.

The External Change Agents

"I think he [Peter Fuda] is quite innovative; he really does look for solutions for really positive end results. And even the structure that he looked at – I pretty much went to him and said this is the problem and I want these to go through this process and that was my solution. Lets help these people to know what this means so that they can embrace it like we have!" (Leigh Clapham, Senior Vice-President and General Manager, Australasia).

Peter Fuda, the founder and Managing Director, PCD, a boutique change leadership consultancy founded in 2001, was instrumental in setting the course for MasterCard Australia. As the 'external change agents', he and his team worked alongside Leigh Clapham to navigate the journey.

PCD are Human Synergistics Accredited Practitioners and use the Human Synergistics suite of leadership and culture diagnostic instruments as part of their consulting offer. PCD's Organisational Change Model maps the sequence of steps to transform change into sustained performance. In their 'Define', stage PCD conducts a needs analysis which identifies the future state in terms of what the organisation wants to be, what they want to achieve, what their strategy is, what their current state is and reviews the systems and the structures. So PCD is essentially setting up the change imperative or the case for change. This stage lasts six months and delivers four outcomes to the client:

1. **A clear picture of the future state.** This is made up of agreed purpose, values, vision, objectives, measures and targets. A common language for management in their organisation is created through a process of engaging with all stakeholders which creates momentum and energy.
2. **Executive team alignment for that future state.** PCD work as process experts in this strategy process, rather than content experts. The client is responsible for providing the content and articulating their strategy of who they are, what they want to be and be aligned to that view. The result is very committed and passionate people, who have defined for themselves this future state, rather than consultants doing it for them.
3. **Engage people through the process.** Momentum and buy-in is created through focus groups, completing OCI surveys to understand the culture and systems reviews right from the outset because stakeholders have been part of the whole process.
4. **A road map.** PCD provides the client with their view of the challenges facing them using a balanced scorecard approach (financials, customer, product, process,

leadership and culture), which paints a picture of where the client wants to be, where they are and the key things they need to do to get there.

The interesting thing with PCD is that they crafted an approach for MasterCard Australia that was practical and commercially oriented. As a change agent being able to formulate and translate the change into a business outcome is vital and something that is sometimes overlooked. In our zeal, we at times get 'lost' in or become seduced by the excitement of designing a program or an approach and 'forget' to link it to business outcomes in an overt way. PCD however took an eclectic approach using a number of different concepts and tools. *"He [Peter Fuda] nicely worked out the four stages of the program getting them to understand what this is. But then saying 'so what's the commercial application?' after that. The fact that he had a commercial focus has been terrific"* (Leigh Clapham, Senior Vice-President and General Manager, Australasia).

Peter in a lot of ways has the same attributes as Leigh – action-oriented, business savvy and possessing a determination to make a difference to his clients.

Lessons Learnt

The lessons MasterCard Australia has learnt reinforce many concepts and heuristics that exemplify how to approach organisational transformation. Highlighted here are the salient points which have been weaved throughout this story.

HAVE A FOCUSSED, INSPIRATIONAL & INTUITIVE LEADER

"I think if a leader embraces it, his behaviour then impacts on others and I think Leigh took it very seriously. He opened up the thing, he led the thing, he drove it and I guess the rest of the organisation embraced it. Certainly he was leading the change and he was demonstrating the behaviours that he was meant to and it's very easy to follow that sort of leadership" (Focus Group Member).

Leigh Clapham's energy and drive has been largely responsible for MasterCard Australia's amazing story. People have sighted Leigh's philosophies and his strategy of 'win-win' as one of the most significant contributions to MasterCard Australia's turnaround. He engendered enthusiasm and buy-in to his direction and vision and was able to garner and harness the collective energies towards a common purpose and direction.

> **... he was leading the change and was demonstrating the behaviours... it's very easy to follow that sort of leadership**

HAVE A COMMERCIAL FOCUS TO TRANSFORMATION

"Rather than run another program that focussed mainly on the before and the after and some of the generic learnings, he [Peter] got it boiled right down to the commercial realities and asked us questions such as 'why aren't you doing your job to the maximum effectiveness at the moment?', 'what are the external forces that are causing the organisation not to be as good as it was or as good as it should be?' We identified those key issues and then said in this current state how do we address these?" (Leigh Clapham, Senior Vice-President and General Manager, Australasia).

Putting the transformation imperative into context with the business challenges has been a factor that has been highlighted throughout this story. Constantly reminding people of the business rationale for moving ahead with an initiative is key in focusing energies towards business outcomes. This may seem obvious, but it's a subtle but powerful concept that may be overlooked – continually refocusing the organisation reminds people of the 'business case' for the various initiatives.

ADOPT A 'BUSINESS AS USUAL' APPROACH

"… it was more Humanistic-Encouraging, but was more subconscious… a bit more time to under-stand other people's pressures, points of view. A few more staff lunches, nothing really that you could put your finger on. This process changed the way people behaved and also brought them into line in terms of the way we wanted to move forward. Leigh had been through it before so he very much led the process. In terms of personal accountability, there was the action plan for the whole office, we really did embrace that" (Andrew Cartwright, Vice-President, Finance).

Embedding the initiatives in the day-to-day running of the business ensures that they are not seen as a 'one-off' or as something that is separate from your 'day job'. MasterCard Australia operationalised the learnings and implemented actions

This process changed the way people behaved…

swiftly. The sense that one gets from MasterCard Australia was that the initiatives brought a realisation that it was a common sense way of running a business that they had not previ-ously appreciated. The danger with having a 'special change program' is that it is seen as a once-off, with the attendant risks of the changes never becoming truly integrated, but rather being seen as something that needs to 'ticked off' before moving forward.

The 'business as usual' approach highlights the notion of change leadership – that is the process of leading change and pursuing continuous organisational renewal.

HAVE COMMITTED & PASSIONATE PEOPLE

"Everything fell into place. It was a perfect organisation to do this, [it was] small, quite dexterous, [people that] could change quickly, enthusiastic individuals that formed good teams. You know how often do you have a task force and they leave the meeting enthusiastically and you say to them two months later: 'How's that task? We must get together and meet again'. These people used to meet every week" (Leigh Clapham, Senior Vice-President and General Manager, Australasia).

Throughout this story, Leigh pays tribute to the commitment and dedication of people at MasterCard Australia. His genuine respect and admiration for their commitment to the journey was palpable and points to the importance of this ingredient in progressing a trans-formation effort. The embracing of and dedication from employees to the change at all levels was foreshadowed and reinforced by a Leadership Team who were seen as role models.

ENABLE PERSONAL INSIGHT AND SHIFTS IN MINDSET

The circumplex struck such a chord with almost every leader as they experienced it, to the extent that some leaders pinned their circumplexes up on their walls as a constant reminder of their challenge and as a symbol of how they had embraced the change. It provided them with, as one Focus Group Member termed it *"a higher level of consciousness of how people reacted and interacted with others – rather than saying 'no' up front, they changed their attitude to being more positive."* This type of paradigm shift is critical to facilitate shifts in mindset at the personal level and in turn organisational transformation.

MAINTAIN MOMENTUM

"… and Leigh said to me 'I am sensing that we are coming off the boil a little'. Now that is the sign of a very Achievement-based CEO. He said to me 'There is a smell in the air – we are still ahead of Visa but I am starting to feel that we are not increasing at the same rate – so if we were moving ahead at 50 knots it feels like 15 knots now and I am uncomfortable with that. I am starting to see cracks'" (Peter Fuda, Managing Director, PCD).

This points to a key learning for MasterCard Australia around how to ensure that the momentum and energy keeps the transformation journey going. The challenge is how to keep it 'top of mind' and ensure it keeps going but also how to ensure that the transformation 'burden' does not solely reside in the charismatic and inspirational leader. So perhaps there is a lesson here in the danger of an organisation suffering from change fatigue and a need to remember that it's

I would definitely take new senior recruits through the process…

important to devolve influence to and empower all employees, so that the 'baton' continues to be passed from one person to the other. In addition, it's important to think about how to engage new people that are brought into the organisation, as alluded to here by Leigh: *"I would definitely take new senior recruits through the process and help them understand what the rest of the team had been involved in and learning from that and the applications of those learning, the influence we felt it had on our business. In effect there probably should have been a case study presented to each new senior employee to let them know what was going through the minds of their colleagues, what their colleagues had been through and to help them understand what was going through their minds and why they did things in a certain way."*

Future Challenges

"There needs to be some sort of structure around maintaining the momentum and making it 'top of mind' and that's the challenge because we are all under a lot of pressure. There's always a crisis, there's always an emergency that we're having to work on, everything's important, everything needs to be done yesterday and everything gets pushed aside" *(Focus Group Member)*.

When conducting the interviews in early 2006 for this case study and reflecting on where MasterCard Australia is today, there was agreement from all parties that there has been a sense of lost momentum about the change journey: *"It was quite extraordinary when I spoke to three or four of the people who had been on this journey and where we are now... they all said we are not 'firing on all cylinders'. If we had put in as much effort in our working groups, focussed on certain outcomes between here and here and now we would have continued to grow our effectiveness. Our effectiveness on a scale of one to ten, if it was an eight in May 2004, has probably slipped to a seven. Our team members who had been involved in the process noticed the difference and they acknowledged that we didn't have task forces working between May 2004 and February 2006 on maintaining those levels of effectiveness and recognising the impact of leadership on the culture and eventual outcomes of new people coming in as well"* (Leigh Clapham, Senior Vice-President and General Manager, Australasia).

And this from Andrew Cartwright: *"... the feedback from this get-together that we had just last week was that we have sort of lost a bit of momentum, we got a little bit comfortable and actually we did a very quick score and it wasn't quite as good as it was here so maybe it was a little bit Green and Red. Leigh and I were talking about the session we had in May 04. I would say we only actioned about 50% of the items to come out of that meeting and I am most probably being a little bit kind. Maybe we thought it was easy so we didn't do it religiously. Whereas back here [in 2003] I would say back we actioned 90% of the action items."*

This storyline of lost momentum parallels other similar storylines of organisations. This pattern has been replicated time and time again – that of an abundance of enthusiasm and energy at the outset; a renewed vigour and excitement at the first Re-Test and then somehow a gradual slowing down and complacency begins to settle in, to the point that the next Re-Test is the tangible representation of that complacency and that 'taking the foot of the pedal', with a decrease in the Constructive norms and an increase in the Defensive norms. And MasterCard Australia appears to have replicated this predictable pattern. The key challenge for MasterCard Australia moving forward is sustaining this stunning story of transformation.

Whilst MasterCard Australia has not formally Re-Tested its culture as yet by completing the OCI again, this intuitive, 'gut feel' of where they are at today has been enough to spur them into action and re-engage with the process with a renewed vigour and determination to 'course correct' and continue navigating this never-ending journey.

Chapter **5**

A Fresh Approach

Yarra Valley Water

human synergistics

Contents
Yarra Valley Water

Written by Corinne Canter

Executive Summary

The public sector has provided fertile soil for jokes and jibes about the alleged lower levels of performance and sophistication. Yarra Valley Water, a retail utility company owned by the Victorian government, however, shatters many of these stereotypes. This case study documents the extraordinary journey of Yarra Valley Water as it transforms its organisation from a Defensive, old-style public service instrument into a dynamic, energized organisation.

Industry	Utilities
Customers	1.6 million
People	395
Assets	A$1.3 Billion
Revenue	A$381.5 Million
CEO	Tony Kelly
Internal Change Agent(s)	Anne Farquhar, Tony Kelly, Senior Executive Team
External Change Agents(s)	Ian Pimblett, Strategic Growth Pty Ltd
HSI Tools Used	Organizational Culture Inventory® (OCI), Oragnizational Effectiveness Inventory™ (OEI), Life Styles Inventory™ (LSI)

Culture Results

Organizational Culture Inventory Test (2001)

Organizational Culture Inventory Re-Test (2005)

 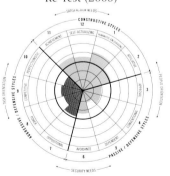

Outcomes	Increased staff satisfaction, staff retention and egagement; increased efficiency and customer service

1995-2000

Yarra Valley Water

Pre-Test

Phase **1**

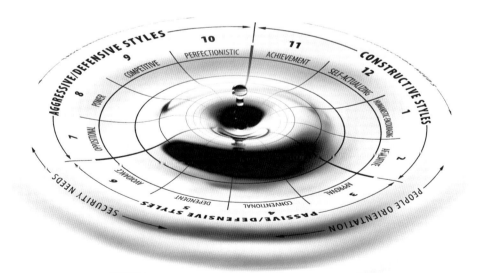

About Yarra Valley Water

Introduction

"We invest in the replacement of our infrastructure, knowing that it will reap benefits in the future, there will be less burst water mains, less leaks and so on. The work we do on the HR side of the business is not dissimilar… you know that it will have benefits. We are a happier company, a more productive company. Staff are the happiest they have been in their history and I believe that makes them more productive"
(Tony Kelly CEO Yarra Valley Water).

The number of stereotypes surrounding public sector or government related organisations has for a long time provided fertile soil for jokes and jibes about the alleged lower levels of performance and service that could be expected from organisations within the sector. However, Yarra Valley Water a retail utility company owned by the Victorian government shatters many of these stereotypes. This case study documents the extraordinary journey of Yarra Valley Water as it transforms its organisation from a Defensive, old style public service instrument into a dynamic, energized organisation with highly engaged people whose eyes are firmly on the goal of achieving the highest levels of effectiveness and efficiency for their customers.

While Yarra Valley Water began this journey in the belief that it would lead to great business results, one of the hallmarks of this case study is the depth of change at all three levels of the organisation; at the individual, group and organisational (system) levels. The process of transformation has tapped into and managed to harness the collective and diverse wills of its entire workforce to create a vibrant organisation focussed on achieving excellence in customer service, the environment and in their business through effective and optimal level of team work. It also stands as a shining example of how engagement of employees is significantly driven by the leadership. This is a great story about how the leadership re-built and earnt the trust of their people and how this process built a momentum of its own that resulted in a more effective, happier, more productive and higher-performing organisation.

Background

Yarra Valley Water is a retail water company that provides water supply and sewerage services to 1.6 million people who live and work in the Yarra River catchment area of Melbourne. In delivering to its customers, Yarra Valley Water *"strive(s) to lead the global water industry in serving the Customer and environment supported by a high performing business culture"* (Annual Report 2004/2005).

The company began operations as one of three retailers for Melbourne, on 1 January 1995, following the restructure of Melbourne's water industry in 1994. Owned by the State Government of Victoria, Yarra Valley Water operates commercially under a Board of Directors appointed by their shareholders, and subject to Corporations Law.

Figure 1. Yarra Valley Water Business

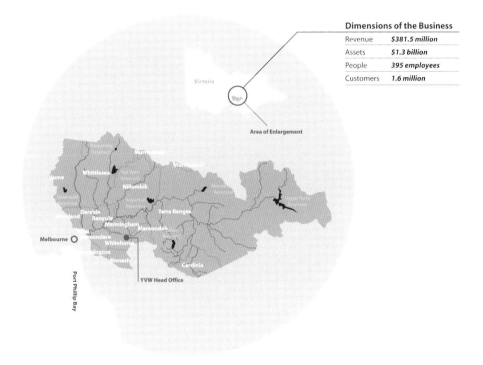

Dimensions of the Business	
Revenue	*$381.5 million*
Assets	*$1.3 billion*
People	*395 employees*
Customers	*1.6 million*

External and Internal Operating Environment

Yarra Valley Water's establishment in 1995 was driven by the Victorian Government's intention to privatise the water industry. The organisation's structure, functions, time and resources were invested in gearing up for the greatly anticipated increase in competition and eventual sale of the organisation.

Getting ready for competition and sale was at the core of how the culture developed over the years 1995–1999. The need to be competitive, implicitly and explicitly, was woven into an Aggressive/Defensive culture. It was led by a Managing Director and Executive Team that, at the time, were operating within the more traditional framework of management, one of centralised hierarchy and a strong command and control approach to managing people.

General Manager Operations, Pat McCafferty says: *"There had been a culture that had been established to 'win' and to maximise the business if it was sold. So we were doing all sorts of things to develop non-regulated revenue."*

Managing Director, Tony Kelly agrees: *"We were very competitive internally. The culture of the place was that you would set one group up against the other competing for budget in a very overt way, it was win /lose. So we were competing with each other, rather than with the water industry; so that was really unproductive."*

The culture of the place was that you would set one group up against the other …it was win /lose

The Aggressive/Defensive element in the culture was responsible for developing a culture of Passive/ Defensive employees. A culture where people did not make decisions and were encouraged to refer all issues up to management. This created a great deal of Avoidance by staff in the way they approached their work and relationships with others. The combined forces of these Aggressive/Defensive and Passive/Defensive elements produced an organisational environment where staff were not encouraged to use their initiative, internal competition was high and departmental silos were very strong. Fuelling this situation was a low level of trust between the Executive Team and employees, reinforced by limited quality interpersonal communication.

The Case for Change

In 1999 when it became clear that the company would not be sold, as the Victorian Government had originally intended, a sense developed internally that the organisation had lost some direction and purpose. While Yarra Valley Water was delivering good results, it was not moving forward. The Managing Director at the time intuitively believed that the lack of innovation was somehow related to the culture of the organisation, but did not know how to approach the problem. In 2001 he hired Anne Farquhar as General Manager, Human Resources and gave her a mandate to change the culture.

At the same time that these events occurred, some doubt about the current approach (or lack thereof) to culture had already taken seed in the minds of a few of the members of the Executive Team. While the team as a whole had not demonstrated any real collective awareness of the issue, some did feel that there was a major gap in how culture was developed and managed. While as a team they had undertaken some work on developing a set of values, there was a sense that it was more of a 'laundry list'. It did not hold meaning for anyone, not even those who contributed to its development. There was a belief held by some of the team that for the business to move to the next level, a change was required in the way they led and managed their people - but they did not know how to approach the issue.

At this point Anne Farquhar – with the input and support of external consultant Ian Pimblett of Strategic Growth Pty Ltd – decided that the Organizational Culture Inventory®

(OCI) tool developed by Human Synergistics could be useful in supporting the organisation in cultural change. The tool provided the Executives and organisation with the opportunity to identify their Preferred culture or their 'cultural benchmark', as well as measuring the Actual operating culture to establish the gap between the two. The scientific, evidence-based foundation of the tools appealed to the Executives who had accounting and engineering backgrounds. They believed that it would give them a benchmark and something to aim for. It also had the capacity to give meaning to new behaviours required throughout the organisation. The Executive Team agreed to support the first test on the basis that it might provide more specific information for analysis and action planning to occur.

2001

Yarra Valley Water

Test

Phase **2**

The Approach

Yarra Valley Water chose to begin the change with measuring the culture. The rationale was to identify a baseline of where the culture was currently operating in order to facilitate an action plan. While the organisation did go on to implement the Life Styles Inventory™ (LSI) process with all their leaders (as will be discussed), the initial thought was to use the Organizational Culture Inventory® (OCI) as means of identifying the organisation's Preferred culture or cultural benchmark and then by 'mapping out the landscape', identify the most pressing issues for the organisation.

The Culture Survey Results

WHAT WAS YARRA'S PREFERRED CULTURE?

The survey results of the OCI in 2001 as shown in Figure 2 provided a great deal of information and some context for understanding why the organisation seemed to have become stagnant. The results showed an organisation with strong Defensive behavioural norms, specifically, the predominance of Avoidance, Oppositional and Competitive styles strongly backed by the Conventional style. In short, people avoided responsibility and action by delegating upwards, blocking new ideas, competing with one another and using policy and procedures as a way of managing insecurities and inhibiting change and innovation.

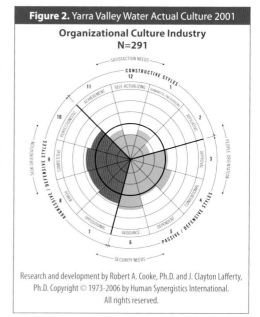

Figure 2. Yarra Valley Water Actual Culture 2001

The survey results were intended to and did create a 'disturbance factor', which was crucial in getting staff to recognise the need to change. One member of staff described its impact as being, *"hard for us all, sobering but the first realisation about how we were being"*.

A disciplined and rigorous process of communicating the OCI results to staff began. All results, good bad and ugly were shared with staff. A systematic process of communicating results on a team by team basis was implemented. Each team was debriefed on both the overall organisational results and their own team's results. This was facilitated by the external consultant, Ian Pimblett, and was undertaken one day at a time. Ian guided each team through a process of 'unpacking' the results and their implications. Each session also incorporated an improvement process which the teams would generate themselves with his assistance.

People were keen to learn more. They could see what was possible and wanted to be part of a better place

This communication process had the effect of creating a great deal of enthusiasm. There was a feeling in the organisation that people wanted to change and that this was a concrete, tangible way of helping them achieve change.

Often we speak about change initiatives as if they happen after the initial measurement phase, it is important however to appreciate that the Test period is a golden opportunity to begin a change process. The communication of the event, the enrolment of staff in the process is actually part of the intervention. Done properly it gives the organisation a 'head start' on the education process that any such intervention requires. It is also equally important to take the time to thoroughly debrief employees for a number of reasons. Firstly employees need to see how their effort in completing the surveys has actually impacted the organisation. This incidentally is a great way to promote an Achievement orientation, to demonstrate to people that their effort actually does make a difference. Secondly it offers the organisation an opportunity to start mobilising and harnessing the motivation and energy of employees as it did for Yarra Valley.

As one Yarra Valley Water Team Leader experienced: *"People were keen to learn more. They could see what was possible and wanted to be part of a better place. Why suffer in a 'not so good culture' if you can have a better one?"*

The Leadership – Culture Connection

The sobering effect of the results of the OCI was felt at all levels of the organisation and subsequent to the OCI being conducted, the decision was taken to measure the individual thinking styles of Yarra's leaders to provide them with some feedback and insight into how they may have contributed to the Aggressive/Defensive norms operating in the organisation. In 2002 the LSI results of the Executive Team revealed that there was in fact a close relationship between the Executive Team's group circumplex and that of the organisation's as is highlighted in Figure 3.

The circumplexes share a somewhat similar overall pattern. The Avoidance style is the primary style operating at the Executive team level as it is across the organisation, with the Oppositional style as the back up style in both circumplexes. The Constructive styles are at a higher level in the Executive Team than appears to operate in the organisation as a whole, although the Constructive styles are under the 50th percentile in both circumplexes. The types of behaviours that were driven by this kind of circumplex at the Executives level included a reluctance to make decisions, referring most decisions to the Managing Director.

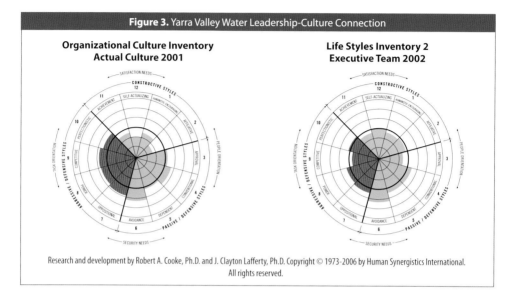

Figure 3. Yarra Valley Water Leadership-Culture Connection

Organizational Culture Inventory
Actual Culture 2001

Life Styles Inventory 2
Executive Team 2002

This may have fostered a dependency on his involvement in all issues across the board and would have contributed to a risk averse, conventional mindset that led team members to oppose new ideas, thereby inhibiting self development and growth. Leading from this type of Defensive position limits success and achievement due to a predominant focus on avoiding failure. The resulting impact was that the Executives, without realising, were inadvertently promoting norms that led to a feeling of stagnation throughout the organisation.

Yarra Valley Water

Phase **3**

Action

The Cultural Change Strategy

Yarra Valley Water embarked on their journey of change in 2001. Their goal was to build a high performance business culture that they defined as: 'One in which the members display constructive behaviours that facilitate high-quality problem solving and decision making, teamwork, productivity, and long-term effectiveness' *(Anne Farquhar, 2003)*.

Although the actual program of change initiatives was very structured and purposeful in design and execution, there was no initial pre-formulated strategic plan that guided the transformation process. Rather the process was guided by a clear vision of what the organisation might look like if it had a high performing culture. This vision was also underpinned by some key assumptions, beliefs and values including:

- People are inherently good and want to do a good job; therefore if they are provided with the right conditions they will be motivated to perform
- The belief that it is important to link an individual's personal transformational journey to that of the organisation
- People need to have personal responsibility, accountability and integrity in relating to oneself and to others
- The need to create and reinforce trust is both a condition and outcome of the transformation process
- Obtaining and sustaining Executives commitment for the process is also a foundation and continuing requisite

In summary, since 2001, when Yarra Valley Water began the transformation process, the aim of the Culture Strategy has been to build and retain a high performing business culture by:

- Identifying cultural goals and measuring progress
- Providing tools and support to promote self awareness and improve leadership capabilities
- Integrating preferred behaviours into processes and policies such as performance management, reward and recognition and succession planning
- Recruiting for cultural fit
- Providing appropriate learning and development opportunities
- Promoting cross functional co-operation and team goals
- Encouraging clear, constructive and open communication across the business
- Providing Human Resources services that efficiently deliver effective advice, information and support
- Providing employee programs and benefits that support work/life balance
- Making a commitment to Re-Testing every two years initially to evaluate the progress and impact of the transformation program

"The key elements are an emphasis on achievement of realistic stretch targets and an open, honest approach in everything we do" (Anne Farquhar, General Manager, Human Resources).

The Program of Initiatives

As Yarra Valley Water's journey unfolded, numerous initiatives and actions were taken to support the cultural transformation. Examples of how several of these initiatives were implemented are detailed in this section and summarised in Table 1 (page 203).

The OCI results provided Yarra Valley Water with both a cultural benchmark for the organisation in terms of what kind of culture it wanted to create, as well as a gap analysis in terms of which styles needed to increase in order to close the gap. The range of initiatives to close these gaps centred around self awareness, building trust, developing basic leadership skills, opening

An emphasis on achievement of realistic stretch targets and an open, honest approach in everything we do

communication channels, creating a shared vision and developing understanding of culture and how it impacts performance.

In reviewing the impact of this program of initiatives, it is clear that:

- The initiatives targeted most of the key 'Causal Factors' highlighted in Dr Rob Cooke's 'How Culture Works' Model shown below. Causal Factors in this context

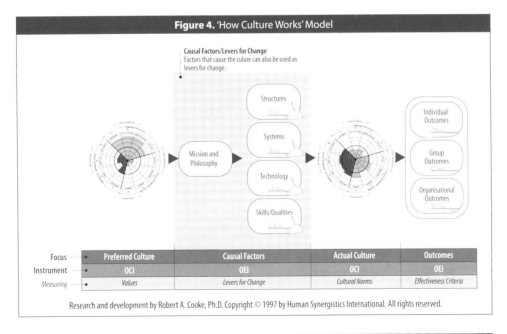

Figure 4. 'How Culture Works' Model

Research and development by Robert A. Cooke, Ph.D. Copyright © 1997 by Human Synergistics International. All rights reserved.

Table 1. Summary Table of Initiatives 2001-2005					
Levers (Causal factors)	**2001**	**2002**	**2003**	**2004**	**2005**
Mission & Philosophy Initiatives that relate to clear articulation of the organisation's identity and values	■ New values determined by staff ■ OCI measurement ■ OCI feedback workshops		■ Launch of Strategic Intent & the 'House' ■ 2nd OCI measure ■ OCI workshops ■ 1st OEI		■ Review of the Strategic Intent ■ 3rd OCI measurement ■ 2nd OCI measurement ■ 2nd OCI measurement ■ OCI/OEI feedback workshops
Structures Initiatives that relate to how people, roles and activities are ordered to create Organisation	■ Cross-functional Teams ■ Skip Level interviews	Delegation of responsibility for financial and other business decisions were increased dramatically	Introduction of HRIS		
Systems ■ Human Resource Systems ■ Selection & Placement ■ Training & Development ■ Performance Management	**T&D** ■ Departmental Open Days ■ Mt. Eliza Leadership program Selection and Placement	**T&D** ■ 'Channels of Change' workshop ■ **Leadership Development** · LSI data capture · LSI Individual feedback · LSI Group workshops · Coaching Training (Co-Achieving) ■ In-house recruitment commenced **Performance Management**	**T&D** ■ 'Blue Zone Days' for all staff	**T&D** ■ In-house L&D strategy launched ■ **Leadership Development** · 2nd LSI data capture · 2nd LSI Individual feedback · 2nd LSI Group workshops Communication Breaktrhough program (leaders)	■ Quarterly communication coaching for teams ■ 'Blue Zone' workshops ■ Requisite Organisation framework introduced
Technologies Methods to transform effort (input) into outcomes (output)					
Skills/Qualities Including methods of communication (up, down and for learning)	■ Symbolic Events ■ Skip level interviews ■ Comms with MD	■ 8th Employee Opinion survey		■ 9th Employee Opinion Survey	

refer to the thirty one factors distributed across five categories which have been shown to be causally linked to driving cultural norms and behaviours. The value of this model comes into its own when the causal factors have been identified, they are then used as levers for bringing about changes to the culture. This enables an organisation to target their resources in specific areas which they know (through the OCI/OEI results) will drive change.

- They were implemented using a variety of different methods including:
  - Symbolic actions and events
  - Leadership development and coaching
  - Formal and informal training opportunities
  - Systems and process reviews
  - Job design and team process initiatives

The ensuing discussion elaborates on these initiatives and their importance in driving cultural transformation. To enable stronger linkage to their impact on culture the initiatives are not presented in chronological order but rather as the 'levers for change' described in the How Culture Works Model mentioned above. Table 1 on page 203 however summarises these initiatives in chronological form.

Using the Causal Factors as Levers for Change

Mission & Philosophy – Clarifying the Organisation's Strategic Intent

At the beginning of the change process action was triggered by a belief at the Executives level that the organisation was not moving forward and that the secret to releasing its potential and improving its performance somehow lay with the cultural dimension of the business.

In 2003, the cultural change process received an additional injection of commitment when the incumbent Managing Director resigned and Tony Kelly assumed the role. As an Executive team member he had already supported the culture measurement introduced by Anne Farquhar in 2001. This old culture had been at odds with his own natural style and with how he wanted to lead or believed it was necessary to lead. His appointment to the role in 2003 provided additional support for the new model.

"I understood that there was a win/win in this… there was an awful lot of avoiding decisions and delegating upwards and that wasn't good for them and it was never going to be good for me either. So we desperately needed a new model, we needed a new way of operating. … it was certainly going to solve my problems and it was going to solve a lot of problems we were experiencing with staff."

To this end Tony Kelly developed a new Strategic Intent to clearly state the direction of the company and to provide clarity and purpose for staff. The Strategic Intent integrated the organisation's success as a customer-focussed, efficient business that values its people, with a strong recognition of the increasing emphasis on the environment by key stakeholders. Together, the four elements of the Strategic Intent combine to provide a strong foundation for the company to play a lead role in helping to manage Melbourne's water resources in a sustainable way.

Yarra Valley Water's Strategic Intent was symbolised as a house and has become a key element of a broad communication plan to help staff understand the Company's direction (Figure 5).

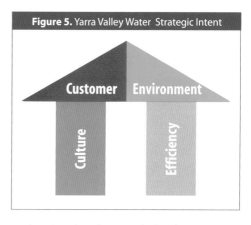

Figure 5. Yarra Valley Water Strategic Intent

Tony Kelly again: *"Our strategy has four key elements – continuous improvement in customer service, building a high-performing business culture, improvements in efficiency, and reducing our impact on the environment."*

The impact of 'the house' was to provide the organisation and its people with a single unifying sense of purpose. It integrated all the hitherto disparate streams of work being undertaken by the people in the organisation into a clear, concise, symbolic language that anchored the organisation's vision of a Constructive culture in the business outcomes the organisation was seeking.

Structures – Empowerment – From Rhetoric to Practice

Anne Farquhar General Manager, Human Resources reflects: *"The underlying thing was, it was important to transfer the principles into policies and procedures. A fundamental assumption was that people come to work to do good, therefore if we provide the right conditions we can let them do their job."*

The systems and structures which implicitly and explicitly encode the norms and expectations of the organisation were also changed to ensure that they promoted more Constructive behaviours and norms: encouraging behaviour that was Achievement-oriented, Affiliative and Self-Actualizing. Specifically:

- Delegation and approval processes that seemed artificial were removed. This opened everything up for much more questioning.
- Skip level interviews were introduced. Skip level interviews provide staff with the opportunity to speak with the manager of their manager. Their introduction at Yarra Valley Water impacted the established power structures, increasing the staff's access to senior management in a way that didn't compromise the line manager's authority, but enabled staff to be heard by key decision makers of the company.
- Cross functional teams were encouraged within the organisation as a means of promoting collaboration as well as a means of harnessing the corporate knowledge of staff. Critical processes that supported the organisation and cut across functional or departmental lines were identified and cross-functional teams established to work on process plans. This created and required a great deal of interdependence across the organisation since the budget lines are still allocated on a departmental basis. The high level of trust in the organisation facilitated this cross-functional approach.

Systems – Embedding New Norms

Part of the change process was transforming the Human Resources Team from a transactional to strategic function. Integral to this was changing the people management systems and processes that had been in place. Anne Farquhar effectively overhauled these and introduced a range of new initiatives and measures such as:

- Centralised Recruitment – ensuring that the right people were in the right roles
- Adapting the performance appraisal system so that it reflected both 'Blue Zone' objectives and targets as well as 'Blue Zone' principles in its execution
- Centralising the Learning and Development function and developing a robust learning and development strategy and implementation plan that would focus on building capability across the organisation

Examples of how these initiatives worked and how they contributed to the cultural evolution of the organisation follows.

RECRUITMENT – GETTING THE RIGHT PEOPLE INTO THE RIGHT ROLES

Recruitment was centralized as a means of injecting integrity and consistency into the process of selecting new employees. In addition to the need to demonstrate competencies, the recruitment process also assessed cultural fit in terms of 'Blue Zone' (Constructive) qualities and behaviours to ensure a successful fit to the values of the organisation and the on-going maintenance of the culture – this was done by incorporating behaviourally oriented questions based on agreed 'Blue Zone' Behaviours.

TRAINING AND DEVELOPMENT

Once the direction of the cultural change had been established, Yarra Valley Water made an enormous investment in developing its people.

In 2004/05 there were more than 180 learning and development opportunities for staff. On average, Yarra Valley Water employees took part in approximately 38 hours of structured learning and development opportunities with more than 90% of these held on-site. More than 30% of this training was dedicated to cultural change, leadership and interpersonal skill development including but not limited, to 'Blue Zone' days, performance management, service leadership, and negotiation courses.

Some of the training initiatives were developed specifically in response to the results of the OEI conducted in 2003, which identified a need for a more in-depth focus on customer service. A specific customer service improvement program was developed, called 'SPLASH', which looked at service, culture and behaviours targeted at improving customer service. Training ranged from opportunities to increase individuals' level of self-awareness, to deep personal learning experiences related to specific customer service incidents.

Open Days

The concept of 'Open Days' was implemented across the organization and now occurs on a semi-regular basis throughout the company. At 'Open Days' staff are involved in introducing and sharing with others what they do, how they do it, their achievements and explaining how their work contributes to the organisation. The result was a series of creative, fun inter-actions that also provided a forum for learning about each other and about all facets of the business. The 'Open Days' concept has been a very successful way of breaking down silos and encouraging collaboration.

'Blue Zone' Days

"When we first went through this, there was a feeling around the organisation that the 'Blue Zone' was about being nice, soft and accommodating and we had to make the point several times that it's not about those things. It is about being productive and successful. It's about trying to improve the business... If you need to be brutally honest then you have to be brutally honest" (Tony Kelly, Managing Director).

To support behaviour change towards the Constructive style, or 'Blue behaviours', Blue Zone Days were introduced. These days are almost compulsory and are conducted annually. The intention is to demonstrate and clarify expectations around appropriate cultural behaviours through fun and engaging activities. These activities explore the 12 styles associated with the OCI and the LSI tools. This initiative provides a common understanding and agreement about what 'Blue Zone' means, where people define a new understanding and develop their ability to translate this new understanding into their every day work.

> **There was a feeling around the organisation that the 'Blue Zone' was about being nice, soft... It is about being productive and successful...**

PERFORMANCE MANAGEMENT

- The LSI feedback and improvement process was incorporated into individual performance management development plans. The intention was to encourage individual commitment to working on specific Constructive behaviours and improve personal development in line with the organisation's focus.
- Yarra Valley Water currently conducts two informal and two formal performance appraisals a year. It is currently working towards replacing these with a continuous conversation-based approach to performance management, where appraisals do not occur as an event but rather as a day-to-day, business-as-usual process. Such a system would also be an effective means of encouraging and promoting the Achievement mindset. By having conversations regularly around performance, the organisation is encouraging individuals to be focussed on their performance and the performance of the organisation all the time not just on a once or twice a year basis.
- Reward and recognition systems were revamped, so that they were linked to and reinforced 'Blue Zone' behaviours and outcomes.

Skills/Qualities

COMMUNICATION – ENGAGING HEARTS AND MINDS OF STAFF

"Communication around the organisation changed. Suddenly more information became available, and people were speaking with each other more and talking about the whole thing as if it was a breath of fresh air" (Yarra Valley Water Focus Group Member).

The process of debriefing the OCI results to all staff included a range of communication initiatives designed to fulfil a number of objectives such as:

- Establishing a two-way communication and feedback process and increasing interaction between management and staff
- Providing an introduction and on-going training in the kind of Constructive behaviours associated with being in the 'Blue Zone' which is where the organisation aspired to be
- Breaking down the silos in the organisation and increasing contact and interaction amongst staff

SKIP LEVEL INTERVIEWS

As previously mentioned, Skip Level interviews involve staff members speaking with their manager's manager about a range of issues. Skip Level interviews were introduced all the way up the line at Yarra Valley Water, so that direct reports of General Managers could speak with the Managing Director and direct reports to the Divisional Managers could speak with their General Managers. General Manager, Strategy & Communication, Pat McCafferty confirms this: *"I schedule about 30-40 interviews, people come in and talk to me about things like their understanding of strategy and direction, their role and I speak to them about leadership and communication and the feedback feeds straight into an annual review. It takes a lot of time but it's of enormous benefit."*

MEETINGS WITH THE MANAGING DIRECTOR

Every month the Managing Director's Assistant chooses six or seven staff at random to come and talk to him as a focus group about issues in the business.

Leadership

With the strong belief that management performance is a major influence on culture, Yarra Valley Water used one of Human Synergistics' individual level diagnostic tools, the Life Styles Inventory (LSI) to give individual feedback to the people managers of the organisation and to show the link between good leadership and positive cultural outcomes. Underpinning this initiative was the fundamental assumption that leaders could not lead unless people trusted them.

> **You can't lead anyone who doesn't trust you**

" … You can't lead anyone who doesn't trust you. There was a lack of vision and leadership anyway but

even if you did have a vision, you weren't going to lead anyone anywhere without trust" (Anne Farquhar, General Manager, Human Resources).

Yarra Valley Water invested greatly in the process of debriefing and explaining the LSI results with their managers. Over 70 managers received key feedback from those they worked closely with in February 2002. Their results were delivered in 'one-on-one' sessions with the external consultant, Ian Pimblett. Further more, managers, including the Executive Team, attended group workshops to share their results with their peers. They also shared their results with their managers and their staff. Key actions were put in place for each manager's personal improvement.

"Managers who were avoiding the issues in their team were brought face-to-face with the feelings of their peers and subordinates", says one Yarra Valley Water Team Leader. *"There was nowhere to hide or avoid - it had to be addressed."*

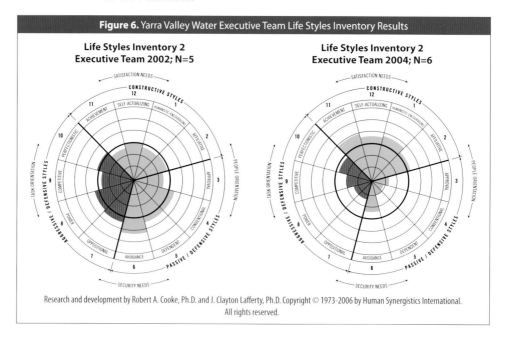

Figure 6. Yarra Valley Water Executive Team Life Styles Inventory Results

The LSI provided a structured observation process, making managers aware of personal issues that may otherwise have gone unnoticed or ignored. This had the effect of triggering their own personal journey of change moving towards more constructive ways of relating and leading their people.

It was this visible public change process at the individual leadership level as can be seen in Figure 6, that ultimately increased the level of confidence and trust of staff in their managers.

This was perhaps the most powerful catalyst in motivating change in others and mobilising corporate will. It had a significant ripple effect through their individual teams and across the organisation. Referring to the impact of change in their business unit, one team leader commented: *"Our GM led the change. He had said previously 'I am too old to change.' His change was an inspiration to everyone within the group. Everyone thought if he could change then we could as well."*

In addition, over a two-year period, managers attended a coaching skills workshop, an internal leadership behaviours course and a tailored senior leadership program at a prominent business school, comprising four three-day modules. Yarra Valley Water also conducts a Leadership Team meeting every two months. This is a half-day session and has two parts. One section focuses on business issues and another part is focussed on further learning about leadership.

CREATING NEW STORIES THROUGH SYMBOLIC ACTION
One of the very first objectives of the transformation strategy was to get the Executive involved with all levels of the organisation. The intention was to humanize them and in so doing encourage staff to see them as accessible and personable. Actions often speak louder than words and a number of symbolic events occurred that demonstrated to all staff that things were changing.

"Regular visibility and events occurring…so that every three or four months there was something happening… it has to be continuous" (Anne Farquhar, General Manager, Human Resources).

Some of these events are highlighted below.

Executive Team in the Yarra Valley Water Corporate Games
The organisation had an event called the Corporate Games. The Executive formed a team and entered the challenges. In one challenge the team spray-painted the hair of the former Managing Director and then persuaded him to leave it that way for the rest of the day while he walked the floors around the building carrying on with business. The former Managing Director was a very traditional, hierarchical, command and control leader. This behaviour was highly out of character for him, and previously unheard of, so it had a great impact on staff.

Another time, the Executive team dressed up as the Village People and performed one of their songs with the words changed to reflect life at Yarra Valley Water in a humourous way at a Corporate Games talent competition.

Tearing Up the Mission Statement and Values
The former Managing Director and the Executive Team had developed a mission statement and set of values without any input from staff. A group of line managers returning from a leadership development course conducted by a prominent business school banded together as a coalition to challenge the Managing Director on these values and mission statement. On their return Anne had become aware that they were unhappy that the mission and values had been developed without their input. She collaborated with the Managing Director and Executive Team to use it as another opportunity to demonstrate that things were changing.

At the business school, the group of leaders were introduced to the Fish Tales (Lundin, Paul, Christensen 2003) which promoted ways of getting employees engaged and motivated. It had resonated strongly with the group. Anne organized for the Managing Director to wear a fish tie for the meeting he was to have with this coalition of managers. When it was time for the meeting, the group of managers entered the room facing the Managing Director who was wearing the symbolic fish tie. They were a little taken aback but raised their concerns about the values and mission. In response the Managing Director listened silently and customarily stern faced, after they spoke, stood up and in another symbolic gesture tore up the values and mission statement and gave them the mandate to go develop a new set.

Car Parking for the Executive Team
Car parks at the front of the building were reserved for members of the Executive Team. This stopped. Parking at the front was allocated on a 'first in, first served' basis.

The New Managing Director Breaks Down the Wall
The first thing Tony Kelly did was to tear down the wall to his office and replace it with glass. This approach was a deliberate strategy by the organisation.

It was not so much about planning and 'stage managing' certain events so much as seizing the opportunities as they naturally presented themselves in the course of business.

"We wanted to create an atmosphere that things were about to change, that something was happening that wasn't just people talking. They could actually see… [and they would be saying] 'Oh that has never happened before'" (Anne Farquhar, General Manager, Human Resources).

These events provided staff with evidence that the organisation was serious about its commitment to do things differently. They were visible statements about the way the Executive Team was changing the way they related to staff. They were also signals indicating that the power structures and distribution of influence were changing as well. Where once upon a time staff were implicitly educated in the divide between them and the Executive, in the new world the walls of status and control were dissolving and were being replaced by more permeable and flexible boundaries based on direct, constructive communication and personal responsibility. Staff were encouraged to be actively involved and to communicate more directly with the Executive Team.

We wanted to create an atmosphere that things were about to change, that something was happening that wasn't just people talking

2003-2005

Yarra Valley Water
Re-Test

Phase **4**

Overview

Yarra Valley Water embarked on a journey of cultural transformation because the leaders recognised that the culture was inhibiting individual performance and productive work relationships which in turn limited the organisation's overall progress and success.

For the purposes of evaluating the outcomes of Yarra Valley Water's cultural transformation the 'Re-Test' period includes all of the data gathered through the OCI and OEI tools between 2001, 2003 and 2005.

The specific outcomes assessed are divided into two broad categories.

CULTURAL OUTCOMES

Moving from security to satisfaction, from Defensive to a Constructive culture indicated by:

- An increase in satisfaction and overall Constructive clusters (Blue) compared to the baseline OCI measure in 2001
- A decrease in overall Defensive cluster (shift below the 50th percentile)
- The shift in the senior leadership team's circumplex in 2005 compared to that in 2001
- Specific Outcomes related to culture over time as measured through the OCI , such as employee satisfaction, role clarity, role conflict and customer service
- Positive shift in causal factors (from undesirable to desirable)

BUSINESS OUTCOMES

How has Yarra's investment in achieving cultural transformation translated to business outcomes?

- Business measures, such as retention, staff engagement and customer satisfaction will be reviewed and discussed.

OCI Re-Test Data 2003, 2005

The circumplexes in Figure 7 show the OCI results in 2005 against the original Preferred culture Yarra identified it wanted in 2001. Figure 8 then highlights the journey involved in closing the gap by showing the OCI Re-Test results from 2003 and 2005 against the baseline measure initially taken in 2001. The Re-Test results show the cultural transformation in process. Since it embarked on this journey, the Constructive styles have more than doubled as Figure 9 shows. The greatest increase has been recorded in the Humanistic-Encouraging and Self-Actualising styles in 2005 having increased by a total of 97% and 164% respectively. On the other hand, there were substantial corresponding decreases in both the Passive/Defensive and the Aggressive/Defensive styles. Four years after the initial OCI Test the Passive/Defensive styles had decreased by 63% and the Aggressive/Defensive styles had decreased by 53%. Interestingly the style that has recorded the greatest shift across all clusters is the Dependent style having

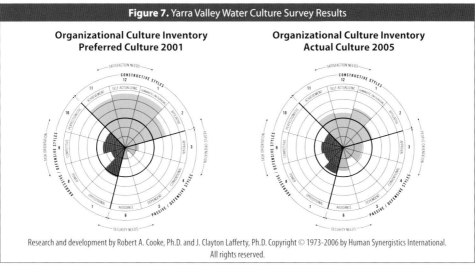

Figure 7. Yarra Valley Water Culture Survey Results

Organizational Culture Inventory Preferred Culture 2001

Organizational Culture Inventory Actual Culture 2005

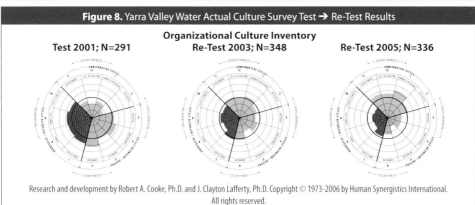

Figure 8. Yarra Valley Water Actual Culture Survey Test ➔ Re-Test Results

Organizational Culture Inventory

Test 2001; N=291   Re-Test 2003; N=348   Re-Test 2005; N=336

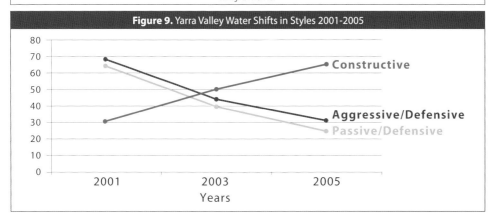

Figure 9. Yarra Valley Water Shifts in Styles 2001-2005

decreased by 20%. The greatest decrease in the Aggressive/Defensive styles was recorded for the Power style having decreased by 62%.

This decrease in Power and Dependent makes sense when one remembers that initially staff were not empowered or encouraged to make decisions, in fact they were reproached for it. This suggests that the increased emphasis on Achievement and Humanistic-Encouraging norms expressed through a more coaching style of leadership combined with a robust learning and development strategy was effective in increasing both the confidence and competence of employees in performing their role.

This overall shift in culture towards more Constructive norms resulted in positive outcomes. As Figure 10 below shows, the organisation's outcomes shows a year on year improvement at individual and organisational levels.

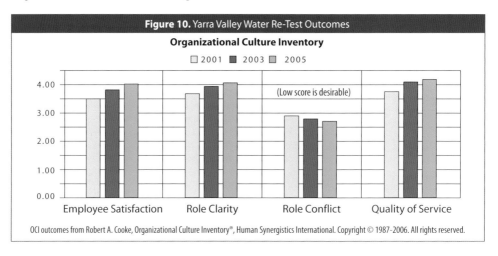

Figure 10. Yarra Valley Water Re-Test Outcomes

Organizational Culture Inventory

☐ 2001 ■ 2003 ■ 2005

(Low score is desirable)

Employee Satisfaction · Role Clarity · Role Conflict · Quality of Service

Organisational Effectiveness Outcomes

In 2003, Yarra Valley Water conducted a combined OCI/OEI culture survey in an effort to provide more specific information about what factors were driving the norms within the culture. This information was then used to target specific initiatives to address the situation. The Re-Test data from the OEI in 2003 and 2005 as shown in Figure 11 and 12 once again reflect the positive shift in culture with the causal factors also showing a positive shift. It is interesting to note that the positive shift in causal factors appear to be related to the areas that Yarra Valley Water targeted in terms of its programs. That is all the causal factors relating to articulation of mission, communication, systems, redistribution of influence (empower-ment, employee involvement) have recorded a positive shift. Their program of initiatives emphasised personal and professional awareness and development, leadership development, redistribution of influence and 'power'; meaningful collaborative relationships among team members; training and development and communication. Opportunities for improvement at Yarra Valley Water remain in the area of job design - how work is organized.

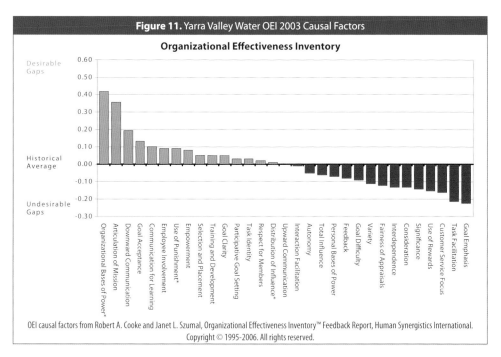

Figure 11. Yarra Valley Water OEI 2003 Causal Factors

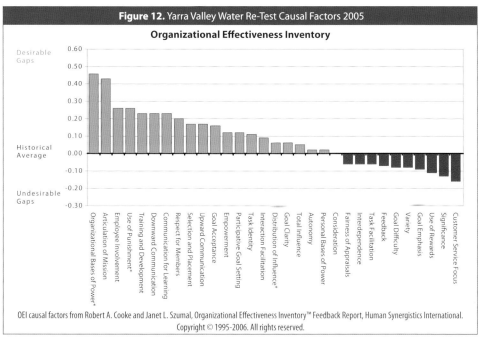

Figure 12. Yarra Valley Water Re-Test Causal Factors 2005

Business Outcomes - Measures of Organisational Effectiveness

One way of understanding the relationship between culture and performance is to frame it in terms of three broad organisational Key Performance Indicators:

- **Execution** – the extent to which the business strategy and tactical operational plans are efficiently and effectively deployed in achieving the organisation's goals. This is because deployment is always about people working with one another. Without people nothing happens, plans are not executed.
- **Engagement** – the extent to which the organisation's employees are well integrated into the organisation and motivated to perform their jobs to optimal levels (maximum discretionary effort); the degree of commitment and loyalty to the organisation.
- **Reputation** – the extent to which the organisation's brand and identity elicits or is associated with a positive response from customers, and consumers.

Over the past five years Yarra Valley Water has improved its business results across these three broad areas.

Execution

- 65% of vacancies are filled internally – retaining corporate knowledge and decreasing training and development costs.
- Decrease in controllable operating costs by 2.4%.
- Re-design of IT Architecture savings of 6.6%.
- The centralization of recruitment has resulted in a 75% reduction in recruitment costs over time and also ensures that Yarra Valley Water is able to successfully provide opportunities for staff when filling vacancies. 65% of all vacancies are filled with internal people. This is a testament to Yarra Valley Water's Learning and Development strategy and cross-functional team ways of working.

Engagement

Staff turnover down from 26% to 6%.

- Reduction in sick leave
  - July 2000 – June 2001 Avg. Sick Days per employee = 6.43
  - July 2001 – June 2002 Avg. Sick Days per employee = 5.35
  - July 2002 – June 2003 Avg. Sick Days per employee = 5.9
  - July 2003 – June 2004 Avg. Sick Days per employee = 5.3
  - July 2004 – June 2005 Avg. Sick Days per employee = 4.5
- Zero industrial action

- Employee Engagement (Overall satisfaction levels from external employee opinion survey)
  - Feb 2001 – 57%
  - Oct 2002 – 64%
  - Oct 2004 – 76%

Reputation

Customer Service (as reported in the Millwood Brown Survey)
- Staff efficiency and promptness increased from 60% to 92%
- Achieved a 56.9% 'excellent' and 'very good' result for customer satisfaction by the end of 2004-05
- 'Politeness and courtesy' increased from 80% to 88%
- Staff competence increased from 90% to 98%

Additional Key Performance Indicators of Improved Customer Service
- Handled more than 600,000 calls from customers related to billing emergencies and water restrictions with over 90% of calls answered in 30 seconds.
- Achieved first contact resolution rate of 98.82%.
- Achieved a 14% reduction of avoidable customer billing contacts.
- Awarded Customer Service Institute of Australia national and state awards for excellence in customer service in the Government sector. These are peak awards for Customer Service in Australia.

Table 2. Customer Satisfaction Index results - overall quality of service											
Customer satisfaction	Dec 99-May 00	Jun 00-Nov 00	Dec 00-May 01	Jun 01-Nov 01	Dec 01-May 02	Jun 02-Nov 02	Jan 03-May 03	Nov 03-Dec 03	Jan 04-Jun 04	Jul 04-Dec 04	Jan 05-Jul 05
Residential customers (%)	51.5	52.3	52.5	52.5	56.0	55.9	56.9	55.5	54.5	53.9	56.9
Business customers (%)	44.9	47.7	48.0	51.9	54.1	56.4	48.7	n/a*	52.4	n/a*	54.0

Source: Millward Brown Australia, 2004 * An annual survey of business customers has replaced the ongoing surveys.

Phase **5**

Yarra Valley Water

Review

Change Agents | Lessons Learnt | Future Challenges

Overview – Change Agents

Internal Change Agents	Tony Kelly - Managing Director
	Anne Farquhar – General Manager, Human Resources
	Yarra Valley Water's Executive Team
	Peter Harford - Managing Director (1995-2002)
	The Board of Directors

| **External Change Agents** | Ian Pimblett, Strategic Growth Pty Ltd |

Successful cultural transformation is a team effort involving often a cast of hundreds and sometimes thousands including everyone from the Board, the leadership, internal and external consultants, staff and customers. While the effort and commitment to change is ultimately a shared contract, it all has to begin somewhere. Someone has to recognise and articulate the case for change such that it will compel individuals to risk moving beyond their comfort zones and into a new and often unfamiliar way of being and working. Without disregarding that it is the employees' commitment that creates the change in the organisation, it is also true that in successful transformation there are key individuals and teams of individuals that can be identified for their contribution to initiating and sustaining the transformation.

'Change Agents' is a broad term used liberally when discussing cultural change and transformation. Here the term is used specifically to refer to a number of individuals who played a prominent and active role in initiating, leading and supporting the transformation.

The individuals who played the active role of change agents included:

- **Anne Farquhar** – General Manager Human Resources.
- **Tony Kelly** - Managing Director
- **Yarra Valley Water's Executive team**
- **Ian Pimblett** - External Consultant, Strategic Growth Pty Ltd

In introducing the specific change agents of Yarra Valley Water and discussing their role and the dynamic operating between them, it is important to acknowledge the contribution of the former Managing Director and the Board in terms of the support and opportunity they provided for the work to begin.

- **Peter Harford** - Managing Director (1995-2002)

  While it could reasonably be argued that Peter was part of the history of Yarra

Valley Water, it is also true that he initially identified the need to begin work on the culture. He hired Anne Farquhar in 2001 and gave her the mandate to bring about cultural change. He supported the early initiatives and as the process gathered momentum he stepped back and allowed Anne, Tony and the executive team the space to do what needed to be done. Staff saw him as *"getting better towards the end and pulling back to allow the transition to occur."*

■ **The Board**

The Board of Directors, with the legal responsibility for Yarra Valley Water, supported the transformation process both in terms of the various initiatives, but also more importantly through their acceptance that it was a long-term proposition. The original business case suggested it would take five to six years before the degree of desired change would eventuate. This acceptance freed the management team from having only to deliver against short-term expectations which enabled a focus on the best long-term, sustainable solutions.

The Roles of the Change Agents

Anne Farquhar joined the organisation in 2001 with a specific brief to change the culture. The Human Resources function had, at best, a chequered history within the organisation. There was a credibility gap that existed: the legacy of five different Human Resource Managers in as many years. Her 'straight talking' style, and ability to build relationships relatively quickly enabled the Executives to feel comfortable with her. In the early days, when her competence had yet to be proven, her 'fit' within the Executive Team at this level gave her the latitude and support to explore some new ways of doing things.

Anne's role in the transformation process was akin to that of a cultural architect. The Executives played a dual role, in that they were her clients and also they resourced her to enable the transformation process. Most importantly and significantly, they supported Anne by walking the talk: by actually doing the work and doing the work visibly and publicly.

As the primary architect, Anne held the initial vision. She sold it to the Executives who bought in. Without the Executive Team supporting the vision and visibly prepared to work alongside her to 'build the house' and live the vision, the transformation process would not have succeeded.

The external consultant, Ian Pimblett was one of a few sub-contractors. He had the skills, tools, and the knowledge in the OCI and OEI to partner alongside Anne and the Executives to bring to life the vision. Anne and Ian had a dynamic partnership, drawing and bouncing off each other.

The collective impact of the contribution of these individuals and their impact as a team and the associated program of initiatives created a psychological safety zone which encouraged and enabled staff to change.

Change is difficult and challenging. It requires people to shift their attachment to often deeply held values, assumptions, beliefs and behaviours, which to all intents and purposes have 'worked' for them. Change is voluntary, it needs to be inspired, and it cannot be forced against an individual's will. In order to change, employees need to know that they are in 'good hands'. They need a certain amount of 'proof', that the leadership can be trusted. This trust is gained and lost in the cut and thrust of the day-to-day interaction of doing business. If there is any shadow of doubt about the sincerity of the leadership, if behaviours are inconsistent with the company line, trust is eroded, defences go up and change will not occur.

One of the key factors in the success of Yarra Valley Water's transformation has been the Executive Team's courage to be seen to do their own personal transformation work. Another important factor has been their understanding that the success of significant transformation hinges on the capacity of the organisation to get the balance right between the business imperatives driving the change and the capacity of the individuals within the organisation to actually break from established patterns. Once established patterns have been broken, people can adopt new behaviours. These new behaviours often represent a significant departure from 'the way we have always done it around here' and require new capabilities not contained in people's existing 'repertoire'.

"The pace of change and the timing and type of initiatives will always be influenced by the capacity of the people to effect and adopt change." Says Anne Farquhar and: "It will also be impacted by the rate of acceptance and success of prior initiatives, external factors such as changes to shareholder policy or technology and social factors such as an ageing workforce and global issues. The role of Human Resources staff and the Executives is to identify the prevailing conditions, interpret impacts on culture and adopt the strategy accordingly."

The pace of change and the timing and type of initiatives will always be influenced by the capacity of the people to effect and adopt change

Overview – Lessons Learnt

The most powerful lessons to be learnt however are in the 'how' they did it and the 'why' it succeeded. Some of the important lessons that this case study teaches include:

THE IMPORTANCE OF THE CAPABILITY AND EMOTIONAL MATURITY OF THE CHANGE AGENT(S)

- The change agents were all individually, personally committed to making the change happen. They were all individually competent in each of their roles and carried their own weight throughout the journey. Importantly they also operated as a high-performance team, goal oriented and committed to getting everyone across the line.
- The change agents were able to define the problem precisely, and conceive a vision that simultaneously responded to the problem, while inspiring staff.
- Through their personal commitment to their own individual journey of transformation and through their actions and decisions the change agents actually 'held a space', a psychological safety zone, in which the change process of individuals, teams and the organisation could occur and align with one another. It was a top down, bottom up approach.
- The persistence of the team of change agents in maintaining the psychological safety zone meant the organisation could develop new systems and enable new behaviours to emerge and become established.

THE STRENGTH OF THE VISION

Also vital to Yarra Valley Water's success was the strength of their vision of what it would be like to have a high performance culture. While the culture strategy had a series of objectives, the vision referred to here is not the traditional concept of vision we have come to associate with companies. Yarra Valley Water's vision was not so much content or goal specific in terms of the business (e.g. become the market leader), it was about the type of environment they wanted to create and the behaviours that such an environment and workplace would promote and engender. It was a process vision underpinned by specific intentions with regard to Constructive behaviour and authenticity, and personal responsibility in the way individuals and teams approached their work and each other.

THE ROLE OF LEADERSHIP -
A VISIBLE COMMITMENT TO PERSONAL AND ORGANISATIONAL CHANGE

It is well known and accepted that leaders play the most crucial role in determining the culture of an organisation. In cultural transformation this role is even more important.

The commitment of the leadership team in the process of cultural transformation needs to be unswerving, consistent and most importantly *visible and genuine*. It is simply not possible to create long-term change by 'faking it'. The main issue here is the relationship between safety, trust and the congruent behaviour of leaders. People are unlikely to change if they do not feel safe. In fact, they are more likely to hold even more firmly to familiar patterns of defensive behaviour.

The level of psychological safety is linked to the level of trust people have in their leaders and the work context that their leaders create for them. The simple test of leadership is whether people follow, not because they have to, but because they want to. People are not likely to follow unless they trust. One of the ways people assess whether a situation is 'safe' or whether someone is to be trusted is by watching for congruence between what that person says and what they do. If these aspects of a leader's behaviour conflict or are inconsistent with one another, people naturally become suspicious and are reluctant to trust them.

In the case of Yarra Valley Water the trust in leadership was rebuilt and earned by the action of the Executive Team. Symbolic events played an enormous role in encouraging staff to open their minds to the possibility that things were going to be different. The leadership team did not start out with a 'big bang sell job' about how much better everything would be. Their approach was both more pragmatic and more subtle; it also allowed staff to contribute to the development of the culture change strategy. The leaders of Yarra Valley Water admitted to staff that there was a problem in the way the organisation operated. This acknowledge-ment was accompanied by an explanation backed by action of how they planned to respond to the problem. They then demonstrated through a number of events their on-going commit-ment to getting themselves and the organisation to a more constructive place.

THE IMPORTANCE OF LINKING PERSONAL TRANSFORMATION TO ORGANISATIONAL TRANSFORMATION

Through the sharing of their own individual personal journey experienced via the LSI process, the leaders of Yarra Valley Water demonstrated a willingness to change themselves before asking, demanding or requiring anyone else change. In the final analysis, it was their leader-ship in personal transformation and behavioural change that was the most powerful catalyst in motivating staff to undertake their own journeys, and as such it was the most powerful driver of cultural transformation.

TRANSITIONS AND TURNING POINTS - MANAGING INDIVIDUAL TRANSITIONS THROUGH THE CULTURAL TRANSFORMATION PROCESS

The success of a transformation process is predicated on the capacity of the organisation to tap into the collective of individual wills, and harness the aspirations, talents and needs of their people - with all the diversity that this entails - into a unified positive force. It is this 'force' that lies behind the transformation process and supplies the energy and fuel that moves the organisation from the old state to the new state.

In Tony Kelly's experience it did not 'take many bad eggs to make a disproportionate effect on the culture'. The subsequent impact of individuals behaving counter to the organ-isation's stated values, principles and beliefs around the Constructive styles threatened the integrity of the organisation's stated commitment. To allow a group of individuals to thwart or undermine Yarra Valley Water's values would imply that the organisation was prepared to adopt double standards and by default was not truly committed to what it said it wanted to create. This inconsistency left unchecked has the capacity in and of its own (regardless of what other 'good' the organisation is doing) to undermine the trust of employees in the leadership. This is an untenable position for any organisation.

In some cases it became clear to both the individual and Yarra Valley Water that these individuals were not going to be able to transition with the organisation for a multitude of different reasons. In some instances, individuals did not want to change their behaviours and decided to leave. There were others who were resistant to the initiatives that Yarra Valley Water was endeavouring to usher in. In these cases, honest conversations were held with these individuals and they were provided with the opportunity, resources and support to demonstrate a change in attitude and behaviour over a period of time. Where this change did not happen and the individual's behaviour and/or attitude continued to conflict with Yarra Valley Water's Preferred cultural aspiration, these individuals were managed out of the organisation appropriately.

> **The commitment of the leadership team needs to be unswerving, consistent and most importantly visible and genuine**

In many cases this was negotiated with the individual in a way which maintained their dignity. These were tough decisions but the development of Blue Zone principles and behaviours enabled management to make these judgement calls and to respond to the individuals concerned with honesty, compassion and respect in managing their exit from the organisation.

"The Exec and management got accountability. They stopped the blame culture, we all had to take responsibility. It is like we found our conscience. With that, the courage to make hard staff decisions which has freed us up. We let go of ego" (Yarra Valley Water Focus Group Member).

Yarra Valley Water underwent a number of restructures and changes throughout this five year period. These types of changes are very challenging turning points for an organisation undergoing a cultural transformation. From a staff perspective, it's 'crunch time'. These situations become 'moments of truth' a way of assessing the organisation's word and integrity. Staff watch leaders at these turning points to see if they will in fact 'walk the talk'. While challenges are an inherent fact of transition, management within a broader cultural transformation process, there has been an acknowledgement from Yarra Valley Water staff that change and transitions have been managed relatively well.

"Greater accountability in [the] management team around culture. Reducing staff fear at change. A change in culture to one more conducive to performance" (Yarra Valley Water Focus Group Member).

THE USE AND APPLICATION OF HUMAN SYNERGISTICS' TOOLS
In this case study, Yarra Valley Water used the OCI, the OEI and the LSI as to initiate and support the desired changes.

Organisational Culture Inventory

The OCI was used as a catalyst for change. The function it served was to reflect back to the organisation in a very tangible way what their culture looked like and how different this was to what they actually said they wanted. There was also a realisation that this gap between their Preferred Ideal and Actual operating culture highlighted conflict between behaviour and their personal values. The OCI created a disturbance factor. This disturbance factor is described by Edgar Schein (2005) as being critical in getting people to recognise the need for change.

Life styles Inventory 1&2

The success of Yarra Valley Water's transformation was defined by the emphasis on personal change and personal responsibility. This emphasis began with the Leadership Team in 2002 with the use of the LSI and was gradually rolled out to all people managers. The impact of the LSI was to provide structured feedback to the Leadership team on how they saw themselves and how others experienced their behaviour. This provided them with valuable information about how their own behaviour contributed to and created the dysfunctional Defensive culture they all acknowledged was not serving the business. As the OCI was conducted first they had a benchmark for assessing and monitoring their own personal change and development towards the Constructive styles. The message and intent was simple – to create their Preferred cultural Ideal the leaders needed to behave in the styles they said they wanted to characterize the organisation as a whole.

Yarra Valley Water's approach to the process of personal change and transformation was characterised by an extensive commitment to providing support to the individuals and teams in understanding results. Significant time and energy was invested in individual debriefing and coaching, and team sharing. Workshops translating the Constructive styles into appropriate behaviours were also important to individual growth and development.

Organisational Effectiveness Inventory

In 2003, the OEI was conducted in association with the Organisational Culture Inventory. The OCI would provide feedback on whether the culture had changed, while the OEI would provide more specific information on what factors were driving the culture. This additional information informed Yarra Valley Water's decisions in terms of how the causal factors would need to be addressed to create a supportive environment for the emerging culture to continue to grow. The OEI also provided feedback to the leadership on the impact they were having.

The three tools were used in an integrated approach to initiate and sustain continuous improvement and maintain the transformational process.

Future Challenges

"As the culture improves, staff expectations increase as well. Their expectations of us as managers is probably more critical. They are not so worried about the basics, they become more worried about the icing on the cake… so the better you become, the harder it is. Our improvement strategies need to be more sophisticated from now on, that's for sure" *(Tony Kelly Managing Director, Yarra Valley Water).*

Keeping the cultural transformation on track and 'fresh' – ensuring that it is continually being embedded deeper into the day-to-day business after five years – will be a very real challenge moving forward. There is a chance that Yarra Valley Water may get to a stage where the tools and strategies it uses may feel too familiar and people may unintentionally slide towards becoming Conventional or moving towards complacency.

As Tony Kelly states, as the culture improves, the bar gets lifted even higher in terms of staff expectations of the both the leadership and the organisation.

Yarra Valley Water has in place a roadmap of initiatives it is planning to implement which will continue deepening the work of the cultural transformation.

"We will continue to integrate appropriately timed opportunities for improvement through self-awareness, development of leadership competencies, measurement of progress and recognition of achievement. There will be an emphasis on communication, particularly to develop understanding of the way we unconsciously process information and use our personal filters to alter reality" (Anne Farquhar, General Manager, Human Resources).

This plan will be supported by specific initiatives focussed on:

- Improving internal service between work teams and across divisions
- Emphasis on common external service goals and improving processes to get better results for customers
- Utilising job design techniques to reduce the repetitiveness of tasks in some roles
- Improving planning processes
- On-going review of organisational structures in determining whether they support or hinder the organisation's cultural style

THE JOURNEY CONTINUES

"It is now a much better place to work and everyone sees the benefits of working in the 'Blue Zone'. We still push for very high levels of achievement but people are now much more confident and relaxed and believe in their ability to achieve and grow. Senior managers will continue to put more trust in their people and make it possible for them to keep on improving our processes and business outcomes. Simultaneous improvement in customer service, our environmental performance and efficiency is a very real challenge. But our staff are now prepared to take on this challenge themselves rather than waiting for senior management to tell them what to do. Their improved levels of work satisfaction and the company's improved performance create a true win-win outcome" (Tony Kelly, Managing Director).

Chapter **6**

kitche cafe

Raising the Bar

TIGERS

Contents
Balmain Leagues Club

Written by Corinne Canter

Executive Summary

This case study follows Balmain Leagues Club's journey from the virtually hand to mouth existence, struggling to keep their doors open, to the emergence of a strategically-responsive, thriving organisation. We track Balmain's cultural metamorphosis as it harnessed its leadership's capacity to engage and energise their people in delivering a turn-around in performance that exceeded even the most optimistic expectations; and which ultimately has led to a viable future.

Industry	Hospitality - Clubs
Customers	35,000 per month
People	100
Assets	25 million
Revenue	$18 million per annum
CEO	Danny Munk (1995-2006), Tim Camiller (2006-Present)
Internal Change Agent(s)	Danny Munk, Wayne Forrest, Executive Team, Duty Managers
External Change Agents(s)	Roma Gaster, Karibu Education International Pty Ltd
HSI Tools Used	Life Styles Inventory™ (LSI), Leadership/Impact® (L/I), Organizational Culture Inventory® (OCI), Organisational Effectiveness Inventory™ (OEI)

Culture Results

Organizational Culture Inventory
Test (2000)

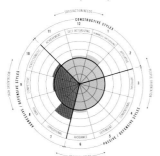

Organizational Culture Inventory
Re-Test (2002, 2004, 2005)

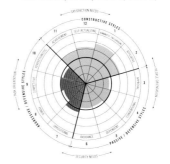

Outcomes	Business growth, decrease in operating costs, increased staff retention and satisfaction, increased brand currency

Balmain Leagues Club
Pre-Test

Phase **1**

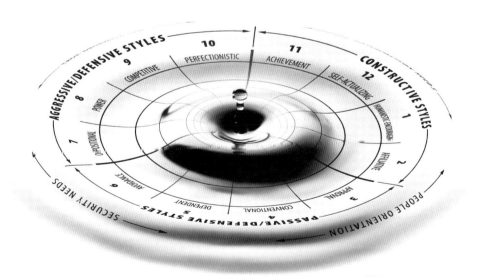

About Balmain Leagues Club

Introduction

"We don't have ten million dollars in the bank to say that we are successful, but we have a business that is solvent, we have a business that a bank is prepared to lend money to, we have a business that the local council and the community are prepared to back in a redevelopment program, in an area where the word 'redevelopment' might as well mean funnel web. We have a business that delivers a profit, so for us, the change process has enabled us to create an organisation that is proactive, deals with issues and has individuals who are prepared to grow" (*Danny Munk, CEO 1995-2006*).

Leagues clubs as we know them today with their child friendly, economically priced family bistros, their drinking bars and gaming lounges had their beginnings in the humble origins of the working class community. In Balmain, one of Sydney's oldest suburbs, Balmain Rugby League Club (football) was established as a result of a public meeting of 600 workers in 1908. During the football season, if the players were badly injured and could not work, their families lived on the proceeds of donations from other workers gathered by passing a hat around. Just after World War II this support was formalised with the establishment of premises that could provide cheap meals and drinks to workers and their families with a special emphasis on returned servicemen (Sydney Morning Herald, 2005).

Balmain has been engaged in the process of cultural change for almost ten years and of all the case studies in our data set, Balmain arguably stands alone in terms of the intensity of their 'burning platform' for change. While other companies have certainly been prompted into change to improve business performance, in this case, not only was the platform smoking, it was clearly scorching, precariously balanced between solvency and dissolution and literally operating on a day to day basis.

Danny Munk recalls: *"In 1999 prior to GST and BAS statements and before the casino significantly changing gaming laws we had an EBIT of 10.5% and a profit of about 1.6 million. We saw our gaming turnover in late 2000, 2001 drop 2 million per month within six months so we faced a loss of players, loss of revenue, and we also had to face putting in 2 million dollars in the merger when we didn't expect that we would have to; we had to upgrade the property and start to find new property for the redevelopment. So needless to say the outlook for the organisation during this period was less than promising."*

Confronted with circumstances that most organisations would consider their worst nightmares, the Executive Team of the organisation under the auspices of Danny Munk learnt how to relate and work with one another in a way that established a deep trust in one another's intention, enthusiasm and abilities to turn Balmain Leagues Club around. This willingness to learn how to become Constructive, and to believe that developing and maintaining constructive relationships in circumstances that would normally have generated a defensive response, had an enormous cascading effect throughout the organisation which resulted in the evolution of high performance teams.

This case study follows Balmain Leagues Club's journey from the virtually hand to mouth, day to day existence, struggling to keep their doors open, to the emergence of a strategically responsive, thriving organisation with a future. Although for ease of explanation this case study describes the process of cultural transformation in terms of its components; to understand how Balmain brought about this significant transformation is to understand Balmain's success as a true team endeavour. There was no single hero nor one definitive system change, moment of truth, tool or individual that 'made it all happen'. Indeed that was why

We faced a loss of players, loss of revenue, so needless to say the outlook for the organisation was less than promising

they succeeded. The team ethic of the staff and managers of the organisation demonstrated a real understanding that the whole was indeed bigger than the sum of its parts. To elaborate, there are some situations and organisations whose idea of team is akin to that of a cricket team. A group of highly talented individuals playing a team sport. In cricket however while at its best, the 'whole is greater than the sum of its parts', it is possible for an individual – a great bowler or great batsman – to dominate or drive the success of the entire team. This stands in contrast to rugby league however in that the success of the team is predicated on highly talented individuals working as a team not just performing their individual best. It was Balmain Leagues Club's ability to operate as a true team (in the rugby sense) that enabled it to transform its culture from an Aggressive/Defensive one to a Constructive one.

We track Balmain's cultural metamorphosis as it harnessed its leadership's capacity to engage and energise their people in delivering a turn-around in performance that exceeded even the most optimistic expectations.

Background

The heartland of the Balmain Leagues Club has always been a membership base grounded in a rich working class tradition with an absolute and undying passion for rugby league.

As a leagues club, it is principally a not for profit organisation with its revenue distributed back to members through the club's services and its support and development of rugby league. Balmain Leagues Club is the sole funder of the Balmain Tigers which is a 50% owner of Wests Tigers. The remaining 50% required to run the West Tiger's rugby league team is shared by two other clubs. Balmain's 50% contribution in 2004 amounted to $1.4 million dollars of the $10.5 million required to run a team in the NRL. The revenue base is supported through two key lines of business, Gaming and Food and Beverages.

External Operating Environment

"The evolution of this organisation has always been based on the need to change in order to move forward... some of that is because everything around us has always been changing, we've never had a three year plan purely based on improvement or tweaking, it's always been monumental change. The environment we've operated in is very dynamic, almost too dynamic, where every facet under which you operate business has changed for us... it was the recognition that we had to become proactive in order to survive" (Tim Camiller, formerly CFO/Newly appointed CEO).

Balmain Leagues Club operates in an extremely volatile sector. Over the past ten years it has had to work tirelessly, initially just to keep the club solvent and then to transform it into a sustainable on-going concern. Balmain, and clubs like it have been (and continue to be) vulnerable to the machinations of a multitude of external factors that each in their turn and collectively could have forced its doors to shut. The major factors that impacted on them between 1995-2006 include:

THE COMMODITISATION OF 'THE GAME'

The advent of Super League in 1995 intensified and fast-tracked the commoditisation of rugby league. The influence of high powered media players transformed the sport into a high stakes entertainment industry, inflating players' salary and placing a great deal of financial pressure on clubs. Clubs went from being able to cover operating costs with $1 million dollars to suddenly needing five times that to be able to continue supporting its rugby league teams. Clubs hoping to move forward on the strength of tradition were faced with the very real and the imminent prospect of dissolution if they did not respond quickly and effectively to the changing landscape. In Balmain's case, a merger in 1999 with the Wests Magpies Football Club created Wests Tigers enabling both of them to literally 'stay in the game'.

CHANGING SOCIAL DEMOGRAPHICS AND INCREASED COMPETITION

While its origins were steeped in working class tradition, since the 1960's Balmain has slowly and steadily undergone a process of gentrification.[1] The social demographics have shifted from being predominately working class to predominantly middle class.[2] Accompanying this shift in demographics has been a proliferation of restaurants, pubs, bars and cafes, all chasing the same customer base as Balmain Leagues Club.

NEW LEGISLATION – THE IMPACT OF GAMING AND ANTI-SMOKING LAWS

Typically about 80% of revenue generated by clubs comes from gaming (Sydney Morning Herald, 2005). Of the $17.4 million dollars of Balmain's revenue in 2004 for example, $12.9 million was generated by poker machines.

Around 1997 Balmain faced a significant threat when competition in the gaming market intensified. Not only was the Casino established a stone's throw away but poker machines were introduced into hotels increasing the number of poker machines in the area by 2,000 in a very short space of time. Indicative of the devastating effect this had on the club, was the dramatic drop in gaming turnover between 2000 and 2001 – $2 million dollars per month within a six month period! The club lost many of its gaming players because it was not able to meet their needs due to the regulations governing gaming in clubs, the likes of which did not apply to the Casino.[3]

Every facet under which you operate business has changed for us... it was the recognition that we had to become proactive in order to survive

Changes in legislation and social trends continue to impact the club's financial prospects. In 2004 for example, the New South Wales government introduced a new tax on poker machines that will gradually increase Balmain's gaming machine tax to 49.09%. The Clubs Association of NSW estimates that the combined impact of this tax with the implementation of new anti-smoking legislation (by 2007, all indoor areas of the club must be smoke free) will cost the club millions of dollars in lost revenue while at the same time, they will need to pay an additional $9.2 million tax revenue in the years to 2011. The high impact of gaming legislation forced Balmain to acknowledge its vulnerable financial position in relying on revenue from gaming. Part of its strategic intent in embarking on a cultural change program was to strengthen revenue from non-gaming sources such as the food and beverage business. This would ensure it was at least in part buffered from the impact of such legislation and others of its kind. In order for this to come to fruition, the business needed to undergo a significant transformation.

1 ABC Asia Pacific Broadcasting Web Page – Henderson, P *Living History* March 8, 2006
2 ABS Statistics from Census 2001 and ABS Average weekly earnings for that same period. The data shows that almost 50% of people living in Balmain earn at or above the average weekly wage. Further 35% of inhabitants in Balmain earn between 1.5 & 2 times the average weekly wage.
3 For example, Clubs were not able to advertise; they could not offer cash promotions and all winnings over $1,000 had to be paid by cheque whereas none of these limitations applied to the Casino.

The Case for Transformation

When in 1995, Danny Munk joined Balmain Leagues Club as Chief Executive Officer; he found an organisation anchored in functional silos and an environment low in trust with a number of personal agendas driving behaviours and actions. Danny inherited an organisation that was likely to pay the cost of an internal environment that resisted the changes being demanded by the industry and market.

In 1995 Balmain Leagues Club's ability to adapt to the environment was being hijacked on a number of levels by competing agendas based on self interest.

"It was an old style business broken into fiefdoms, you had the leagues club and the football club, and you had the leaders and the followers. In the leagues club, for example, it was the principle of the Animal Farm. We're all equal except some are far more equal than others. There was a culture of 'we will do as we're told as long as they see what we're doing'… By the end of 1995 we had lost a lot of good staff and that hit home to me because I had spent a fair amount of time encouraging people and thought we were heading in the right direction… Suddenly by December a stack of good quality staff left and when people go, who you think could have added to your business you have to ask yourself… what's going on here?"

We had people with talent but they didn't believe anything that came out of our mouths, or anything that was written

When Danny investigated the situation further it became apparent that processes he thought were in place were not in place, his own management team were high on lip service but low on action and this ultimately led to a significant change and turnover in his management team.

The first eighteen months of his tenure was a very difficult period. Externally, the club was facing threats on all fronts and internally, morale was low, turnover was high and capable senior management was thin on the ground. The external environment demanded his time, but the lack of solid management experience and skills at the coalface meant that Danny was spending too much time micro-managing club issues.

Enter Wayne Forrest in 1997. With a solid background in management in the club industry in New South Wales, Danny appointed Wayne to the role of Operations Manager (eventually being promoted to General Manager – Operations) and was given the brief of implementing robust operational systems to improve the performance of the club. This did not prove to be easy, with such a long history of being a command and control, punishment oriented culture all management efforts directed at change were tarnished with the brush of their predecessors. They struggled to get the message across.

"We had people with talent but they didn't believe anything that came out of our mouths, or anything that was written… we found that no matter what we said and how we said it we were getting the little bouncing doggy effect in the car, the head going up and down but you know that by the look of the little doggy that there's nothing there… so at that point we had to find a mechanism where people could start understanding the story but also finding some way to get people to believe the story" (Danny Munk, CEO 1995-2006).

2000-2002

Balmain Leagues Club

Phase **2**

Test

The Approach

Balmain Leagues Club did not move directly into measuring its culture, its journey began In 1997 when Wayne Forrest had been personally introduced to Human Synergistics' Life Styles Inventory™ (LSI) tool through Peter Donnan a KPMG consultant working with Balmain at the time. Initially the impact of the LSI feedback on Wayne was to facilitate a deep personal realisation that his own behaviour (that which he had been rewarded and promoted for throughout his career) was fundamentally counter to his core values.

It was through this personal learning that Wayne began to see the potential of the LSI and OCI to support the changes he, Danny and the rest of the Executive Team had been attempting to usher in. The impact of Wayne's initial and early exposure to the LSI was to kick start a comprehensive approach to culture change under the collective leadership of the Executive Team that struck a fine balance between process and behaviours. Initially, Balmain engaged a number of accredited consultants to conduct a few workshops introducing the LSI 1 & 2 to the organisation.

After a period of about eighteen months since arriving at Balmain and encouraged by the initial positive impact the LSI seemed to be having on the business, Wayne began to evolve his thinking about change further. Although he did not have a master plan, intuitively he was clear about the next step.

People walked away saying, 'you know I have a bit more understanding of why some of the things around me happen and how I contribute'

"I think I knew instinctively where we were heading, but the actual plan only went as far as the next stage because we were learning as we went and that learning was so significant that there was no way I could plan as much as I normally would. New information was becoming available to me so quickly... from the accreditation process, other interaction within the group, my own personal experiences and input of other people. One of the things that I did know or that became logical to me was that we needed to measure it, measure the culture" (Wayne Forrest Operations Manager/General Manager 1997-2004).

Wayne convinced Danny Munk and Tim Camiller (the CFO at the time, now CEO) to invest in conducting an Organisational Culture Inventory® (OCI) to measure where the culture was at. Measurement occurred at the end of 1999 and the debriefing of results occurred in 2000.

Danny Munk comments that: "The exercise was interesting I can't say that we were fully sold at that time but a number of people walked away saying, 'you know I have a bit more understanding *of why some of the things around me happen and how I contribute' or 'I can see where you may want to take this business and I may not fit.' It was not an outcome I expected but it was a good outcome… Out of that Wayne became very passionate about LSI and OCI because it enabled him to provide a vehicle for people to see how they impacted others and how others impacted them and the outcomes of this impact without using the words 'right or wrong.'"*

Culture Survey Results

The diagnostic tools Balmain utilized throughout the six years of their cultural transformation journey were:

Year	Diagnostic	Target Group
2000-2005	Life Styles Inventory™ 1 & 2 (LSI)	Executive Team, Duty Managers, Supervisors and other Administrative Managers
2000, 2001	Organizational Culture Inventory® (OCI)	Conducted across the organisation
2002	Organizational Culture Inventory® (OCI)/ Organizational Effectiveness Inventory™ (OEI) Combined	Conducted across the organisation
2004, 2005	OCI/OEI Combined	Conducted in subsets of the organisation: IT, Operations, Administration
2003, 2005	Leadership/Impact® (L/I)	Executive Team

The intention of this section is to establish Balmain's cultural and leadership style baseline. For the purposes of this section the initial 'test' period is defined as 2000-2002. The results in 2000 are initially spotlighted because they really set the benchmark and created the strategy for the cultural transformation of the club, although some of the test data on leadership are drawn from between 2001-2002.

Balmain conducted its first OCI in 1999. The survey identified the organisation's Preferred culture, the 'best it could be' and then measured the Actual operating culture 'as it is now'. This information then provided a basis for informing the change strategy and planning initiatives.

Balmain's Preferred culture (see Figure 1) showed a strong aspiration towards a highly Constructive or 'Blue' culture which is consistent with data across Australia and New Zealand. Most organisations' Preferred culture places all Constructive styles well above the 50th percentile and shows the Defensive styles well under the 50th percentile. Balmain's preferred primary style was Humanistic-Encouraging, closely followed by Achievement, Self-Actualizing and Affiliative Styles.

By way of contrast, the Actual Culture results identified that the primary cultural style of the

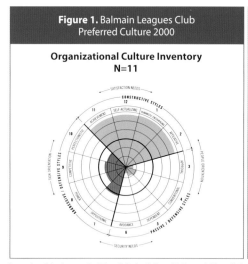

Figure 1. Balmain Leagues Club
Preferred Culture 2000

Organizational Culture Inventory
N=11

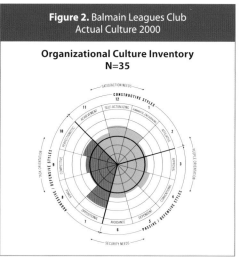

Figure 2. Balmain Leagues Club
Actual Culture 2000

Organizational Culture Inventory
N=35

organisation was Oppositional (see Figure 2). Staff indicated that they experienced the culture as implicitly or explicitly encouraging them to 'look for mistakes', 'point out flaws', and 'oppose new ideas'. Strongly backing the Oppositional style was the Perfectionistic style with staff indicating that they were encouraged to 'persist and endure', 'keep on top of everything' and 'appear to be competent'. The results also showed the Passive/Defensive styles of Avoidance and Conventional, encouraging staff to 'fit in', 'make a good impression' and 'not take chances'. The combination of Aggressive/Defensive and Passive/Defensive behaviours created a dynamic interplay which explained the difficulties senior management were experiencing in bringing about change. The collective impact of this dynamic was a Defensive culture focussed on maintaining a facade of being in control and competent, while at other levels changes that would enable the organisation to adapt to the environment were actively resisted and undermined.

On the positive side, despite this interplay between the Defensive styles, the Constructive styles of Self-Actualizing, Humanistic-Encouraging and Achievement styles were above the 50th percentile. Better still, there was a reasonably high level of agreement among staff indicating that their experiences of these styles were shared. This indicated that Balmain had a fairly solid basis on which to build its cultural change program. This foundation was important given the need for fast change.

The Leadership-Culture Connection

Leadership impacts Culture. Culture impacts leadership. They both impact performance. One of the fundamental ways in which leaders impact the organisation is through their leadership style and the way in which their behaviour affects the environment or context in which their staff operate (Cooke, 2003).

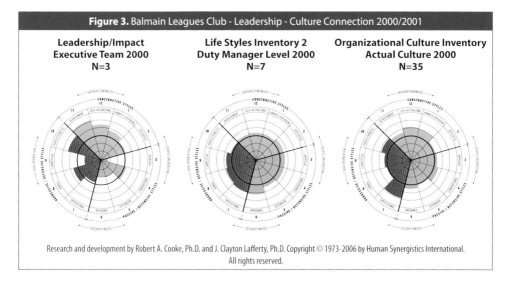

Figure 3. Balmain Leagues Club - Leadership - Culture Connection 2000/2001

Balmain has been measuring the styles strategies and impact of its leadership team since 2000 through both the LSI and Leadership/Impact. The circumplexes in Figure 3 show the original OCI test results in relation to the Leadership/Impact composite circumplex for the Executive Team and the LSI composite circumplex of the Duty Managers. Briefly, the Leadership/Impact tool differs from the LSI diagnostic in that it focuses on the 'shadow' cast by the leaders – that is how their leadership strategies impact or drive the behaviour of their direct reports and other members of the organisation (cause and effect), while the LSI focuses on the description of the focal individual's behaviour as seen by others (the meaning others attribute to behaviours). Both are used in improving leadership effectiveness.

These circumplexes show that the influence of the Duty Managers overall is likely to have been more pervasive than the influence of the Executive Team in terms of driving the primary Oppositional style of the culture. This is indicated by the fact that members of the organisation described Duty Managers' observed behaviours as primarily Avoidance and Oppositional (see Duty Managers' LSI 2 in Figure 3); however, the Leadership/Impact results for the Executive Team do not indicate that the Executive Team encourages this behaviour.

The Leadership/Impact feedback on the Executive Team however, shows that staff believed the Executive Team was causing them to behave in Perfectionistic ways, and as such it is also likely that the expectations for Perfectionistic behaviour by the Duty Managers contributed to the Aggressive/Defensive elements and the Conventional style of the overall organisation.

Both levels of leadership then impacted and likely drove the overall strength of the Aggressive/Defensive behaviours reflected in the culture. The factors that drive Aggressive/Defensive behaviours in organisations relate to goal-setting practices, job insecurity and disempowerment at the individual level, methods of reinforcement, sources of power and influence at the group level, respect for individuals and cultural values at the organisational

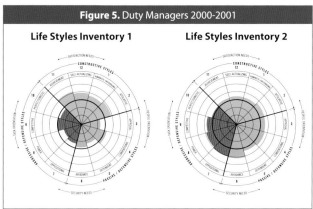

level. The data obtained through the combined OCI/OEI later in 2002 (discussed in more detail in the Re-Test section of this case study) support this point.

Juxtapositioning the Duty Managers' LSI 1 (self concept) and LSI 2 (description by others) results against the L/I results of the Executive Team permits examination of the leadership-culture connections (see Figures 4 and 5). Given that the LSI 'Self' circumplex describes how the Duty Managers see their own behaviours and thinking styles and the Leadership/Impact circumplex describes the impact the Executive Team has on Duty Managers (their direct reports) behaviour:

■ The motivation for the Duty Managers to behave in Perfectionistic and Conventional ways may have led to staff describing the Managers' styles as Avoidance and Conventional.

■ It is likely that the Executive Team positively influenced the strength of the Constructive styles in the Duty Managers' LSI 1 and 2 circumplexes.

One of the greatest insights these data provide, however, is that the Duty Managers' thinking styles and possibly their intentions, (as shown by the LSI 1 circumplex) were much more constructive than there behaviours (LSI 2).

Balmain's cultural transformation was spearheaded by developing the capability of both its Executive Team and its team of Duty Managers.

THE EXECUTIVE TEAM – "CHANGE STARTS AT THE TOP"

In the early years of the cultural transformation process, Wayne Forrest had begun working intensively with the Duty Managers in the operations area. While the Executive Team at the time were supportive of the initiatives in operations, it is fair to say that this type of leadership development was not yet wide spread throughout the organisation. Interestingly the very success of the work began to cause some tensions with other managers and sections of the organisation. The impact of one group of people operating differently in the way they approached and did business inadvertently placed pressure on other groups within the organisation that were still operating in the same way.

This emerging issue highlighted the need for Executive Team input and participation in leading an organisation-wide cultural change process. Danny Munk, as CEO, led a small core group of three Executives: Wayne Forrest as Operations Manager, Tim Camiller as Chief Financial Officer and Marcelle Proper as IT Manager (evolved into IT and Marketing Manager). All of the executives came from diverse backgrounds, experiences and brought with them different talents. They were all also strong personalities with distinct and at times, quite different views about how things should be done. This made for some interesting tensions at the top level. It was determined that the Executive Team would benefit from having an outside expert work with them. Roma Gaster was engaged for this purpose. She is the founder and Managing Director of Karibu Education International Pty Ltd. With a diverse knowledge base spanning economics, languages and organisational change, and over twenty years working in the field of organisational effectiveness across a number of industries, Wayne found in Roma a like-minded and enthusiastic partner to support him and the club on their journey. As the early work with Roma Gaster proceeded, it became clear that the Executive Team needed to work on their relationships with one another and their effectiveness as a team. As a result, the

> # There was no point in just using the words, unless people were prepared to get involved in the process

Executive Team went off-site for a two and a half day workshop with Roma as the facilitator. Held at Wiseman's Ferry, the workshop was called 'Raising the Bar' and it was at this workshop that the four leaders began to work at a very deep level on the dynamics within the team and how this affected the team's overall performance and leadership of the organisation.

"… here you had these four dynamics, we all had individual strong personalities with our own issues and we really needed to get that team working a lot stronger, Roma had already done some leadership stuff with us… people were starting to use the words but weren't necessarily living the process, it was the first time that the group started to learn that there was no point in just using the words, unless people were prepared to get involved in the process" (Danny Munk, CEO 1995-2006).

This workshop represented a turning point not just for the individuals at a personal level but for their team and especially for the club. At the workshop, the team of individuals was provided with an insight into the 'real person' behind the mask or persona that was presented at work and to the world. They each began to understand what drove each other, what pushed each other's buttons and appreciate where they were all coming from. The workshop helped them create a level of safety in how they related to one another by enabling each person to show something of their vulnerability without judgement or blame.

Roma introduced the team to a number of processes and tools that enabled them to learn how to give each other feedback directly and honestly. In one such exercise an individual would leave the room while the other team members discussed that individual's impact on the team in terms of their behaviour. When the individual came back into the room, their team mates would explain to them which of their behaviours caused them to act constructively and which of their behaviours caused the greatest problems to the team and staff throughout the organisation. The individual then left the room to reflect on the feedback they had been given. When they returned they explained to their team members how they wanted to be 'called' on their behaviour. They referred to this process 'calling the line'. This analogy of above the line behaviours and below the line behaviours has been used across many organisations to facilitate this kind of feedback, however its success depends on individuals within the team committing to the process.

This experience expanded their collective tolerance and acceptance for behaviours they saw in one another, which initially may have triggered a defensive or angry response. All left Wisemen's Ferry with a very clear understanding and appreciation for the essence of communication, the ability to 'hear the message under the noise' and the understanding of how this could impact on the leadership of their respective teams. They all made a commitment to work much more constructively with each other and their teams. More importantly, they left having established a commitment to each other that they would 'call the line' individually but that in some cases if it seemed too daunting or difficult (in terms of giving such feedback to the CEO, for example) their commitment was to seek the assistance of a team mate and to provide feedback in a pair or a trio.

The impact of this commitment and learning about teams and how to be a team resulted in each member of the Executive Team becoming more involved in each other's areas. Tim Camiller, for example, stepped out of the confines of Finance and got more involved in Administration; Marcelle Proper got more involved in Operations. A blending and inclusiveness of talents and ideas began to occur, so that they operated as an ecological system.

This was not to say there was a fairy tale ending. It's not that they left Wisemen's Ferry and 'lived in harmony happily ever after' – behavioural change isn't that easy. The impact of the team's renewed understanding of their team dynamics and the conscious commitment to being Constructive, created a basis to begin to practise the change. The stated commitment was not in and of itself enough. They had to also consciously work the behaviours – as Danny says 'get involved with the process' every moment of every day. They chose to continue to work in the Constructive, even when every instinct compelled a habitual defensive reaction. To help them get through this learning and practise, Danny played a crucial role (as did Wayne on occasion) in facilitating this change process by acting as go-between when individuals in the team were grating up against each other's style. This role was not a planned decision but rather something that emerged as the team practiced improving their relationships. While it often goes unrecognized in organisational change studies, it is an important function. The 'go-between' plays a 'connector' role when the team is under stress. They enable the communication lines to stay open and to facilitate understanding of the message behind the behaviour. It keeps everyone on track and moving forward to their goals and commitments and serves as a constant reminder to the team of their goals and commitment. It ensures that any progress gained is maintained and continues even in the most trying of circumstances. While this role need not be played only by the CEO, it is arguably most powerful and of most value when the CEO assumes this position. To explain why this is, it is useful to think about an organisation as a ship. While most of the crew are quite comfortable for the first mate to steer, there is an added level of security and comfort when the captain is at the helm. There were other roles, however, which were as essential. Danny describes Marcelle and Tim as being 'safety zone' people, they became the 'go to' people if staff had issues or concerns about the behaviours of Danny and Wayne. They enabled and encouraged staff to claim their voice. In some instances staff requested to work with an independent external party. In these instances, Roma came to work with teams to tease out issues and their solutions. In this sense, the Executive Team made it clear that if staff needed access to Roma directly as a mentor to facilitate their growth, they were not about to stand in their way. Rather they facilitated and enabled the process.

The work that the Executive Team did on themselves individually and as a team was key to the success of the Club's cultural transformation process. Each of these individuals made a personal and professional commitment to lead in a constructive way. They took on board the responsibility of not just walking the talk but living the talk. The impact of this unified commitment was to create a 'safety zone'. Staff saw their leaders visibly change and witnessed the increased possibilities that this brought. Staff in the focus groups conducted for this research project referred to this as being 'inspiring'. That the top team was prepared to start the change by changing themselves held a lot of currency with encouraging staff to get on board and trust the rhetoric coming from their leadership. Further evidence of the top team's commitment to sustaining a Constructive culture came in 2004, when just after Wayne's departure from the club, the team decided that Danny was probably best placed to become accredited in the LSI and OCI tools. He was not a lone operator though, as he continued the work, Tim and Marcelle were intricately involved in determining the direction and nature of the initiatives to be conducted. It is a rare thing for a Chief Executive Officer to take a substantial amount of time out of his busy schedule to educate himself in tools and processes that facilitate organisational change and effectiveness. This action speaks volumes about the degree of commitment shown by Danny to ensure the continued growth of both his people and the club.

GETTING THE DUTY MANAGERS INVOLVED

The OCI results helped to clarify and shape the strategy with regard to the Duty Managers. The combination of low Humanistic-Encouraging and high Oppositional cultural norms led to the decision to focus the next twelve to eighteen months on increasing the Humanistic-Encouraging style and decreasing the Oppositional style. The results also helped Wayne determine where the resources needed to be invested. Wayne worked on the principle that – if the fundamental behaviours that are associated with the Humanistic-Encouraging style are training, coaching, mentoring and helping each other learn and grow, then he did not have the correct structure or the correct capabilities within his people to promote this cultural norm.

"In the past we had always tried to rectify things by changing structure in isolation to anything else, but now we had come to the recognition of that old catch phrase of 'strategy before structure', was what we had to deal with. It was a really simple question, if leadership was about helping people to grow, then the only people we didn't have involved in that process was the people who were in a direct leadership role – the Duty Managers – nor did we measure it nor was it part of their performance criteria… so we set about putting some things in place to address that gap" (Wayne Forrest, General Manager Operations 1997-2004).

Balmain Leagues Club

Phase **3** Action

Levers for Change

Viewed in its entirety, Balmain's cultural transformation was anchored by a behaviourally-based strategy reinforced by systems and processes that were designed to provide staff with the opportunity to practice the new behaviours and values the organisation had stated it wanted to see.

Overall, the effect of this program of initiatives was to shift Balmain Leagues Club from being reactive to proactive and from being tactical to strategic, while building their capacity to be more agile and responsive to the environment. Adaptability was clearly identified as a desirable strategic capability. There were eight key elements to Balmain's cultural change strategy:

- Leadership Development
- Recruitment and Selection
- Induction
- Performance Management
- Training and Development
- Reward and Recognition
- Planning and Decision Making
- Consequence Management – The importance of reflection and learning from mistakes

LEADERSHIP DEVELOPMENT

Just after the 2000 OCI debriefing of results, Wayne decided to become accredited in the LSI process. It was while he was on the accreditation course that he met Roma Gaster. From first contact with the Balmain Leagues Club people, Roma could see that Balmain was different.

"It takes huge commitment and courage to make this happen. The fact that Balmain Leagues Club is smaller enables it to be more agile and nimble which generally helps to facilitate change a little faster than larger organisations with thousands of employees. At BLC they have broken my perception of what club employees are like because they are so hungry for development and growth. In the last 6 years I have been positively challenged by the team because they continually want more – meaning I am constantly looking for new ways to take them above and beyond."

The bedrock of the transformation strategy was grounded in the assumption and belief that leaders' behaviours were the difference between dissolution and survival. The leadership development programs co-created by the Wayne and Roma at that time focussed primarily at two levels – the Executive Team and the Duty Managers. The intent was to develop an adaptable, high performance culture by engaging leaders, managers and supervisors in the process of building Constructive thinking and behavioural styles through the Club.

RE-INVIGORATING THE DUTY MANAGERS

In the first twelve to eighteen months, the focus of the program was to increase the Humanistic-Encouraging and Achievement Styles. The target group identified as pivotal to turning the club culture around were the Duty Managers because their leadership directly impacted front line staff and thus, customers. A number of systems changes were required in order to facilitate the engagement of the Duty Managers (outlined in further detail throughout this section). These changes were not insignificant and accelerated the cultural change process. It began with Wayne re-thinking and re-positioning the role of Duty Managers. The rhetoric around this repositioning was backed by additional resources. In one of the most financially difficult times, when most companies would have rationalised positions and employee numbers, Balmain Leagues Club decided to invest in and expand the ranks of the Duty Managers. In order for the strategy to work Wayne had to redistribute the workload of the Duty Managers and re-organise the distribution of influence to ensure that they could take on a more empowered and strategic role in the leadership of the Club, in particular of the front line staff.

To step up to the challenge, the managers needed considerable training and development. Over the next two years, Wayne developed and implemented a comprehensive training program for the group which involved club specific knowledge, skills and experience, but also primarily behaviour-based workshops facilitated by Roma that covered a breadth and depth of content.

> **We would look at skills development around behaviours... to drive the business outcomes required and to give something back to them personally**

"At every stage we would review our performance and in conjunction we would look at skills development for them (Duty Managers) around behaviours, so more skills around listening and coaching and mentoring, problem solving and decision making and team development. We ran a whole series of workshops for the managers to develop them to drive the business outcomes required, but also give something back to them personally" (Wayne Forrest, General Manager Operations, 1997-2004).

The impact of these behaviour-based, transformational workshops built trust and engagement through honest discussions about the individual, the team and the organisation and how these three levels impacted on each other. The team became stronger by sharing the highs and lows of their individual and team experiences, both in business and in their personal lives.

RECRUITMENT AND SELECTION

An integral part of the cultural change process required Duty Managers to become more involved in the decisions around selecting and hiring staff. To facilitate this, a two pronged approach was adopted.

Firstly, the existing job descriptions were re-developed to clearly outline the specific roles and responsibilities of all positions across the club. The job descriptions were developed in a manner whereby the focus was taken from the actual tasks and duties and placed on the outcomes and standards required of each position – both at a task level and a behavioural level. This established a set of objective criteria which defined the skills and attributes required and the standards at which people were expected to perform.

Secondly, the interview process was enhanced by the inclusion of and an emphasis on behavioural questions and assessment. The ultimate objective in this approach was to assess, as far as reasonably possible, the likelihood of this person 'fitting in' to the culture.

The aim is always to find a person who comes with the capabilities to perform the tasks required of the position as well as the personal qualities that align with the Preferred culture.

Irrespective of the task capabilities, the overriding selection criteria is always the personal and interpersonal attributes.

A key part of this process, involved the Duty Managers being involved in interviewing staff and the interview process and then the subsequent follow-through with the induction and ongoing training processes. The interview process is the first step in the development of an ongoing relationship with each employee, with the people who will be leading them on a day-to-day basis.

INDUCTION PROCESS

Balmain also recognised that the first few days, weeks and months of a new employee's service is arguably the most important time in establishing the relationship between employer and employee. It is at this time that new employees begin to learn about the culture implicitly (by watching and noticing how others work with one another, how they are treated and supported) and explicitly by what is communicated and how this is communicated to them. A new process of induction was introduced to the club which involved assigning every new employee to the 'care' of a Duty Manager. The Duty Manager was responsible for ensuring that the new employee received all the information and support they required to perform their role, including one to one job instruction (refer to Tigers Training Program, p. 250). From their very first day, new staff were led by example and taught about the culture that Balmain Leagues Club was growing and cultivating.

Again, a multi-faceted approach was adopted to ensure that the approach taken within the induction process supported the ongoing development of a Constructive culture.

It was recognized that the 'standard' system of inducting new people into the organisation was fundamentally working against the development of a Constructive culture and in fact was likely to be driving some of the Defensive behaviours.

In particular, Balmain challenged the notion of issuing an employee handbook and having new employees sign off on their acceptance and understanding of the contents. Balmain believed that this is likely to – either explicitly or implicitly – send the message of 'follow the rules' and 'do it perfectly' or 'we will use this document to discipline you with later – when you stuff up'.

The employee handbook was not done away with in total, rather, the approach that provided some balance to the message sent to a new employee at that time.

Wayne activated a three hour induction program for all existing employees in the first instance and then ongoing for all new employees. This induction session was conducted by

Wayne as General Manager and contained the Vision for the Club, the internal and external environment and challenges. It also contained a session on the values and behaviours that are expected and promoted at the Club. This part of the program was underpinned by the use of the *Understanding the OCI & the 12 circumplex Styles*™ workbook and a 4m² circumplex mat that was used to facilitate role plays and discussions around the culture.

Another 'standard' characteristic of the Induction process is to send the new employee around the club for a 'tour'. It was realized that, the intended message about 'how we do things around here' was always being sent accurately. Balmain set about ensuring that they selected and trained the people who were conducting the tours to ensure that the 'right' message was being sent.

> **Reviews stopped being about what you did right and wrong and what you've done well, reviews started being about stop start continue, about job design**

PERFORMANCE MANAGEMENT

As the cultural transformation continued, one of the issues that had emerged relatively early on was the need for the Club's systems to provide opportunity for staff to live and practise constructive behaviours. In the early stages of the change process, people were using the words of Constructive styles but this was not necessarily translating through their behaviour.

"That fell back very much on us, for them to be using the words but not live the words meant that we (the Executive Team) had not sold the message because this meant that they didn't believe that we would honour our side of the bargain which was to allow people latitude to live this thing. So from 2001 and 2002 we changed the way we did reviews. Reviews stopped being about what you did right and wrong and what you've done well, reviews started being about Stop-Start-Continue, about job design, if the review was on a negative basis then unless you knew about it, it was not going to be discussed, we started to set a policy… if for 364 days you were good, you couldn't be bad on the 365th so that was one big thing" (Danny Munk CEO 1995-2004).

Prior to the cultural change process, performance appraisals were a one-way communication event in which most of the feedback was reactive and carried out in a 'Management by Exception' manner. They were also inconsistent in terms of timing and rigour. A new approach to assessing performance was introduced as highlighted in Figure 6, primarily focussed on delivering on the Achievement and Humanistic-Encouraging styles. It integrated the learnings from the work with the circumplex in its process. It was conversation based and started with a group review of the business in which all managers were involved before cascading the appraisal process down to individuals. It was simple but very robust and comprehensive. The way the process was organized and debriefed created a level of safety and comfort which limited the level of anxiety that employees may have otherwise experienced around appraisals. As a result of this environment, the process was also extremely challenging to the individuals.

The process involved two workshops. The first one was a group review of the business and the strategic objectives and the second one focussed on individual performance.

"We relied on two tools to review business and individual performance – the Constructive styles of the 'HS Circumplex' together with 'The Debrief Formula' to focus on task (results) and behaviours (relationships). At the Strategic Review, the group and functional teams presented a summary on what they had achieved and what they were going to do. At the second workshop, the Individual Review, each person presented their own appraisals on flip-chart paper. Everyone walked around the room looking at each others' flip-charts. Then people gave each other feedback in a group setting specifically about the individual's leadership style (using a process called 'Stop-Start-Continue')" (Roma Gaster, Karibu Education International).

For the Individual Reviews, the process used simple, open questions that focussed on supporting the individuals' development of the Constructive styles, while balancing the task and behavioural aspects of their work. For example, the question asked regarding the individual's development was 'what can I say about myself this year that I couldn't say about myself last year?' At each review, employees and employer committed to delivering a set of objectives in service to one another's objectives.

We have quite a few different roles now because it met the need of the growth of people

Whilst this process was implemented initially as an annual activity, over time the performance review process (as shown in Figure 6) was facilitated on an 'as needed' basis. It recognized that for people to perform well and maintain a high level of satisfaction, their individual needs needed to be met. Some people in the organisation required more feedback or more frequent feedback and support than others.

Invariably the review process was supported by a workshop designed to address the development of the team's capabilities around one of the four Constructive styles.

PERFORMANCE MANAGEMENT AND JOB DESIGN IN GROWING PEOPLE

As the new performance review process got traction in the organisation a new type of conversation was occurring around performance.

Danny Munk reflects: *"It was quite confrontational for people to talk about. We were saying, 'OK this is what we said at the beginning of the year, this is where your LSI was then, now lets take a look at your Stop-Starts and Continue from 12 months ago: What are the changes that you have made, let's have a look at the Re-Test and take it from there'. A lot of people found this confronting but on the other hand they found that if they started saying 'if I could just work a little different my life would be different.' We started to say yes to a lot of that."*

Through these performance review discussions, people started identifying some of the barriers and limitations they experienced in their roles. These discussions invariably led to redesigning a number of jobs to enable people to continue to develop and grow. While the Executive Team were, in principle, supportive of the need to do this, they anticipated that it would not necessarily be easy to bring about change. In the end it was easier than they thought, as Danny explained.

"We thought it would be hard but it was surprisingly simple, because it was administrative staff who wanted to work differently, some who had families wanted to work 40 hours but not necessarily in

five days, when people said they weren't money driven, they actually meant it, but they needed other things and these could be education, support and our willingness to give them a taste of another role, which technically speaking, they shouldn't have been involved in. By giving them a taste of another role to see if there would be an opportunity for them to grow, meant that when positions came up they could absorb some of the parts of that job. In some cases we would break positions up to enable others to take up the opportunities. Every time someone left the organisation we didn't automatically fill the position, we sat down with the team and asked them 'what should happen with this role?'. We now have quite a few different roles because it met the need of the growth of people. The redesign of jobs was all about allowing these people to grow and in turn allow them to hand over parts of their job to let others grow."

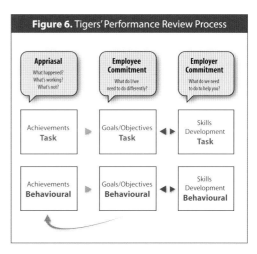

Figure 6. Tigers' Performance Review Process

There are numerous examples now of how job design was used to further grow and develop individuals, as well as a means of shoring up the capability in the organisation. Balmain's IT manager, for example, also looks after Marketing. One of the best examples is the changes to the original cellarman position. Over the past ten or so years this role has evolved from moving, counting and storing kegs to purchasing officer.

"Our current cellarman is actually our purchasing officer and he uses the manual side of the job as relaxation from all the purchasing of all goods into the club. And the assistant to the cellarman, who would have previously been taught to stock kegs is now going to courses on stock control, systems and accounting so it is now a skilled position as opposed to being an unskilled position and interestingly our cost of goods has dropped and consistently dropped and we've seen some very tough times since 1999. There are lots of things we cannot control and the things we could control was the stock control" (Danny Munk, CEO 1995 -2006).

TRAINING AND DEVELOPMENT

Balmain implemented a new system with regard to training its people, the system is shown in Figure 7 on the next page. The measure of success for the training system when initiated was to support the Humanistic-Encouraging and Affiliative styles.

In 2001, Balmain Leagues Club developed its own internal training program. The Tigers In-house Training program consisted of eleven internal courses and/or training programs, delivered and assessed by a manager with the relevant experience and qualifications.

The Club has also developed a relationship with the Club Managers Association Australia (CMAA) through their Education arm, Club Management Development Australia (CMDA), that enables its employees to undertake recognition of prior learning for nationally recognised units within and up to the Advanced Diploma of Hospitality (Club Management) qualification level.

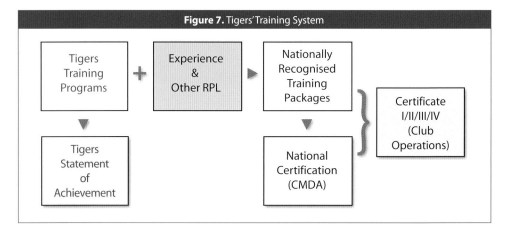

Figure 7. Tigers' Training System

The training program covers the Induction Program (consisting of 4 stages), apprenticeships, management traineeships, work experience as well as providing conduits to achieve the nationally recognised Certificate IV Hospitality (Operations).

Other training supported and/or sponsored by the Club included employees undertaking courses such as a Bachelor of Business in Management & Psychology (Charles Sturt University), Gaming Management Development Program (Leagues Club Association NSW), Microsoft Certification/Accreditation and a M.B.A. Human Resources (U.N.E.).

In addition, all Duty Managers were trained to Certificate IV Training and Assessor Qualification and the practical application of the skills acquired through this process was integrated with other people management processes such as Induction, Recruitment and Performance Management.

REWARD AND RECOGNITION

When Danny and Wayne first started at the Club, the reward program extended to the issuance of a 'Christmas Bonus'. There was no criteria for any rewards that were given, and in fact there were no real rewards for anything other than 'turning up'. Over time, a credible rewards and recognition system grew and eventually included, but was not limited to the following:

- **Professional Development Recognition** – employees were recognized in an ongoing manner through the successful completion of internal 'training' activities and the subsequent issuing of in-house certification and nationally recognized certification and qualifications (see Tigers Training System, Figure 7).
- **Mid-year Service Awards and Training Awards Presentation Event** – this was usually in the form of a dinner or cocktail party held within the venue to reward and recognize achievement of 'time in' and training achievements. Service Awards are issued for 3, 5, 10, 15 and 20 years service.
- **Tigers Team Tournament** – a series of up to 6 events per year, including golf, lawn bowls, ten pin bowling, trivia, tennis etc. The employees were members of one of

3 or 4 teams which participated in these events – usually with modified rules, over the course of the year. Points achieved were predominantly team focussed, rather than individual. A key to the success of these events was the explicit expectation that people behave in line with the four Constructive styles – therefore, quite often challenging people to deal with their competitive tendencies.

■ **Annual Awards Presentation Dinner** – usually held off-site and focusing on recognizing individual, team and organisational achievements for the year. Individuals were recognized through a staff and management nomination process based around some clear qualifiers. Teams were recognized through the presentation of trophies for achievements in the Team Tournament.

STRATEGIC AND OPERATIONAL PLANNING

While the emphasis in the cultural change strategy was on increasing the Humanistic-Encouraging style and decreasing Oppositional, a fair amount of work was also done on increasing the team's Achievement orientation. As part of this focus all leaders and Duty Managers were invited to participate in Strategic Planning sessions facilitated by Roma Gaster.

"Importantly, and in parallel to the culture and leadership focus, the Executive Team, the Board and the Duty Managers were also involved in creating the Club's strategic plan. This was not done as a separate initiative; rather the strategic plan was viewed as being an important piece in the jigsaw puzzle of building and sustaining a high performance culture" (Roma Gaster, Karibu Education International).

These sessions included the Executive Team, Duty Managers, Managers of the Football Club and frequently members of the Board. These workshops included scenario planning and developing the strategic intent, goals and objectives for both the Leagues and the Football Clubs.

Instead of the strategy being driven by CEO and Executive Team, this process was co-created and owned by the Board, the Executive Team and Duty Managers. Through effective communication and engagement – ownership of the planning process was and continues to be evident within the Operational Teams at Balmain Leagues Club. The outcomes of the Strategic and operational planning processes were then, as appropriate, incorporated into each manager's job description and/or used to underpin future performance reviews.

DECISION MAKING

In addition, at the individual level each Leagues Club Manager was supported and coached by Wayne Forrest to understand the impact of his/her decisions – using the HS Decision Making model (see Figure 8). In this way, individuals became, and continue to be, much more aware of how their efforts contribute to the bigger picture Balmain Leagues Club Strategy and to the results of the Club.

Firstly, managers where asked to consider the two key elements of effective decision making using the aforementioned HS model.

Figure 8. Framework for Effective Decision Making

$$ED = Q \times A$$

Effective Decision = **Quality** X **Acceptance**
making of the decision is a result of   of the decision   of the decision

They were then presented with and trained to use a process that was focussed more so on the 'quality' of the decision:

- Outcome
- Alternatives
- Pros and Cons of each Alternative
- Preferred Option/Alternative

Having determined the preferred course, the managers were then expected to ensure that there was a rigorous action planning process in place, i.e. what needs to be done, by whom and in what timeframe, and who else needs to be involved?

All this in the context of the greater framework of Plan, Implement, Review (verify and validate), and Adjust/Change.

In a short time, the Planning and Decision-Making processes became a cultural expectation at Balmain Leagues Club – they became part of the unconscious operating style – woven into 'the way we do things around here'.

CONSEQUENCE MANAGEMENT – LEARNING FROM MISTAKES

One of the key tools Roma Gaster introduced to the Balmain Leagues Club team during the workshops was 'The Debrief Formula' which was and is still currently used as a means of discussing issues and learning from mistakes – and, as mentioned above it also forms the basis of the Individual Performance Review.

The formula is quite straight forward, whenever there is a problem, the issue is discussed in terms of four questions:

- What happened?
- What worked?
- What did not work?
- What will I/we do differently?

The power and impact of applying this formula to any issue at any level cannot be understated. With everyone consistently adopting this approach, Balmain Leagues Club was able to turn their culture around from one that punished mistakes to one that valued mistakes as a learning opportunity.

One staff member confirms: *"When something happened I was encouraged that the focus was not on right/wrong or 'good or bad' rather on what we needed to ensure that we learnt from the experience and what commitments needed to be made to do things better or differently. In the future, decisions were debriefed which allowed the individual to reflect and decide alternatives."*

In addition to realising the learning opportunities inherent in mistakes, this 'time out' for reflection has evolved into a mechanism that facilitates 'double loop learning'. Introduced by Argyris and Schon in the seventies, double loop learning refers to the organisation's capacity to strengthen and extend its capabilities by questioning the assumptions and beliefs underpinning their actions (Argyris & Schon, 1974).

"We have an environment and a practice that whenever there is an issue we apply our learned HS skills to address these issues, and we have a debrief that says what's working, what's not working. Even in our performance appraisals we talk about this and 'what can you say about yourself that you couldn't say last year'. We apply it in lots of circumstances, instead of just working in the business, we are working on the business, it's about saying 'I know that I have 20 tasks to perform this week but I need to find time to reflect on how I can improve the business – sit back and design systems, sit back and grow people'" (Tim Camiller, Newly Appointed CEO).

It's about saying I know that I have 20 tasks to perform this week but I need to find time to reflect on how I can improve the business – sit back and design systems, sit back and grow people

2002-2005

Balmain Leagues Club
Re-Test

Phase **4**

Overview

It has been over six years since Balmain began this journey. What has it achieved? What can be said about Balmain now that could not have been said prior to the cultural transformation?

This section evaluates the Club's progress in creating cultural change and achieving transformation against two key outcome areas:

CULTURAL OUTCOMES
Moving from Security to Satisfaction, from a Defensive to a Constructive culture indicated by:
- Movement towards their Preferred culture as indicated by an increase in Satisfaction and overall Constructive clusters (Blue) compared to the baseline OCI measure in 2000
- Increase in the Humanistic-Encouraging and Achievement as the specific styles Balmain targeted for change (positive shift above the 50th percentile)
- Decrease in Defensive cluster, with a specific emphasis on the Oppositional style as per Balmain's strategy (shift below the 50th percentile)
- Improvement in specific Outcomes related to culture over time as measured through the OCI

ORGANISATIONAL EFFECTIVENESS AND BUSINESS OUTCOMES
- Positive shift in the causal factors that were identified as creating a Defensive culture
- Improved Business measures relating to efficiency, effectiveness such as customer satisfaction and financial indicators
- Strengthening of this cultural transformation has strengthened Balmain's ability to adapt effectively to the external environment as measured through the Organisational Effectiveness Inventory™ (OEI)

As this section unfolds, the results speak for themselves. Balmain Leagues club has achieved against all the evaluation criteria above.

BASELINE – THE JOURNEY BEGINS...
The Re-Test data shows us that over the seven years since Balmain first measured its culture, it has shifted significantly from a predominantly Security-oriented, Defensive culture to a predominantly Satisfaction-oriented Constructive culture (see Figure 9 and 10).

The Constructive styles have increased by 13% with the strongest overall improvements over this period recorded in the Achievement style which increased by 23% and the Humanistic-Encouraging style which increased by 21%. The Oppositional style which was the primary cultural style in 2000 decreased by 54%. Interestingly the Dependent style characterized by items such as 'never question superiors' and 'accept orders without question' decreased by 77%. This indicates that the initiatives implemented by Balmain increased

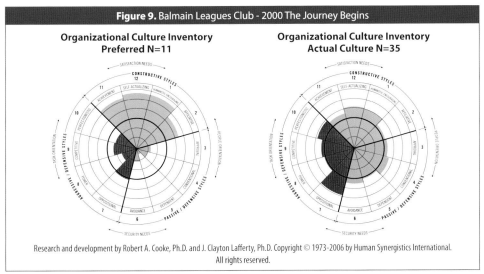

Figure 9. Balmain Leagues Club - 2000 The Journey Begins

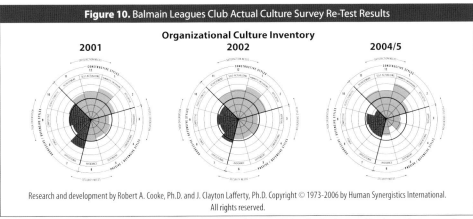

Figure 10. Balmain Leagues Club Actual Culture Survey Re-Test Results

*NB the 2004/2005 circumplex represents data gathered across sub sets of the organisation that has been combined to produce an overview of the organisation for the purposes of this case study

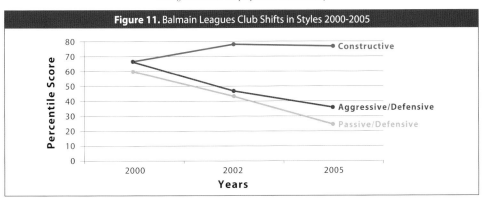

Figure 11. Balmain Leagues Club Shifts in Styles 2000-2005

the confidence, skill and autonomy of teams. The greatest overall shift however has been recorded in the Passive/Defensive styles which have decreased by 42% as highlighted in the figure below. It is noteworthy that Balmain's initiatives and strategies, which were targeted to specifically increase Humanistic-Encouraging and decrease Oppositional were successful.

The OCI measures four types of outcomes associated with Culture :

- Employee Satisfaction
- Role Clarity - the degree to which people are clear about their roles
- Role Conflict - the degree to which individuals receive conflicting messages about what they should be doing
- Customer Service

Figure 12 shows that six years after the initial test period there has been a positive shift in all of these outcomes although 'Role Conflict' (for which a lower score is desirable) increased in 2001. This may perhaps be explained by the fact that there was some significant changes implemented during this time in the role of Duty Managers which could have initially caused some confusion. It is to be expected that in the process of adjusting to new expectations, new responsibilities and new ways of relating with colleagues that some confusion may occur.

Also of note is that in 2002 there was a distinctive leap in the outcomes. By 2002 the cultural change initiative had been in place for over two years. In that time up to eight workshops had been conducted and managers had had sufficient time to adjust to their new responsibilities. During this time the 'bar was constantly being raised' particularly in relation to role modelling Constructive styles by being accountable for relationships and results. Most people rose to the challenge and stretched beyond their comfort levels. Some, however, were not as comfortable in this new world of accountability and over a period of time left the Club.

In fact, at various stages during the change process, members of the team became overwhelmed and struggled with ongoing demands of maintaining a high performance team, to the extent that some members became quite Perfectionistic around their expectations of themselves and others, which manifested itself into an intolerance of any deviation from the high standards that had become the norm.

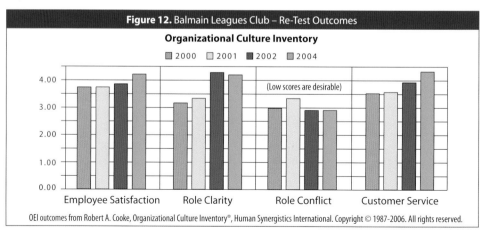

Figure 12. Balmain Leagues Club – Re-Test Outcomes

Organizational Culture Inventory

2000　2001　2002　2004

(Low scores are desirable)

Employee Satisfaction　Role Clarity　Role Conflict　Customer Service

Organisational Effectiveness

In 2002 and 2004/05 Balmain administered the Organizational Effectiveness Inventory (OEI) along with the Organizational Culture Inventory (OCI). The OEI measures 31 causal factors that drive culture. The bar graphs in Figure 13 and 14 show the causal factors for 2002 and 2004/05 respectively. The graph outlining the results of 2002 shows that two years into the program of change, there were 12 factors still below the historical average. The historical average reflects the median of the responses of members from the research database of 1084 organisational units. In general, organisations seeking to move their culture to Constructive norms should aim to score above the historical average. Scores below the historical average indicate that Defensive norms may be operating.

Of the 12 causal factors below the historical average, 7 belonged to two categories:

Supervisory/Managerial Leadership
- Interaction facilitation (people oriented)
- Task facilitation (task oriented)
- Goal Emphasis (task oriented)
- Consideration

Systems - Goal Setting Practices
- Goal difficulty
- Participative goal setting

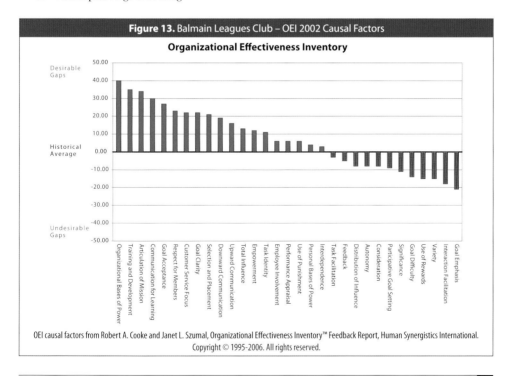

Figure 13. Balmain Leagues Club – OEI 2002 Causal Factors

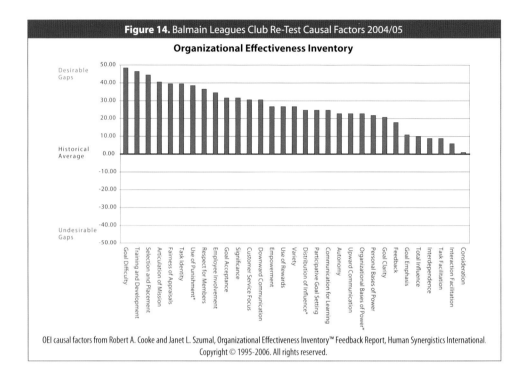

Figure 14. Balmain Leagues Club Re-Test Causal Factors 2004/05

Organizational Effectiveness Inventory

Noting this is useful when reminded of the leadership-culture-performance connection and the LSI circumplexes of the Duty Managers (Avoidance and Oppositional strongly backed by Power). It is likely that these specific causal factors drove the Aggressive/Defensive elements of the culture, remembering that in 2002 the Oppositional style, although on the decrease, was still above the 50th percentile. Further, it supports the initial leadership test results which indicated that the culture was greatly impacted by leadership style.

These factors may have played out in the organisation through a lack of inclusiveness. Managers may have been imposing goals and objectives on team members rather than jointly participating in determining them. One of the staff members commented, *"The culture of the organisation had changed from a 'punishment' to a 'reward' focus. Personnel were treated as important and people started speaking with each other, rather than demanding things get done. Communication and tone and how things were said changed positively"*

At this time Balmain was about twelve months into the change program involving Duty Managers. Over the course of 2000-2005, ten workshops were conducted for the Duty Managers focusing on a combination of performance management, coaching, mentoring, and interpersonal skills. By 2004/05, two years after the first OEI, this intensive work with the Duty Managers paid off. All of the causal factors were rated above the historical average.

ORGANISATIONAL EFFECTIVENESS OUTCOMES

Arguably one of the most important indicators of Balmain's cultural transformation program is whether it contributed to or increased the organisation's ability to adapt to the external environment – its principal reason for embarking on the journey. One of the measures of this success is how an organisation's people rate its ability to adapt. Figure 15 shows the outcome results in 2002. Note that 'External Adaptability' is the outcome highest above the historical average. External Adaptability includes:

- Timely and efficient implementation of new programs
- Proactive Identification and adjustment to change
- Effective response to external opportunities and threats

The 2005 results show an improvement in External Adaptability. It is likely that the measure of external adaptability is high because two years into the process, staff would have begun to feel the ripple effect of the changes being implemented in an around the Duty Managers role.

The outcome with the lowest score and the most opportunity for improvement is Organisational Level Quality. Organisational Level Quality is measured by:

- Your organisation will get repeat business from its present customers
- You would recommend this organisation to potential customers
- The quality of products and /or services' meets customers' expectations

While the cultural tide had a visible and tangible feel to it and was impacting in a broad

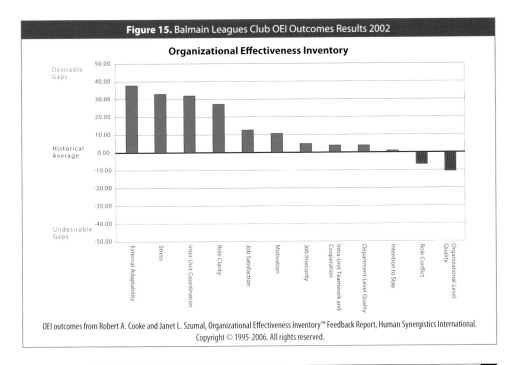

Figure 15. Balmain Leagues Club OEI Outcomes Results 2002

OEI outcomes from Robert A. Cooke and Janet L. Szumal, Organizational Effectiveness Inventory™ Feedback Report, Human Synergistics International. Copyright © 1995-2006. All rights reserved.

way in 2002, it is likely that the changes in day-to-day management practices in relation to the food and beverage business were still in process.

By 2005, the latest Re-Test measures show that all outcomes were rated above the historical average. Note particularly that the outcome 'External Adaptability' increased as had 'Organizational Level Quality'. How does this progress compare with the Constructive benchmark set by our research data set of 1084 organisational Units? The results in Figure 16 speak for themselves. The intent of the organisation in embarking on this journey of change was to improve its capacity and agility in adapting to the external environment. Through its program of change, Balmain Leagues Club has achieved a transformation of great proportion that enabled it to exceed the measure of External Adaptability reflected by the Constructive benchmark.

At the very beginning we outlined that our evaluation of the success of Balmain's transformation would depend on what we could say about them now, that we could not say about them in 1995, prior to the change initiatives. In this regard the data are clear: they have improved their capacity to adapt their external environment, they achieved their goal. To test this we next explore how this capability has improved their business performance.

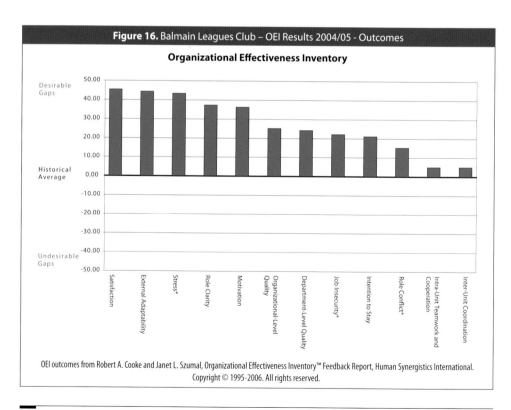

Figure 16. Balmain Leagues Club – OEI Results 2004/05 - Outcomes

Organizational Effectiveness Inventory

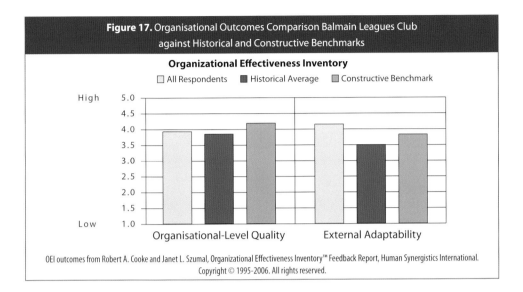

Figure 17. Organisational Outcomes Comparison Balmain Leagues Club against Historical and Constructive Benchmarks

OEI outcomes from Robert A. Cooke and Janet L. Szumal, Organizational Effectiveness Inventory™ Feedback Report, Human Synergistics International. Copyright © 1995-2006. All rights reserved.

Business Outcomes

In reviewing the club's business performance between 2000-2005 it is apparent that it has improved its performance across a range of measures, year after year. It is also clear that Balmain's management feels that the cultural change process was integral to this turna-round. In real terms, however, it is difficult to draw a direct linear relationship between the change and the results (that is, it is difficult to compare figures year on year) due to the range of quite extensive external factors impacting the club's bottom line, operating costs and visi-tation trends. The wide range of factors below provides a good indication of this difficulty:

- **Change in trading hours** due to legislative restrictions (Mandatory shut down periods), i.e. between 2000 and 2004 Balmain has traded:
  - 24 hours by 7 days per week
  - 18 hours by 7 days per week
  - 18 hours by 5 days and 21 hours by 2 days per week
  - 21 hours by 7 days per week
- **Changes (restrictions) in Smoking Legislation**
- **Introduction of Harm Minimisation Measures (Gaming)** including:
  - Restrictions on the maximum cash payment of $1,000 on prize winnings (Remainder must be by cheque)
  - Ban on Gaming-Related advertising
  - Restriction on Gaming Promotions:
    - Prizes not to exceed $1,000
    - Cash prizes not permitted

- Problem Gambling Awareness initiatives: Signage, brochures and stickers from Club Entry to Gaming Machines
- Mandatory Self-Exclusion program and Counselling services
- Cheque Cashing restrictions: 1 cheque per person per day (up to $400)
- ATMs not available in Gaming area
- **Reduction in the amount of NRL "Home Games" played at Leichhardt Oval**
- **Trade influenced (positively and negatively) by "on field" performance of the NRL Football Team.** E.g. West's Tigers winning the Grand Final in 2005 had a positive impact, revenue wise, of nearly $1 million

EXTERNAL ADAPTABILITY

While it may be difficult to demonstrate a direct link, there are numerous events and facts that attest to the link between performance and culture. Balmain's enhanced capability to adapt to the environment was particularly tested in 2004 and 2005. They were extremely tough years for the industry in general with newly introduced Government Legislation (smoking laws, responsible conduct of alcohol compliances together with a severe poker machine gaming tax) and increasing competition. While the club had always been acutely affected by market forces, it's bottom line at this stage was beginning to be severely impacted.

"In January 2005, the Management Team all got together, we reviewed the strategy and recognised what we could and couldn't control, as well as considering potential threats. Subsequently we put in place expenditure controls (e.g. salaries, marketing, promotions, procurement etc.). In February 2005 the plan was put to the Board who gave approval and stepped back. By May 2005 revenue had improved and we were back on budget."

Danny Munk goes on to say that: *"There is no way this could have happened without the influence of the Management Team within their own teams – i.e. all teams bought into process and all teams were consciously paddling in one direction. Then the football team started to get on a roll towards winning the premiership… and with their success came unexpected revenue. Club maximised use of revenue. We refitted three areas in the Club without borrowing from the bank. Also during a very challenging year I gained my HS accreditations and personally facilitated remeasures for LSI, L/I & OCI/OEI. None of the above could have been possible in a 'Red' or 'Green' culture!"*

Another example that testifies to Balmain's enhanced capacity to be more agile and strategic, lies in the implementation of their strategic plan that positions Balmain Leagues Club as a more diversified business with less reliance on gaming.

None of this could have been possible in a 'Red' or 'Green' culture!

The Club has submitted plans for a major redevelopment of the existing premises into a new mixed use facility that again diversifies the interests of the Club while also integrating with and reinforcing its community ties. The Club's change and growth doesn't stop there. The Club has an application to open a second site at Sydney Olympic Park. One of the ways in which the club has been supported in achieving its strategy has been through the relatively low turnover of staff. Lower attrition levels stems the flow of corporate knowledge which enables the organisation to build on and extend on its strength.

TURNOVER

It is no surprise that turnover in the entertainment and hospitality can be much less stable than other industries due to transient and seasonal nature of Hospitality staff, and changes to base rosters as a result of the changes in trading hours. While the organisation has not kept year on year figures tracking turnover, Balmain appears anecdotally at least to be holding their own with regards to operational staff.

"Turnover readily comes to mind and the best example I can give you is the kitchen… one of the outcomes of changing the management was that we have had one staff turnover in 18 months and this was in the period of great hospitality opportunity. There is a shortage of trained chefs; they enjoyed working for someone who has this capacity of creating an environment where people want to learn from him. Over 18 months we have had one person turnover compared to 100% turnover prior to his being promoted" (Tim Camiller, CFO 1997-2006).

With regards to Management and Administration staff, turnover has been extremely minimal for the last 3 to 5 years, with a turnover rate of less than 5% resulting in the need to recruit only six times during this time period.

GROWTH IN BUSINESS

According to Tim Camiller: *"The Function business has grown consistently year on year by 15% that is largely to do with our community awareness and more importantly our community appreciation. I think we are more respected in the community because most of our function clients are community business, the consistency of our brand is much more widely recognised in the community marketplace."*

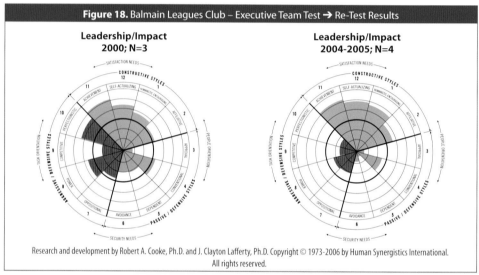

Figure 18. Balmain Leagues Club – Executive Team Test → Re-Test Results

Leadership/Impact
2000; N=3

Leadership/Impact
2004-2005; N=4

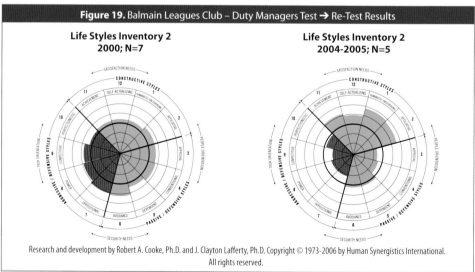

Figure 19. Balmain Leagues Club – Duty Managers Test → Re-Test Results

Life Styles Inventory 2
2000; N=7

Life Styles Inventory 2
2004-2005; N=5

Leadership-Culture Connection

How did the leadership change? The circumplexes in Figure 18 and 19 show the 'before and after' snapshot of the Executive Team and the Duty Managers.

The circumplexes of both the Executive Team and the Duty Managers captures their extraordinary development over the years since they first began the journey in 1999. At both levels there has been a significant increase in the Constructive styles and a substantial decrease in the Defensive styles. This is significant because the primary style shown in the Duty Managers' 2004 LSI 2 circumplex is Humanistic-Encouraging. This is important because the Duty Managers were targeted as the group that needed development if Balmain Leagues Club was going to increase the level of Humanistic-Encouraging in the culture. This increase is evidence that the strategies employed to boost the Humanistic-Encouraging style through the Duty Managers hit their mark.

Phase **5**

Balmain Leagues Club
Review
Change Agents | Lessons Learnt | Future Challenges

Change Agents

Internal Change Agents	Danny Munk, Tim Camiller, Wayne Forrest, Marcelle Proper, Rod Neilsen, Duty Managers
External Change Agents	Roma Gaster, Karibu Education International Pty Ltd

COURAGE AND COMMITMENT TO SHIFT THE PARADIGM

This case study brings into sharp focus the story of an organisation, which, although successful in its sector had to 'eyeball' the issue of survival by virtue of the sheer number of external forces that 'merry-go-rounded' into and out of its business.

In this story rather than cut headcount and strip back employee-centred programs as a primary means of supporting the business through tough times, Balmain Leagues Club, under the leadership of Danny Munk, Wayne Forrest and the rest of the Executive Team, increased the investment in these areas at a time in the club's history when it could least afford to.

It takes a great deal of courage to risk in a very real way an organisation's limited resources by investing in an outcome that is not cast in iron from the start. They did this in the belief that it was people not product, or tasks, that are the front-line defence in the battle to survive. This shift in the operating paradigm of the time initiated a chain of events and actions that led to the increased resilience of the organisation. It all started with a belief, a step change in consciousness and the courage to back it.

PARTNERSHIP AMONG INDIVIDUALS – A STRONG TEAM ETHIC

Balmain's success is about teamwork, it's about individuals carrying their own weight, it's about bringing their unique talent and qualities to the team and it is about the team tackling reality head on, in a collaborative way. The collective strength of all the individual players demonstrated a long held belief about team effectiveness.

It is within this team context that the qualities of the change agents are reviewed and discussed.

MUTUAL TRUST AND BELIEF IN EACH OTHER'S POTENTIAL AND CAPABILITY

Balmain was spurred to launch this process by virtue of the fact that if they did not do something they would certainly be faced with dissolution. However compelling this is, it is also an extremely large burden to carry. The margin for experimenting with resources and or mistakes was not great and yet the organisation needed to take a leap of faith that this dive into uncharted waters was going to result in something better. The transformation was borne out of and created a high level of trust between the key change agents and their teams. At a time when Danny Munk and Tim Camiller could have understandably reigned in Wayne's enthusiasm and belief in the potential of the LSI and OCI as springboards for positive change by restricting access to financial resources, they chose instead to step back and allow the space for something new to happen. They put their money and their trust in Wayne's capability. This built momentum and trust became a fundamental building block of the cultural change process. The ability to trust an individual's capacity, intent and enthusiasm to do the 'right thing' by the organisation and do a 'great job' was not stated explicitly, but was implicitly demonstrated through the action and attitude of leaders towards their people.

THE ART OF STORY TELLING IN HARNESSING AND MOBILIZING THE COLLECTIVE WILL OF STAFF

"Our teams started paddling in the same direction once our management learnt the art of story telling" (Danny Munk CEO 1995-2006).

Executive led story telling is one of the most effective ways of creating connections between individuals and between individuals and the organisation. This is certainly the case with Balmain. Argument and rational reason sometimes are not sufficient to sustain motivation and energy when times are tough. There will always be some way of finding flaws in a rational argument. Mastering the art of telling a good story is another way of calling people to action. The best stories engage employees in a higher sense of purpose, a better future (Self-Actualizing) and create a link between the individual's effort and capacity to positively bring about change (Achievement). Most people have a 'passion for significance' this manifests as the desire to make a difference and for their life to have some greater impact. Stories are a great way of engaging employees and encouraging them to commit to the possibility of a future on the basis that they have the power to make it happen. Balmain as a business was virtually on its knees trying to keep the doors open. They needed to engage the belief and trust of their people if they were ever going to move forward. The change agents, Danny and Wayne in particular, were able to inspire others to see the vision of the future they held, at times when rational argument would have had the louder voice.

LEADERS OPENNESS AND WILLINGNESS TO CHANGE

"Probably the biggest change was, as much as we used HS to sell the story about changing behaviour, it also got people including myself to understand the significant difference between reactive and proactive. We talk about behavioural models in the HS tools but one of the biggest issues in it is 'Do you want to follow? Or do you want to lead?' It doesn't mean everyone is a leader but everyone leads within their position. My role became about owning the strategic plan, and I had to report against it. Moving into the strategic part of the role was difficult and I struggled with it. There are things I love to do like gaming, IT and being with staff and the membership. I had to accept that to stay in this chair, I had to move into this role and in turn step back and let Wayne, Marcelle and Tim run the business. But I also got far better at telling stories, and that was a big shift for me and it was a big shift for the others. They had to work differently with their teams" (Danny Munk, CEO 1995-2006).

Organisational transformation is not a function of command but rather a result of individuals preparedness to change. Mobilising the organisation's collective will is the most important prerequisite for successful change. This success is predicated on individuals agreeing to own and direct their own personal change process. Initially it was Wayne Forrest who modelled this self-reflection and act of will. In speaking to the managers who reported to him for this research project, it became clear that the point at which they began to believe that something different in the organisation was possible was when they saw Wayne change before their eyes. This was then followed by a gradual but visible change in the Executive Team and the Duty Managers as they went through the leadership development program designed by Wayne and Roma. While the development programs provided some structure, and a safe journey, the management team including all the Duty Managers across all functional areas, did the transforming. Had they not committed to and bought into the vision, Balmain Leagues Club would very likely be in the same position it was in 1997. Balmain has been engaged in this effort for ten years and many of the managers of this team have participated from the very beginning. The sustained program of change is a testament to their emotional maturity self mastery, and personal commitment to the community and making a difference to each other, the business and their members.

> **'Do you want to follow? Or do you want to lead?' It doesn't mean everyone is a leader but everyone leads within their position**

ENGAGEMENT AND INCLUSIVENESS

One of the interesting qualities of Balmain's story is the inclusiveness with which the cultural change strategy was approached and implemented. Although there were definite architects in mapping the route to the envisioned destination, a great deal of room was allowed for the Duty Managers to be involved in developing and implementing the cultural change. This inclusiveness engaged all managers in a dynamic and ever evolving 'live' process. The alchemy of change that emerged can initially be traced to a 'meeting of minds' and values between Wayne and Roma (and subsequently Danny and Roma when Wayne left in 2004). The intention underlying the design of the workshops was anchored in Wayne, Danny and Roma's values-based approach and a belief in 'minessence' which involves stripping complication away and allowing simple, intuitive-based solutions to emerge through a process of group engagement and dialogue. The work Roma did with Balmain created question- based processes that were both functional in terms of furthering the individual and the organisation's knowledge as well as process oriented, teaching and modelling the ways in which the Constructive styles translated into behaviour. Her contribution as an external consultant has been to guide and in some ways anchor, the navigation process throughout the journey, providing the necessary support, debriefing and providing a depth of skill needed to keep the initiative on an even keel. Furthermore, Balmain's approach to leadership development had the knack of sensing where the team was at and via the workshops helped to ground their development and growth at key points throughout the process by leading and pacing the programs to match where individuals and the team were at.

Lessons Learnt

The lessons to be learnt from Balmain Leagues Club reinforces much of what we already know about some of the critical success factors required for a successful cultural transformation: Leaders 'walking the talk'; the power of communication and the need for people management processes and systems that create opportunities for people to practice new behaviours. This section however focuses on some of the more distinctive aspects of Balmain's journey that sets it slightly apart from other stories.

SOCIAL RESPONSIBILITY – IT'S ABOUT MAKING A DIFFERENCE

"There is a big sense of community – they are giving a lot to the community. Some of the footballers from when Balmain won last time, are on the current Board. The youth, the elderly – they all take enormous interest. Skin contact from the ground up is phenomenal. It is more than a nine to five job for some of these people. It is a love and a passion" (Roma Gaster, Karibu Education International).

Staff at Balmain are keenly aware that their organisation is part of the fabric of the community, it always has been. The level of responsibility for stakeholder returns in a community- oriented organisation can be a much heavier load to bear and a far less cut and dry proposition than the drive for shareholder return. The additional emotionally loaded, public expectations invested in the organisation becomes as much of a driver in running the business than just 'product, price, place and promotion'. (Just watch the thousands of people congregate outside a club when it wins a grand final and you will see the truth of this statement!). It is a responsibility that motivated staff with its sense of purpose and greater good.

"Being a community-based organisation and one patronized almost entirely by members of our local community, if we become or are something that the community doesn't like then we will cease to exist. Our constructive, proactive culture is reflected in our customer service and staff relations. You have to continually work on it though – the community and hospitality market demand it," says Tim Camiller.

KEEPING IT SIMPLE

While Balmain Leagues Club did introduce a number of formal systems and processes to enhance its operations, one of the hallmarks of their success is the largely conversation-based processes they integrated into their formal systems. In a conceptual and technological age where we are inundated with information, models, buzz words, and ever increasing claims of new and more sophisticated ways of optimising performance, it is refreshing to consider the power of the simple yet robust processes introduced at Balmain. The performance manage-ment process for example, is comprised of methods that are direct and to the point, broken down to its very basic functional purpose. This approach made things easy. This is in stark contrast to most organisations where there is often as much training (if not more) involved in using the forms associated with performance management than there is in having the conversation, which we seem prone to forget is actually the main game! It is also important to acknowledge that while simple, the processes did not lack depth. Rather than complicating and 'overcooking' the format, Balmain's investment was directed at training and supporting individuals to bring depth to the conversation.

BUILDING MOMENTUM FOR ORGANISATIONAL CHANGE THROUGH SMALL GROUPS

While Balmain involved the entire organisation in the measurement phase of the process, it used it as an opportunity to concentrate their efforts in thin slicing the areas or target groups in the business that would deliver the breakthrough they were after. Given their limited resources a targeted approach was the most effective and rapid way of achieving change. This focus also created pockets of readiness within the organisation that prompted a ground floor momentum generating interest from the other areas of the business in terms of what was going on. As the programs gradually rolled out to other groups, there was a sense of anticipation rather than suspicion because they had already witnessed the changes in their colleagues. As the program rolled out, the different teams were able to maintain their individual functional diversity while they aligned with a common focus.

> **This wasn't a bonding group hug stuff, this was about getting stuff on the table and really dealing with some issues**

"The sense is that it is touching everyone. The functional groups all did their thing but it was all aligned, through brand, strategy and Constructive styles. The brand is very important and we underestimate how the brand can affect the employees within the organisation" (Roma Gaster, Karibu Education International).

STRENGTH IN VULNERABILITY

The team development workshops conducted with the Duty Managers through the years as previously discussed, included a range of issues. Some were skill based, some were process but all included activities that encouraged honest, authentic communication. To trust one another, the team needed to know one another. This part of the workshop enabled personal transformation at the individual level.

Wayne Forrest emphasises, *"… this wasn't a bonding group hug stuff, this was about getting stuff on the table and really dealing with some issues and on any number of occasions there were tears and significant emotional events… but we did it in such a safe environment that people generally survived them."*

One of the questions the research has been seeking to understand is to what degree is this kind of deep interaction between team members required to support personal transformation and cultural change. In the case of Balmain, both Wayne and Roma believe that it is an integral part of the process.

"I think the OCI shift would have happened anyway but I believe it was more marked and sustained because of the personal transformation of their leaders – personal transformation made the organisation change more core" (Roma Gaster, Karibu Education International).

Wayne Forrest (former Operations Manager 1997-2004) agrees: *"If we don't push people through or if we don't challenge them to a particular level then we don't see their full potential... it's about a true level of understanding about what makes people tick. Redefining trust and being very clear on what trust looks like in terms of behaviours."*

Numbers aren't controlled by you; You can't always win on the numbers. At the end of the day, growing your people into the business in a way that will meet and exceed your stakeholders expectations is the best way to achieve the business goals short term and long term

---

SHORT TERM NEED vs. LONG TERM SUSTAINABILITY

The economics of our society and the structures that operate within it, place a lot of importance and value on short term financial gains. Many companies plan as far as the next quarter or next financial year. Too much focus on the numbers in the short term can threaten the ongoing success of the organisation. If there were ever an organisation that had an argument for only focusing on the short term it was Balmain and yet they chose to invest their resources in a process that they knew would take time and believed would lead to better results –which it did. How does Danny Munk respond to challenges from other CEO's about the need to focus on the numbers? Danny advises them: *"Enjoy the moment, because what you are growing is short-lived. Numbers aren't controlled by you; about 90% of numbers are controlled by others, factors outside your control... You can't always win on the numbers. You can control your understanding of the stakeholders in your business, what their needs are and the type of outcomes they seek. You can control how you go about meeting these expectations. At the end of the day, growing your people into the business in a way that will meet and exceed your stakeholders expectations is under your control and is the best way to achieve the business goals short term and long term. As a manager you need to accept that you will change people's lives and what I learnt was that this required a more holistic vision of the business."*

Future Challenges

Balmain Leagues Club is in a highly competitive and volatile sector, its challenge has always been and remains to be 'future fit' so that it can actually catch and respond to the curve balls it will be thrown by its environment. They have extremely strong competitors in every aspect of their business.

In terms of their food and beverage business they are flanked by trendy restaurants, bars, pubs and cafes strewn along the main street in the fashionable inner suburbs of Balmain and Rozelle. In nearby Leichhardt, they are surrounded by another of Sydney's oldest suburbs whose main attraction is its reputation as the 'Italian quarter' also offering rich Italian food, cafes and gelato bars, movie theatres. Other recreational and leisure options, such as bookstores and specialist shops that provide ample opportunities for retail therapy are also competing for the consumers' leisure dollar.

As far as gaming goes, there are many pubs that all offer poker machines to their patrons. If this was not enough, Star City within close proximity operating under very different regulations. Throw into the mix a raft of legislative changes and the emotional investment of its stakeholders and it is clear Balmain Leagues Club survival will never be able to be taken for granted.

Their challenge then is to continue to maintain the skill base and learning capability that has enabled it to increase its agility in the face of such strong opposition. It must continue to build, develop and extend simple and robust systems and processes that will remain flexible enough to change with the external demands, but encoded enough so that its longevity is not dependent on personalities or the personnel of the time.

Balmain is now facing this challenge because its key change protagonists in initiating and promoting the transformation, Wayne Forrest and most recently, their leader Danny Munk have left. Balmain is lucky in that Tim Camiller, Marcelle Proper, Rod Nielsen and their management teams were also a part of the core team that delivered the transformation and so their capacity to continue and extend the transformation to the next levels is more certain than might otherwise be the case. They have become the current culture 'stewards' has little to do with luck.

The next level of achievement for Balmain is to broaden and diversify its revenue base through the redevelopment being planned. That it has survived let alone prospered over the past ten years sufficiently to undertake such an ambitious project testifies to the impact of cultural change on its business. As Tim Camiller says: *"Every aspect of our business has as strong a competitor as any business does. Without the cultural change of our organisation we wouldn't be here today. We have had to build an organisation that employs and promotes superior performance and we needed to reach that next level of development in order just to survive."*

Although Danny Munk has moved from Balmain, his experience at Balmain is still very much with him and has enabled him to 'shorten' the conversation in working with his new team to work to deliver improved outcomes. Asked to comment on Balmain's future, Danny says:

I am as sure of Balmain going forward tomorrow as I am sure that there will be air to breathe, and the wonderful thing about that is, no one can take the credit, but everyone can and the great thing for me is that there is community ownership of the club once again

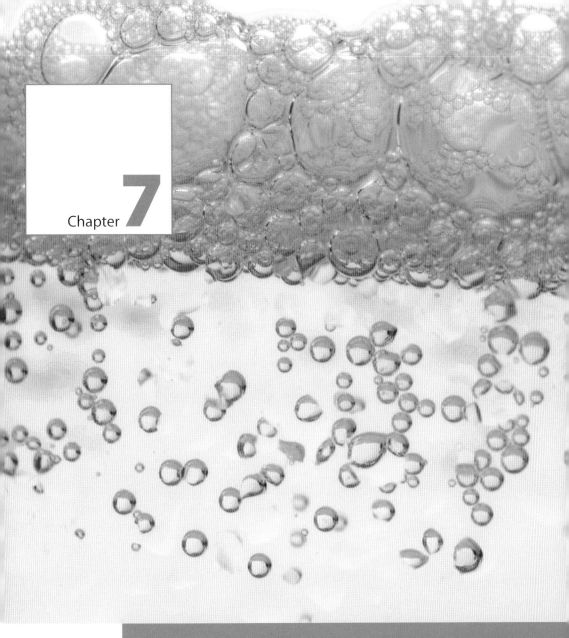

Chapter **7**

Making Our World
A More Social Place

LION NATHAN

human
synergistics

Contents
Lion Nathan

Written by Corinne Canter

Executive Summary

This case study charts an organisation's emerging strategic capability to do continuous change. There are many lessons to be learnt from what is the longest running case study on cultural transformation in our data set. Key among these lessons is what it takes to maintain the journey over a long period of time, and how a robust and Constructive culture precipitates resilient and courageous leadership.

Industry	Fast Moving Consumer Goods (FMCG)
Customers	30,000
People	2,800 Australia, New Zealand, USA, UK
Market Capitalisation	A$4.3 Billion
Revenue	A$1.8 Billion
CEO	Rob Murray 2004-Present; Gordon Cairns 1997-2004; Douglas Myers 1988-97; Lion Nathan formed by the merger of Lion Breweries and LD Nathan in 1988
Internal Change Agent(s)	Bob Barbour, People & Culture Director; Gordon Cairns, CEO 1997-2004; Lion Nathan Senior Leadership Team; Lion Nathan Human Resources Team; Rob Murray, CEO 2004-Present
External Change Agents(s)	Carolyn Taylor 1996-1998
HSI Tools	Organizational Culture Inventory™ (OCI), Life Styles Inventory™ (LSI)

Culture Survey Results

Organizational Culture Inventory Test (1998)

Organizational Culture Inventory Re-Test (2004)

Outcomes	Increased profit, employee engagement and customer satisfaction.

Phase **1**

Lion Nathan
Pre-Test

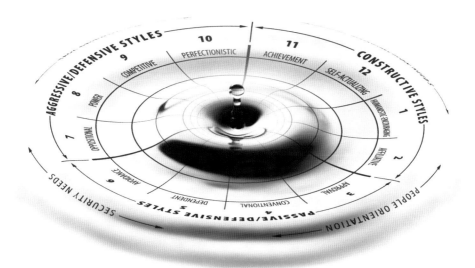

Right Here Right Now

It might just look like the drink you've always loved.
But a lot's gone on behind the scenes to keep it that way.
Little changes, subtle stuff. You probably didn't notice.
Good, you weren't meant to.

If you're one of our team, we don't need to tell you what's
gone down and how much things will continue to change.
'Cos that's probably why you joined.
Because you like the edginess of being just a little unsettled.
And if you're a shareholder, is there any such thing
as the perfect result? No, there's just a point when you say
'that's OK - for now'.

For all these reasons, we believe in refreshment.
We're committed to business transformation.
We look to surprise and delight, and keep wiggling
the boat a little. Satisfaction never sticks.
You have it. It passes and you set new goals.

(Lion Nathan Annual Report 2004)

About Lion Nathan

Introduction

"We have a very strong strategy. We have a group of people deployed around making it happen. We're honest enough to call whether the results are good or bad and honest enough or brave enough to throw away some of the paradigms we have had about how you measure success" *(Rob Murray, CEO).*

Lion Nathan's name has been synonymous with successful cultural transformation for almost ten years. During that time, the company has championed the business case for creating a Constructive, Achievement-orientated culture, as a means of engaging their people and delivering results. Its enduring commitment to strengthen and embed its culture has resulted in some staggering statistics in terms of effort deployed for change:

- 4 administrations of the Organizational Culture Inventory® (OCI) – conducted every two years since 1998
- 51 of its own staff becoming accredited in using the Life Styles Inventory™ 1 & 2 (LSI 1 & 2)
- Over 600 individuals receiving individual feedback through the Life Styles Inventory 1 & 2 (including Board Members)
- Total LSI 1 participation N=3,156 (individuals going through the process several times)
- Total LSI 2 participation N=15,213

While these statistics reflect only one aspect of Lion's on-going culture and capability program, they provide some indication of the 'cultural tide' and the momentum the company has built around its transformation process.

Ten years do not pass however without the world changing quite dramatically. Lion has had to adapt to the ebb and flow of these waves of change in order to sustain its passion for achievement and excellence. One of the most significant events has been the 'changing of the guard' at CEO level with the departure of Gordon Cairns in 2004 and Rob Murray's appointment to the top job in October that year.

To have sustained the journey for more than ten years is, in and of itself, a significant achievement. This case study reviews Lion's expedition of cultural transformation from its beginnings in 1996 through to the present time.

For the purposes of this case study and for ease of explication, four distinct periods have been identified and will be discussed within our analytical framework of Pre-Test → Test → Action → Re-Test:

- 1990-1995 – Lion's expansion into Australia
- 1995-1998 – The case for change
- 1998-2004 – 'The Lion Nathan Way' - Cultural Transformation
- 2004 – Renewal - Deeper into the 'Blue'

Although the story of Lion Nathan's cultural journey is relatively well known, the spotlight has focussed largely on their success - the positive cultural outcome of the transformation. High profile organisational achievements are often at risk of being diminished in some way when exposed to the public eye. That they have made it to the 'other side' might give the impression that everything just fell magically into place, or that conditions were somehow different for them, giving them an advantage over other companies. In actual fact, the journey has not always been smooth, nor has the terrain been easy. In recent years in particular, Lion Nathan has at times endured quite intense public scrutiny and speculation about its business. Despite some heckling from the sidelines, Lion has stayed true to its values and beliefs, stepping up to the challenges irrespective of the headlines.

This case study locates Lion's cultural transformation in the broader context of the story behind the headlines. It is a story that charts an organisation's emerging strategic capability to 'do change', and continuous change at that. There are many lessons to be learnt from what is the longest running case study on cultural transformation in our data set. Key among these lessons is what it takes to maintain the journey over a long period of time, and how a robust and Constructive culture precipitates resilient and courageous leadership.

Background

Lion Nathan is an Australian-based alcoholic beverages company, with operations primarily in Australia and New Zealand. Lion's core purpose is 'To make our world a more sociable place', and its vision is 'To be the leading alcoholic beverage company in Australia and New Zealand'. Its portfolio of beer brands includes Tooheys, XXXX, Hahn, West End, Emu, Swan, James Squire, Lion, Speights and Steinlager. It brews and distributes around 900 million litres of beer annually.

Lion Nathan also has a global premium wine business formed through the combination of leading Australian and New Zealand fine wine producers Petaluma, Banksia and Wither Hills.

In addition to its beer and wine businesses, Lion Nathan is involved in a number of related businesses in Australia and New Zealand. These include the distribution of licensed wine and spirits brands, the production and distribution of Ready-to-Drink beverages (RTDs), liquor retailing, and malt extraction for home brewing and the food industry.[1]

---

1 Lion Nathan Website March 2006

Figure1. Lion Nathan Business

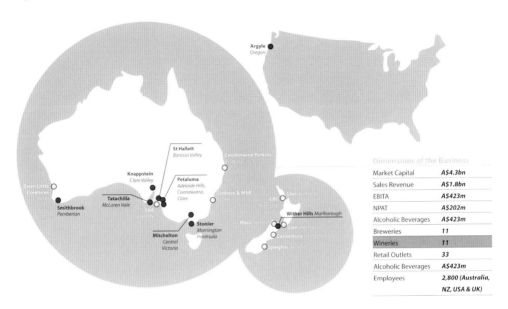

Dimensions of the Business	
Market Capital	A$4.3bn
Sales Revenue	A$1.8bn
EBITA	A$423m
NPAT	A$202m
Alcoholic Beverages	A$423m
Breweries	11
Wineries	11
Retail Outlets	33
Alcoholic Beverages	A$423m
Employees	2,800 (Australia, NZ, USA & UK)

External/Internal Operating Environment

Originally a New Zealand company, Lion completed the acquisition of Natbrew Holdings, which owned Alan Bond's brewing assets in Australia, during the period from 1990 to 1992. In 1993, the company added the Hahn Brewery and The South Australian Brewing Company to their operations. Together, these acquisitions significantly extended Lion's footprint in the Australian market.

Initially, the company was quite successful in the marketplace as a result of its efforts in revitalising the acquired brands and in realising the operational efficiencies delivered by economies of scale. This success did not last however, and in the lead up to 1996, Lion's profits, revenue and market share started to go backwards. In response to this, a team led by a senior manager reporting to Douglas Myers, the CEO at the time, was charged with the task of reviewing the entire business. With the support of McKinsey & Co., they critically evaluated the effectiveness of the business in terms of existing capabilities in key functional areas, organisational structure and brand strategy (Taylor, 2005).

Amongst other things, the review team found that while Lion had developed some good capabilities in operations, they needed to bridge the capability gap in sales and marketing.

The Case for Transformation

In response to the findings of the review, a change program was launched between 1995-1996, incorporating a number of initiatives aimed at turning the performance of the business around. Some fairly significant restructuring was on the agenda, prompted by the number of autonomous businesses operating within the Group - five in Australia and a further four in New Zealand. Over time, it became clear that this structure inhibited rather than supported company success. A practical example of the limitations of the structure is described by Bob Barbour, Lion's current People & Culture Director, who was with one of Lion's businesses at that time. *"It became quite complicated in terms of leveraging [our] strengths against one national competitor with three brands. We had fourteen brands and five different businesses. You make a mistake in one, like for example Castlemaine XXXX ran a commercial that didn't work, and then we'd run it in Tooheys and it wouldn't work again, and we'd try again in Victoria. People just weren't leveraging the learnings. There'd be the same useless thing happening all over the place."*

> **If we were going to invest all this effort and money we really needed to focus on behaviour if we were going to make it permanent**

The imperative of needing to significantly restructure the business, and at the same time to build capability in sales and marketing, forced the company to focus on changing its culture:

"We figured that if we were going to invest all this effort and money in restructuring the business, and in building [the] capability of sales and marketing, we really needed to focus on behaviour as well, if we were going to make it permanent" (Bob Barbour, People & Culture Director).

Lion became interested in discovering what was required to improve the culture and make it more adaptable. The first initiative was a series of change workshops in 1997 for about 100 of Lion's leaders. Lion engaged the services of Carolyn Taylor from Corporate Vision to support it in this process, and to conduct the workshops. The workshops had a number of components, one of which involved leaders receiving feedback on their behaviour through Human Synergistics' Life Styles Inventory 1 & 2. In addition to this, they received a lot of information on what was required to change organisations. Three key insights emerged from these workshops. Bob Barbour observed *"... a realisation that we needed to get clearer on some sense of purpose, and so be clearer on a vision, ... and that we needed to get clear on values in the business. Ever since I had joined we'd had about ten, and I could never remember any of them. We went through a process of getting clearer on a vision and agreeing three values from a list which the 100 leaders had identified. [There were] about eight potential ones and the top leadership chose three after much discussion."*

Those three values were:

■   Act with integrity
■   Face reality
■   Passion for the business

Subsequently, for the period from 1996-1998, Lion invested time and resources into further developing, confirming and refining its values and its sense of purpose. It also extended the LSI process to the next level of leadership (over 500 people) across the business.

Phase **2**

Lion Nathan

Test

The Approach

In the 1990s, Lion had begun a journey that revealed insights into the business along the way. Lion did not begin its cultural change process by measuring its entire culture, or by surveying all its people. Rather, it began by piloting the LSI 1&2 with its top leadership group as a means of acquiring some knowledge on how to develop the organisation's capacity to change. By 1998, the LSI process had been rolled out to over 500 leaders. By combining all the individual leaders' circumplexes, Lion was able to start building a picture of what its culture looked like. This picture indicated that Lion Nathan had an Aggressive/Defensive culture, which generated some interest, and so in 1998, Lion decided to conduct its first organisation-wide survey.

At this time, Gordon Cairns was the CEO, and Bob Barbour was Group Human Resources Director. They were confronted with two pieces of evidence indicating that the organisation was not doing well. The financial results were disappointingly poor, as shown in Figure 2, and the results of the first OCI indicated that Lion Nathan had a highly internally Competitive and Perfectionistic culture.

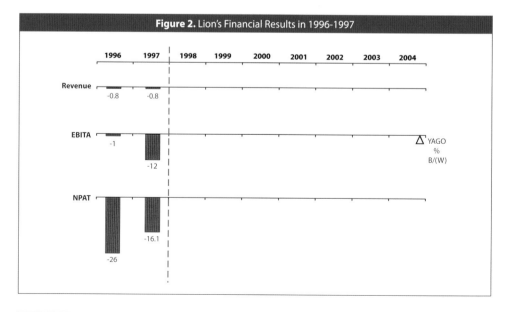

Figure 2. Lion's Financial Results in 1996-1997

Culture Survey Results

The results of the 1998 culture survey (Fig. 3) showed a profile of an organisation whose operating culture was predominantly task-focussed and Aggressive/Defensive, with a primary style of Competitive. Staff were encouraged to, implicitly or explicitly: win against others; be seen and noticed; and out-perform their peers. These results confirmed what Gordon Cairns had heard from some of the employees he had spoken to when he first joined Lion as CEO. *"When I joined the organisation and started talking with people, they didn't enjoy working there. Morale was poor, turnover was high, people were dispirited, there were no clear values, people who were doing well had the wrong values. There was an entitlement culture, it was internally competitive and personality driven."*

Figure 3. Lion Nathan – Actual Culture 1998

Organizational Culture Inventory
N=1192

These sentiments were echoed by Jamie Tomlinson, the current Chief Financial Officer (CFO), who has been with Lion Nathan for 22 years.

"We were very internally competitive, almost promoting the individual at the expense of the team. It's [now] a much more Constructive style. The way the business is run now, you don't get the feeling that people are out there to advance their own career at the expense of yours" (Jamie Tomlinson, CFO).

The Leadership-Culture Connection

Leadership impacts culture, culture impacts leadership, and they both impact performance. The truth of this hit home for Gordon Cairns, who realised that change would need to start at the top. All the while he had empathised with employees who shared their unhappiness with him about working in a highly competitive culture, he had been quite unaware of the degree to which he was contributing to their unhappiness. He was, in fact, leading in a way that encouraged a set of values and behaviours that were essentially counter to what he believed was right, and in a way that was having a different effect than the one he thought he was having. He had fallen victim to what Pfeffer referred to as the 'knowing-doing' gap - a state where, while we know the theory of what we should be doing, we actually do very little to action it (Pheffer & Sutton, 2000). In Gordon's case, the gap was revealed to him through the LSI feedback process.

'FOR THINGS TO CHANGE, FIRST I MUST CHANGE' - TRANSFORMATION GETS PERSONAL

"This kind of profile gets rewarded in most businesses as you climb up the ladder. It gets rewarded because you get things done. So here's what happens; you get told that you are like that but you keep getting promoted, so what does that do? It reinforces the view that this behaviour is acceptable, and this is why a lot of people fail, because they don't adapt. I looked back on my Myers Briggs and all the other tests. I have done every test known to man, and the feedback has always been hugely consistent. I never took any notice of it until I realised that this type of profile could lead to failure. You see,

> ## We were very internally competitive, promoting the individual at the expense of the team

as you come up through management ranks, there is a high task orientation. This kind of profile is high task. Then you get to the top and surprisingly, you don't do any work yourself - you get things done through people. You can't KPI someone to change their culture, because it's a cause, not a task, which means you have to convince people's hearts, not their minds" (Gordon Cairns, CEO 1997-2004).

As Gordon points out, his LSI 2 circumplex shown in Figure 4 had much in common with CEOs and managers across Australia and New Zealand. Figure 5 shows the Australian and New Zealand LSI data collected from approximately 50,000 people describing their managers. This is the typical profile that currently prevails, and is encouraged, in most organisations across Australia and New Zealand. Individuals with high Aggressive/Defensive behaviours are often rewarded and promoted on the basis that they 'get things done' (task orientation).

Figure 6 testifies to the fact that Aggressive/Defensive behaviours are rewarded. The table shows a positive correlation between Aggressive/Defensive styles and salary at the individual

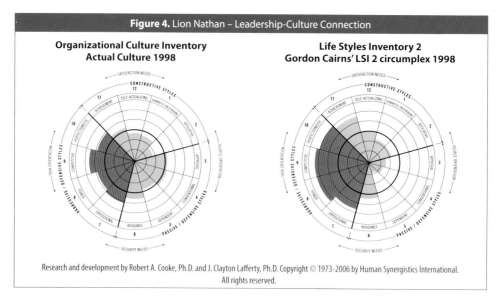

Figure 4. Lion Nathan – Leadership-Culture Connection

Organizational Culture Inventory Actual Culture 1998

Life Styles Inventory 2 Gordon Cairns' LSI 2 circumplex 1998

Research and development by Robert A. Cooke, Ph.D. and J. Clayton Lafferty, Ph.D. Copyright © 1973-2006 by Human Synergistics International. All rights reserved.

level, despite the fact that the evidence shows no positive relationship between Aggressive/Defensive style and managerial effectiveness. This is in contrast to the significant positive relationship between Constructive styles and managerial effectiveness, however there is no significant relationship between the Constructive styles and salary.

Ironically, even though an individual gets promoted for 'getting things done' (task focus) as they are climbing the corporate ladder, when they reach the 'top job', it's not the ability to get things done that they need, it's the ability to get things done *through people*. In this sense, a high task orientation can be a limitation for a CEO. Highly task-oriented and Aggressive/Defensive behaviours are associated with an inclination to place more importance on 'things' rather than people. It can lead to de-emphasising feelings, setting unrealistically high, and in some cases unachievable, standards and behaviours that, although they may secure some results in the short term, are actually self-defeating in the long term. The results typically come at quite a high cost, in terms of 'burning' relationships and de-motivating people along the way,

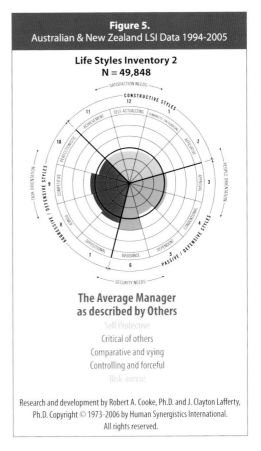

Figure 5.
Australian & New Zealand LSI Data 1994-2005

The Average Manager as described by Others

resulting in a high attrition rate, and the loss of talent and corporate knowledge that is associated with staff turnover. The actual and opportunity costs of this impact do not feature on a balance sheet.

A profile high in Aggressive/Defensive behaviours is also likely to be motivated by a desire to 'look good', appearing to be in control and on top of everything. When a CEO has too much invested in their image and reputation, it is likely that they will be reluctant to admit to mistakes, and that the need to be seen as a 'winner' will override the need to face reality when times get tough. When times do get tough, those needs may manifest in driving staff hard to perform tasks and activities that employ risk-averse tactics to avoid failure, rather than strategies that focus on achieving success for the organisation.

While Gordon Cairns did not like getting this feedback, he understood that if the culture was to change, he and his senior reports needed to make it happen by role-modelling a new approach and new ways of working.

Figure 6. Outcomes associated with Life Styles Inventory			
Factor	Constructive	Passive / Defensive	Aggressive / Defensive
Managerial Effectiveness	++	0	
Quality of Interpersonal Relations	++	+	–
Job Satisfaction	++	--	
Psychological/Physiological Health	++	-	–
Problem-Solving Effectiveness	+	-	
Interest in Self-Improvement	++	+	–
Organisational Level	+	--	
Salary	0	--	+

+ Indicates positive significant relationship; 0 Indicates non-significant relationship; - Indicates negative significant relationship   Copyright © 1987 by Human Synergistics International. All rights reserved.

Most people [leaders] recognise that you can't get good results without a great culture, but they think culture is something that's out there and doesn't start with them; that's the difficulty. They say 'we need a culture transformation program and oh, by the way, I'm not going to participate in it [as CEO] and neither is the senior team'... The whole point about that is it reinforces the belief that it is just another quick fix, another feel good, because the person/people who need it most are not taking part. There is no such thing as 'the company'. The company is individuals. And it's individuals that have to change

(Gordon Cairns, CEO 1997-2004).

Lion Nathan

Phase **3** Action

Overview

Following on from the results and new learnings, Lion Nathan invested a good deal of time and effort in researching all available literature and practices on implementing change in organisations. The knowledge gained from this exercise enabled it to develop a comprehensive model for change that it has refined into a strategic capability over the years.

This model incorporated the following key characteristics:
- Clear expectations about what was required from leaders
- On-going and specific measurement and evaluation of progress
- The search for 'best practice', and an evidence-based approach to change
- Thoughtful and inclusive planning, involving the active participation and buy-in of the top leadership teams
- Experimentation through pilot programs
- Disciplined execution of programs
- Consistency of messages and tools
- Reflection and evaluation
- Renewal - continuous improvement

The research Lion Nathan conducted on change, and its participation in a series of change workshops in 1997, combined with a collaborative approach to problem solving, provided some key insights which led the company to develop its cultural transformation strategy around three pillars:
- Creating a sense of purpose, vision and values
- Developing leadership capability
- Reinforcing the desired behaviours through people management processes and systems

Creating a Sense of Purpose

As was previously mentioned, one of the primary insights to emerge from the initial change workshops conducted in 1997 was the need for change to be anchored in a sense of purpose and values. Input from employees about what values should be core to the company was followed by intense discussion and debate among the senior leadership team. Eventually, they agreed that the company's core purpose should be 'To make our world a more social place'. This did not represent the ever-popular 'Big Hairy Audacious Goal' (BHAG) but rather, was a higher-level aspiration, the outcome of people connecting over Lion's products – a drink at home with a partner, or in a pub with mates, at special functions with colleagues or at dinner with friends; people having fun, socialising with one another and relaxing – feeling good about life.

Lion came to the conclusion that in order to really engage with its people, it needed to inspire them to a cause. Gordon Cairns elaborates on this idea as he explains the notion of an organisation as a social network, where people volunteer their talent: *"I can't force you to come to*

You inspire people by making what they do meaningful, and also something they can believe in

work, I can't tell you to come here, I can't command you to work harder. You are a human being, you voluntarily give up your talent to come to work. The only way I can reach you is to inspire you. You inspire people by making what they do meaningful, and also something they can believe in."

To Lion, it is important for the company that this sense of purpose is reflected in the day-to-day working lives of its people. Its aim is that Lion people have a great time while they do their work. Lion does not perceive that fun and working efficiently and effectively are mutually exclusive constructs.

Lion's core purpose, together with the three values identified earlier (Act with Integrity, Face Reality, Passion for the business), formed the foundation and context for all the work that was to come – not just in terms of how change would be implemented, but also in relation to how business decisions would be made.

These values have stood the test of time, although insight and reflection have led to the inclusion of two additional values: 'Achieving Together', and 'Being Sociable'. Meanwhile, 'Face Reality' has become a sub-set of 'Act with Integrity'.

In 2004, 150 of Lion's top leaders came together to test the values and core purpose. They 'voted' using hand-held portable machines, and their levels of commitment were:

Core Purpose	**94%**
Act with Integrity	**97%**
Passion	**98%**
Achieving Together	**98%**
Being Sociable	**98%**

The core purpose and values of the company have formed and continue to form the bedrock of Lion's approach to leadership and cultural development, and as People & Culture Director Bob Barbour says, *"We have never yet laminated them and stuck them on the walls."*

The leadership team also did a lot of work in arriving at Lion's core purpose and vision. This sense of purpose, mission and values were incorporated into a one-page blueprint that is used to filter decision making (see Figure 7).

Lion's commitment to using this blueprint as a 'filter' for making decisions about the business has been tested over time. In 1999 for example, Lion considered the prospect of poker machines as a possible profit generator. *"Fosters were into it in a big way, making over $100 million"* says Bob Barbour. *"We decided not to get into it because we decided it was not consistent with our core purpose of making the world a more sociable place."*

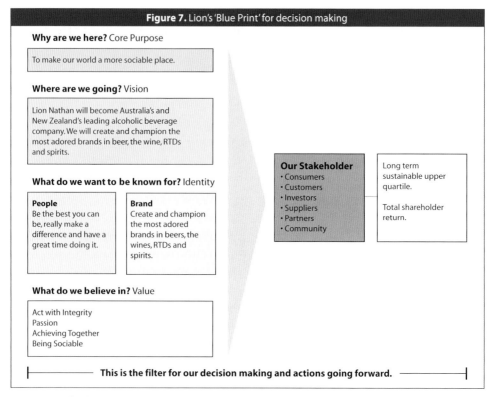

Figure 7. Lion's 'Blue Print' for decision making

Why are we here? Core Purpose

To make our world a more sociable place.

Where are we going? Vision

Lion Nathan will become Australia's and New Zealand's leading alcoholic beverage company. We will create and champion the most adored brands in beer, the wine, RTDs and spirits.

What do we want to be known for? Identity

People
Be the best you can be, really make a difference and have a great time doing it.

Brand
Create and champion the most adored brands in beers, the wines, RTDs and spirits.

Our Stakeholder
- Consumers
- Customers
- Investors
- Suppliers
- Partners
- Community

Long term sustainable upper quartile.

Total shareholder return.

What do we believe in? Value

Act with Integrity
Passion
Achieving Together
Being Sociable

This is the filter for our decision making and actions going forward.

Once it had determined its core purpose and values, Lion had to communicate these to its people. They realised that the primary conduit had to be the leadership teams across the organisation, and so Lion set about developing the first of its leadership programs, aimed at extending the capability of its leaders to deliver the new messages effectively.

Leadership Drives Cultural Transformation

Bob Barbour realised that if leaders were the key to effective culture change, they needed to understand more about what constituted effective leadership, in order to determine what 'leadership' would mean for Lion. His team researched the available literature on effective leadership, and eventually the Lion leadership team identified and agreed that essentially, great leadership came down to four levers:

- A motivating sense of purpose
- Talent management
- Future focus
- Creating a high performance culture, using the OCI as the template.

Lion's view was that the primary determinant of the culture of a team was the leadership style of its leader. Using the insights gained from their research, Lion developed and delivered its own leadership development program based on these levers. The underlying principle was that in order to change the culture, the leaders had to change, and for the leaders to change, they needed to understand what Lion wanted from them. The program was delivered by Lion's senior leadership team.

According to Bob Barbour, *"Getting your own leadership to deliver it has a couple of benefits. One is you get really clear in your own mind what this is all about, because you're standing up there talking about it and getting questions. It really helps you to think about areas that you've got gaps in, or that you could do something about personally. Secondly, as it happens, a lot later on there was a lot of research that shows the most effective form of training is delivered by leaders within the business, [as] it's more credible."*

TRANSFORMATION GETS PERSONAL

The credibility pay-off that Bob referred to relies, of course, on the quality of the message being delivered, and on the capability of the leader delivering it. Lion's starting point therefore was to engage its leadership group in the process by making the case for change personal. Bringing the message home to them initially through the feedback provided via the LSI process, Lion's approach to turning their Defensive culture into a Constructive one rested on increasing the awareness of individual leaders regarding their personal style, and the impact they had on their teams and on the organisation as a whole.

> **It creates change in people because it creates a bit of pain… it causes you to want to move**

The decision to use the LSI 1&2 tool was made on the basis that the leadership team had experienced its impact, and had also seen it create change in others. Bob Barbour recalls the rationale: *"It creates change in people because it gives you feedback you don't like. It creates a bit of pain. You get feedback saying people are observing these behaviours, and by the way here are some more Constructive behaviours, so it causes you to want to move. We saw it change quite a lot of people"* (Bob Barbour, People & Culture Director).

Lion invested a great deal of time and effort in ensuring that all leaders were properly de-briefed on what the results meant. This was crucial, because individuals tend to experience myriad reactions when they receive their initial LSI feedback.

Gordon Cairn's initial reaction, for example, was anger, and to dismiss it as 'not being him': *"As soon as you get the LSI you go 'that's not me, that's how other people see me. It's not who I am.' So you go home and you show your wife and she says to you, 'that is who you are, and quite frankly, I and the kids have been telling you that for a long time.' …So in a nice way your wife is saying look we'd like you to change as well… [it] seems to me, what more is there than a successful marriage and a successful career? That's a compelling reason to change"* (Gordon Cairns, CEO 1997-2004).

The initial pain experienced in receiving feedback indicating that others see you less constructively than you see yourself seems to be an important step towards personal change. This 'disturbance factor', often backed up by feedback from family members, seems to create a dissonance, a 'moment of truth' situation, and a compelling motivation for change, as individuals realise that the impact of their behaviour is often counter to how they see themselves and, more importantly perhaps, counter to their personal values. Jamie Tomlinson, Chief Financial Officer summarizes: *"The personal circumplex I think is a very powerful device. I've done it now five or six times and personally made a change. It's because it hits you pretty hard when you get a bad one. You take it home and show it to your wife and say 'look what they're saying about me and she says well actually that's pretty accurate… it's that kind of internal resonance that really hits you, and then every day you make subtle changes and when a whole bunch of people do that there's no question that it brings about positive change."*

Open sharing of LSI feedback - suddenly [the] Emperor's new clothes became significantly more apparent

The initial LSI debrief was also accompanied by a process of sharing individual results with peers in the leadership team. People were encouraged to show their circumplex to their peers (although it was their choice). In what might be deemed quite a controversial move, their peers then provided feedback, to which the only response they were allowed to make was, 'Thank you'. It was quite a challenging and confronting process. This initial debriefing process was then followed up with one-on-one coaching to ensure that leaders were supported in taking action to move from Defensive behaviours to Constructive behaviours. The act of leaders sharing their circumplex with team members and peers had an enormous impact in terms of creating goodwill, as evidenced by this series of comments made by individual members participating in a research project focus group:

"Initially there was a very high emphasis on the need to change the culture from the very senior leaders. The CEO particularly was leading by example. This meant that the OCI/LSI was very powerful, because it was personal."

"Change starts at the top. The top leaders were coming out and sharing their circumplexes, and it was like they were saying 'If I can, you can too' - The whole process became very personalised."

"Culture starts at the top and so the leaders had to show a positive example of commitment to culture change. It wasn't that Gordon was perfect or that he actually demonstrated Constructive behaviours, it was that he was prepared to go public and say that he was not perfect and was trying to change."

"Open sharing of LSI feedback - suddenly [the] Emperor's new clothes became significantly more apparent."

(Focus Group Members)

The organisation's challenge to leaders to become more Constructive was made highly visible to everyone. Leaders were being held accountable for their behaviour, and the new expectation of personal responsibility and accountability became 'how we do things around here'. One of the ways Lion highlighted their leaders' responsibility for shaping the culture of their team was by providing each leader with a breakdown of the OCI results for their area, so they could track and pace the impact of their leadership style on their team. As one of Lion's line managers commented, *"Personal accountability took the arbitrary dimension out of it... there was no wriggle room."*

Building the Infrastructure to Keep Transformation on Track

The fundamental premise underpinning Lion's initial approach was that the most important unit of change was the individual. Once the process gathered speed however, the change needed to be supported by Lion's people-management practices, processes and systems if it was to be sustained over the long term. To this end, Lion developed a number of robust processes, referred to as 'The Lion Nathan Way', relating to its leadership development framework, competency models, performance management, talent review, and remuneration and reward practices.

The design of these processes was based on Lion's values, cultural vision and business goals. The overall framework was defined by Lion as 'Competency × Results' (C × R). This formula captured the belief that effective leaders focus on how they do things in order to get the right results. The notion of 'how' (competency) and 'what' (results) underpinned all of Lion's key processes, giving them the capacity to ensure that the desired behaviours were being put into practice.

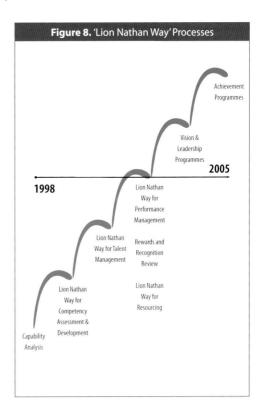

Figure 8. 'Lion Nathan Way' Processes

Achievement Programmes

Vision & Leadership Programmes

2005

1998

Lion Nathan Way for Performance Management

Lion Nathan Way for Talent Management

Rewards and Recognition Review

Lion Nathan Way for Competency Assessment & Development

Lion Nathan Way for Resourcing

Capability Analysis

COMPETENCY ASSESSMENT AND DEVELOPMENT

Lion has developed nine competencies which are used in the process of assessing individuals and designing development plans. These competencies were developed in conjunction with the leadership team to ensure a high degree of ownership, and are grouped according to the C × R framework. For example:

Competency
- Developing Solutions
- Personal Awareness
- Coaching & Developing Others

Results
- Achieving Results
- Functional Excellence

In 2006, as part of their evolving approach, Lion changed the framework to Behaviours × Results, which served to reinforce the underlying principle.

TALENT MANAGEMENT

The Talent Management Review is a very important part of Lion's business process. This is the process by which an individual's development needs are discussed and agreed on, and also the means by which the organisation can identify and develop key talent and key contributors. The talent management review process involves managers engaging in a one-on-one discussion with their staff, during which they discuss the individual's strengths, and areas requiring development. They also discuss the employee's 'Best Imaginable Career Path'. This process results in a development plan that includes experiences and competencies required to close the gap between current performance and future aspirations.

The information that is gathered through this process is then collated into organisational 'bench charts'. This enables Lion to facilitate career development for staff and allows them to track and address the company's capabilities and skills shortages.

Developing this process further, Lion Nathan has created a 'Talent Matrix' tool, which is particularly useful for identifying Lion's high-potential talent. It focuses on achieving results through functional excellence and learning agility. The latter is characterised by problem solving, personal awareness, and emotional intelligence.

> **Individuals are rewarded on the basis of achieving results in the right way**

ACHIEVEMENT REVIEW

The Achievement Review refers to Lion's performance management and remuneration review process. Again, individuals are assessed against a matrix that reviews performance against the Competency × Results framework. Individuals are rewarded on the basis of achieving results in the right way. In fact, Lion regards people who are high in results but low in competency and values as 'needing improvement'. Remuneration is based on high competency × high results, achieved in line with Lion's values.

Over the years, people who have consistently delivered high results, but in ways contrary to Lion's values and stated competencies, have been managed out of the organisation. This only happens after a long process of discussion, coaching, and an opportunity to improve their behaviour. In the early years of the transformation process, a couple of very high profile members of the senior leadership group were asked to leave. This sent a very powerful message to staff that Lion was serious about its commitment to its values, and that individual behaviour that ran counter to those values was unacceptable, no matter how good your results, or how senior your position.

RESOURCING

Lion Nathan's recruitment process is thorough and robust. It is based on the insights, gained from research, that 'a great company and a great job is more important to people than remuneration and lifestyle', and that 'people leave leaders, not companies!' As People & Culture Director Bob Barbour says, *"Free massages and lunches won't help if the relationship with the leader is not working."*

Lion focuses laser-like on attracting talented leaders as a key part of their strategy to attract and retain talented staff. The process itself is anchored in competency assessment and cultural fit, including whether individuals are 'sociable'. The process involves:

- 5 or 6 structured interviews
- Ability testing (verbal reasoning, numeric reasoning)
- Dinner (beer/wine)
- Motivation questionnaire

Appointing a New Leader 2004

Lion's approach to hiring talent was put to the test in 2004 when they set about recruiting a replacement for Gordon Cairns, who was leaving after seven years at the helm. When reflecting on his reasons for stepping down, Gordon responded candidly, and with great personal insight that demonstrated an on-going commitment to Lion's values and cultural vision: *"I am not the right person to take the next step for Lion Nathan. I believe a CEO's best work is done in the first years. My primary role is to hold up the mirror and make bold decisions. After seven years I have built a reputation I now want to protect. This is likely to make me risk-averse"* (Taylor, 2005).

The appointment of a new CEO is a crucial decision for any business, and arguably even more important when a company has invested as heavily in a cultural transformation program as Lion had. Culture, and the shaping of it, is a core function of the CEO role, and it is not unusual for incoming CEOs to 'throw the baby out with the bath water' in their enthusiasm to own the culture program, and bring their own style of leadership to the organisation. After seven years of sustained effort in the area of organisational development, Lion needed a CEO who not only would 'fit' Lion's existing culture, its aspirations, and its Constructive behavioural values, but who could develop it, and take it to the next level.

When Lion first approached Rob Murray in 2002, he was the CEO of Nestlé Oceana. He had a demonstrated track record in building high-performing businesses, and extensive experience in the fast-moving consumer goods sector. He had been responsible for building Nestlé's key brands such as Milo, Nescafé, Kit Kat and Maggi. When Rob was asked to consider being a candidate, he indicated that, as attractive as the prospect of discussions might be, he had given an undertaking to stay with Nestlé for four years, and that prohibited him from considering any other job prospects. Rob reflects: *"I went away thinking what a shame, and thinking [that for] 90% of companies that would put them off. The first thing that gave me a clue that Lion might offer something different was that they came back and said 'Well we think that's great that you view the world that way. Actually, now Gordon has decided to stay a couple of years longer, would you consider going on the Board as a kind of long process of you getting to know us and us getting to know you?'"*

Rob duly agreed to join the Board, and when Gordon announced his retirement date two years later, Rob went through a competitive process prior to being confirmed as Lion's choice to succeed Gordon as CEO. By then, Lion had the opportunity

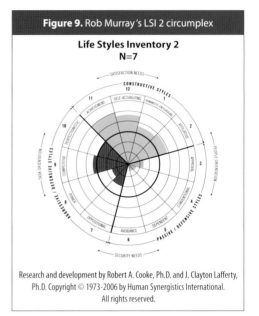

Figure 9. Rob Murray's LSI 2 circumplex

to observe Rob's style and approach, and had also been given permission to access Rob's circumplex, as seen here.

Rob Murray's profile showed a leader who was perceived by others as being very Constructive, with a primary style of Achievement, supported by a secondary style of Self-Actualizing. Rob was perceived as leading by example, and setting realistic and challenging goals that encouraged everyone to give their best throughout each project. The impact of the Constructive profile is likely to encourage team work by eliciting input from subordinates, and encouraging them to think for themselves within the context of specific values and principles. The combination of Achievement and Self-Actualizing styles is also likely to manifest in strong problem-solving skills, with the capacity to think laterally and at a big picture level. When discussing his views on balancing the 'hard edge' with the 'soft skills' in people management, Rob's comments reflect another aspect of the interplay between the goal-focussed Achievement style and the highly principled Self-Actualizing style: *"I just fundamentally don't believe people respond to fear… It's just not my right to drive fear into another individual. I really don't see this as my job, and I don't think it's my right on a human level. I try and show people some kind of compassion, that I am prepared to listen and think, but when I think results are unacceptable, I try to call that… I don't do it in a way that drives fear or negativity into them, I try to say it as I see it. You've got to be prepared to remain objective…"*

In the first year following Rob's appointment, Lion faced a number of tough strategic decisions, such as selling its Victorian Hotels, leaving China, and revising profit forecasts from what had been double-digit growth to a more conservative 5%, to enable the company to re-invest in itself in the interest of long-term sustainability. To have tackled so many issues so quickly is further evidence of Rob's Achievement and Self-Actualizing orientation at work, and also of Lion's courage under his leadership. CFO, Jamie Tomlinson, says: *"Rob's style is very open. He is very strategic, and trusts and wants people to do the right thing. In that kind of environment, people are happy to talk; there's no fear. He's prepared to take the medicine to the market. It's a courageous thing to do; he could have carried on as usual, which is what the market wants."*

Members of the focus group we ran when gathering material for this case study also commented that 'Rob Murray has taken Lion Nathan to new levels of honesty'. This level of honesty was revealed to the public in November 2005 when Rob announced that Lion had decided to stop the practice of 'Trade Loading'. This is the practice of stimulating sales of beer through discounting in times of high demand. The practice had been in use for seven years, and while it had come to be expected by customers, the leadership team decided that it did not align with the company's values, nor was it good for the business. Rob was quoted in the Australian Financial Review at the time saying: *"Increasing the amount of beer stocked in the trade through discounting at busy times or towards the end of a financial year raised production costs and caused problems with retail pricing. Lion would be a better company in the long run by ending trade loading."*

While there was a reasonable amount of speculation in 2004/05 about where Lion would head strategically under a new CEO, Rob's perspective on the role of a leader is clear. It is more to do with maintaining the health and long-term sustainability of the organisation than auctioning off its future in the interest of short-term gain, or acquiescing to the expectations of the market. Rob reflects: *"As a leader, you have to decide whether your role is your four or five years in the business, and your personal reputation related to that, or whether your role is you're a custodian of the business for this period of its life, and you need to hand it on to the next person healthier than you found it."*

It's just not my right to drive fear into another individual. I really don't see this as my job, and I don't think it's my right on a human level

The purpose of exploring Rob's character is not to validate him as a leader. Apart from the fact that this is not required (his achievements are already on the public record), the point of interest relates more to the role that Lion's cultural transformation from a Defensive to a Constructive culture played in the selection of its new CEO.

In seven years, the organisation had evolved to a point where part of the selection criteria for recruiting a new CEO was the degree to which they demonstrated Constructive behaviours. This research project has shown us that as the organisation transforms, the bar gets progressively raised year after year in terms of what is expected of its leadership. Given its cultural evolution over the past ten years, along with the strength of the Constructive elements of its culture and the enormous buy-in of its people, Lion could not, and would not, have chosen a leader who could not, as part of their natural orientation, 'walk the talk'.

Lion Nathan

Phase **4** Re-Test

Overview

Over the ten years since Lion began the transformation process, it has conducted thousands of Tests and Re-Tests in terms of individual LSI, and has conducted four organisation-wide culture surveys using the Organizational Culture Inventory (OCI).

For the purposes of evaluating the outcomes of Lion's cultural transformation, the Re-Test period refers to the data gathered, using the OCI tool, in 2000, 2002 and 2004.

The specific outcomes, which will be assessed below, are divided into two broad categories, cultural outcomes and business outcomes.

CULTURAL OUTCOMES

Moving from security to satisfaction, from a Defensive to a Constructive culture indicated by:

- An increase in satisfaction and overall Constructive clusters (Blue) compared with the baseline OCI measure in 1998.
- An increase in the Achievement style, one of the specific styles targeted for change (positive shift above the 50th percentile).
- A decrease in overall Defensive cluster (shift below the 50th percentile) with a specific emphasis on the Competitive and Perfectionistic styles, as they were the strongest styles in 1998.
- The shift in the senior leadership team's LSI 2 circumplex in 2005 compared to that in 1998/1999.
- Specific outcomes related to culture over time as measured through the OCI, such as employee satisfaction, role clarity, role conflict, and customer service.

In addition, Lion included supplementary questions with each OCI survey, conducted every two years, related to the following areas:

- Sense of Purpose
- Talent Management
- High Performance Culture

BUSINESS OUTCOMES

Business measures, such as those relating to engagement, profit, customer satisfaction and staff engagement, are reviewed and discussed.

Figure 10 highlights Lion's progressive transformation as seen through the lens of the organisation's circumplex. As can be seen, Lion has shifted steadily from a Security-oriented culture to one that is satisfaction-oriented. Overall, in the period 1998-2004 the Constructive styles increased by 53%. This increase has been accompanied by a substantial decrease in Aggressive/Defensive styles by 37%, with Passive/Defensive styles also decreasing by 33%.

Figure 10. Lion Nathan – Culture Survey Test ➜ Re-Test Results

Organizational Culture Inventory

1998   2000   2002   2004

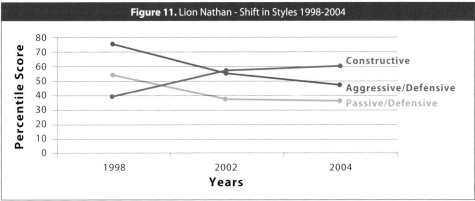

Figure 11. Lion Nathan - Shift in Styles 1998-2004

Constructive

Aggressive/Defensive

Passive/Defensive

The greatest shift occurred in the Power style, which decreased by just over 50%, followed interestingly enough by a decrease in the Competitive style, which by 2004 had decreased by just over 37%. This may indicate the effect of the organisation's emphasis on leaders motivating staff through a sense of purpose and teamwork, rather than through command and control. It may also reflect the impact of the strong push to live the organisation's values, especially that of 'Act with Integrity'.

The greatest increase in the Constructive style was recorded for Humanistic-Encouraging, which increased by 86%. The Achievement style also increased by 16%. Although, on the face of it, this may not seem like a large increase (given that Lion targeted it as a style it wanted to increase), its baseline was higher than the other Constructive styles, and it was therefore more difficult to achieve an increase in this area. In addition, while Lion promotes an Achievement-orientated culture, it is promoting achievement of tasks through people, as opposed to Achievement of tasks on their own - hence its Competency × Results model.

In 1998, Lion was predominantly task-oriented. To have focussed on Achievement at the exclusion of the other Constructive styles would have only reinforced this focus on tasks (Achievement being the most task-orientated of the Constructive styles). The increase in Humanistic-Encouraging style reflected both a re-balancing of task and people orientation, and the transformation of the leaders, translating into a move away from command and control and towards coaching. By way of example, the following quote refers to the experience of one of Lion's line managers: *"Leaders increased their focus on coaching others. Coaching workshops were run to ensure that leaders had the skills to coach, and as a result more time was spent in talking to people about behaviours. In my team I have also done Group Styles Inventory™ (GSI) and reviewed team styles and the circumplex on a regular basis. This has provided some incentives for changing the way we work, and has changed the culture"* (Line Manager).

Without over-playing the lower level increase of the Achievement style in comparison to the other Constructive styles like Humanistic-Encouraging (because any increase is a success), it is nevertheless interesting to note that the reasons for this may be linked to some of the views expressed by staff. The focus group of team leaders we interviewed for this research project saw the cultural transformation process as an anchor for the business in the midst of great change, and also as the main driver of staff retention over the years. There was a sense in this group that the discipline and consistency with which this strategy was implemented was not always reflected in other areas of the business. According to a Line Manager: *"The human resources strategy stayed consistent, while the other [business] strategies and leadership changed significantly – it was not a fly-by-night thing."*

Leaders increased their focus on coaching others… more time was spent in talking to people about behaviours

The view was also expressed that the adoption of this new approach of emphasising teamwork was in some ways a double-edged sword. The collective view was that the organisation was still feeling its way in terms of balancing what they perceived to be a tension between including the team in decision making, and the advantages of an individual-based decision-making process: *"[I'm] not sure that we challenge as much as we can, and sometimes we take consultation too far; lots of people gathered in rooms achieving consensus, which can sometimes take the edge off a decision."*

In any case, assisting people to achieve integration, or a synthesis, between individual and team, task and behaviour, and creative difference and conflict, represents an opportunity for Lion. Using what is now its combined strength in the Humanistic-Encouraging style (results through people) and its focus on Self-Actualizing (authenticity and values as supports to achievement) may well provide further opportunity to reinforce and eventually further increase the Achievement style.

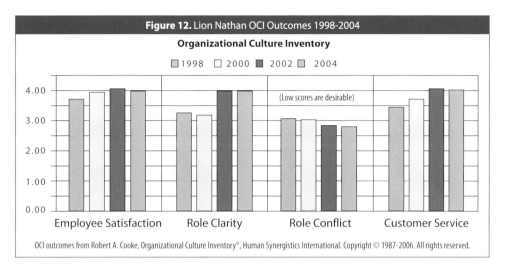

Figure 12. Lion Nathan OCI Outcomes 1998-2004

Organizational Culture Inventory

■ 1998   □ 2000   ■ 2002   ■ 2004

(Low scores are desirable)

Employee Satisfaction   Role Clarity   Role Conflict   Customer Service

OCI CULTURAL OUTCOMES

Given the increase in Constructive styles and decrease in Defensive styles, what impact did this have on the organisation's outcomes?

Figure 12 shows that in general, all the outcomes associated with the OCI measure showed an upward trend between 1998-2004, with employee satisfaction and customer service showing a slight decrease in 2004. This decrease is due to a response to one of the five questions that make up this outcome: 'Does the organisation respond effectively to the changing needs of customers and clients?' Employees rated this at 3.40 in 2004 compared to 3.41 in 2002. For all other questions in that category, the scores were higher than in the 2002 OCI Test.

Figure 13 shows the responses to the supplementary questions Lion added to the OCI. The questions were divided into a number of major headings. There were more categories than those that are shown here (e.g. 'stretch goals', 'renewal'), however the categories of 'Sense of Purpose', 'High Performance Culture', and 'Talent Management' were consistent throughout 2000 to 2004, whereas the other categories were not. Of note is that these measures are linked to Lion's three pillars in terms of their leadership development program. It can be seen once again that there is an upward trend, although in 2004 there was a decrease in 'Talent Management'. This decrease was the result of several factors, the primary one being the decision by Lion to limit the category of questions in 'Talent Management' in 2004.

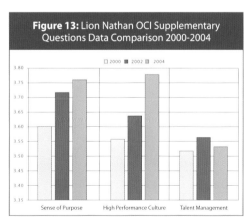

Figure 13: Lion Nathan OCI Supplementary Questions Data Comparison 2000-2004

□ 2000   ■ 2002   ■ 2004

Sense of Purpose   High Performance Culture   Talent Management

The Leadership-Culture Connection

Lion's leadership team has gone through many changes in this ten year period. Still, operating on the principle that there is a relationship between leadership and culture, it is interesting to note where the leadership team sits today compared with where the team sat in 1998 (see Figure 14).

In comparing the organisation's OCI circumplex with that of the Senior Leadership Team's LSI circumplex, it is possible to see the relationship between leadership and culture.

Overall, the pattern of each circumplex is relatively similar, although the leadership circumplex shows higher levels of Constructive behaviours and lower levels of Defensive behaviours. Encouragingly, all

> **When you get people to really buy into this, they become very, very sensitive to how they are led; you need leaders who do it well. Any inconsistencies will be pointed out to you**

Defensive behaviours are below the 50th percentile (third dark circle from the centre) in both circumplexes. The level of constructiveness of the leadership team is not just a function of individual development, effective recruitment and selection, but also reflects one of the 'by-products' of a cultural transformation process, which is that once people really commit to the vision of a Constructive culture, their expectations of leaders get higher and higher.

Rob Murray says, *"When you get people to really buy into this, they become very, very sensitive to how they are led; you need leaders who do it well. Any inconsistencies will be pointed out to you."*

In such an organisation, leaders who don't 'walk the talk' are not an option. This has a downside in that individuals can feel a little impatient with having to tolerate a leader who is transitioning from leading through Defensive behaviours to leading through more Constructive behaviours.

Having established that Lion's cultural transformation process did achieve an increase in Constructive styles, and that this had a flow-on effect on the outcomes associated with culture as measured by the OCI tool and its leadership team, the big question is, 'has this translated into business performance?'

Business Outcomes

Overall, Lion Nathan's business shows a reasonably high level of success across financial, employee engagement, and customer satisfaction indicators. The on-going challenge to those of us working in this field is to endeavour to explain the nature of the relationship between culture and business performance. While there is a growing body of evidence that demonstrates a direct relationship between profit and culture, it is often difficult (in Lion Nathan's case in particular) to draw the same conclusion.

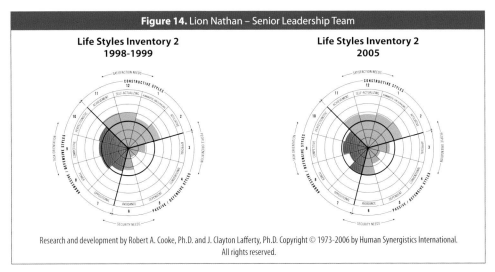

Figure 14. Lion Nathan – Senior Leadership Team

Life Styles Inventory 2
1998-1999

Life Styles Inventory 2
2005

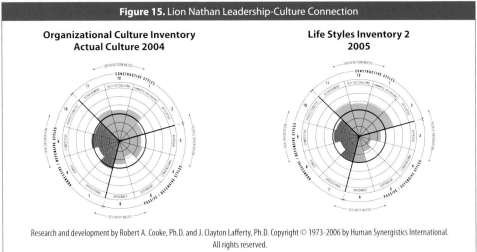

Figure 15. Lion Nathan Leadership-Culture Connection

Organizational Culture Inventory
Actual Culture 2004

Life Styles Inventory 2
2005

At various times during the ten year period after it embarked on its transformational journey, Lion implemented a series of initiatives that pulled a number of different levers in terms of business performance, strategy, recruitment and investment in other markets. Arguably, all of these played some role in turning around the performance of Lion over that ten-year period. What is undeniable however, is that in 1996 and 1997, Lion's financial results were poor. By 2004, it had steadily improved its performance in terms of profit, EBITA, and shareholder returns. The share price is a particular case in point, having risen from $3.34 to $7.38 in that time. At the same

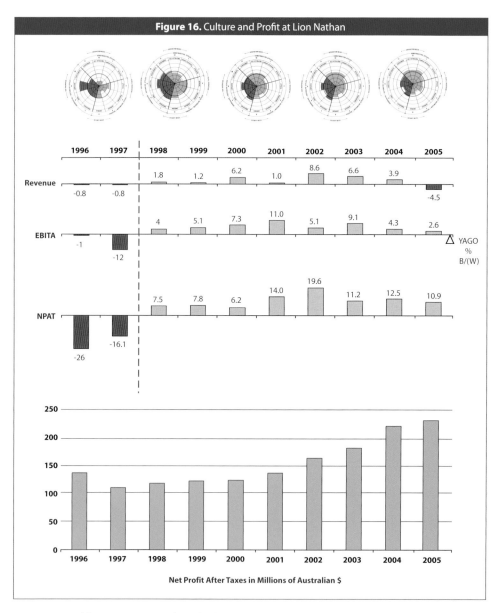

Figure 16. Culture and Profit at Lion Nathan

time, it was able to maintain relatively high employee engagement and customer satisfaction scores, even though these fell just short of Lion's own expectations and goals.

Was it simply coincidental that this progress occurred, and has been maintained, concurrently with the culture becoming more Constructive? In light of the available evidence, this would be a hard argument to maintain. The results would indicate that a great culture produces great results.

A Constructive culture contributes to great results by ensuring that everyone is working at optimal levels in a collaborative and effective manner to achieve business results. Culture promotes an internal cohesiveness that enables people to 'get on with the job'.

According to CFO, Jamie Tomlinson: *"It promotes an external focus rather than an internal one. It helps people focus on what's important."*

While most leaders agree that culture is integral to business success, there is still a fair amount of pressure to prove the value of this work, in terms of its direct return on investment, and its impact on the bottom line. In our pre-occupation with doing so, it is easy to overlook the fact that, as the primary mechanism for adapting to the environment, culture, in a sense, is the bottom line.

> ## It promotes an external focus rather than an internal one. It helps people focus on what's important

Whether they realise it or not, rapid and effective adaptation to the environment should be the primary concern of leaders and boards. Without an agile culture, one that can flex and change with the ebb and flow of market forces, an organisation will not survive, and neither will shareholder returns. So in this sense, has Lion developed a culture that supports its adaptation to the environment and delivered results? The evidence from the past ten years suggests that it has.

EMPLOYEE ENGAGEMENT

Lion has been participating in the Hewitt Best Employers survey since 2000. While Lion has maintained a reasonable level of engagement since 2000, in recent years this has decreased slightly. For the last two years, it has achieved an engagement score of 68%. Although the score sits just below its target of 75%, Lion Nathan is still well-positioned relative to other companies.

One of the assumptions associated with staff satisfaction, and, indirectly, with high engagement, is that happy, productive staff are more likely to produce higher levels of customer satisfaction. While Lion continues to seek improvement in both its engagement and customer satisfaction scores, both are already high.

"Lion is a tough company to leave; it's got a cultural attraction that creates an internal pull. People are approachable and open, it's a democratic organisation. These are indicators that are impacted by the culture" (Jamie Tomlinson, CFO).

CUSTOMER SATISFACTION

Figure 17 outlines the results of customer satisfaction surveys conducted since 2001 by social research firm TNS. It shows Lion Nathan's customer satisfaction scores with respect to different areas of its business. Over the course of the five years since Lion commenced using this survey, the organisation's overall performance in terms of customer satisfaction has consistently been around 80%.

Figure 17. Lion Nathan Customer Satisfaction	Performance Score				
	W1 Sep 01 (n=1000)	W2 Mar 02 (n=977)	W3 Sep 02 (n=996)	W4 Sep 03 (n=1244)	W5 Sep 04 (n=1219)
Tap Beer Servicing	7.1	7.4	6.7	7.0	7.5
Field Sales Force	7.7	7.9	7.7	7.8	8.0
Commercial Terms and Billing	8.6	8.5	8.5	8.6	8.5
Product Delivery	8.5	8.6	8.5	8.5	8.3
Ordering Placing Process	8.6	8.3	8.4	8.4	8.4
Brands	8.3	8.3	8.1	8.3	8.2
Product Quality	8.6	8.7	8.6	8.7	8.6
Overall Performance	8.1	8.1	8.0	8.2	8.1

Significant increase in area of Tap Beer Servicing and some improvement though not statistically significant in Field Sales Force (sig at 90% only). Satisfaction with Product Quality and Product Delivery has declined. The decline in these areas has offset improvements in Tap Beer Servicing and Field Sales Force leading to no improvement on overall satisfaction.

Significantly LOWER than previous wave at 95% confidence interval
Significantly HIGHER than previous wave at 95% confidence interval

Lion Nathan

Phase **5**

Review

Change Agents | Lessons Learnt | Future Challenges

Change Agents

Internal Change Agents	Bob Barbour - People & Culture Director
	Gordon Cairns - CEO 1997-2004
	Lion Nathan Senior Leadership Team
	Lion Nathan Human Resources Team
	Rob Murray - CEO since October 2004

External Change Agents	Carolyn Taylor - Corporate Vision (her company at that time) in the early stages of the process.

Cultural transformation, almost by definition, is the collective achievement of a group of individuals, including all employees, who have chosen to follow where their leaders suggested they go. In the face of external pressures and internal challenges, someone, sometime, must initiate the process. This usually happens when an individual has glimpsed something of the way forward. In Lion's case, the individual responsible for choosing this particular road to walk down was Bob Barbour.

With the support of external partners such as Carolyn Taylor in the early days, and in particular, his highly dedicated team of human resource professionals, Bob had enough information to go to Gordon Cairns with a suggestion on how Lion should move its change initiative forward. While Bob initially led the way into what was uncharted territory, there is no doubt that it was the collective efforts of the Lion Nathan leadership team that led the company towards its destination. Rather than focusing on individual contributions, it is useful to reflect on the qualities that created the impact that in turn resulted in transformational change throughout the organisation.

COURAGE AND THE ABILITY TO FACE REALITY

Jim Collins, in his high-profile book *Good to Great*, demonstrates how the most successful companies' leadership teams share the quality of being able to face the truth (no matter how brutal). Any organisation seeking to transform from a good company to a great company needs to first go through a point of awareness, a realisation, and then acceptance that the company could do better, could be better. Between 1995 and 1998, Lion had already started the journey of exploring change, but in 1998, faced with the incontrovertible evidence of its poor financial performance and Aggressive/Defensive culture survey results, it reached the point of awareness. What it had been doing was not working, and it needed to do something completely different. The Leadership Team's courage was in moving away from the familiar towards something different and untried, which, at some level, always involves a leap of faith. This courage was mirrored in the personal transformation of the leaders. Confronted with information that caused a level of pain, their response was to experience it, rather than deny it, and use it as a means to move towards a more Constructive way of behaving.

EMOTIONAL MATURITY AND SELF DISCIPLINE

Being a leader is not easy. Leaders have enormous responsibilities, not just in terms of their functional commitments to the organisation, but in terms of their duty of care to their team members.

Lion's cultural transformation was achieved by its leaders demonstrating a level of emotional maturity and personal discipline that is not commonplace in the corporate world. Emotional maturity incorporates the ability to hold the view, and work with the fact, that the standards placed on you as a leader are necessarily much higher than on your team members or other employees (no matter what their behaviour). It is the capacity to lead by example and master one's emotions and 'baggage' – in even the most trying of circumstances – that in part determines whether people will follow you willingly. In addition to emotional maturity, this kind of leadership demands a high level of personal insight and self-discipline in order to persist with areas that, by virtue of having developed over many years, are resistant to, and extremely difficult to, change.

THE WILL AND MOTIVATION TO EXCEL

Lion Nathan's change agents' motivation is for the company and all its people be the best that they can be. In bringing its products and services to the market, it seeks to improve on and better its achievements, always stretching towards higher principles. This motivation to excel is not just reflected in the goals Lion sets for itself, but even more so in their approach to implementing new initiatives. Their process highlighted a dedication to seek the most up-to-date learning and best practice research in the world, and to develop the ability to translate them into principles relevant to Lion Nathan via the 'Lion Nathan Way'.

THE CONTRIBUTION OF THE HUMAN RESOURCES TEAM – PACING AND EMBEDDING THE TRANSFORMATION

Working away behind the scenes, designing, developing, trialling and evaluating new tools, was Bob Barbour's Human Resources team. That their tools and processes have largely stood the test of time indicates a thorough knowledge and understanding of their client groups. They also had a particular ability to pace the evolution of systems and tools in a way that enabled innovation and adaptation while building on the prior phases. They anchored the strategy, and provided consistent support to line management in their efforts to lead the team to 'Bluer' pastures. The consistency across the organisation can be attributed to the partnership between the leadership team and their human resources business partners.

Lessons Learnt

One of the extraordinary things about the Lion Nathan transformation process is the consistent use of messages, tools and methodologies. Reviewing communication and presentations from the past ten years, what is striking is that the values, key messages and ideas have not changed. Rather, Lion has built on this foundation year after year, so that the result is a deepening of the knowledge, awareness and experiences of its leadership teams and its people.

Over the years, Lion has reflected on each stage of its on-going transformation, and identified a number of insights and key learnings:

- CEO and Leadership Team must be involved and committed
- Leaders are the key
- Understand your current culture and the link to performance
- Articulate a clear plan
- Be consistent and focussed in your efforts over a long period (it's a marathon, not a sprint).
- Behaviour change takes time and commitment
- Congruence of behaviour. Don't say it if you're not prepared to do it! (Barbour, 2005)

THE ROLE OF PAIN IN ORGANISATIONAL TRANSFORMATION

There is one item that is not on their list, but is extremely important, and has been acknowledged by all those interviewed for this case study. There is a level of pain that goes with the process of change, and there is value in that pain. Gordon Cairns summarised what he had learnt in three concise points: *"[1] There is value in suffering. Parts of the experience have been very painful, parting with friends, looking in the mirror... [2] The acceptance of responsibility. I did not really understand what this meant, and I see many of my peers in the business community seek to avoid it. I have come to understand what it really means. I have come to believe that no matter how big the problem, we can solve it... [3] Dedication to the truth. When a mirror was held up and I saw myself from another person's perspective, I came to accept that was the truth. My quest became to change the behaviour that caused another person to see me that way..."* (Taylor, 2005)

In reviewing Lion's story, it is also clear that underpinning the company's transformation was a set of assumptions that adopting a methodical, collaborative and inclusive approach to problem solving was necessary to deliver the required insights and actions.

ASSUMPTIONS AND BELIEFS
Determining Core Purpose and Values are Key

One of the first things Lion Nathan did when it knew it was about to embark on a significant journey of transformation was to define its core purpose and values as a company. While the Competency × Results framework underpins Lion's people management processes, it was conceived within the context of the company's core purpose and values - the 'why'.

One of the best ways to motivate people to deliver great results is to inspire them to a cause, a sense of purpose - to help them see the significance of their work within the bigger picture. Core purpose, vision and values are about direction and reason for being. As author Stephen Covey says, 'If the ladder is not leaning against the right wall, every step we take just gets us to the wrong place faster' (Covey, 1989).

In discussing the work Lion is continuing to do on exploring the benefit and impact of values in the workplace, Bob Barbour explained their reasoning this way: *"We believe that if people are really clear about what's important to them, they will be much more effective inside of work and outside of work. They will be far more self-actualised. I think the Self-Actualizing style is the keystone in the OCI and LSI tool, that's why it sits at the top. If you can really build Self-Actualizing behaviour and thoughts, then you become much more Constructive and less Defensive, because why would you need to be? If you can do that as a leader, you build a culture in the*

> **If you can really build Self-Actualizing behaviour and thoughts .. as a leader, you build a culture in the team around you.. which is highly Constructive... which ultimately builds marketplace success**

team around you, and the people you have contact with, which is highly Constructive, which we know will build high engagement, which we know is a good basis for external engagement, which ultimately builds marketplace success."

Individuals Form the Basic Unit of Change and Transformation

Individual change is a prerequisite of cultural transformation. When a company undertakes a process of cultural transformation, whether it is aware of it or not, it has undertaken a quest which cannot be achieved unless individuals accept the invitation to change and transform with it. This concept is fundamental to the success of transformation efforts. Things don't transform, people do.

Decision-based Change vs Behaviour-based Change

The distinction between decision-based change and behaviour-based change as an approach to organisational development and/or cultural transformation is an important one, because it has implications for the process of transformation that is adopted. This insight arose from reflecting on the nature of change, and how Lion had previously implemented change. Decision-based change is driven from the top, and by a business imperative. As an approach, it too can be useful, and sometimes necessary. However, in a cultural change program, behaviour-based change is more appropriate. This recognises that in order for change to be effective and sustained, the individual must see the need for change as compelling, and must 'own' their own process.

Connectivity
In the final analysis, the way to deliver great results is to nurture a great culture. A great culture is defined by high levels of emotional connection (engagement) between an individual, their role, their leader and the organisation. Great results are achieved when there is a high level of connectivity between the organisation (as a living system) and the 'market' – their customers and consumers.

Consistency and 'Stickability'
To borrow from Gordon Cairns, 'organisational change is not really rocket science'. There are copious texts on how to do change, all of which essentially say the same thing; set clear expectations, make sure the right people are in the right roles, communicate the vision, integrate values into your people-management systems, and so on. The knowledge that these things work has been around for more than fifteen years. However, these texts often leave out the secret ingredients: consistency and stickability. The use of consistent tools in a consistent way, so that messages are consistently conveyed, enables changes in behaviour to emerge. Stickability means persisting with the effort of making all this happen, even in the face of external pressures, internal flux and personal doubt. One of Lion's greatest achievements is not just that it achieved transformation, but that it stuck at it for ten years!

Congruence between Rhetoric and Behaviour
Lion was able to harness the collective will of its people because it could demonstrate a commitment to its espoused values and beliefs. For example, Lion publicly proclaimed and institutionalised the notion that how you did things was as important as what you did. Indeed the notion has become enshrined in its internal formula for success:
success = competency × results (recently revised to behaviour × results).

From an employee perspective, it is very easy to test an organisation's commitment to its stated values and its credibility. You just watch how the organisation treats the people who, although they behave appallingly, and in ways counter to the stated values, produce great results for the company. If these individuals survive, and indeed thrive, without being called to account for their behaviour, or without any change in their behaviour, employees know that their organisation is not serious about its commitment. Worse, employees know that the organisation and its leaders cannot be trusted. Lion's commitment to maintaining this level of congruence was, and is, very public. If, as a Lion employee, your values and behaviour are out of alignment with the organisation's values, and if this is still the case after you have had opportunities to improve, you will be asked to leave.

"... at the centre of it is this belief that if you actually really want to change your culture, it's important to be clear - it's not just important to us what you achieve, but its important to us how you behave, and how you achieve these results- and that's an enormous step. Taking it to its extreme, we could have people in the company who deliver really quite strong results, but who do it (if I can put it like this) in the wrong way, exhibiting the wrong behaviours. We'd ask them to leave the business" (Rob Murray, CEO).

Future Challenges

Lion's journey continues. Having made great strides forward in terms of organisational development and culture, its focus moving forward is to explore how it might enhance its overall connection to the marketplace. Lion is investigating how it might use the capability it has developed internally around culture to more effectively understand and engage its customers and consumers. The fourth iteration of its leadership development program focuses on the concept of engagement, and what this means for effective leadership, both internally for the team, and externally for customers and consumers.

BEHAVIOURS × RESULTS

While Lion's transformation process has always focussed on promoting behaviours consistent with its corporate purpose and core values, it is now raising behavioural change to another level, encouraging authenticity in its people through further clarification of their values. The operating assumption and rationale is that values drive people's motivations. Lion is seeking to facilitate a process whereby its people can reflect on, refine and confirm their own set of values, with the aim of ultimately enabling them to understand how their values impact on their behaviour. People & Culture Director, Bob Barbour says, *"What we want to do is try and help them connect the values they have identified for themselves to their thinking styles through the LSI 1, to the behaviours that people see, on the basis that it will provide a powerful motivation to change."*

While Rob Murray is committed to continuing Lion's transformation, he is also committed to moving more deeply into the 'Blue' by encouraging staff to really work and live their values in a way that hits closer to home, rather than through competencies as measures of skill.

"Genuine people, authentic people, behave in certain ways and that drives results," says CEO Rob Murray. *"I'm not sure that pre-prescribing it as competencies is the right approach. To me, it's more a process of lining up what people are about, what they are driven by, what values they've got and whether these values are compatible with the business, then helping them to live those values in a business context. People then feel more comfortable, in work and outside of work. But whether it's competencies or behaviours × results, the key thing is that people understand that how you do things is as important as the results you get."*

STANDARDISATION – THE DISCIPLINE OF EFFECTIVE EXECUTION

The key to Lion Nathan's future success lies in the disciplined execution of its strategy, taking the company forward to the next stage of its development. The collective impact of a carefully considered strategy focussed on market connectivity, together with its effective and deliberate deployment, will produce sustainable long-term results.

"The next stage of our journey is linked to standardising the way we do things. The 'Lion Nathan Way for sales; the Lion Nathan Way for brand; building the Lion Nathan Way for fast change and managing change, just standardising the way we do things" according to Rob Murray, CEO.

Conclusion

In recording any company's journey of transformation, it is quite easy to lose sight of the forest for the trees. In detailing and elaborating on what the company did, and how it did it, in an effort to understand the actual drivers of cultural transformation (the subject of our research), we may miss the opportunity to respond to what is arguably one of the big questions in the area of organisational transformation - of what strategic value to the organisation is cultural transformation? Does it, in real terms, deliver a competitive advantage beyond the obvious staff retention, customer focussed and financial measures (not insignificant boons in themselves)?

Through implementing its cultural transformation, Lion Nathan has developed a strategic capability to integrate continuous change, and to see change as an everyday business activity.

In a world where we are bombarded with moment-by-moment reminders that 'the only constant is change', a company that is able to respond to these changes without outwardly disturbing its day-to-day operations must surely have a competitive advantage. This is particularly the case in light of the evidence available, which indicates that most companies fail in their efforts to change (McCarthy, 2003, 2004, 2005).

Possessing this capability now does not mean that Lion can rest on its track record of success. In fact, all indications are that the goals have moved on to the next frontier, and Lion's gaze is fixed firmly on stretching towards its next achievement:

"We are raising the bar, so that we are good at doing what we say in the marketplace. Ultimately, that's where you get not just financial performance but also massive satisfaction, because you achieve and deliver the results that you have promised" (Rob Murray, CEO).

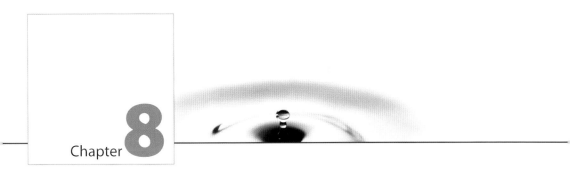

Chapter **8**

Epilogue

Epilogue

So, did we answer our clients' challenge? How do organisations transform their cultures? What creates transformation? What is the evidence about what works?

At the beginning of this research project, Dexter Dunphy predicted that we would find little that was fundamentally new in the practice of cultural transformation. Returning to our discussion of the 'knowing-doing gap', most of the processes we have written about here were already known, and published in articles and recipe lists of 'the 10 steps to transforming your organisation's culture'. Our consulting experience clearly showed that organisations were *doing* many of these processes, with varying degrees of success.

We are delighted that Dexter's prediction proved to be wrong, and that he went on to conceptualise a new process model for cultural transformation. I believe this model goes a long way to answering our clients' challenge, and adds significantly to the practice of transformational change.

Human Synergistics and our network of Accredited Practitioners now face the challenge of translating this model into practical tools and insights for managers to use in their transformational efforts.

> **We shall not cease from exploration**
> **And the end of all our exploring**
> **Will be to return to the same place**
> **And know it for the first time**
> (T.S. Eliot)

GOING BEYOND KNOWING AND DOING

At a personal level, a significant 'Aha' moment occurred when reviewing the concept of 'reflexivity' and its role in creating personal and organisational transformation. 'Aha' moments classically occur when an answer you have been searching for, often associated with a state of confusion, suddenly becomes clear. For me, it was one of those rare moments of clarity, an emotionally satisfying integration of years of experience and questioning.

Many years ago, I was deeply impacted by Jack Mezirow's book, *The Transformative Dimensions of Adult Learning*, where he posits that to be effective in a rapidly changing world, we need to not only learn in the 'knowing and doing' domains, but to go deeper and learn in the 'being' domain. In 'being' domain learning we examine our consciously and unconsciously held beliefs, assumptions and worldviews. This deep and often difficult learning is at the heart of personal and organisational transformation.

Whether we are specialist change agents or managers, without this depth of learning, it is unlikely that we can support the depth of change in others that creates transformation. We need to see ourselves as the instruments of change, and our effectiveness is determined in no small part by how well we learn in all three domains: knowing, doing and being.

So, my challenge to you, in whatever role you find yourself, is to go beyond your current worldviews, to challenge your organisation's status quo, and to be 'unreasonable', as George Bernard Shaw once put it, in the pursuit of a greater vision; a vision of Changing the World— One Organisation at a Time™.

In addition, should we meet sometime in the future, I look forward to hearing your stories of transformation.

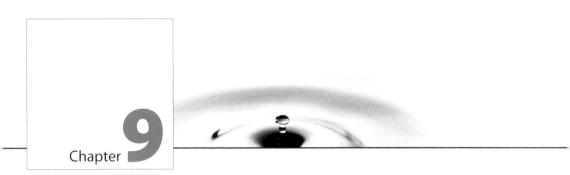

Chapter **9**

References

Argyris, C. (1990). *Overcoming Organizational Defenses: Facilitating Organizational Learning.* Allyn & Bacon, Boston.

Argyris, C. (1992). *On Organizational Learning.* Blackwell, Oxford.

Australian Bureau of Statistics Census (2001)

Balkundi, P. & Harrison, D. (2006). Ties, Leaders, and Time in Teams: Strong inference about network structure's effects on team viability and performance. *Academy of Management Journal*, Vol. 49, No. 1, pp. 46-68.

Bate, P. (1994). *Strategies for Cultural Change*, p.243. Butterworth-Heinemann, Oxford.

Bennis, W. Leadership of Change, in **Beer & Nohria** (2000). *Breaking the Code of Change*, Harvard Business School Press, Boston, Mass., pix.

Charan, R. (2006). Home Depot's Blueprint for Culture Change. *Harvard Business Review.*

Cohen, A.R. (2000). Initiating Change: The Anatomy of Structure as a Starting Point. In Beer, M. and Nohria, N., *Breaking the Code of Change.*

Cooke, R.A. (1987). *Organizational Culture Inventory Leader's Guide.* Human Synergistics International, Plymouth, MI.

Cooke, R.A. (1996). *Leadership/Impact.* Human Synergistics/Center for Applied Research, Arlington Heights, IL.

Cooke, R.A. (1997). *How Culture Works.* Human Synergistics International, Plymouth, MI.

Cooke, R.A. (1997). *Organizational Effectiveness Inventory.* Human Synergistics/Center for Applied Research. Arlington Heights, IL.

Cooke, R.A. (2005). *7th Australian Culture and Leadership Conference*, Sydney, Australia.

Cooke, R.A., & Lafferty, J.C. (1987). *Organizational Culture Inventory.* Human Synergistics. Plymouth, MI.

Cooke, R.A., & Rousseau, D.M. (1988). Behavioral Norms and Expectations: A Quantitative Approach to the Assessment of Organizational Culture. *Group & Organization Studies,* 13, pp. 245-273.

Cooke, R.A., & Szumal, J.L. (2000). Using the Organizational Culture Inventory to Understand the Operating Cultures of Organizations. In Ashkanasy, N. M., Wilderom, C. P. M., & Peterson, M. F. (Eds.), *Handbook of Organizational Culture and Climate.* Thousand Oaks, CA, Sage.

Cooke, R.A., & Szumal, J.L. (2003). *Organizational Culture Inventory and Organizational Effectiveness Inventory Feedback Report.* Human Synergistics International, Plymouth, MI.

Cooke, R.A., & Szumal, J.L. (1993). Measuring Normative Beliefs and Shared Behavioral Expectations in Organizations: The Reliability and Validity of the Organizational Culture Inventory. *Psychological Reports*, 72, pp. 1299-1330.

Covey, S. (1989). *Seven Habits of Highly Effective People: Poweful Lessons in Personal Change.* Simon & Schuster.

Cummings, T.G., & Worley, C.G. (1993). *Organizational Development and Change.* West Publishing Company, Minneapolis, Minn.

Dunphy, D., & Dick. (1981). *Organisational Change by Choice*, McGraw Hill, Sydney.

Dunphy, D.C., & Griffiths, A. (1998). *The Sustainable Corporation: Organisational Renewal in Australia.* Allen and Unwin, Sydney.

Dunphy, D., & Pitsis, T. (2003). *Wisdom*. In **Coy, R.** (ed), *The Seven Heavenly Virtues of Management*, McGraw Hill and AIM, Sydney.
Evans, S. (November 5, 2004) Lion Boss Takes Stock. *Australian Financial Review*.
Farquhar, A. (2003). *Culture strategy paper*, Yarra Valley Water.
French, W.L., Bell, C.H., & Zawachi, R.A. (1993). *Organizational Development and Transformation*. Irwin McGraw-Hill Ed 4, Boston, Massachusetts.
Gladwell, M. (2000).*The Tipping Point: How little things can make a big difference*, Abacus, Little Brown & Co, London.
Henderson, P. (March 8, 2006). *Living History*. [Online], Available: http://abcasiapacific.com/nexus/livinghistory/s1575173.htm.
Heracleous, L. & Barrett, M. (2001). Organisational Change as Discourse: Communicative action and deep structures in the context of information technology implementation, *Academy of Management Journal*, Vol. 44, No. 4, pp. 755-78.
Hock, D.W. (1999). *Birth of the Chaordic Age*. Berrett-Koehler, San Francisco.
Horrigan, L.M. (2005). A *Paradox-based Approach to the Study and Practice of Organisational Change*, PhD thesis, Faculty of health, Department of Psychology, Griffith University, Bathurst.
Klein, M.I. (1992). *Corporate Culture and Store Performance: Differences Among High Performance and Low Performance Stores*. Ph.D. dissertation. Philadelphia,Temple University.
Kotter, J. (1996). *Leading Change*, pp. 51-52, Harvard Business School Press, Boston, Mass.
Kotter, J.P. & Cohen, D.S. (2002). *The Heart of Change*, Harvard Business School Press, Boston, Mass.
Lafferty, J.C. (1987). *Life Styles Inventory*. Human Synergistics International, Plymouth, MI.
Lundin, S.C., Paul, H., Christensen, J., & Strand, P. (2002). *Fish! Tales: Real-Life Stories to Help You Transform Your Workplace and Your Life*, Hyperion, New York.
Marshak, R.J. (1993). Managing the Metaphors of Change, *Organizational Dynamics*, Vol 22 no 1, pp. 44-56
McCarthy, S. (2001). *Building High Performance Cultures – Measuring Organisational Culture Through the Organisational Culture Inventory*. Human Synergistics Australia/New Zealand Publication, Wellington.
McCarthy, S. (2002). *Leading High Performance Cultures – Measuring Leadership Style Through the Life Styles Inventory*. Human Synergistics Australia/New Zealand Publication, Wellington.
McCarthy, S. (2005). *The Culture-Performance Connection. The Research Results Book 2003-2004 Australia and New Zealand*. Human Synergistics Australia/New Zealand Publication, Wellington.
Miles, R. H. (2000). Accelerated Organizational Transformation, pp. 381-389 in **Beer & Nohria**. *Breaking the Code of Change*, Harvard Business School Press, Boston, Mass., pix.
Palmer, I., Dunford, R., & Akin, G. (2006). *Managing Organizational Change - A Multiple Perspective Approach*, p.294, McGraw-Hill Erwin, New York.
Pfeffer, J., & Sutton, R.I. (2000). *The Knowing-Doing Gap: How Smart Companies Turn Knowledge into Action*. Harvard Business School Publishing, Boston.
Quade, K., & Brown, R.M. (2001). *The Conscious Consultant*. Jossey Bass, San Francisco.

Quinn, R. E., (1996). *Deep Change: Discovering the leader within*, p. 9, Jossey Bass/Pfieffer, San Francisco.

Roberts et al. (2005). *Composing the Reflected Best-Self Portrait*.

Saville, M. (October 10, 2005) Balmain Not Out of the Woods Yet. *Sydney Morning Herald*.

Schein, E.H. (2004). *Organizational Culture and Leadership*. Wiley Publishers Ed. 3, New York.

Senge, P.M. (1990). *The Fifth Discipline: The Art and Practice of the Learning Organisation*. Century Business,London.

Stace, D., & Dunphy, D. (2001). *Beyond the Boundaries: Leading and Re-Creating the Successful Enterprise*. McGraw Hill, Sydney.

Stace, D., & Dunphy, D. (2001). *Under New Management: Australian Organisations in Transition*, McGraw Hill, Sydney.

Szumal, J.L. (1998). *Organizational Culture Inventory Interpretation and Development Guide*. Human Synergistics International, Plymouth, MI.

Taylor, C. (2005). *Walking the Talk-Building a Culture for Success*. Random House Business Books, United Kingdom.

Turner, D., & Crawford, M. (1999). *Change Power: Capabilities that Drive Corporate Renewal*. Woodslane, Sydney.

Weick, K.E. (1995). *Sensemaking in Organisations*, Sage, Thousand Oaks, California.

Xenikou, A., & Furnham, A. (1996). *A Correlational and Factor Analytic Study of Four Questionnaire Measures of Organisational Culture*. Human Relations, 49, pp. 349-37.

Chapter **10**

Appendices

Appendix 1 – Glossary of Terms

Term	Explanation
Causal Factors	In Human Synergistics' model, How Culture Works, causal factors include organizational systems, structures, technologies, and members' skills/qualities that lead to and reinforce cultural norms. (These causal factors or 'levers for change' are measured by the Organizational Effectiveness Inventory™.)
Change	To alter, to move from one state to a new state, to behave differently to established patterns.
Change Agent	Key individuals, internal and external to an organisation, who have been integral to initiating, promoting and maintaining the transformation process.
Circumplex	Circumplex models arrange variables, such as behavioural styles, in a circular manner based on their degree of similarity. The Human Synergistics' Circumplex identifies 12 specific patterns of thinking and behaving, which cluster into three general orientations: ■ Constructive Styles ■ Passive/Defensive Styles ■ Aggressive/Defensive Styles
Culture	Human Synergistics views culture as the behavioural norms and expectations (based partly on shared values and beliefs) that guide members in how they should approach their work and interact with one another.
Leadership/Impact® (L/I)	Leadership/Impact is a circumplex-based, diagnostic inventory that measures the impact of leaders on the behaviour of others. Additionally it provides feedback on the leadership strategies, positive and negative, that account for this impact.
Life Styles Inventory™ (LSI 1&2)	Self Description (LSI 1) - Measures an individual's self-reported thinking and behavioural styles and provides feedback on those styles organized around Human Synergistics' Circumplex. Description by Others (LSI 2) - Parallel to the LSI 1, LSI 2 provides feedback from others on the focal individual's behavioural styles.

Term	Explanation
Organizational Culture Inventory® (OCI)	The Organizational Culture Inventory is a research-based and validated survey used to measure the operating cultures of organizations in terms of behavioural norms and expectations. The survey measures the strength of three types of cultures (Constructive, Passive/Defensive, and Aggressive/Defensive) and is used to initiate and guide organisational transformation as well as to assess cultural change. A special form of the OCI is available to identify the preferred culture for an organisation-that is, the type of culture that would promote effectiveness and lead to positive outcomes.
Organizational Effectiveness Inventory™ (OEI)	The Organizational Effectiveness Inventory is a 'climate' survey that is often administered along with the culture inventory. The OEI measures outcomes of culture and therefore shows how the current culture of an organization is promoting or inhibiting its effectiveness. The OEI also measures causal factors (that is, factors leading to cultural norms) and therefore identifies 'levers' for constructively changing the cultures of organisations.
Test → Action → Re-Test	This is the research framework used to analyse the change processes and describe the cultural transformations experienced by the five organisations studied for this book. The framework involves the initial administration of the OCI or OCI/OEI (Test), followed by individual and organisational development initiatives (Action), and finally the re-administration of the OCI (Re-Test).
Transformation	For the *In Great Company* study, transformation is defined as the redirection of an organization's culture from one dominated by Defensive norms to one oriented towards Constructive norms. On Human Synergistics' Circumplex, such transformations are represented by a shift in colour from red and green (Aggressive/Defensive and Passive/Defensive) to blue (Constructive).

Appendix 2 – Human Synergistics Diagnostics

The five organisations that participated in this research used Human Synergistics' integrated diagnostic system to support their culture transformation initiatives. Each of the organisations used two or more of the following diagnostic inventories:

- Organizational Culture Inventory® (OCI and OCI-Preferred)
- Organizational Effectiveness Inventory™ (OEI)
- Life Styles Inventory™ (LSI 1&2)
- Leadership/Impact® (L/I)

These inventories, summarized in Table 1, are based on Human Synergistics' Circumplex which brings together twelve distinct yet inter-related sets of behaviours. These behaviours or 'styles' are organized around a circle based on their degree of similarity. Behaviours that are similar to one another are placed close together on the Circumplex, while those that are different are placed further apart. The twelve sets of behaviours are defined and located around the circle based on two underlying dimensions: (1) the extent to which they reflect a concern for people versus tasks and (2) the extent to which they are associated with higher-order satisfaction needs versus lower-order security needs.

Table 1. Summary of Human Synergistics Diagnostics

Focus of Measurement		Instrument
Organisational Level Measurement & Feedback	Preferred Culture	Organizational Culture Inventory® (OCI-Preferred)
	Actual Operating Culture	Organizational Culture Inventory® (OCI)
	Organisational Structures, Systems, Technologies and Skills/Qualities of leaders	Organizational Effectiveness Inventory™ (OEI)
	Organisational Outcomes at the Individual, Group and Organisational levels	
Individual Level Measurement & Feedback	The impact of those in top leadership positions – how the individual leads others to behave	Leadership/Impact® (L/I)
	Individual Thinking Styles	Life Styles Inventory™ Self-Description (LSI 1)
	Individual Behavioural Styles	Life Styles Inventory™ Description by Other (LSI 2)

The twelve styles cluster into three general factors—Constructive, Passive/Defensive, and Aggressive/Defensive. The styles and clusters are as follows:

Table 2. Summary of Styles and Clusters

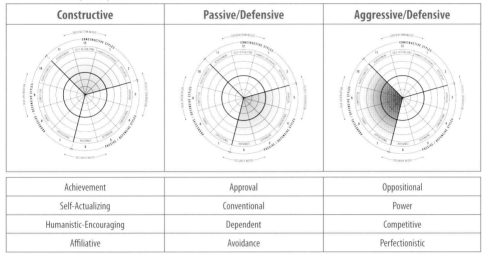

Constructive	Passive/Defensive	Aggressive/Defensive
Achievement	Approval	Oppositional
Self-Actualizing	Conventional	Power
Humanistic-Encouraging	Dependent	Competitive
Affiliative	Avoidance	Perfectionistic

The Organizational Culture Inventory measures norms and expectations for these twelve styles. The Life Styles Inventory measures the extent to which individuals exhibit each of the twelve styles, based on self reports and descriptions by others. Leadership/Impact assesses the degree to which leaders encourage or drive people to behave in each of these Constructive and Defensive ways. These inventories will be discussed below and descriptions of the twelve styles provided as they relate to organisational culture.

ORGANIZATIONAL CULTURE INVENTORY® (OCI)

The Organizational Culture Inventory (OCI; Cooke & Lafferty, 1987) measures culture in terms of behavioural norms and expectations. The inventory presents 120 statements that describe some of the behaviours and personal styles that might be expected or implicitly required of an organisation's members. Based on the Circumplex, some of the cultural norms measured by the OCI are positive, and supportive of constructive interpersonal relationships, effective problem solving and personal growth; others are dysfunctional, and can lead to unnecessary conflict, dissatisfaction, and symptoms of strain on the part of organisational members. More specifically, the OCI measures twelve cultural norms that are organised into three general types of cultures corresponding to the Circumplex clusters:

Table 3. Description of Clusters

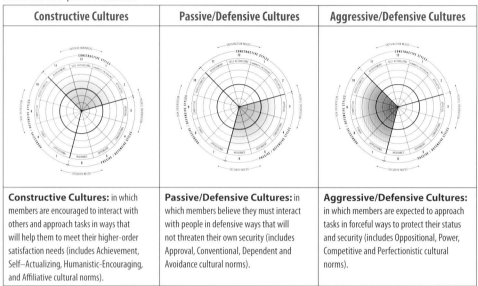

Constructive Cultures	Passive/Defensive Cultures	Aggressive/Defensive Cultures
Constructive Cultures: in which members are encouraged to interact with others and approach tasks in ways that will help them to meet their higher-order satisfaction needs (includes Achievement, Self–Actualizing, Humanistic-Encouraging, and Affiliative cultural norms).	**Passive/Defensive Cultures:** in which members believe they must interact with people in defensive ways that will not threaten their own security (includes Approval, Conventional, Dependent and Avoidance cultural norms).	**Aggressive/Defensive Cultures:** in which members are expected to approach tasks in forceful ways to protect their status and security (includes Oppositional, Power, Competitive and Perfectionistic cultural norms).

Descriptions of the twelve culture norms, along with examples of items from the inventory, are provided in Table 4. Ten items are used to measure each of the twelve culture styles. Scores along the ten items are added together, scores across respondents are averaged, and the results are then plotted on a statistically-normed Circumplex. When the unadjusted (or 'raw') score for each style is transferred to the circumplex, it is converted to a percentile score that provides a more realistic picture of the culture. The bold centre ring on the Circumplex represents the 50th percentile. Scores falling below the 50th percentile are low relative to the current culture scores of other organisations; scores that fall above the 50th percentile are high relative to the current culture scores of other organisations.

Table 4. Descriptions of the Twelve Styles Measured by the Organizational Culture Inventory® (and Sample Items)

Constructive Norms	Cultural Styles Promoting Satisfaction Behaviours
Achievement	An Achievement culture characterizes organizations that do things well and value members who set and accomplish their own goals. Members are expected to set challenging but realistic goals, establish plans to reach these goals, and pursue them with enthusiasm. (Pursue a standard of excellence; Openly show enthusiasm)
Self-Actualizing	A Self-Actualizing culture characterizes organizations that value creativity, quality over quantity, and both task accomplishment and individual growth. Members are encouraged to gain enjoyment from their work, develop themselves, and take on new and interesting activities. (Think in unique and independent ways; Do even simple tasks well)
Humanistic-Encouraging	A Humanistic-Encouraging culture characterizes organizations that are managed in a participative and person-centered way. Members are expected to be supportive, constructive, and open to influence in their dealings with one another. (Help others to grow and develop; Take time with people)
Affiliative	An Affiliative culture characterizes organizations that place a high priority on constructive interpersonal relationships. Members are expected to be friendly, open, and sensitive to the satisfaction of their work group. (Deal with others in a friendly, pleasant way; Share feelings and thoughts)
Passive/Defensive Norms	Cultural Styles Promoting People/Security Behaviours
Approval	An Approval culture describes organizations in which conflicts are avoided and interpersonal relationships are pleasant—at least superficially. Members feel that they should agree with, gain the approval of, and be liked by others. ('Go along' with others; Be liked by everyone)
Conventional	A Conventional culture is descriptive of organizations that are conservative, traditional, and bureaucratically controlled. Members are expected to conform, follow the rules, and make a good impression. (Always follow policies and practices; Fit into the 'mold')

Dependent		A Dependent culture is descriptive of organizations that are hierarchically controlled and do not empower their members. Centralized decision making in such organizations leads members to do only what they are told and to clear all decisions with superiors. (Please those in positions of authority; Do what is expected)
Avoidance		An Avoidance culture characterizes organizations that fail to reward success but nevertheless punish mistakes. This negative reward system leads members to shift responsibilities to others and avoid any possibility of being blamed for a mistake. (Wait for others to act first; Take few chances)
Aggressive/Defensive Norms		**Cultural Styles Promoting Task/Security Behaviours**
Oppositional		An Oppositional culture describes organizations in which confrontation and negativism are rewarded. Members gain status and influence by being critical and thus are reinforced to oppose the ideas of others. (Point out flaws; Be hard to impress)
Power		A Power culture is descriptive of nonparticipative organizations structured on the basis of the authority inherent in members' positions. Members believe they will be rewarded for taking charge, controlling subordinates and, at the same time, being responsive to the demands of superiors. (Build up one's power base; Demand loyalty)
Competitive		A Competitive culture is one in which winning is valued and members are rewarded for outperforming one another. Members operate in a 'win-lose' framework and believe they must work against (rather than with) their peers to be noticed. (Turn the job into a contest; Never appear to lose)
Perfectionistic		A Perfectionistic culture characterizes organizations in which perfectionism, persistence, and hard work are valued. Members feel they must avoid any mistakes, keep track of everything, and work long hours to attain narrowly defined objectives. (Do things perfectly; Keep on top of everything)

The cultural norms measured by the OCI have a direct bearing on the activities of members and the functioning of organisations, and are related to outcomes such as member satisfaction, motivation, teamwork, product/service quality, and other criteria of organisational effectiveness (e.g. sales performance and profitability). Research consistently indicates that the Constructive styles are positively related to these outcomes while the Defensive styles tend to be negatively related to them (Cooke & Szumal, 2000). Furthermore, research shows that the cultural norms result from, and are reinforced by, organisational structures, systems, managerial styles, and other factors that can be changed, at least to some extent, by those in leadership positions. These factors therefore can be targeted as levers for changing the cultures of organisations.

Finally, the OCI is also used to measure the preferred or ideal culture for organizations. Respondents are asked to review the same 120 items that appear on the regular form of the OCI but to answer in terms of the extent to which the behaviours should be expected of members to maximize the effectiveness of the organization. The resulting profile, based on the values and beliefs of respondents, typically shows strong extensions along the Constructive styles and weak extensions along the Defensive styles (particularly the Passive/Defensive styles). The preferred profile can be compared to the current OCI profile to identify gaps and targets for change.

ORGANIZATIONAL EFFECTIVENESS INVENTORY™ (OEI)

The Organizational Effectiveness Inventory (OEI; Cooke, 1995) allows organisations to measure both the causal factors that are likely to drive and shape their cultures and the impact of their cultures on members, groups/teams, and their organisations as a whole. The questions included in the survey are based on research in the areas of human resource management and organisational behaviour. Some of the questions focus on the entire organisation while others are specific to the respondent's department, supervisor/manager, or job.

Unlike the other diagnostic inventories from Human Synergistics, the OEI is not directly based on the Circumplex. Instead, this survey is keyed to the Circumplex-based Organizational Culture Inventory and measures factors that are systematically related to the twelve culture styles. Thus, the OEI provides organisations with feedback on the causal factors (levers for change) and outcomes (effectiveness criteria) included in Dr Cooke's model of How Culture Works (1997).

OEI Causal Factors – Levers for Change

Behavioural norms within an organisation represent members' collective learning regarding what it takes to get things done and to succeed – or at least to survive – in the system. Members infer what is expected or implicitly required on the basis of cues or signals they receive on a day-to-day basis. These cues and signals may be associated with the organisation's mission and philosophy but are also related to the organisation's structures, systems, technology, and the skills/qualities of members. These factors, which may or may not be in alignment with the organisation's values, determine whether members come to believe that they should behave in Constructive versus Defensive ways and therefore shape the true operating culture of the organisation.

Dr Cooke and Dr Szumal's research (2000) has shown that these factors are causally related to cultural norms and are important to consider when identifying levers for change in organisational development programs. The OEI was therefore designed to measure and provide systematic feedback on 31 specific causal factors in five categories:

- Mission and Philosophy
- Structures
- Systems
- Technology
- Skills/Qualities

The specific causal factors measured by the OEI are described in detail in the OCI/OEI Feedback Report (Cooke & Szumal, 2003) and are summarized here.

- **Mission and Philosophy** are the mechanisms by which organisations explicitly communicate their values to members. The OEI measures the extent to which the organisation has successfully defined and communicated its values to its members in terms of: Articulation of mission \ Customer service focus.

- **Structures** refer to the ways in which people, roles and activities are ordered and coupled to create organisation. Aspects of structure that can influence an organisation's operating culture and which are measured by the OEI are: Total influence \ Distribution of influence \ Empowerment \ Employee involvement.

- **Systems** refer to the interrelated sets of procedures that an organisation uses to support its core activities and solve problems. Human resource management, appraisal and reinforcement, and goal setting systems are among the most powerful factors for shaping - as well as redirecting – the operating culture of an organisation. The OEI addresses these systems as follows:

  - **Human Resource Management Systems** are examined in terms of the extent to which they maximise the performance and development of employees, and do so in a fair and equitable manner. To do this, the OEI measures: Selection and placement \ Training and development \ Respect for members.

  - **Appraisal and Reinforcement Systems** are assessed in terms of their fairness and emphasis on rewards rather than punishment: Fairness of appraisals \ Use of rewards \ Use of punishment.

  - **Goal Setting Systems** are assessed in terms of the extent to which members' goals are designed to be positive and motivating. Specifically, the OEI measures: Goal clarity \Goal challenge \ Participative goal setting \ Goal acceptance.

- **Technology** refers to the methods used by the organisation to transform inputs into outputs. Aspects of technology that have been found to have an impact on the operating culture of organisations, and that are measured by the OEI, include job design and interdependence: Autonomy \ Skill variety \ Feedback (from the job) \ Task identity\ Significance \ Interdependence.

- **Skills/Qualities** refer to the skills and qualities exhibited by organisational members, particularly those in leadership positions. Skills and qualities that can have an impact on culture revolve around communication, leadership behaviours, and bases of power.

- **Communication** refers to the effectiveness with which members send and receive ideas, opinions, attitudes and information (about the organisation, its environment and members) within the organisation. Specific communication measures include: Downward communication \ Upward communication \ Communication for learning.
- **Supervisory/Managerial Leadership** is considered in terms of the extent to which managers and supervisors exhibit an effective balance of people- and task-oriented leadership behaviours. Specific dimensions of leadership include: Interaction facilitation (people-oriented) \ Task facilitation (task-oriented) \ Goal emphasis (task-oriented) \ Consideration (people-oriented).
- **Supervisory/Managerial Sources of Power** explain why organisational members do what their superiors ask them to do. The OEI measures the extent to which managers and supervisors rely on positive, neutral and negative sources (bases) of power. Two different types of bases are measured: Personal bases of power (positive) \ Organisational bases of power (neutral to negative).

OEI Outcomes of Culture

Drs Cooke and Szumal's research (2000) has identified various criteria of organisational effectiveness that are influenced by the operating cultures of organisations. While it is clear that organisational outcomes are shaped by a range of variables, the focus of their research has been on identifying factors associated with long-term organisational success, and then examining the impact of the OCI culture styles on these factors. Their research has converged on twelve outcomes that are organised into three general categories and measured by the OEI.

- **Individual Level Outcomes** focus on the extent to which the organisation has a positive rather than a negative impact on the personal states and attitudes of its members.
  - **Positive Indices:** The OEI measures the extent to which organisational members report pleasurable and productive personal states and attitudes: Role clarity \ Motivation \ Satisfaction \ Intention to stay.
  - **Negative Indices:** The OEI measures the extent to which members report excessive organisational demands, pressures, and/or negative conditions (stressors), as well as psychological responses to those conditions (stress or strain) Role conflict \ Job insecurity \ Stress.
- **Group Level Outcomes** focus on the extent to which the organisation effectively integrates and co-ordinates the efforts of its members within and across units. Intra-unit teamwork and co-operation \ Inter-unit co-ordination \ Departmental-level quality.
- **Organisational Level Outcomes** focus on the organisation's effectiveness with respect to its clients and external environment. Specific measures include: Organisational-level quality \ External adaptability.

Feedback and Benchmarks

Organisations are provided with OEI results on the 31 causal factors and twelve outcomes, as well as the individual survey items associated with these scales, based on the mean responses of members who completed the inventory. To facilitate interpretation, organisational and subgroup results (if requested by the organisation or consultant) are presented along with the Historical Average and the Constructive Benchmark.

The **Historical Average** represents the median of the responses of members of 1084 organisational units in Human Synergistics research data base. Results that are more positive than these averages are desirable and likely to be associated with a more favourable culture profile.

The **Constructive Benchmark** is based on the median scores of 172 organisational units identified by the OCI as having predominantly Constructive operating cultures. OEI results for these Constructive units are more positive that the Historical Average along both the causal factors and outcome measures.

By comparing their organisation's results to the average and benchmark, managers and consultants can systematically identify reasons for initiating culture change (based on the outcomes) as well as levers for bringing about that change (based on the causal factors).

LIFE STYLES INVENTORY™ (LSI 1&2)

The Life Styles Inventory (LSI; Lafferty, 1986) is an integral part, and the original component, of Human Synergistics' multi-level diagnostic system. The LSI is an individual feedback tool, designed to provide insights into a manager's (or individual contributor's) thinking and behaviour styles. The feedback generated by the LSI focuses on how these personal styles impact the individual's effectiveness in his/her current role; the Self-Development Guide accompanying the feedback focuses on the types of changes that could enhance his/her performance, well being, and satisfaction.

Like the Organizational Culture Inventory, the LSI is designed around Human Synergistics' Circumplex. While the culture survey focuses on norms and expectations for the twelve styles, the LSI measures the extent to which the individual exhibits each of those styles. The LSI measures individual thinking and behavioural styles through the use of 240 items—20 corresponding to each of the twelve styles. The LSI includes two separate but complementary surveys: LSI 1 (Self-Description) and LSI 2 (Description by Others).

- **LSI 1 (Self-Description)** – LSI 1 is a self-report inventory designed to measure an individual's thinking styles and self-concept. Thinking styles are viewed as a combination of values and needs (both security and satisfaction) and concerns (for people versus tasks), which lead to behaviours and have consequences for the individual's perceptions of his/her relations to the environment. These factors contribute to self-concept – the intellectual, social, psychological and physical image that people have of themselves. Thinking styles thus have consequences for job performance, the quality of interpersonal styles, leadership effectiveness and the individual's ability to cope with stress.

■ **LSI 2 (Description by Others)** – The LSI 2 includes the same 240 items as the LSI 1 but is completed by other people who know the focal individual well. The descriptions provided by others are combined and profiled on a Circumplex which can be compared to the individual's self-report profile. Given that the responses of others are based on their observations, the LSI 2 tends to focus more heavily on behavioural styles than thinking styles. (The two are not always consistent.)

As noted above, the LSI includes a self-development guide and process designed to assist individuals in reconciling inconsistent LSI 1 and 2 profiles, identifying the thinking styles and behavioural styles that contribute or detract from their effectiveness, and creating plans for personal development and improvement. The LSI is critical for organizational change given that cultural transformation generally requires personal development on the part of members at all levels of the organisation.

LEADERSHIP/IMPACT® (L/I)

Whereas most leadership surveys measure the respondents' perceptions of the leader's behaviours, Leadership/Impact (L/I; Cooke, 1997) measures people's beliefs about how their own behaviours are shaped and influenced by the leader. L/I thus focuses on the impact of leaders and the way in which they create a culture and influence the performance of the people around them. Mirroring the Organizational Culture Inventory and the Life Styles Inventory, the impact of leaders on the behaviours of others is assessed and profiled by L/I through the use of Human Synergistics' Circumplex.

Dr Cooke's research on leadership and the characteristics that differentiate effective from less effective leaders led him to focus on leadership strategies. The strategies used by leaders determine the impact that they have on others, and their strategies and impact together determine their effectiveness (see Figure 1).

At the most general level, leaders are likely to exhibit a combination of two different

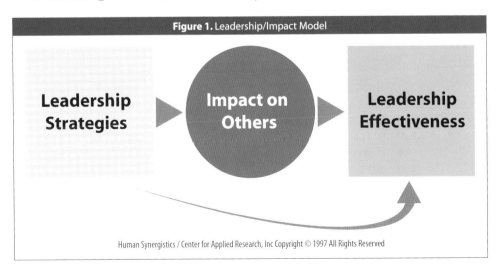

Figure 1. Leadership/Impact Model

Leadership Strategies → Impact on Others → Leadership Effectiveness

Human Synergistics / Center for Applied Research, Inc Copyright © 1997 All Rights Reserved

Leadership Strategies – Prescriptive and Restrictive (see Figure 2). Prescriptive strategies are those that guide or direct the activities and behaviours of others toward goals, opportunities and methods for task accomplishment. Restrictive strategies are those that constrain or prohibit activities and behaviours with respect to goals, opportunities, and methods. These different strategies pervade the way in which the leader approaches and carries out leadership activities such as envisioning, mentoring, providing feedback, and creating a setting. Each of these domains of leadership can be carried out in Prescriptive and/or Restrictive ways—and L/I measures and provides the leader with feedback on their current strategies.

Figure 2. Leadership Strategies (Leadership/Impact)

DOMAIN	RESTRICTIVE	PRESCRIPTIVE	
Envisioning	Delimiting ◄──► Defining		Personal
Role Modeling	Circumscribing ◄──► Exemplifying		
Mentoring	Passive ◄──► Active		Interpersonal
Stimulating Thinking	Vertical ◄──► Lateral		
Referring	Negative Referents ◄──► Positive Referents		
Monitoring	By Exception ◄──► By Excellence		
Providing Feedback	Negative ◄──► Positive		
Reinforcing	Punishment ◄──► Reward		Organizational
Influencing	Unilateral ◄──► Reciprocal		
Creating A Setting	Constraining ◄──► Facilitating		

DEFENSIVE (IMPACT) CONSTRUCTIVE

Prescriptive strategies are generally more effective than Restrictive strategies. This is partly because the former serve to define a direction for the system, establish structures for organizational learning and adaptation, and support processes for problem-solving and the integration of organisational components. Possibly most importantly however, Prescriptive strategies on the part of leaders create and reinforce an organisational culture that communicates Constructive norms and expectations to members.

As shown in Figure 3, a leader's impact on others can be either Constructive or Defensive. Ideally, most leaders prefer to have a Constructive impact on the people around them; in practice, their actual impact tends to be more Defensive. Leaders with a Constructive impact motivate people to think and behave in achievement-oriented and cooperative ways that emphasise growth and development. In contrast, leaders with a Defensive impact drive people to think and behave in either Aggressive or Passive ways to protect their status and position. Constructive behaviours not only lead to better performance than do Defensive behaviours, they also result in higher levels of personal satisfaction and lower levels of stress. More generally, leaders who can use their L/I feedback to move toward more Prescriptive strategies will, in effect, redirect the culture of their organisations away from Defensive and toward Constructive styles.

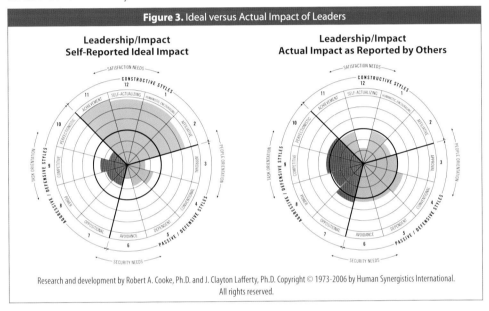

Figure 3. Ideal versus Actual Impact of Leaders

Research and development by Robert A. Cooke, Ph.D. and J. Clayton Lafferty, Ph.D. Copyright © 1973-2006 by Human Synergistics International. All rights reserved.

Appendix 3 – Understanding the Drivers of Cultural Transformation
The Research Project — Written by Rosalie Fishman

CONTRACTING

Dexter Dunphy and Rosalie Fishman were engaged to provide research expertise and an independent viewpoint for the design and conduct of a research study into the drivers of cultural transformation. The central question of 'What created the transformation in the five target organisations?' was broadened to encompass the generation of a deeper understanding of the nature of corporate cultural change and results-based guidelines for how organisations can proactively direct their change efforts.

In initial consultations, the theme, scope, research design, and opportunities for reciprocal learning and capability development were determined. To this end, a research group was set up that comprised a team of five from Human Synergistics, including the Australian director, two senior consultants, a project manager and executive assistant, two external academic researchers, and public relations and communications support.

It seemed from the onset that there was a learning potential for the Australian office of Human Synergistics. Though Human Synergistics International has carried out extensive research on the OCI and factors related to culture, most of this research has been directed and conducted by Human Synergistics staff in the United States. Therefore, there was an opportunity to develop the qualitative research skills of the staff in Australia. It was determined that research capability would be built by engaging the Human Synergistics team in all stages of the project, including project design, research design, development of research instruments, and collection and collation of data, and through taking the lead role in writing up the case studies and drawing the project together into its final presentation format.

The external researchers agreed to provide the qualitative research expertise and the academic leadership needed to guide the project, and to create a consolidated report drawing out the key findings, and their implications for the management of transformative change.

PR and communication support was to be used to guide the design and produce the final product.

A fluid partnership emerged, and a strong bond was formed between all parties, based on the constructive and collaborative nature of the emerging relationships. Learning was evidenced through the exchange of ideas, milestones being reached effectively, and the quality of the final product.

The research objectives that were set at the beginning of the project were to:

1. Identify the key drivers of culture change in five organisations that reported significant shifts in their OCI results from time-period one to time-period two
2. Create individual case studies for each of these five organisations
3. Create a consolidated report/book covering all five organisations, with a focus on drawing out the key findings and telling the story
4. Present the findings at the 2006 Australian Culture and Leadership Conference

5. Develop qualitative and case study research capabilities on the part of the Australian staff of Human Synergistics

RESEARCH DESIGN

Given the intent of the project, the decision was made to use a qualitative research framework to undertake in-depth studies of the five most transformational organisations as measured by their OCI results (see Looking for Evidence of Cultural Transformation above).

In framing the research questions, and designing the study and the instruments to be used, two major sources were drawn on. The first was Human Synergistics' comprehensive body of research and empirical findings, including the model of 'How Culture Works' (Cooke 1997) and quantitative research, involving thousands of organizations, leading up to the model (Cooke, 1987; Cooke & Rousseau, 1988; Cooke & Szumal, 1993), validating the framework (Cooke & Szumal, 2000; 2003), and applying it to organisations in Australia and New Zealand (McCarthy, 2003; 2004; 2005). The second was Professor Dexter Dunphy's extensive body of work in organisational and cultural change (Dunphy, D., & Stace, D. (1990). Dunphy, D.C., & Griffiths, A. (1998).) and his extensive research experience. It was agreed to focus on the drivers of cultural change as outlined in Dr Cooke's model, and to explore what had in fact occurred in the targeted organisations over the nominated time periods. It was felt that gaining insight into what was going on in each organisation immediately prior to the first OCI (Pre-Test), what was occurring at the time of the first OCI (Test), what occurred in the interim period between the first and second OCIs (Action phase), and what was going on at the time of the second OCI (Re-Test) would best facilitate answering the research question posed.

Fundamentally, an applied research question was being asked, one that can best be addressed within the applied qualitative research tradition. The value of such qualitative research lies in its utility, and its validity is measured not only by the findings it puts forward, but also by the success or otherwise of the decisions that are made based on those findings. In effect, qualitative research allows for descriptions of what is salient, enables the story to be told in context, and facilitates the generation of ideas as to the 'what' and 'how' of events and the possibilities of 'where to from here'.

Qualitative research adopts an analytical orientation to describe and clarify events, draw conclusions, and generate hypotheses. It is an iterative process, where the researcher's focus drives the data collection, and is an integral part of the analytical process of data reduction, analysis, data display, conclusion drawing and verification (Miles & Huberman, 1984). In-depth interviews, focus groups, review of relevant organisational records and performance data, internal communications and researcher observations are standard methodologies used within a qualitative research framework.

Power in qualitative research lies in the rigour of the work, the use of varied instrumentation – both quantitative and qualitative – the gathering of data from a diversity of viewpoints from actors with differing roles at different organisational levels, and a philosophical stance that acknowledges grounded research in the field of social science as a valid form of knowledge-building.

Examples of the iterative process inherent in this type of research evidenced in our study include: seeking added information from the client organisations to validate or complete missing pieces of data at the writing stage of the project; fine-tuning interview schedules on the basis of previous interview material; broadening the research questions as new data comes to light; targeting the interview sample to ensure the gathering of required data; and finally, iterative review of findings and discussions to fine-tune analysis.

RESEARCH QUESTIONS

Effective field methodology aims to collect data to address the myriad research questions embedded in the larger question posed in a commissioned piece of work. In our case, the larger question, 'determining the drivers of cultural transformation', was intended to move past a theoretical or best practice prescriptive orientation, i.e. the 'should do', to a potential explanation for what actually happens to allow, support and facilitate cultural change. To address these issues, taking Dr Cooke's model as a starting point, we needed to gather information on what was happening in each organisation with regard to its mission, philosophy, structures, systems, technology, skills and qualities. The research questions aimed to move beyond a validation of Cooke's model to explore more fully the question of how to make such cultural change happen. What was it about these organisations that allowed them to make the transformation? To find clues, we needed to hear the transformational stories told by those involved in the change process. We needed to understand what had changed, the processes involved, the energetic, motivational and emotional interplay, and the perceived costs and pay-offs for what could only be seen as a huge undertaking.

The research questions (outlined below) were designed to guide the construction of the individual and focus group interview schedules, and to generate other data required to address the research issues.

The Research Questions:

- Background and rationale for deciding to measure the organisation's corporate culture in time frame one - marker events, decision-makers and key players involved – the 'Why start?' story
- Impact of the culture survey results at period 1 on the organisation – were any change decisions made, and if so, by whom, and for what purpose?
- Detailed data on the organisation's mission, philosophy, structures, systems, technology, skills and qualities at period one and period two
- Detailed outline of cultural interventions undertaken - with what impact?
- Description of the key change agents - Who were the leaders of change? What allowed others to follow? What brought the organisation along?
- The second organisational culture survey – Why the measure? What was tangibly different? Behavioural examples? Was it worth it?
- Impact on performance
- Challenges - and lessons learned? Would you do it again?

Data Generation

The following data set was targeted:

- Review of relevant organisational data, including internal communications and performance data
- Results of the OCI measures in period 1 and period 2 of the project
- Results of other relevant inventories undertaken
- Interviews with CEO, CFO, and nominated key internal and external change agents
- Focus group interviews with targeted team leaders and line managers

RESEARCH DESIGN CONSIDERATIONS

The following research design considerations were taken into account, and highlight the rationale for the decisions that were made.

1. **Instrumentation:** Interview Schedule and Focus Group Instrumentation: It was decided to develop a comprehensive interview schedule for use with change agents, and detailed focus-group instrumentation to allow for consistency in data-gathering across the organisations studied, and to ensure that data-generation would deliver the material needed to address the targeted research questions specified above.

2. **Flexibility:** Flexibility was built into the research design so that specific questions could be elaborated on or left unaddressed, or new ones generated to meet individual needs, on a case-by-case basis. The question sets acted as a focal point for data-generation, and allowed for a core, standardised body of information to be gathered. However, within this framework, the skilled qualitative researcher had the flexibility to explore specific issues that may have arisen on a case-by-case basis.

3. **Organisational rhetoric:** Given that the rhetoric from the top and in formal organisational communications is often very different to what the lower levels of the organisation hold to be true, it was decided to undertake the internal change agent interviews and the focus groups at the team leader and line manager levels before interviewing the senior team. The data thus generated was then used to inform and fine-tune the individual CEO and CFO interview schedules. This was to ensure that key issues, which may have arisen elsewhere in the organisation would be discussed in greater depth, and that differing perspectives could be addressed.

4. **Triangulation as a validity check:** The research team was deployed in such a way as to allow different team members to be involved in data collection in each of the organisations studied. This allowed for a number of voices and perspectives to be heard, and for the triangulation of data (i.e. when three or more people agree on the data set generated), which is an important validity tool in qualitative research.

   Further, to support the data-recording process and to build the power of triangulation in each case, the interviews were carried out jointly by an academic researcher and a member of the Human Synergistics team.

   The research team met on a regular basis to discuss the data that was being gathered by various team members. These meetings were also part of the triangulation process, assuring the integrity and validity of the findings. One of the stated goals of the research team, and in particular the authors of the case studies, was to be true to the voices of those who gave so generously of their time to tell us their story. Team discussions were part of the research protocol to ensure that this happened.

5. **Gaining Organisation Entry and Buy-In:** Letters of invitation outlining the nature of the research and seeking participation and entry were sent to the CEOs of all five organisations. As part of the agreement, participating organisations were to receive an Executive De-brief Session outlining the findings from their case study prior to the cases being presented in a public forum. Sign-off was obtained on confidentiality issues from all organisations; use of data and the publishing of the final case study report was also a part of the research agreement.

6. **Knowledge Transfer:** Development of the interview and focus group instruments allowed for the transferability of tools and the use of such tools by different members of the research team. This not only supported the deployment of the team members as outlined above, but also generated a learning opportunity for the Human Synergistics team in Australia, and created a knowledge base that could be readily passed on to those involved in future research studies.

7. **The Case Study Sample** – While traditional research on organisational change generally uses the case study approach, they are rarely chosen on any systematic basis, but rather on the basis of the story they can tell. They therefore rarely offer the validity base needed to ensure that the data collected is meaningful. In our sample, the case organisations were chosen from a population data set that had been measured as demonstrating superior performance using the validated Human Synergistics OCI tool. Further, as outlined above, the five organisations chosen for study were drawn from the six top-performing organisations of this population base, thus setting a validity profile that far exceeds most case study-based research. We can therefore be confident that our efforts to codify the learning that has occurred in these examples of successful transformational changes have yielded significant data.

RESEARCH METHODS AND INSTRUMENTS

The following section details the instruments used, the research process followed, and the data-management and analysis protocols employed.

Change Agent Individual Interview Schedule

The change agent individual interview schedule was designed to draw out as much data as possible from the interviewee in the designated time frame, and to ensure that we were generating meaningful data that could be used to address the research questions posed in our study. A one-and-a-half-hour time frame was thought to be adequate to generate the data needed, without fatiguing the interviewee, or taking up too much of their time and generosity in their voluntary capacity.

We were aware that the stories we were trying to capture were complex, and that we would be dealing with a group of highly-skilled change agents who would not only have a story to tell, but could well present as experienced interviewees (ones who are interviewed frequently on a given matter), and who may therefore have been tempted to lead the story-line. To this end, a formal interview schedule was prepared to promote consistency of data-generation, and to ensure that we gathered the material targeted. However, the interviewer was instructed to follow the story-line, and was encouraged to be flexible, in an endeavour to draw out the most salient points. We were also very interested in gathering the real-life experiences of change, and to this end storytelling, the use of metaphor, illustrative quotes, and the individuals' experiences were highly relevant. Finally, we felt that it is in storytelling that learning occurs, and so this axiom was at the heart of our data-collection processes.

A copy of the interview schedule that was used can be found at Appendix 4.

CEO and CFO interview schedules

CEO and CFO interview schedules generally followed the same construction base as outlined above for the individual change agent interviews, however they were tailored to the knowledge bases of those holding these positions. Further, they were designed to generate data that was informed by the individual change agent and focus group interviews, to ensure that relevant issues emerging from those findings were addressed.

Focus Group Interview Schedule and Process

The focus group interview schedule and facilitator notes were prepared to support the more complex task of generating data from a group of people who had been brought together to share their experiences of the transformation process. We were interested in the impact of the change process at lower levels in the organisation. Our initial intention was to undertake a stratified sample to ensure a valid coverage of the population group. However, it soon became clear that the sample group had to be specifically chosen to ensure that we were able to talk to people who had been in the organisation throughout the change program, that is, from the administration of the first OCI to the present time. Further, in some cases, the size of the organisation and time and cost limitations prohibited the use of such a sampling device. To this end, and under instruction, a targeted group of team leaders and line managers was selected by our contact within each organisation. A representative cross-section of potential interviewees who met this criterion were interviewed.

As was the case for the individual interview schedule, the focus group questionnaire was constructed to address the research questions set. In order to allow individual voices to be heard, and to allow for group discussion to deepen understanding and generate added data, the focus groups were dual-structured. Individual reflection time was facilitated by three sets of response sheets that individuals filled out individually and without conferring with other members of the focus group; while group discussion time was facilitated by using a modified Delphi technique (see Focus Group Facilitator notes) for ranking group scores, and by the use of preset tables for ease of data collation. The focus group interviews lasted approximately ninety minutes. Responses during the group interview process were both electronically-taped and recorded on butcher's paper or whiteboards, and they, together with the individual response sheets, were collected for future analysis. Once again, two interviewers were present, to support validation of data through the triangulation process, and as an aid to data-recording.

A copy of the interview schedule that was used can be found at Appendix 5.

Data Management and Analysis

Data management was centralised with administrative support in the HS team. Taped material from individual and focus group interviews, focus group response sheets, and secondary data was collected and transcribed. The writing of case studies demonstrated the iterative process, with numerous drafts and calls to the client organisations for additional information to validate or fill in missing pieces of data. In particular, performance data was a central part of ascertaining whether culture change affected performance. A standardised format (i.e., the Pre-Test, Test, Action, Re-Test model) was developed for analysing data and for writing the case studies. Basic tabular data-handling was used to reduce the focus group material, and as an aid to drawing out the key findings. Finally, storytelling as a learning mechanism was a key axiom that was kept in mind during the writing stage.

The Instruments

Appendix 4 – Individual Interview Schedule

PERSONAL INTRODUCTIONS AND ACKNOWLEDGMENTS

Overview of intent
We are examining changes in this organisation during the period between the OCI Test and Re-Test, and are interested in your perspective on the issues that drove the transformation, and the factors that sustained momentum of transformation and the results.

Process comment
We will require about an hour-and-a-half of your time. There is a series of questions we will be asking you to reflect upon. We will be taking notes and tape-recording. Confidentiality concerns etc. are addressed as outlined in our research project agreement. Are there any questions?

GATHERING OF ORGANISATIONAL BACKGROUND MATERIAL
How would you describe your organisation's culture at the time of the initial test period? What external factors do you think shaped the culture of the organisation at the initial test period? What internal factors do you think shaped the culture of the organisation at the initial test period? What stories were being told? What was your experience of what was happening?

REASONS FOR USE AND CHOICE OF A CULTURAL SURVEY?
What were the reasons for deciding to undertake a cultural survey?

- What where the reasons for wanting to assess the culture?
- Whose idea was it to implement the survey?
- How was the idea taken up, and by whom?
- Was a follow-up survey planned as part of the initial decision-making process, or was that decided later?
- How/why was Human Synergistics chosen?
- Were there any other diagnostic tools used?

IMPACT OF CULTURAL SURVEY RESULTS AND
REASONS FOR IMPLEMENTING CHANGE INITIATIVES
- What impact, if any, did the initial survey results have on the organisation's key stakeholders? Specify.
- Did the results reflect expectations? Were people surprised by any of the results?

- How were the HS survey results treated, i.e. who got to see the results? What use was made of the results?
- Was a clear decision made on the need for change?
- What was this decision based on, e.g. predetermined need for change, or as a result of the diagnostics used?
- Were there any other reasons for the change decision, and if so, what were they?
- Who made the decision?
- Were there any areas of the business (specific business units, for example) where transformation was critical to the performance of the overall organisation?
- In addition to senior managers, were there any individuals or groups within the business who acted as champions of the change process?

CHANGE DECISIONS

- Reflecting on the decision(s) for change in the organisation, could you nominate what they were?
- In general terms, what was the intended purpose and focus of the changes that were planned? For example, was the purpose to (a) change the culture itself? (b) solve existing problems? (c) avoid anticipated problems? (d) pursue new opportunities? (Indicate which, and specify – including financials)
- What was the specific purpose and focus of each of the changes made, i.e. which critical variables did the change program set out to modify?
  - Strategic Focus (vision, mission, philosophy)
  - Capital Base (financials and market targets)
  - Structures (organisational architecture, job design)
  - Systems (communication systems, HR systems, performance appraisal and management systems, etc.)
  - Workforce (skill mix/capability/communication/leadership skills, etc.)
  - Culture (values/attitudes)

DETAILS OF CHANGE INTERVENTION

Reflecting on the set of change interventions you have nominated above, detail the change interventions(s) undertaken between the OCI's Test and Re-Test. For each change intervention undertaken, name and outline the intervention in as much detail as possible:

- Type of intervention – organisation level targeted.
- What was the intended outcome?
- Who initiated the intervention?
- Who where the drivers? Change leaders and managers who led and legitimated the interventions?
- Who were the stakeholders and supporters; opponents and resisters?
- What level of resourcing did the project have?
- Detail the intervention design, sequence of actions taken, and time frame for the intervention to be completed.

- Outline the communication strategies undertaken.
- Were any problems and/or setbacks encountered? How were they handled?
- Were there any strategies for maintaining the change momentum, protecting gains made, and tackling derailers?
- Were there any strategies for monitoring progress? For acting to modify changes if they were not producing the intended results?
- Outline the key intervention outcomes and results (documentation if measured)
- What investments if any were made in the change process (cost, time, resources)?

IMPACT

An OCI Re-Test was undertaken and great changes were observed between your Test and Re-Test OCIs.

- Why do you think this was so?
- How would you describe the major changes in culture that took place?
- Were you surprised, or was this an expected/planned-for outcome? How so?
- Give some examples of actual behaviour changes that show the culture shift.
- How were new behaviours reinforced?
  - direct mandate or directive
  - communication
  - modeling (if so by whom)
  - designed learning experiences
  - personal feedback (e.g. LSI)
  - reward systems
- Can you give some examples of where the change initiatives you describe above relate to the changes reflected in the second survey results?
- Did the impact of the change initiative surprise you?
- Give specific examples of how you experienced the change.
- Have the culture changes improved the organisation's business performance? How? How is this evidenced?

IN HINDSIGHT

- What could have been done differently?
- What was learned from the process?
- Any personal comments or reflections?

Appendix 5 – Focus Group Interview Schedule – Facilitator's Notes

Introductory Statement & Thanks (informal) (5 minutes)

- Welcome and brief introduction.
- Outline intent of group focus and thank participants in advance.
- Outline process – the program is quite structured, so that we can get as much information from you in the shortest time period, and so that we have time for interactive discussions. We are very interested in your opinions.

IDENTIFYING CHANGES (45 MINUTES)
Hand out Response Sheet 1

a Facilitator: *"The first thing we would like to look at is the organisational changes you can identify as having occurred within your own business unit and across the whole organisation (between ---- & ----). Change affects us all in different ways; we are particularly interested in your perspectives about what changes occurred over this period."*

b Facilitator hands out Response Sheet 1: Identifying Changes
Facilitator: *"We will be asking you to give us some written responses, which will be the basis for our discussion. We will hand out three response sheets altogether – this is the first. We will be collecting these response sheets later, and using them in our research. Your responses will be anonymous - you do not need to put your name on the response sheets. On this first response sheet, we are asking you to think about the organisation at around the time the first Organizational Culture Inventory (OCI) was undertaken, and to compare that to when the second survey took place, reflecting on what changes took place over the intervening period of time."*

Response Sheet 1 – questions 1 and 2 (10 minutes)
Facilitator: *"Now please read and answer questions 1 and 2 on this first sheet. You have ten minutes to name and describe the changes asked for."*
   This activity is to be done individually, without conferring with one another.

c List Nominated Changes on Whiteboard (10 minutes)
Facilitator: *"I now want to create a list of all the changes you have written down under both headings. I will take one change from each of you and then go around the group until we have all the changes listed. If a change has already been listed, let me know, and I'll just tick that again."* The facilitator lists their responses on the whiteboard/flip chart (an electronic whiteboard is ideal for this).

Response Sheet 1 - questions 3a, 3b, and 3c. (10 minutes)
Facilitator: *"Now turn to the second page of Response Sheet 1, and complete questions 3a, 3b and 3c. Having looked at all the responses we have on the board, without discussion (to prevent influence processes)*

rank what you now think are the three most important changes that took place in this period. Also, provide a reason for your choice in each case. We will have an opportunity to discuss these later."

d Collate Responses (10 minutes)

Facilitator: *"I will now take all your first choices and allocate 3 points to each change you have nominated as your first choice."* The facilitator does this, and repeats process for second and third choices, allocating 2 points and one point respectively. The facilitator then writes all responses on the whiteboard/flip chart against the relevant change items, and then adds up the score for each item.

e Open Discussion (30 minutes) (see facilitator comment below)

Facilitator: *"So you can see that the changes seen as most important are…"* (read three or four highest scoring items from list on board). *"Starting with the highest scoring item, I would now like you to tell me about this change; What was it about? Why did it take place (impetus and driving forces, including organisational response to an externally driven change)? What was the change intended to achieve?"* (facilitator leads a discussion with group to clarify and confirm input, and obtain examples and illustrations to further demonstrate points being made).

Facilitators please note: Some redundancy invariably occurs when participants are asked to respond to this question and in the open discussion session that follows on implementation processes. I found it valuable to collapse these discussion periods into one, as a way of covering everything we needed, avoiding repetition, and saving time. I outlined the following discussion triggers as a way of structuring the discussion and keeping on track although, as you can imagine, responses generally cut across a number of these categories.

"Looking at each change nominated, could you give:

1. *A brief overview of the change – what it was about*
2. *Drivers for the change – impetus*
3. *The intent, aim or purpose of the change*
4. *Outcome of the change*
5. *Who where the stakeholders*
6. *How was it implemented and facilitated*
7. *Setbacks*
8. *How is momentum maintained"*

IMPLEMENTATION PROCESS (35 MINUTES)
Discussion - as above:

a Facilitator: *"Let's go back to the most important changes we were just discussing"* (refer participants to their list of the most important changes). *"In reflecting on these organisational changes, can you outline:*

- *Who were the critical stakeholders and drivers for the change? What was done to support the effective implementation of this change process? Were there any problems or setbacks?*

How was the impetus for maintaining the change managed? Did the impact vary across organisational units?

■ *What could have been done better or differently?"* (15 minutes)

Hand out Response Sheet 2

b Facilitator hands out Response Sheet 2: Process Interventions

"You will see that on this response sheet, there is a list of 'process interventions'. These are the kinds of tools that managers often use to change things in organisations. Using the list of process interventions, identify the top three processes that made the implementation discussed above most effective. Note that this time you are not asked to rank the items, just check the three you think were most effective. Please respond to the first question only.

■ *Leadership/Management style*
■ *Setting strategic direction and focus*
■ *Communication*
■ *Resources invested*
■ *Level of employee involvement*
■ *Individual/personal changes*
■ *Change in organisational structure*
■ *Change in job design*
■ *Feedback using diagnostic tools, e.g. LSI*
■ *Change in key personnel*
■ *Change in reward structure*
■ *Other (name and specify)"*

Response Sheet 2 – question 1 (5 minutes)

Facilitator: *"Now please read and answer question 1 on this sheet. You have five minutes to identify the three most effective processes."*

This activity is to be done individually, without conferring with one another.

c Collate Responses (5 minutes)

Facilitator: *"Now let's see which process interventions you saw as most effective."* The facilitator writes up responses on the whiteboard, and calculates the final score for each.

Response Sheet 2 - question 2 (5 minutes)

Facilitator: *"Now I want you to answer the next question, which asks you to list the process interventions that had the greatest impact on the overall cultural change process, first at the business unit level, and then at the organisational level."*

This activity is to be done individually, without conferring with one another.

c Collate Responses (5 minutes)

The facilitator writes responses on the whiteboard/flip chart and conducts a general discussion to clarify, confirm, and obtain examples and illustrations.

Note: Facilitator to use prepared chart below to assist the recording of the data.

Process Interventions	Implementation Effectiveness	Total	Impact at Business Unit Level	Total	Impact at Organisational Level	Total
Leadership/ Management Style						
Setting Strategic Direction and Focus						
Etc.						

IMPACT OF CHANGE (30 MINUTES)
Hand out Response Sheet 3

Facilitator hands out Group Response Sheet 3: Impact of Change.

a Response Sheet 3 – all questions

Facilitator: *"You will have 10 minutes to engage in individual reflection, and to respond to all questions. Please think about each of these questions, and answer them succinctly."*

The questions are intentionally open-ended, and designed to generate further information.

1. The first Human Synergistics culture survey was undertaken in ----. A second survey, undertaken in ----, showed very significant changes from the first. Do you think that the survey reflected real changes in the culture of the organisation?
   Yes/No (circle your choice)
   1a. If yes, why do you think this was so?
   1b. If no, why do you think the results were so different?
2. Only answer the next questions if you answered 'yes' above:
   2a. With particular focus on your own experience, and that of your team/business unit, give some examples of some actual behaviour changes that demonstrate the culture shift.
   2b. In the broader organisational context, what examples stand out as significant behavioural changes?
3. Have the culture changes improved the organisation's business performance? How? What evidence do you have for this?

b When everyone in the group has completed their individual reflections (or when time is up) the facilitator asks for their responses.

Discussion To Draw Out Examples (15 minutes)
The facilitator ensures discussion takes place on answers to each question. The focus in this section is to get as many specific examples as possible in relation to the observed changes.

Close (5 minutes)
The facilitator asks participants to fold their three response sheets together, collects them, places them in the large envelope provided, and labels them focus group/name of organisation/date. The facilitator then thanks participants for their attendance and time, and closes the session.

Appendix 6 – Focus Group Interview Summary Data

Table 1. Organisational Changes Experienced between Time Period One and Time Period Two – the three changes ranked as most significant.

What major changes occurred across the whole organisation between period 1 and period 2?				
Adshel	**Balmain Leagues Club**	**Lion Nathan**	**MasterCard Australia**	**Yarra Valley Water**
OCI Feedback	Human Synergistics' feedback tools	Consistency in reinforcing the new culture	Commercial redirection	Leadership
Role Clarity	Business redirection	Leadership	Improved communication	Tools
Employee Involvement		Role modeling and accountability	Leadership	

Table 2. Changes Nominated by More than One Organisation as being Most Important.

Nominated Changes	Ranking × number of organisations
Feedback and use of Human Synergistics' instruments	Ranked as 1 by two organisations and 2 by another
Leadership	Ranked respectively as 1, 2 and 3 by three organisations
Business/commercial redirection	Ranked as 1 by one organisation and 2 by another

Table 3. Three most important Cultural Change Process Interventions at the organisational level – by the focus group.

Which of the process interventions above had the greatest impact on the overall cultural change process?				
Adshel	**Balmain Leagues Club**	**Lion Nathan**	**MasterCard Australia**	**Yarra Valley Water**
Communication	Setting strategy direction and focus	Feedback using diagnostic Tools	Leadership/management style	Leadership/management style
Leadership/Management style	Leadership/management style	Strategic direction	Communication	Communication
Level of Employee Involvement	Leadership/management style Tools	Leadership/management style Leadership	Level of employee involvement	Feedback using diagnostic tools

Table 4. Cultural Change Process Interventions and the number of organisations nominating them in their top three choices.

Process Interventions	Top three across all organisations	Adshel	MasterCard Australia	Yarra Valley Water	Balmain Leagues Club	Lion Nathan
Leadership/management style	5	2	1	1	2	3
Feedback using diagnostic tools	3			3	3	1
Communication	3	1	2	2		
Strategic redirection and focus	2				1	2
Change in reward structure	1					Significant
Level of employee involvement	1		3			

Table 5. Impact of Cultural Change on Performance.

Have the culture changes improved the organisation's business performance? How? What evidence do you have for this?				
Balmain Leagues Club	**Adshel**	**Lion Nathan**	**MasterCard Australia**	**Yarra Valley Water**
Staff retention improved ****	Increased staff effectiveness, motivation and understanding ***	Nicer place to work, however openness and honesty still needs to be more fully developed *	Team work improved ***	Customer Service improved ***
Increased profit/revenue/spending ***	Happier workplace **	Financial performance consistent –relationship to performance unclear **	Communication more open **	Staff more innovative and creative ****
Industry Recognition *	Reduction in money wasted, due in the past to lack of consultation *	Change adaptability increased *	Staff more motivated and achievement-oriented **	Retention rates have increased **
Improved Customer Service **	Increased spending on staff development*	Operational area still often complex and too consensual in style *	Personal empowerment improved ***	Improved cross-functional team work ****
More Effective Communication **	Financial performance steadily improving, although relationship not clear *	Retention of people *		
Financial results have improved *	More pleasant place to work, although at time perhaps too relaxed *			
Increase in Change Adaptability **		Increased personal and business accountability		
denotes the number of participants giving the same response				

Table 6. Changes Reflected in Rob Cooke's Model of Cultural Change.
The following table summarises the changes occurring in each of the organisations using the Cooke model to tabulate the data.

Organisation	Mission/philosophy	Structures	Systems	Technology	Skills/Qualities
Yarra Valley Water	■ Development of Values and mission ■ Strategic Intent & 'House' symbol ■ OCI/OEI Measurement 2001,2003,2005	■ Cross functional teams ■ Delegation of authority changed ■ Introduction of HRIS ■ Skip Level Interviews	■ Centralised Recruitment ■ Centralised Learning & Development Function ■ Blue Zone Days ■ Open Days ■ SPLASH ■ LSI & Leadership Development ■ Co-achieving workshops ■ Communication Breakthrough workshop ■ Performance Review Process ■ Requisite organisation		■ Symbolic events ■ Discussions with the MD ■ Corporate Games ■ Open Days ■ Employee Opinion surveys
Balmain Leagues Club		■ Upgraded Duty Managers roles and responsibilities ■ Duty Managers included with Executive team and Board members ■ Debriefing formula/consequence management	■ Recruitment ■ Induction/Orientation ■ Tigers Training Program and Accredited training system ■ LSI, L/I and extensive Leadership Capability workshops ■ Performance Review Process ■ Reward & Recognition	■ Significant job redesign ■ Duty Managers ■ Role Evaluation as part of the performance review process and as part of the recruitment process.	■ Increased emphasis on inclusion and involvement of staff in planning and decision making ■ Close working dynamics of executive team in supporting each other in functional areas ■ Formalisation of management as coaching and mentoring

Organisation	Mission/philosophy	Structures	Systems	Technology	Skills/Qualities
Lion Nathan	■ Core Purpose ■ Vision ■ Values ■ Consumer Engagement		■ Resourcing ■ Achievement Review ■ Competency x Results ■ Talent Matrix ■ Leadership Development ■ LSI 1&2		■ Annual Roadshow by CEO ■ Values Booklet ■ Engagement Survey
Adshel	■ Establishing cultural vision ■ OCI/OEI	■ Role Clarity – PDs ■ Culture Teams established ■ Some restructuring and reporting changes	■ Remuneration ■ Performance Appraisals ■ Executive Development Programs ■ Personal Effectiveness	■ New panel booking system	■ Focus groups ■ OCI Roadshows ■ New Sales Director ■ CEO behaviour change
MasterCard Australia	■ Establishing cultural vision – Preferred OCI ■ Test - Actual culture ■ Articulating business goals ■ Sharing stories of employees who exemplified the values ■ Re-Test Actual OCI	■ Quarterly team workshops ■ Bi-annual workshops ■ WIP meetings ■ Cross-functional forums ■ Defined roles and responsibilities ■ Common area for employees ■ MasterCard Australia social club	■ Team of Quarter award ■ Employee Recognition Board ■ Joint setting of KPI's ■ Revised Performance Management System – focus on KPI's, values and behaviours	■ Job redesign	■ Two-way flow of communication ■ Cascading L/I to the next level of leaders ■ Leaders undertaking one-to-one coaching ■ Leaders sharing L/I data and action plans

OEI causal factors from Robert A. Cooke and Janet L. Szumal, Organizational Effectiveness Inventory™ Feedback Report, Human Synergistics International. Copyright © 1995-2006. All rights reserved.

Table 7. Evidence of Culture Change

The first Human Synergistics culture survey was undertaken in period 1. A second survey, undertaken in period 2, showed very significant changes from the first. Do you think that the survey reflected real changes in the culture of the organisation? If yes, why do you think this was so?

The general consensus across all companies was that their culture had changed tangibly, with visible changes being demonstrated in (listed below in no particular order):
Individual behaviours, including accountability, respect, empathy, commitment, and employee involvement
Leadership and management style
Awareness of behavioural impact on others
Communication effectiveness, including the use of a new common language evidenced by naming behaviour as 'Red', 'Blue' or 'Green'.
Increased role clarity